# Contents

# BUSINESS
# ORGANISATIONS
# AND
# ENVIRONMENTS
## BOOK 2

### NEW B/TEC SPECIFICATION

MATTHEW GLEW

MICHAEL WATTS

RONALD WELLS

 Heinemann Educational Books

Uniform with this title

*Business Organisations and Environments
Book 1*
  by Matthew Glew, Michael Watts and
  Ronald Wells

Heinemann Educational Books Ltd
22 Bedford Square, London WC1B 3HH

LONDON   EDINBURGH   MELBOURNE   AUCKLAND
SINGAPORE   KUALA LUMPUR   NEW DELHI
IBADAN   NAIROBI   JOHANNESBURG
PORTSMOUTH  (NH)   KINGSTON

First published 1987

**British Library Cataloguing in Publication Data**

Glew, Matthew
  Business organisations and environments.
  Bk. 2
  1. Business enterprises
  I. Title. II. Watts, Michael, *1943–*
  III. Wells, Ronald, *1947–*
  338.7       HD2731

  ISBN 0–435–45906–6

Phototypeset by Gecko Limited, Bicester, Oxon.

Printed in Great Britain by Thomson Litho Ltd, East
Kilbride, Scotland

# Acknowledgements

The authors would like to thank Melvyn Butcher
for contributing Chapters 1, 2, 12 and 13.

The authors and publishers would like to thank
those who gave permission to reproduce copyright material as indicated in the sources.
Crown copyright material is reproduced with
permission of the Controller of Her Majesty's
Stationery Office.

# Preface

This book includes the requirements of the
re-specified Common Core Modules 3 and 4
entitled 'The Organisation in its Environment',
which represent an integral part of the Business
and Technician Education Council National
Award in Business Studies.

In accordance with the revised specification
the book considers the position of the organisation within the wider business environment.
The book fully reflects the emphasis that BTEC
have placed in the re-specification on the areas
of change, technology and management skills.
The book seeks to guide students towards an
understanding of their roles within the business
environment. It therefore provides them with a
basis for understanding and later analysing the
economic, legal, social and political problems
that affect the business world. The material has
been presented in accordance with the underlying BTEC philosophy of an interdisciplinary
approach to business studies courses. A balance
has been maintained throughout the book between the disciplines of economics, law, government and sociology, thus providing a complete view of the operations of the business
organisation.

The book will also prove valuable for students
requiring an introduction or conversion course
to the BTEC Higher National Award. In addition, students engaged upon professional and
managerial courses will find that the wide per-
spective it provides on the business environment can successfully augment their studies.

## To the tutor

To help you we have included several ideas for
integrated assignments on pages 213–18. These
are in line with the requirements of Business &
Technician Education Council, *Business and Finance, Distribution Studies and Public Administration: Core Unit Specifications and Sample Learning
Activities* (BTEC Publications, 1985).

Matthew Glew   Michael Watts   Ronald Wells
July 1987

# 1. The UK System of Government

## GOVERNMENT AND DEMOCRACY

Each nation state needs some form of **government** to regulate its affairs. Government is a function of any organised society, but the form of government differs from nation to nation. One nation's government may be democratic and elected: in another it may be totalitarian and imposed. Whatever the form or structure, all governments have activities and objectives in common, namely law-making and the economic and social development of the country.

The United Kingdom is a **democracy**. It supports a **mixed economy** in which business activity directed both by the state and by the free market is given the opportunity to work and to flourish. The type of environment in which a business organisation operates is determined by the interaction of government policy with market forces and trends. The extent of government intervention in the business environment depends on the government's policies.

Policy-making and implementation are complicated and time-consuming. In a democracy a government can remain in office only by **consent**. The government has to take account of a variety of political, economic and social influences and pressures. Democratic governments *invite* people and organisations to give their opinions, in order to arrive at fair and publicly supported policy ideas and objectives.

Let us consider how a democratic government, like that of the UK, receives opinions, advice and even pressure from people and organisations.

### The democratic system
We live in a **democracy**. Essentially the word means 'the will of the people', but there are many possible interpretations of this. To some people it may mean free electoral choice or the guarantee of certain civil rights. For others it is the opportunity to participate fully in public affairs and to attempt to influence policy. Democracy's main features can be identified as follows:

- freedom of speech, religion and association (i.e. attending meetings and joining groups);
- freedom from arbitrary arrest;
- secret electoral ballots;
- universal adult suffrage (votes for all);
- open debate;
- the government being accountable to the people;
- no punishment for political views;
- no one group unduly privileged politically;
- the police are restrained by the law courts, media, public opinion and Parliament;
- free choice of political parties;
- opportunity to promote causes;
- opportunity to influence public opinion.

### The British Constitution
To exist as a legal entity, a nation state requires a **constitution** – that is, a set of rules of government. It is said that the British constitution is unwritten, but this is misleading because much of our constitution, like statute law (Acts of Parliament), *is* written. What the term 'unwritten' means is that you cannot obtain a single document which outlines the entire British constitution, including such matters as the position and authority of the sovereign, the role of Parliament, the electoral system, the appointment of judges and civil rights. All this information is available, but it means consulting many sources rather than just one. (In contrast, the United States constitution is contained within a single written document.)

The British constitution has developed over the centuries, but it is very much a living and not an abstract instrument, and it continues to change. The constitution is based upon **common law**, **statute law**, **case law**, **conventions** and **precedents**. It has great flexibility, making it possible for government to act within very wide limits without abusing power, to adapt its actions and institutions to meet changing opinions, demands and circumstances. The UK constitution works well in the sense that it has made Britain a relatively stable and free society to live in.

*Checks and balances*

An essential aspect of any constitution is that it contains **checks and balances**. This ensures that no branch of the government system can use the system unreasonably to increase its powers. For example, the government could in theory create laws to suit itself; it could change the Representation of the People Act to increase the maximum life of a government from five years to an indefinite period. The monarchy is constitutional and could be abolished. The power of the House of Lords has been reduced over time, and a government could change it further or abolish it altogether.

So why doesn't government behave in such an extreme way? The answer lies in those checks and balances. Whatever its **theoretical power**, government can function only **by consent**. Even a government which enjoys a large and impressive majority in Parliament and has the ready support of public opinion (as measured by opinion polls) may find it difficult to

itself. Nothing short of a revolution or a military coup is likely to be able to overthrow it.

## INSTITUTIONS OF GOVERNMENT

The following are the main institutions of the UK system of government.

**Parliament**

Parliament consists of the sovereign (at present the Queen) and the two Houses of Parliament – the **Lords** and the **Commons** (sometimes referred to as the Upper and the Lower house or chamber). These three elements have to work together as a partnership in order to carry out the functions of Parliament. Do not confuse Parliament with either the House of Commons or the government; when we refer to Parliament we are speaking about the entire legislative authority vested in the sovereign, the Lords and the elected Members of Parliament. See Fig. 1.1.

**Fig. 1.1: Queen + Lords + Commons = Parliament**

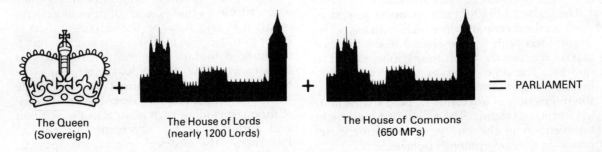

| The Queen (Sovereign) | The House of Lords (nearly 1200 Lords) | The House of Commons (650 MPs) | PARLIAMENT |

get a Bill through the law-making process of Parliament. The courts of law and the monarchy would both speak out if a government tried to increase its power unreasonably. The constitutional rules must be adhered to; vested interests must be given full opportunity to petition government, and time must be allocated so that government proposals can be fully considered.

No UK government could attempt to prolong its own life indefinitely without large numbers of people accusing it of being arrogant and corrupt. All the forces of public opinion and parliamentary procedure would be mobilised to stop the government from carrying out its intention.

In a sense, then, our constitution protects

**The sovereign**

The Queen (the present sovereign) **reigns** but does not **rule**. She does not run the country, nor does she determine government policy. The Queen carries out many ceremonial duties, and it is understandable if some dismiss her as being just a figurehead, an empty symbol of power; but that would be to misinterpret the sovereign's role within the UK constitution.

The UK monarchy is **constitutional** – that is, even our Queen is said to occupy her position and exercise her authority **by consent**. This situation goes back to 1688, the year of the 'Glorious Revolution'. William and Mary were *invited* to take the British throne and in 1689 they became King and Queen. The Civil War earlier in the seventeenth century was due largely to the clash between the King and Parliament over the question of legislative power and authority. Charles I believed in the 'divine right of kings'; he said that God chose the monarch, and so whatever the King did was beyond question and could not be criticised. Since 1688 the monarchy has been said to exist as part of the UK constitution because the British people wish it.

### The Queen's involvement with Parliament

- After a general election, the Queen asks the leader of the majority party in the House of Commons to form a government.
- She formally appoints ministers, judges and bishops of the Church of England.
- The Queen formally assents to laws. A Bill cannot become an Act of Parliament until it has been through both Houses and and presented for the sovereign's signature, known as the **royal assent**.
- The Prime Minister is required to meet with the Queen regularly and frequently. According to custom no report is made of their discussions. The Prime Minister briefs the Queen on current issues and proposals, and the Queen uses her influence and experience to advise and encourage her Prime Minister.
- The Queen visits the Houses of Parliament for the **State Opening** each autumn. On this occasion she addresses the Lords, and the government and opposition front-benchers from the Commons, by reading the **Queen's Speech**. This speech is prepared for her by the Cabinet and contains the intended programme of the government for the forthcoming parliamentary session.
- The Queen dissolves Parliament.

The Queen is also the head of the Church of England and of the armed forces. She makes goodwill tours overseas, receives foreign dignitaries, attends receptions and generally supports a range of public activities. The Queen's role may be without actual power but it carries great weight and influence.

### The Crown

The term **Crown** is often used, and its meaning can be difficult to explain. The Crown is the most important collective symbol for all the institutions of state in the UK. For example,

government property is held in the name of the Crown; legal actions against criminals are taken on behalf of the Crown; officers of the law keep the Queen's peace; officers in the armed forces hold the Queen's commission.

The authority of the government is embodied in the Crown. As a symbol it acts as a constant reminder of the partnership or interrelationship of the sovereign and the two Houses of Parliament.

### The House of Lords

The House of Lords or Upper Chamber comprises nearly 1200 members, who are drawn from four sources:

- Lords of Appeal in Ordinary;
- bishops of the Church of England;
- hereditary peers;
- life peers.

Whilst 1200 may be entitled to take seats in the Lords, the average daily attendance is about 250. The House of Lords is sometimes ridiculed as a place to park worn-out politicians and business men and out-of-touch aristocrats. But its existence within the constitution can be seen as more a strength than a weakness. The Lords provide a forum of lively and positive debate; they have introduced legislation, and have made valuable amendments to Bills coming up from the Commons. The abolition of the House of Lords would remove some of those important 'checks and balances'.

### The powers of the Lords

It would be reasonable to expect the powers of the Lords, the Upper House, to be greater than those of the Commons. At one time that may have been the case, but during the twentieth century the Lords' powers have shrunk, and the Commons has become more and more dominant in the parliamentary system. All Bills originating in the Commons must nevertheless go through the Lords. This may be seen by less patient MPs as unreasonable and ' time-consuming, but it is a useful check on hasty decision-making.

The main power of the House of Lords is its ability to **delay** legislation, but there are limits even on this power. A Finance Bill can be delayed for up to a month; other Bills may be delayed for up to a year. If the Lords believe that the Commons are attempting to push through unpopular or unreasonable legislation, then the Upper House can frustrate the intentions of the Commons by throwing out a Bill. The Lords can do this twice, but after that the Commons have the right to directly seek the royal assent.

This relationship between the Lords and the Commons illustrates how the 'checks and balances' work. It would take the Commons three to five years to overrule opposition from the Lords, and long before then the public and the media would challenge Parliament about any such legislation. In fact, the pursuit of an unpopular measure which is opposed by the Lords could result in the government losing the confidence of the country.

*Other features of the Upper Chamber*
The party system exists in the Lords, although their Lordships are not subject to the same degree of voting discipline as MPs in the Commons. The Whips in the Lords can only pursuade; they cannot threaten. Peers also enjoy a more relaxed life on their benches because they have no constituents to impress. They do not need to worry about getting on television or being reported in the papers. They do not have to bother with 'nursing' a constituency and worrying about the personal outcome of the next election. A peer does not have to take a party whip at all; if he or she wishes to be totally independent of a party, then he or she can sit on the **cross-benches** See Fig. 1.2.

Peers do not receive pay but they can claim an attendance allowance (not a particularly generous one). The only members of the Lords to receive pay are the government ministers and Whips, the leader of the opposition and the opposition Chief Whip.

An interesting feature of the Lords is the wealth of experience and expertise the House has among its active members. The life peers, in particular, are drawn from those who have held powerful positions in industry, commerce, trade unions, the armed forces, politics, law and the arts. They have much to offer, and their debates are often well informed.

Because there is a legal limit of ninety-five members of the government who can be appointed from the Commons, there are generally a dozen or so members of the government in the Lords. Mostly they are junior ministers and they must answer questions and debates on

behalf of the Cabinet ministers in the Commons. If a peer is a Cabinet minister, statements and answers are conducted in the Commons by his or her junior minister(s). The problem facing the Lords is the shortage of government spokespeople; each minister has to speak not just for his or her own department but on behalf of three or four others, too.

The Lords play another important role. They are the highest court of appeal in the land for civil and criminal cases. By convention, the Lords of Appeal in Ordinary hear the cases.

The atmosphere in the Lords is very different

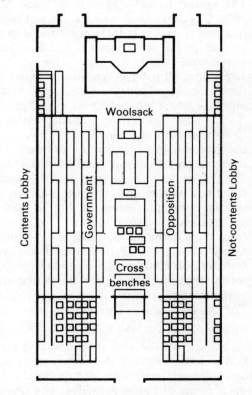

**Fig. 1.2: Plan of the Chamber of the House of Lords, showing the position of the government, opposition and cross-benches**

from that of the Commons. Business is less pressured, passions are more restrained and debaters address each other more politely!

**The House of Commons**
The Commons comprise 650 elected Members of Parliament, each one representing a constituency. An MP is elected for a period of up to

five years, because the maximum life of a government is five years. When, after a maximum of five years, the Prime Minister calls a general election, all MPs must contest their seats.

The public image of the Commons is that of a rowdy place with 650 members noisily debating issues, raising points of order, asking questions, rudely interrupting and even shouting abuse at each other. There are times when feelings run high, but some issues become so important, and the political divisions so great, that they overshadow all other business. Many MPs feel that it is their duty to express firmly-held views on such issues as the Falklands War and the privatisation of British industries.

The House of Commons is the **power-base** of the UK democracy, the place where legislation is forged and the focus of many a crusade. However, a visit to the Commons can often be disappointing, for the House is rarely full; it is on Budget Day, at Prime Minister's question time and for major debates, but visitors are generally amazed to see only a handful of MPs debating some apparently obscure and tedious point. Much of the work of the Commons goes on outside the chamber, particularly in **committees**. All Bills are scrutinised by committees before they are presented for the third reading. MPs are also expected to be aware and knowledgeable, and so some are always away on official visits and delegations – not forgetting the duties imposed upon them by constituency business.

*The party system*

The party system is better organised than in the Lords. All MPs stand for Parliament on a **party ticket**; i.e. they stand as a member of a political party intending to secure, through a majority of the vote, the position of government; or, in the case of the minority parties, intending to obtain sufficient seats to become a significant influence in the Commons.

It is in the Commons that the real confrontations occur between **Her Majesty's Government** and **Her Majesty's Loyal Opposition**. See Fig. 1.3. It is not the function of the opposition to actively and deliberately oppose every suggestion, proposal or Bill of the government. But the opposition, which represents a major body of opinion in the country, must call the government to account. It must also put forward

proposals of its own and debate them with skill, attempting to impress the voters that it is the 'alternative government'. MPs are conscious of the voters, and many questions and debates are raised in order to reach out to the constituencies and to inform them that their representatives are doing their 'duty'.

Our political system has been referred to as a **two-party system**. This does not mean that only two parties exist, but that only two, Labour and Conservative, are in contention for government. The Alliance, formed by the Liberal Party and Social Democratic Party, sees itself as the 'third force' in British politics, which will break the two-party mould.

**Fig. 1.3: Plan of the Chamber of the House of Commons, showing the positions of the government and opposition benches**

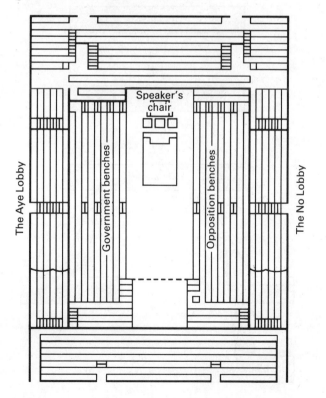

After the 1983 general election, eleven parties were represented in Parliament. See Table 1.1 and Fig. 1.4.

**Table 1.1: Make-up of the House of Commons after 1983 general election**

| Party | Number of seats |
|---|---|
| Conservative | 397 |
| Labour | 209 |
| Liberal ⎫ | |
| Social Democratic ⎬ The Alliance | 23 |
| Scottish Nationalist | |
| Welsh Nationalist | |
| Ulster Unionist | |
| Ulster Democratic Unionist | 21 |
| Ulster Popular Unionist | |
| Social Democratic and Labour Party | |
| Provisional Sinn Fein | |
| **Total** | **650** |

**Fig. 1.4: The UK system of government**

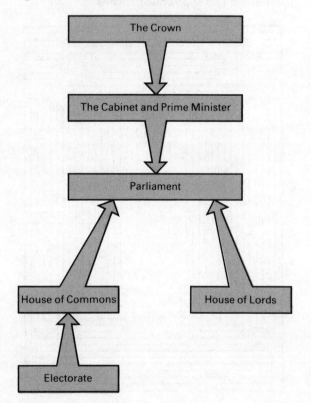

## THE ELECTORAL SYSTEM

### 'First past the post' and PR

The British system of electing a government is relatively simple and is referred to as **first past the post**. In each contested constituency it is necessary for a candidate to win the largest number of votes, although not necessarily the majority (more than 50 per cent). A party wins a general election not because it secures a majority of the votes cast but because it wins the largest number of seats in the Commons.

Many people now feel that this system is unfair, and there is a growing pressure to change to a system of **proportional representation** ('PR'). PR is the system used by many European and Scandinavian nations. The Liberal Party's manifesto for the 1983 general election, for example, said: 'Electoral reform is . . . a precondition of healing Britain's divisions and creating a sense of community.' The criticism is that our present system is unfair, even undemocratic.

The present UK system has worked for many years, so what is the problem? Take a look at this election result. It is not a true one but it is realistic:

| | |
|---|---|
| Conservative | 18,000 votes |
| Alliance | 16,000 votes |
| Labour | 11,000 votes |
| Green Party | 500 votes |
| National Front | 100 votes |
| *Total votes cast* | 45,600 |
| Conservative majority | 2000 |

The Tory candidate has been returned as the MP because he has a 'majority' of 2000 votes. His constituency is a 'marginal' one. His 18,000 votes represent 39.5 per cent of votes cast; a much larger number, 27,600 electors, wanted someone else than the Tory. This is the situation many people say is unacceptable, because the MP has not been elected by the majority.

The supporters of PR would want to see a method which ensured a successful candidate obtaining at least 50 per cent of the votes. Several systems of PR exist; each has the object of electing candidates who have identifiable majority support. At the moment the only par-

**Table 1.2: The 1945 and 1983 general election results**

| Year | Party | Number of votes | Percentage of votes cast | Number of seats |
|------|-------|-----------------|--------------------------|-----------------|
| 1945 | Conservative | 9,972,010 | 39.7 | 213 |
|      | **Labour** | 11,967,746 | 47.7 | 393 |
|      | Liberal | 2,252,430 | 8.9 | 12 |
|      | Others | 903,009 | 3.6 | 22 |
|      | *Totals* | 25,095,195 | 100.0 | 640 |
| 1983 | **Conservative** | 13,012,612 | 42.4 | 397 |
|      | Labour | 8,461,616 | 27.6 | 209 |
|      | Liberal/SDP | 7,776,061 | 25.4 | 23 |
|      | Others | 1,420,590 | 4.6 | 21 |
|      | *Totals* | 30,670,879 | 100.0 | 650 |

liamentary candidates assured of winning a voting majority are in those seats where only two candidates put up.

No UK government since the Second World War has been returned with a true electoral majority. Yet we have always accepted the result, and it has always appeared to reflect public opinion. Table 1.2 compares the results for the 1945 and 1983 elections and offers some interesting data.

These two elections share a similarity. In both 1945 and 1983 the majority party won with a 'landslide' result. The Conservatives' 1983 result was almost the same as Labour's 1945 result, and yet neither party secured a majority of votes. The situation seems worse still if you calculate the winning party's vote as a percentage not of all votes cast but of the total votes which *could* have been cast (remember that only about 80 per cent of electors actually vote in general elections). But how valid is the criticism? It is for you to make up your own mind on this issue.

In Table 1.2 you will see that is was the Liberal Party in 1945, and is now the Liberal/SDP Alliance, which 'suffers' by the electoral system. The 1983 result indicates Alliance support almost as big as Labour's, and yet the Liberals and SDP only won 23 seats, compared with 209 for Labour. The Alliance complains that the 'price' of electing one of its MPs is 338,000 votes, compared with 40,000 for Labour and 33,000 for the Tories.

**Would PR mean coalition government?**

If the 1983 results were recalculated purely on number of votes cast, then the composition of the House of Commons after the election would have looked like this:

| | |
|---|---|
| Conservatives | 276 seats (−121) |
| Labour | 179 seats (−30) |
| Alliance | 165 seats (+142) |
| Others | 30 seats (+9) |

This would have produced an interesting situation and would have presented the Tories with a problem. The Queen might have asked Margaret Thatcher, not 'Will you form a government?' but '*Can* you form a government?' If the opposition parties had voted against the Tories, then government would have been defeated right from the beginning, and the political situation would have been hopeless. The answer in such a situation lies in either 'an arrangement' or the establishment of a **coalition**.

A coalition would result in the dilution of individual party ambitions and programmes. Some would say that this would be a good thing, because it would prevent unpopular or extremist government policies being put into practice. If, for example, the coalition was formed by the Alliance and the Conservatives, neither party could hope to do everything it had promised before the election. Policies would have to be redefined, so that the government (whose Cabinet would include both Tory and Alliance ministers) could appeal to both Conservative and Alliance electors.

Britain had coalition government during the Second World War. Although it worked very well in the unique situation of wartime, there was still political division and controversy. It was a successful period of government, but the country was facing a common enemy. When the end of the war was in sight, party lines were quickly redrawn, and pressure was applied by the Labour Party to call a general election.

If PR is employed there will always be the prospect of coalition, but this is not a natural consequence of proportional representation. It would almost certainly mean that the Alliance in particular would secure more seats. One of the PR systems being considered would involve **multi-member constituencies**. Instead of one MP representing the seat, there could be four – and the constituency would be four times as large. The idea here is that electors could have a real choice of who to vote for. For example, a voter might choose to support two of the Labour candidates, one Tory and one Green Party candidate, voting not so much on party lines but on the candidates' ability and suitability. The final result for a multi-member seat could be, say, one Alliance MP, one Labour and two Tory. One advantage of this system, it is claimed, is that the public will be able to approach whichever of the MPs is more likely to represent their views.

Activity 1.1
Study Fig. 1.5 which shows the voting patterns in the 1983 election compared with those in 1979. Compare these on a regional basis with the 1987 election results. Account for the differences and suggest what lessons the parties might have learned from the results.

## THE MEMBERS OF PARLIAMENT

### Standing for Parliament
To have any chance of becoming an MP, a person usually needs to be an active member of an organised political party. He or she also needs to be selected for a constituency where there is a likelihood of success – where either his or her party holds the seat or where it has a chance to win it.

Many seats are known as **safe**. In these seats there is usually little opportunity of unseating the MP. Those seats where the majority is small, say under 3000, are called **marginals**. Candidates standing for the first time usually have to fight difficult seats and have to oppose large and daunting majorities. This gives would-be MPs excellent experience and may strengthen their claim on a better or a winnable seat next time.

What sort of person becomes a Member of Parliament? The pay is only moderately attractive. The hours are long and tedious. MPs' working conditions would cause strikes in industry. MPs have to ballot for office space and even filing-cabinets. There is no end to the complaints and queries raised by constituents. For some there is no job security. Many serve well but in relative obscurity. The chances of becoming a Cabinet minister are few. There are all-night sittings, lots of travelling and the need to maintain two homes (unless the constituency

**Fig. 1.5: How Britain voted: region by region, 1983.  How the parties' shares changed from 1979.**

| SCOTLAND | |
|---|---|
| TORY | −3.0% |
| LABOUR | −6.6% |
| ALLIANCE | +11.9% |

| NORTHERN IRELAND | |
|---|---|
| Figures do not apply because parties are different | |

| NORTHWEST | |
|---|---|
| TORY | −3.7% |
| LABOUR | −6.7% |
| ALLIANCE | +10.7% |

| WALES | |
|---|---|
| TORY | −1.7% |
| LABOUR | −9.8% |
| ALLIANCE | + 10.6% |

| WEST MIDLANDS | |
|---|---|
| TORY | −2.3% |
| LABOUR | −8.7% |
| ALLIANCE | +11.5% |

| SOUTH WEST | |
|---|---|
| TORY | −0.5% |
| LABOUR | −9.9% |
| ALLIANCE | +10.9% |

| NORTH | |
|---|---|
| TORY | −1.9% |
| LABOUR | −9.7% |
| ALLIANCE | +12.0% |

| YORKS & HUMBERSIDE | |
|---|---|
| TORY | −1.0% |
| LABOUR | −9.2% |
| ALLIANCE | +10.8% |

| EAST MIDLANDS | |
|---|---|
| TORY | −2.3% |
| LABOUR | −8.7% |
| ALLIANCE | +11.5% |

| EAST ANGLIA | |
|---|---|
| TORY | −0.2% |
| LABOUR | −12.0% |
| ALLIANCE | +12.2% |

| GREATER LONDON | |
|---|---|
| TORY | −2.0% |
| LABOUR | −10.1% |
| ALLIANCE | +13.2% |

| SOUTH EAST | |
|---|---|
| TORY | −0.2% |
| LABOUR | −10.9% |
| ALLIANCE | +11.4% |

Source: *Sunday Times*, 12 June 1983.

is within reasonable travelling distance of Westminster). The job has a poor public image. MPs have little home life. Even with all these problems, there is no shortage of people who want to enter the Commons.

A profile of a would-be Member of Parliament might include these points:

- self motivated;
- persuasive speaker;
- strong opinions;
- commitment to the party's policies;
- crusader;
- well informed;
- educated;
- achiever;
- capacity for hard work;
- stamina;
- open personality;
- active in local affairs;
- British subject;
- over 21 years of age.

A **prospective parliamentary candidate** must be adopted by a constituency organisation and then, when the election is announced, be nominated by at least ten electors living within the constituency. A candidate will drop the title 'prospective' only when the election is called; otherwise he or she will incur election expenses.

Any adult citizen may stand for Parliament, except:

- a member of the House of Lords;
- a member of the clergy of the Church of England, Church of Scotland, Church of Ireland and the Roman Catholic Church;
- an undischarged bankrupt;
- convicted criminals still serving sentences;
- people convicted of corrupt practices at elections;
- some civil servants;
- judges;
- ambassadors;
- members of the regular armed forces;
- paid members of the boards of national industries;
- directors of the Bank of England;
- clerks of county courts;
- town clerks or chief executive officers.

## The work of MPs
Very few MPs, however able and hard-working, become Cabinet ministers. So MPs have to develop a role for themselves in the Commons. One MP may be an expert on tax law, another on housing, perhaps one will agitate against blood sports. The MPs participate in the committee system of the House of Commons. It is not unusual for an MP to have 'outside' interests, e.g. sit on a board of directors, run a company, be a barrister, participate in radio and television programmes or write a regular column for a newspaper. All MPs have to register their outside interests and activities and to declare their shareholdings, directorships and companies owned.

Well-known and influential MPs, especially those who have held Cabinet rank, may be offered directorships or chairmanships of companies. Despite the power enjoyed by a major business corporation, it will like to have an MP on its payroll. The MP can provide:

- advice on prospective legislation and how it might affect the company;
- knowledge of Whitehall and how the ministries work;
- personal contacts with ministers, chairpersons of select committees and leading MPs;
- introductions to other influential people;
- leadership for company delegations;
- a way to recruit fellow MPs to the company's cause;
- a sympathetic attitude towards the company in particular and the industry in general.

Other MPs may be involved not with companies but with associations, charities or trade unions. Some Labour MPs are sponsored by their trade unions and they may be given financial help with election expenses and perhaps secretarial assistance. A body like the Police Federation has a spokesperson in the Commons – not a police officer but an MP who is sympathetic towards police issues and problems. These MPs will be expected to represent the views and policies of their sponsoring organisations, to ask questions, to influence other MPs and maybe to initiate legislation.

All this raises the question about an MP's position. He or she is not a delegate but a **representative**. MPs are not told by their electors how to vote in the Commons, what to say or what attitude to adopt on any issue. They are expected to have a broad vision and experience and to work for the better interests of their country, constituency and party. Many MPs argue that their outside interests help them to tackle issues with greater confidence and competence. In this way, they believe, they become better politicians. See Fig. 1.6.

**Fig. 1.6: The MP as representative and the influences on him or her**

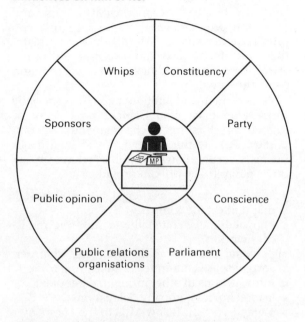

Activity 1.2
Brenda Smith is very active in the college debating society. She is an accomplished speaker with a commanding presence. She is articulate on political issues and in order to gain experience she has canvassed for all the main parties – Tory, Labour and the Alliance. In a recent debating competition, the chairman of judges, when awarding Brenda her much deserved trophy, suggested that she should consider a career in politics.

Since that competition, Brenda has been thinking about the judge's remarks. She likes the idea of becoming an MP. She is fairly certain where she stands politically but at the moment is not a member of any political party. She realises that to get into Parliament will take a lot of work and luck but she doesn't know where or how to start.

Advise Brenda Smith how to go about fulfilling her ambition.

## GOVERNMENT AND CIVIL SERVICE

### The government

We talk of 'the government' but what do we mean by it? Government is not to be confused with Parliament, which comprises nearly 1900 peers and MPs, all representing different interests, backgrounds and political opinions. The government is formed by the party which secures the most seats in the House of Commons following a general election. Not all MPs belonging to the majority party are in the government, although they are members of the government party. Not more than ninety-five MPs can be given government jobs in the ministries and departments; the remainder must come from the Lords. The government usually has between 100 and 110 members, of whom between 20 and 24 form the Cabinet. See Fig. 1.7.

*Ministers*
A **Cabinet minister** occupies a senior and powerful position in the government and will generally head a department, e.g. the Ministry of Defence, the Department of Education and Science. A member of the Cabinet is automatically a member of the **Privy Council** and is entitled to be addressed as the Right Honourable.

Ministers not of Cabinet rank are **junior ministers**. They are known by a variety of official titles: Minister of State, Parliamentary Under-Secretary of State or Parliamentary Secretary. For example, the Department of Trade and Industry is served by seven ministers and has the basic structure shown in Fig. 1.8.
At the time of writing, one of the Department of Trade and Industry's under-secretaries is a member of the Lords. All major departments tend to have a minister drawn from the Upper House. The government has to perform there, and it is essential that there are peers who can contribute to debates and answer questions on departmental issues.

*The Cabinet*
The exact size of the Cabinet is for the Prime Minister to decide. Modern-day Cabinets are likely to hold just over twenty ministers, depending on the relative importance of departments and ministries.

It has been said that politics exists not because

**Fig. 1.7: Formation of the government**

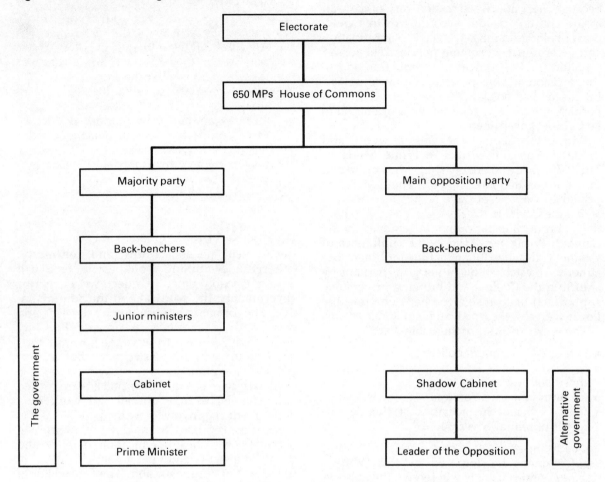

**Fig. 1.8: Ministers of the Department of Trade and Industry**

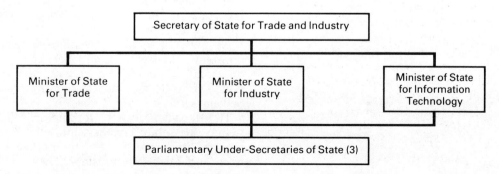

there are two sides to every argument but because there are two sides to every office – an inside and an outside. According to this view, power belongs to those who control information and determine government policies. The nearer a politician is to sources of information and to the decision-making process, the more powerful his or her position is likely to be. This is perhaps why British government is often said to be **Cabinet government**.

Within the Cabinet the most powerful and influential position is that of **Prime Minister**. The PM's style and energy shape the nature and direction of the government. The PM is expected to exercise positive leadership *over* and *within* the Cabinet.

The Prime Minister cannot be removed by the Cabinet. But if the PM loses the confidence of Cabinet colleagues then it is time for him or her either to re-establish his or her grip (perhaps by **shuffling** the Cabinet and bringing in personal supporters) or to resign (perhaps entering the Lords with a well-earned peerage).

The basic functions of the Cabinet are:

- to frame government policies;
- to formulate the laws necessary to support those policies;
- to control the Civil Service;
- to co-ordinate the activities of the departments of central government.

Due to the strength of party discipline within the Commons (as imposed by the **Whips**), Cabinet policies usually will receive the approval of the **back-benchers** (non-ministerial MPs of the governing party). However, the Cabinet (or **Executive**) is always answerable to Parliament. Individual ministers are held responsible for all the activities of their departments, and Cabinet ministers are collectively held responsible for all the activities of the government.

Activity 1.3
(a) Using the resources of your library, find out the names of all the Cabinet ministers. Also find out the names of their 'opposite numbers' in the **Shadow Cabinet**, and on the Alliance front benches.
(b) Present your findings in the form of a chart.
(c) Study recent newspapers and find at least three reports of issues in which some of the people on your chart have been involved. Briefly describe the issues involved.

### The Civil Service

Government needs **stability** and **continuity**. Otherwise everything would grind to a halt during election time. In effect we have two governments: the **political** and the **administrative**. The former is represented by the MPs and peers, and the latter by civil servants. The duty of the Civil Service is to serve the government – not just to carry out instructions but also to advise. Governments rely heavily upon the Civil Service to see that their policies are carried out. This is because not all the work of a department is involved with policy-making; much is concerned with the day-to-day running of our services – health, education, defence, and so on. Ministers do not get involved with every tiny detail of administration. The Chancellor of the Exchequer, for example, is not concerned with managing the officials in the local tax office – that is the job of civil servants.

Civil servants are permanent officials and must remain neutral. They do not support any particular party-political line and are expected to serve whichever government is in power. Until policies of a previous government are scrapped or changed, the Civil Service must continue to follow them.

Not all civil servants are high-powered government advisers. The service employs thousands of people in a wide range of occupations – from clerks and cleaners to Permanent Secretaries.

Those civil servants working in **Whitehall** (where the senior civil servants who head and manage the ministries have their offices) do not fetch and carry for ministers. They are skilled advisers, policy-drafters, writers of papers and composers of speeches and answers to questions; they are expected to assist ministers to frame policies and to come to decisions. A minister cannot carry out his or her function without relying upon a lot of background information and research, which is provided by members of his or her department. It is usual for ministers to draw on another source of advice – the **political adviser**, whose task it is to consider the party-political implications of any measure or policy. Civil servants cannot be asked to do that, which would compromise their impartiality. The political adviser is likely to be an MP of the minister's own choosing.

It is possible for a lazy or weak minister to be influenced or led by civil servants. But it is part of the checks and balances of government that ministers must report not only to Parliament but also to the Cabinet, where policies are thrashed out. Ministers may be given wide powers and authority, yet no one minister can adopt his or her own policies without seeking Cabinet approval. The Cabinet sometimes defeats a minister's proposals or public stand on an issue, and then the minister may feel forced to resign. See Fig. 1.9.

**Fig. 1.9: A minister's relationship with the Cabinet and Civil Service**

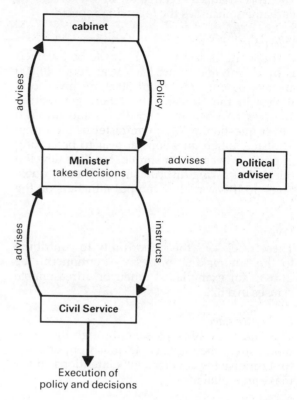

## THE RELATIONSHIP BETWEEN PARLIAMENT AND THE GOVERNMENT

### Opposition and Shadow Cabinet

All members of the UK Parliament, both peers and MPs, have the **duty** of scrutinising the work of government, although this is also specifically the role of the **official opposition**, i.e. the largest opposition party in the Commons. There has to be an effective challenge to government; it must be made to justify itself and has to remember that it is answerable to Parliament and to the electorate. Without any examination of its work and policies, particularly of its spending, a government might be tempted to ignore democracy. Parliament, through its various activities, is the instrument to stop the government from abusing its powers.

With the exception of the government, the most important body in the Commons is the **Shadow Cabinet**. It comprises senior party spokespersons on policy areas who are in effect shadow ministers and would expect one day to be members of the government. Thus the shadow spokesperson on defence would like to be offered the post of Secretary of State for Defence if his or her party won the next election. However, there is no rule which would insist on his or her appointment, because the Prime Minister has the right to choose the ministers.

A lot of media attention is paid to the opposition, and the performances of the leader and Shadow Cabinet are carefully watched and considered. The main opposition party's public image depends on how its leading members are reported. Although the opposition is not there just to oppose for the sake of it, it can be an effective check on the government and would be expected to question the government at every opportunity.

**The role of MPs**

The role that MPs can play in the affairs of Parliament includes the following aspects.

*Questions*

Perhaps the easiest way for MPs to be involved is by asking questions. Each year about 40,000 are asked, but only about 3000 are given oral replies in the House – the others get written answers. An MP may raise an issue through clever questioning of any minister or the Prime Minister. Often questions appear to be lacking in point or even rather simple, but MPs develop the skill of asking difficult supplementary questions. In this way they can put ministers on the spot.

*Debates*

These offer MPs the opportunity to contribute to the law-making process. Attention can be drawn, for example, to unfair or unreasonable clauses in a Bill.

*Committee stage*

This stage of a Bill's passage through the Commons offers the vigilant MP much opportunity to scrutinise the government's intentions and to make amendments.

*Adjournment debates*

At the end of each day the House suspends its business until the next sitting. There is an **adjournment debate** for the last half an hour of the day, and this offers MPs the chance to raise matters of special concern and to get a detailed response from a minister.

*Opposition days*

These were once known as **supply days**, when the Commons discussed the supply of money to the government and its financial estimates; but the opposition used these days to criticise the government's policies that the money would pay for. Since 1982–3 the opposition has been allocated twenty **opposition days** a year when it can directly criticise the government's policies. On seventeen of these days the subject for debate is chosen by the leader of the opposition; the remaining three days are at the disposal of the leader of the second largest opposition party.

*Delegated legislation*

Occasionally an Act is passed which gives power to a minister to make laws affecting his or her area of responsibility. Parliament passes a sort of 'control' or 'parent' Act, and the minister, having decided what is required, lays his or her proposals before Parliament where they may be debated. Effective control over ministers is exercised by MPs' questions and by the **Select Committee on Statutory Instruments**.

*Select committees*

These are essentially committees of investigation which look into government departments. They are an important feature of the Commons. A select committee can call for written evidence and can cross-examine any witness (this is done in public). Having completed an investigation, it is required to publish a report and make it available to the public.

A committee comprises eleven back-bench MPs, and the parties are represented in proportion to the number of seats held in the House. Members are chosen by the House on the recommendation of the Committee of Selection.

No government can spend money or raise revenue without the permission of Parliament. The Chancellor presents his or her Budget in the form of a Finance Bill, which has to become a Finance Act before the government can act on its proposals. A major task confronting Parliament is to ensure that money is spent correctly and that any overspending by a department can be justified. Money matters are scrutinised by the most important select committee: the **Public Accounts Committee**.

*Parliamentary Commissioner for Administration*

If there is the suggestion of maladministration by a government department, then a complaint can be made through an MP to the Commissioner or, as he or she is better known, the **Ombudsman**. If there is a case, the Ombudsman reports and suggests a remedy.

We do not expect our MPs or peers to spend parliamentary time foolishly. They have a positive duty to keep a check on the work of the government.

In summary, MPs can challenge the government by:

● voting against proposed laws;

- making amendments;
- asking questions;
- restricting funds;
- examining work in committees.

Remember: the power of government rests on the **consent of the governed**.

## MAKING THE LAW

Law-making is the primary function of Parliament and it requires the active involvement of both Houses. Bills can be introduced in either House, although almost all major Bills originate in the Commons. All Finance Bills must be raised in the Commons. Legislation comes under two main headings: **Public** and **Private**.

### Public legislation
It is usual for the government to publish its legislative intentions so that the public can comment on its ideas and proposals. Once the government thinks it is ready to develop ideas further, aiming to put them into practice with an **Act of Parliament**, it orders the preparation of a **Bill**. Preparing Bills is the job of the **Parliamentary Counsel's Office** and may take up to four months. The Bill will take the form of a **draft statute** and consists of:

- a long title which covers its purposes and content;
- a short title by which it is generally known;
- an enacting formula;
- schedules containing lists of statutes affected;
- details of machinery and procedure resulting from the main provisions.

The stages through which a government Bill has to pass are as follows.

### First reading
An MP, usually a minister, notifies the House that he or she intends to introduce a Bill. On the appointed day the member's name is called out by the Speaker, and a 'dummy Bill' is presented to the Clerk, who reads out the short title. This act constitutes the **first reading**, and a day is fixed for the second reading. There is no debate at this stage, because the intention is to inform the House of forthcoming business.

### Second reading
On this occasion the member in charge of the Bill explains its main purpose and moves that 'the Bill be now read a second time'. A debate follows, but no discussion on detail is permitted, because only the Bill's general principles are of immediate concern.

### Committee stage
The Bill is referred to a **standing committee** whose task it is to examine it in detail. The committee will comprise about eighteen MPs and they will devote their energies to each word and each clause of the Bill. The committee may sit for several months. While it can make amendments, it cannot destroy the Bill's main principles.

### Report stage
Once the committee has done its job, the whole House must be informed of what has happened to the Bill. The Bill will have been reprinted so that all amendments and changes can be read. The House reserves the right to make further amendments and to insert new clauses.

### Third reading
Usually a Bill is read a third time immediately after the report stage. This reading gives the members an opportunity to look again at the Bill, with all its amendments, and to decide whether they want it to go any further. Other than corrections to printing errors, the Bill cannot be changed in any other way; the House either accepts it or rejects it.

### 'Another place'
As soon as the Bill has completed its stages in the Commons, it is taken by a Clerk to the Lords, where it is 'delivered to the table' (the reverse procedure applies to a Bill originating in the Lords). The Bill passes through the same stages in the Lords although much more quickly. Bills are often considered by a **Committee of the Whole House** rather than going to a small committee.

The Lords may reject or amend a Bill, and if that is the case it is sent back to the Commons for further consideration. Mostly the Commons will accept amendments on non-controversial Bills. But if there is disagreement the Bill may go to and fro between the Houses until agreement is reached. If compromise remains impossible then the Commons would have to reintroduce the Bill in the following parliamentary session.

*Royal assent*

A Bill cannot become an Act without the **royal assent**. In order not to interrupt the business of Parliament, the Royal Assent Act 1967 allows the Speaker and the Lord Chancellor simply to report the Queen's approval. The traditional ceremony is still used on occasion, when the Clerk of the Parliaments announces in Norman French, 'La Reyne le veult' – the Queen wishes it.

Figs. 1.10 and 1.11 show the stages of a government Bill. Even when an Act has received the royal assent it may not come into force immediately. It may be necessary to give those affected full opportunity to adapt to the changed situation. Such Acts require a **government order** before they take effect.

**Fig. 1.11: From Bill to Act**

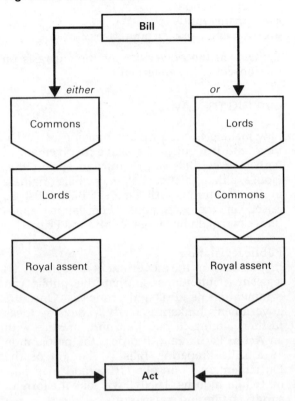

**Fig. 1.10: Stages of a Bill through Parliament**

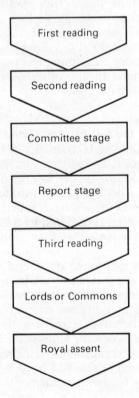

*Private members' Bills*

There are two kinds of public Bill: **Government Bills** (dealt with above) and **Private Members' Bills**. In theory an MP may introduce any Bill he or she pleases, but the chances of success are poor if a proposal cuts across government policy or involves expenditure. The main difficulty confronting MPs is that of obtaining the time to have their Bills debated by the House.

One device for introducing a private members' Bill is by a motion for leave to bring in a Bill on a Tuesday or Wednesday under the **ten-minutes rule**. The member making the motion speaks for ten minutes in favour of his or her Bill, and another member may speak against it for a similar time. The Speaker will then **put the question**. If the House finds in favour, then the Bill is considered to have been read a first time. A day is then announced for its second reading.

Another method of introducing a Bill is for an MP to win a place in the ballot held at the beginning of each parliamentary session. Ten Fridays are reserved for private members' Bills.

Each successful member presents his or her Bill in person and names a Friday for its second reading. MPs have to draft their own Bills, cope with the complicated procedure of Parliament and obtain a quorum of the House on a Friday afternoon. If the Bill offends the government, the Whips will be put on against it. Also, unless it is first on the **order paper** for the day, opposing interests will debate the previous business at length so as to leave insufficient time for the following Bills.

## Private legislation

In addition to passing public Bills concerned with the community at large, Parliament may give particular powers or benefits to an individual, to companies, to local authorities, to public utilities and to nationalised industries. Thus a local authority can seek powers not provided by an existing Act, while a public utility can ask for the powers to make by-laws. There is a detailed and elaborate procedure to ensure that private legislation does not unreasonably harm either national or private interests.

The number of **private Bills** introduced each parliamentary session is not likely to exceed fifty, and most of them are promoted by local authorities. During the nineteenth century private Bills numbered between six and seven hundred each session.

The stages through which a private Bill passes are as follows:

1. Petition, preliminary advertisement and examination.
2. First reading.
3. Second reading.
4. Committee stage.
5. Consideration stage.
6. Third reading.
7. House of Lords.
8. Royal assent.

In addition to private Bills, there are two further aspects of private legislation:

*Provisional order confirmation Bills*
Many progressive local authorities used to promote private Bills in order to extend their general powers. The procedure was expensive until the **provisional order** system was introduced; this provides a cheaper, simpler and shorter procedure. These are practically private Bills but they are termed 'provisional' since they cannot be acted upon until they have received Parliament's approval.

*Special procedure orders*
These tend to supplement the above-mentioned system. They aim at quicker and cheaper preliminary approval of those departmental orders which give effect to decisions of national policy but which might affect private rights.

Activity 1.4
(a) Write down three areas where you feel that there is a real need for a change in the law or for new law.
(b) Compare your suggestions with those of the rest of the class. Identify and discuss the issues with which people seem to be most concerned.

Activity 1.5
During a two-week period, listen to the Radio Four programme *Yesterday in Parliament*. Keep a diary of the major legislation which is being dealt with, and the questions and events being discussed.

# 2. Political Parties, Policies and Public Opinion

office just to please its friends; it has to take decisions which it regards as being in the best interests of the nation.

Government must not be seen as a vulnerable committee easily swayed by public opinion. Much government policy is determined by:

- the need for the government to fulfil its election pledges as set out in its pre-election *manifesto*;
- the government's responsibility to respond to and resolve **current problems** and sometimes unforeseen circumstances.

## POWER AND INFLUENCE

Chapter 1 looked at the structure of government in the UK and some of its processes. Government policies do not just happen; they are the result of currents of public opinion, pressure, policy evolution and changing circumstances. Parliament has an important part to play in determining government policy, but policies that are put into legal form by the Commons and the Lords have sometimes been shaped and stimulated by other, external influences. Policies are discussed and changed by political conferences, by trade unions, by employers' associations and major companies, by pressure groups, by petitions and by individuals. Sometimes the efforts of individuals or groups result in a government-sponsored policy.

The **power** to make and effect policy rests with the government. No organisation outside Parliament has more power, and there is no way any group could achieve it. What pressure groups and lobbyists concern themselves with, however, is **influence**, and there is plenty of opportunity to attempt to exercise that.

There is no single mechanism for suggesting or influencing policies. We live in a democracy, and many ways are open to people who want to express a view, highlight a case or bring about a change in the law; they will use the most suitable means at their disposal. The government does not have to listen to or act upon the ideas put to it, but it would be behaving undemocratically if it attempted to stop individuals or groups expressing their opinions. It may be that a Conservative government is more inclined to respond favourably to business, whilst a Labour government will tend to listen to the unions. However, no government is in

## PARTIES AND POLICIES

One of the most effective channels for influencing policy is the political party. Parties are more than just associations of like-thinking people; they are instruments for securing Parliamentary power. The leading parties are well organised and strong, and their administrative leadership is highly professional and motivated. Running an effective and modern party involves a lot of money, so plenty of local constituency time and effort is spent on raising funds.

Political parties need **funds** in order to:

- maintain a head office, preferably within easy reach of Westminister;
- offer various services to their MPs;
- offer services to the constituencies;
- organise national publicity;
- mount campaigns;
- produce leaflets and brochures;
- fight local-authority and general elections.

Political parties need to be run like businesses if they are to survive. Their 'market' environment is highly competitive – i.e. the struggle to win public support and to secure the reins of government.

The **grass-roots** of a party are as important as its leadership. Without the willing and committed involvement of volunteer members who give their money and time, the structure of a party would soon disintegrate. Without active constituency organisation no candidate could hope for success in a local or general election.

Apart from securing representation at Westminister through elected MPs, local party organisations seek:

- to win seats on parish, district, borough and county councils;
- representation on school managing and college governing bodies;
- representation on any public committee in which they have an interest;
- to promote their views and policies on local radio and television and in the newspapers.

### Party leadership

The structure and purpose of a party may be democratic, but the active and effective control is usually in the hands of a small number of activists and party officials. How many party members can give much free time to the party? How many are skilled in debate and writing? How many enjoy committee work? How many are motivated to seek power and influence for themselves? The answer to all these questions is 'only a few'.

This is not to criticise but to underline the reality of party organisation. The direction and policy of political parties are usually controlled by the totally committed. A party is likely to have a complex structure of committees running from local **ward** level to the very top. Those who want political power need to work their way through the system.

### Parties and elections

Political parties tend to represent particular interests (see pp. 20–23), and people generally vote according to what they believe is in their best interests. Apart from the main party candidates, however, people who want to promote particular causes often become candidates at either local or national elections. They do so in an attempt to attract media attention and hope to sway some opinion in favour of their ideas (usually knowing that electoral failure is certain). However, the majority of the electorate votes for the main parties, especially at general elections. Table 2.1 shows the voters' choices over the past century.

Protest votes are sometimes recorded in favour of minority groups, and this is often a feature of by-elections. It may be that a campaigner against lorries, a motorway, an airport or a housing development will stand for either the local council or parliament. He or she may even be elected, but without a structured political organisation he or she is unlikely to have any influence; membership of committees may

**Table 2.1: General Election Results 1885–1983 (elected MPs)**

| Year | Conservative | Liberal | Labour | Others | Total MPs |
|---|---|---|---|---|---|
| 1885 | 249 | 335 | | | 584 |
| 1886 | 294[1] | 191 | | | 485 |
| 1892 | 315[2] | 273 | 1 | | 589 |
| 1895 | 411[3] | 177 | | | 588 |
| 1900 | 402 | 268 | 2 | | 672 |
| 1906 | 157 | 377 | 53 | | 587 |
| 1910 | 273 | 274 | 40 | | 587 |
| 1918[4] | 383 | 161 | 73 | 90 | 707 |
| 1922 | 344 | 115 | 142 | 14 | 615 |
| 1923 | 258 | 158 | 191 | 8 | 615 |
| 1924 | 412 | 40 | 151 | 12 | 615 |
| 1929 | 260 | 59 | 287 | 9 | 615 |
| 1931[5] | 521 | 37 | 52 | 5 | 615 |
| 1935[6] | 429 | 21 | 154 | 11 | 615 |
| 1945 | 213 | 12 | 393 | 22 | 640 |
| 1950 | 299 | 9 | 315 | 2 | 625 |
| 1951 | 321 | 6 | 295 | 3 | 625 |
| 1955 | 345 | 6 | 277 | 2 | 630 |
| 1959 | 365 | 6 | 258 | 1 | 630 |
| 1964 | 304 | 9 | 317 | | 630 |
| 1966 | 253 | 12 | 364 | 1 | 630 |
| 1970 | 330 | 6 | 288 | 6 | 630 |
| 1974 | 297 | 14 | 301 | 23 | 635 |
| 1974 | 277 | 13 | 319 | 26 | 635 |
| 1979 | 339 | 11 | 269 | 16 | 635 |
| 1983 | 397 | 23[7] | 209 | 21 | 650 |

[1,2,3] Includes Liberal Unionists.
[4] Coalition.
[5,6] National Government.
[7] Includes both Liberal and SDP.

be denied; there will be no seconder to his or her motions, and the reason for his or her being elected may be overshadowed by more pressing and longer-term problems.

### Party policy

Political parties spend a lot of time on policy-making. Issues are debated as a continuing activity. Since local and national governments are drawn from one or more political parties government policies will be those largely developed from within the party organisations – although any government will also rely upon 'outside' bodies which support its party financially and ideologically.

### Conferences

The period late September to early October is

known as the 'conference season', and the annual **party conferences** that take place then attract interest and attention. The conferences are stage-managed media occasions, when each party tries to get its message across not just to its one or two thousand delegates but to the nation as a whole. There is always the impression, created by the leading politicians who perform at the conferences, that they are addressing not an immediate and faithful audience but every one of us watching TV at home.

Motions are submitted by constituency parties and policy matters are discussed by the conference. The motions that are passed or adopted, thus becoming **conference resolutions**, are generally considered by the party managers and the national executive to see whether or how they might be developed as official party policy. Particularly at Labour Party conferences, the left-wing tends to want conference decisions to bind the parliamentary party; on the other hand, voting at Conservative Party conferences is sometimes discouraged to avoid any appearance of disagreement.

Conferences are the time when leading party figures address the members on key issues. At the end of a successful conference the delegates go back to their constituencies politically refreshed and fired with enthusiasm.

The objects of the party conference can be summarised as:

- to reassure the 'faithful' that the party has positive policies and is moving in the 'right direction';
- to impress the uncommitted and floating voters that the party is worth supporting;
- to put over to the nation current policy thinking;
- to present the party as either firmly in control of government or the best alternative party to govern Britain;
- to offer a clear statement of intent;
- to display party unity.

Activity 2.1
The government consults people through **Green Papers, White Papers** and feedback through the media, MPs, public meetings, pressure groups and so on. Despite having a majority, the government needs to keep in touch with public opinion, but none the less it is elected to take decisions without having to consult the general public on each and every issue.

Timothy Johnson reckons that there are a number of issues which the government should discuss directly with the public. He feels strongly, for example, that the government should seek the opinions of people about nuclear weapons, nuclear power and European Community food mountains.

Karen Cook says that Timothy doesn't understand a thing about politics. She says that surely the government was elected on a clear set of policies, and the people were consulted through the ballot box. She thinks the government should be left to get on with the job.

Advise Timothy and Karen on your views on the matter.

## THE MAIN POLITICAL PARTIES

### The Conservative Party

This party enjoys a long history and it has its roots in what was known as the Court Party, those who supported King Charles II in the seventeenth century. It was nicknamed the 'Tory' Party by its opponents; the word 'Tory' was a corruption of an Irish term meaning thief or rogue. The Tories are seen by many as the 'party of government', and it has been said that their success in promoting this image is due largely to their ability to change direction without changing basic principles. Many Conservative thinkers argue that Conservatism is not about dogma or philosophy but more about a way of thinking and dealing with issues, a way of responding to events.

In the nineteenth century the Tories saw themselves as the true patriots. Under **Disraeli**'s clever leadership the party 'adopted' the monarchy. **Queen Victoria** was a popular sovereign, and her popularity overflowed on to the Tories. The Conservative Party became identified in people's minds with the Crown, the British Empire and active foreign policy.

The early Tories were in the main high Anglicans and landowners who resented the Nonconformists and the rise of the merchant class. Disraeli thought that the upper classes had the right and duty to govern, provided they did so in the interests of the people as a whole. The Tories resisted universal suffrage, i.e. giving the vote to all adults regardless of class and property. Disraeli made the point that he believed in a *House of Commons*, not in a *House of the People*.

The Tories used to be **interventionists**. That is, in the nineteenth century they supported social reforms and believed in paying for them through taxation. The modern Conservative Party tends to hold the opposite views.

The popular image of the Conservative Party is that it is a party for the wealthy, the successful, up-and-coming young professionals, the upper classes, people with private incomes and public-school education, and so on. Many of the party's leadership tend to reflect this image, and it is one that its opponents like to develop.

Support for the party comes from a wide spectrum, however, and has always done so. The Tories owe their election successes not just to the landowners and the bankers but to the willingness of the ordinary people to vote them in. It is reckoned that some 40 per cent of trade union members regularly vote Conservative. Not all working-class people are staunch unionists and socialists; similarly, not all wealthy and professional people are committed to Toryism. Nevertheless, much of the party's financial support comes from the business community.

### The Labour Party

This is a much younger party than the Conservative and Liberal parties. Its roots lie in the growing need during the nineteenth century for some representation in Parliament of what we can broadly call the 'working people'. Many efforts were made to involve people in forms of practical socialism like the co-operative movement and the trade unions, and by the end of the nineteenth century left-wing political organisations had been established and were making themselves heard: the **Social Democratic Federation**, the **Fabians** and the **Independent Labour Party**. In 1900 the **Labour Representation Committee** was formed, which sought to get MPs into Parliament who represented the working class. The committee changed its name to the Labour Party in 1906, and in the general election of that year 53 Labour MPs were elected (22 of whom were sponsored by trade unions).

The Labour Party was therefore born out of the trade union movement – a point which should not be overlooked when criticising the party's reliance on funds from the unions. The unions founded and nurtured the Labour Party and so they have a right to be involved in its management.

The first Labour government was formed in 1924 but it did not have much success. Real parliamentary power, and the first major Labour government, came with the **1945 general election** when the party won a landslide victory over the Tories with a majority of 180 seats. The party pledged itself to creating a fairer society and to rebuild a war-torn Britain. The period 1945–51 is regarded as one of social and economic regeneration. It is known for the development of state education, the setting up of the National Health Service and the nationalisation of many important industries, e.g. gas, electricity and the railways.

The image of the Labour Party, despite many of its leading members being university educated and wealthy, is considered 'cloth-cap' – a enduring reference to the party's working-class origins. The party is seen as committed to expanding the public sector (state ownership) , to eliminating private education and health service, and to economic and taxation policies which – its opponents say – will stifle initiative and enterprise. Supporters of the party claim that it stands for a fairer society.

The Labour Party attracts its support, like the Tories, from a wide variety of opinion and backgrounds. It has had to come to terms with the fact that many working-class people are much better off now than they were half a century ago. The idea of council housing estates being 100-per-cent Labour supporters is nonsense. The parliamentary party has its share of the well-to-do, lawyers, teachers, business people, public-school and university-educated people. It tries to appeal to all, not just to the people of Clydeside or Tyneside, to the workers in the coal mines, shipyards and steelmills.

### The Liberal Party

In the nineteenth century the Liberals represented the right wing in British politics. They were committed to *laissez-faire* (letting people do what they think best) and condemned the Tories' interventionist policies. The attitude of the Liberal Party was summed up by **Sir Robert**

**Walpole** as 'Let sleeping dogs lie.' This meant a government of non-activity and non-interference.

**Gladstone** argued in 1868 that government intervention through taxation and legislation was an interference with people's lives and with their freedom. The Liberals believed in the 'watchkeeper state'; there should be as little government as absolutely necessary.

Forty years later **Lloyd George** created a revolution in Liberal thinking. He argued that the freedom from legislation and regulation had produced a good life for a few but 'dire poverty' for a third of the British population. Lloyd George proclaimed the new Liberal direction: a change from the freedom from taxation and regulation to the freedom to enjoy a better standard of living for all. His policies and the fundamental change in Liberal attitudes drove some of the more traditional party supporters towards Conservatism.

During the nineteenth century the Liberal Party often held power, enjoying the fruits of a two-party system. The emergence of the Labour Party seriously challenged the Liberal Party's position, and since the 1920s it has not done very well in general elections. The party attracts a lot of voters, but the number of parliamentary seats has been small for the last half-century. The 1983 general election witnessed a considerable upsurge in voting support for the Alliance (Liberals and SDP), which attracted one vote in four and yet resulted in only one seat in twenty-eight.

The image of the Liberals has in recent years not always been strong. The party has often been the butt of political jokes: for example, that they hold parliamentary group meetings in a taxi or a telephone box. For some people, the Liberals have had their day; they regard the party members as keen and pleasant idealists with unworkable ideas. Yet the 1983 election did show plenty of support. The party has claimed to be 'radical non-socialist', and since the formation of the Liberal/SDP Alliance it looks forward to holding the balance of power in Parliament.

### The Social Democratic Party

This is the youngest party. It was formed in 1981 by the so-called **gang of four**: Roy Jenkins, Bill Rodgers, Shirley Williams and David Owen, who each held office in a Labour government.

The decision to form the SDP was prompted by dissatisfaction among right-wing Labour Party members who felt that the Labour Party was pursuing outmoded and divisive policies which would not enjoy general favour with the electorate. The founders of the SDP felt that the middle ground or consensus held the key to the political future; in their opinion the Labour Party was too far to the left of the voting public.

Membership of, and support for, the SDP is not drawn solely from disillusioned Labour voters. The party has encouraged the involvement of many who have never been politically active before, and there are many former Conservatives in its membership – especially those called '**wets**', i.e. Tories who believe in 'capitalism with a human face', government intervention in health care, unemployment, etc.

The SDP and Liberal Parties have formed the Alliance, but they remain separate political entities with their own leadership and party organisations. The Alliance is primarily based upon an electoral agreement: the two parties share a common manifesto, and no SDP candidate will stand against a Liberal or vice versa. The Alliance partners seem to incline towards coalition, and their objective is success in a general election and subsequent power-sharing.

### 'Left' and 'Right'

The terms 'left' and 'right' are used as a kind of shorthand to describe a person's or a party's political views. Table 2.2 illustrates the general

**Table 2.2: 'Left' and 'right'**

| Broad left | Broad right |
|---|---|
| • Social ownership | • Free enterprise |
| • Equality | • Freedom |
| • Collective rights of the community | • Individualism |
| • State control or direction of the economy | • Non-intervention |
| • Taxation as the means of redistributing resources | • Pricing as the means of distributing resources |
| • Democracy | • Oligarchy |
| • Civil rights | • Law and order |
| • Nuclear disarmament | • Nuclear deterrent |
| • Government spending to resolve economic problems, e.g. unemployment | • Control of money supply, free-market resolution of economic problems |

philosophy and ideas associated with both the left and the right.

Fig. 2.1 relates the main political parties and groupings to the left–right spectrum. If you want to compare detailed party policies, you will have to look at party leaflets and manifestos.

> Activity 2.2
> (a) Write to the secretaries of the major political parties in your area, inviting them to your college or school to give a talk on the aims of their organisation and how they try to achieve those aims.
> (b) After the talks, write a report discussing the objectives of each organisation and their activities.

## PUBLIC OPINION

Government exercises its function by consent. Electors are consulted through the ballot box, but voting is just one aspect of democracy. **Consent** includes the government's willingness to recognise the various channels through which people may voice opinion. The consent to government, then, is based on the encouragement, formation or education of opinion.

### Opinions are personal things

Most people have opinions on most subjects and issues, but how have they come to their conclusions? Are a person's ideas and opinions

- the result of experiences and of thoughtful decision, consciously arrived at after considering all the evidence through logical argument? *Or*
- reflections of their personality, determined largely by irrational influences and motives and not really open to logical argument?

The question is easier to ask than to answer. Political opinions are not in-born; they have to be learnt, and this is generally done through some kind of social conditioning. Each person is susceptible to one kind of influence or another, and we respond to ideas according to our willingness to believe or disbelieve and the way we choose our information and material. Some people consider themselves totally objective and rational in the formation of their views, when often they are irrational and subjective. Table 2.3 shows how differently we may see ourselves and our opinions, on the one hand, and our political opponents and their views, on the other.

**Table 2.3: Views of ourselves and our opponents**

| Self | Opponents |
|------|-----------|
| • Highly intelligent | • Lack of intelligence |
| • Emotionally stable | • Emotionally unstable |
| • Integrity | • Doubtful motives |
| • Outstanding personal qualities | • Chronic selfishness |
| • Well read | • Inability to grasp the truth |
| • Country before self | • Self or class before the interests of all |

**Fig. 2.1: The left–right spectrum**

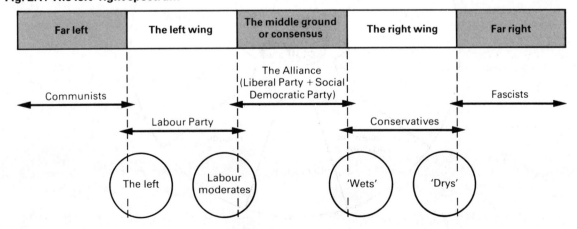

## Influences on the individual

Some people are more objective than others. They will apply logical argument to issues and wrestle with facts and other people's ideas until a reasonable view emerges. For others, opinions are resolved simply by determining or calculating what they have to gain or to lose. But however a person chooses to arrive at his or her opinion, he or she is subject to many influences, some obvious, some subtle. Look at Fig. 2.2. It shows a number of major influences, each of which contributes to the formation of our opinions and perhaps also of our characters.

The mass media in particular – radio and TV, newspapers and magazines, books and films – are very persuasive opinion-makers. We live in the 'media age' when it is almost impossible to escape their influence. Answers to political and economic problems are often presented through the media in an oversimplified form. Despite all the effort the community puts into education, people still tend to respond to the politician who claims to have all the answers and promises positive and quick results. So much of the news is pre-packaged in an oversimple, easy-to-digest way which prevents us from getting at the more complicated truth behind the instant media image. This makes people vulnerable to politicians, lobbyists, pressure groups, opinion researchers and clever advertising. However, the media also provide a more responsible level of reporting and discussion for people who are prepared to make the effort to think about the political issues of our time.

## How public opinion is expressed and estimated

Public opinion – what the majority of people think about a particular issue or situation – varies according to age, race, religion, occupation, sex or membership of a particular organisation. It is therefore difficult to measure or assess. Most of the UK's population forms the so-called 'silent majority' which determines which party is in power but whose opinions are rarely heard. However, if people's feelings are ignored, the government may pay the price; it takes only a shift in support of 1 per cent from one party to another to cause a switch of eighteen seats, and hence a drop of thirty-six in the ruling party's majority.

There are a number of ways in which the government may attempt to gauge public opin-

**Fig. 2.2: Influences on the individual**

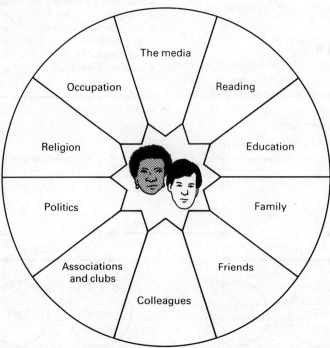

ion. See Fig. 2.3. First, the **public opinion polls**, which deal with a variety of different social, economic and political issues, provide a useful source of reference. The most significant are those held just before a general election in an attempt to forecast the possible result. Between 1945 and 1966 and in both 1979 and 1983 these were successful in their predictions, but in 1970 and the two elections of 1974 they were wrong. However, even when they failed to achieve the correct result their forecasts were generally within the statistical limits of their samples.

### Fig. 2.3: The measurement of public opinion

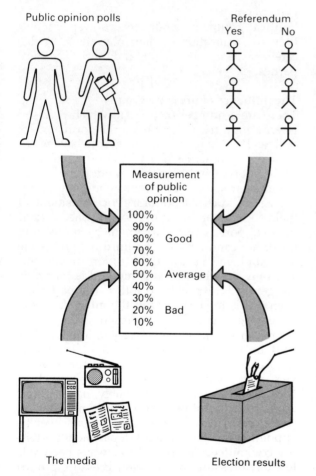

Public opinion polls

Referendum
Yes    No

Measurement
of public
opinion

100%
90%
80%  Good
70%
60%
50%  Average
40%
30%
20%  Bad
10%

The media                    Election results

Secondly, a **study of the media**, such as an assessment of readers' letters in the press, or of the questions being asked on 'phone-in' programmes, may help to reveal some of the issues which concern the general public.

Thirdly, the results of **by-elections** may be considered as an indicator of public opinion. However, they are not as helpful as might at first be thought, because the results show the public's preference for a particular party without revealing the factors determining that preference. The value of elections as a means of determining public opinion is down-graded still further when it is considered that 60 per cent of the electorate always vote the same way.

Finally a **referendum** may be used to measure public opinion on a particular issue. This was first tried in 1975 when a national referendum was held on the question of Common Market membership. It was tried again in 1979 to decide upon the question of devolution in Wales and Scotland. This is a fairly accurate method of measuring public opinion, although its accuracy depends upon the number of people who take part in the referendum. Problems also arise in determining whether an absolute or merely relative majority should be taken as a true reflection of public opinion.

Many government policies have been created on the basis of what is supposed to be a fair estimation of public opinion. Two examples have been the decisions concerning the siting of the third London airport and membership of the EEC. When the suggestion for a third London airport was first raised in the 1960s, both the major political parties favoured its siting at Stansted. This met with considerable local opposition, although it was not until the Roskill Commission reported on the siting in 1971 that Stansted was dropped, and Cublington in Buckinghamshire adopted. Tremendous opposition was aroused in Cublington, which encouraged the Conservative government to switch their attention to Maplin Sands in Essex. Again public opinion reacted there, and the 1974 Labour government turned its attention once more to Stansted. The question was then temporarily shelved, but was reopened in 1979. Stansted still remains the most likely location.

In the case of the decision to join the European Community, this seems to have been taken without much consideration being given to public opinion. When Britain entered in 1973 the Gallup poll revealed that 38 per cent were against and 26 per cent were 'don't knows'. These results hardly suggest resounding support. The referendum in 1975 represented a belated attempt to include public opinion in a decision which would ultimately shape the future business environment. The fact that it attracted so much attention reflected how public opinion had largely been ignored when the decision was originally taken in 1973.

> **Activity 2.3**
> During a one-month period, study the letters appearing in both the national and local press. With which events, issues and problems are people particularly concerned? Suggest the type of action the government should be taking in order to satisfy public opinion.

## PRESSURE GROUPS

The *Guardian Directory of Pressure Groups* (Wilton House Publications) defines a pressure group as 'an association of individuals joined together by a common interest, belief, activity or purpose that seeks to achieve its objectives, further its interests and enhance its status in relation to other groups, by gaining the approval and co-operation of authority in the form of favourable policies, legislation and conditions'.

Potentially any group of individuals who feel sufficiently strongly about a particular issue are capable of acting as a pressure group. For example, a group of villagers might react very strongly if they were suddenly confronted by heavy lorries passing through their main street in order to get to a new motorway spur. They would probably form themselves into an action group, affiliate themselves to any relevant national organisation and agitate for the building of a bypass.

There are three main types of pressure group that are likely to try to influence the formation of government policies. They may be classified as **interest, promotional** and **political** groups.

### *Interest groups*
**Interest groups** try to agitate and act as spokespersons for social or economic causes. Those which have had the greatest impact are the employers' associations, like the Confederation of British Industry (CBI); the trade unions, through the Trades Union Congress (TUC) and the major unions, including the miners, railway workers, seamen, engineers and electricians; the professions, for instance, the Royal Institute

of British Architects, the British Medical Association and the National Farmers' Union (NFU) and the various consumer groups.

### *Promotional groups*
**Promotional groups** are generally concerned with the achievement of one particular goal or the solution of one particular problem. A good example would be the National Society for the Prevention of Cruelty to Children, environmental-protection groups such as Greenpeace and Friends of the Earth, and development charities like Oxfam and War on Want.

### *Political groups*
**Political groups** generally seek power first and then the realisation of their objectives. In this category come the major and minor political parties.

### The influence of pressure groups
There are a number of ways in which pressure groups may try to influence the formation of policy. They may attempt to get their views or their case put across in Parliament by enlisting the support of an MP, either by adopting him or her as their spokesperson, or giving him or her a position such as honorary vice-president of their society, or by trying to put one of their own supporters into Parliament by sponsoring his or her candidature. The third method is the one employed by the trade union movement. The only drawback to this method is that MPs are generally expected to follow the party line even if it is in conflict with the interests of the pressure group that they represent.

Pressure groups may also try to influence the content of a private member's Bill by lobbying the MP who is responsible for its launching. A very well-established pressure group, such as the CBI or the TUC, will probably make a direct approach to a minister or Cabinet minister. In certain cases a group spokesperson may even be appointed to a government department's advisory committee. The NFU has always been able to exert pressure in this way. Pressure groups also try to employ the media to put their case across. For example, the major commercial banks spent a large amount of money on publicising their views on the question of nationalising all commercial banking activities. Groups like CND, Oxfam and Greenpeace also work hard to publicise their views through the media.

### The business environment

Much of the activity of pressure groups influences the business environment. The largest impact on policy formation comes from those groups representing workers, owners and consumers. See Fig. 2.4.

### *The TUC*

Individual trade unions, with the exception of some of the very large ones, are unable to exert much pressure on policy. However, collectively, as part of the **TUC**, their power is considerable. The TUC was formed in 1868 as an association of trade unions. It has about 10 million members in affiliated trade unions from a very wide spectrum of British industry, and it is accepted by government, industry and the labour force as the spokesperson for workers' affairs.

The basic objective of the TUC is to improve the economic and social conditions of workers generally. It is also pledged to co-operate with other organisations with objectives similar to its own and to assist in solving industrial disputes. The TUC tries to achieve these objectives by acting as a pressure group in its own right. It also works on a number of advisory committees alongside the government. The TUC is represented on many official and unofficial bodies concerned with matters of interest and import-

**Fig. 2.4: Major pressure groups influencing policy formation**

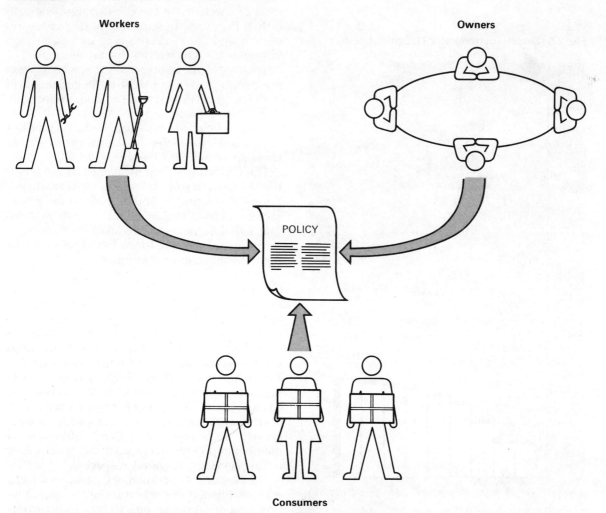

Workers

Owners

POLICY

Consumers

ance to trade unions. Its representation ranges from the Economic and Social Committee of the European Community to the St John Ambulance Association.

As the TUC represents about half of the total work force its views are considered to be fairly authoritative and its powers extensive. However, the TUC's membership has been falling in recent years as unemployment has risen. It could be argued that its influence is weakening as it has failed to impress the government with its arguments on solving unemployment. See Fig. 2.5.

The TUC's major weakness is that it has to represent diverse interests which sometimes come into conflict. For example, if it was involved in the formulation of a policy for an integrated transport system which involved a shift from road to rail this would cause friction between the Transport and General Workers' Union, representing the road haulage lorry drivers, and the British Rail unions.

*The CBI*

By grouping together in the same way as trade unions, employers' associations within the **CBI** are able to have a considerable impact on policy formation in the business environment. The CBI was founded in July 1965 by the merger of the British Employers' Confederation, the Federation of British Industries, the National Association of British Manufacturers and the Industrial Association of Wales. Its membership is made up of approximately 12,000 firms and 200 employers' and trade associations. The basic objectives of the CBI are to act as spokesperson for British business, to support the free enterprise system and to create the type of business environment in which industry may flourish.

To achieve these objectives it acts as a pressure group in its own right by negotiaing with both the government and the trade unions and it is also represented on around 140 wide-ranging official and unofficial bodies. The CBI is recognised by the government as the spokesperson for business.

The CBI suffers from the same weaknesses as the TUC in trying to represent very diverse interests, ranging from the public to the private sector and from multinational to small business. The CBI has nevertheless made a major contribution towards the formation of policies relating to the business environment.

*Consumers*

Individual consumers are able to influence policy by forming pressure groups. Two of the most effective consumer groups are the **Consumers' Association** and the **National Federation of Consumer Groups**. The former was started in 1957 when it published *Which?* magazine and it has since grown to around 7000 members. Its basic objective is to provide an impartial testing of consumer goods and services and to promote greater consumer protection. Although its membership is relatively small the results of its testing services are widely respected.

The National Federation of Consumer Groups was established in 1961 with the backing of the Consumers' Association. It has sixty groups

**Fig. 2.5: Unemployment and TUC membership**

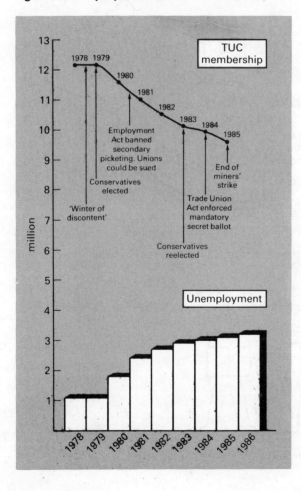

with over 11,000 members. It is basically concerned with consumer protection and has lobbied for standard packaging, the banning of exclusion clauses in service contracts and the setting up of a small claims court.

Consumers groups are now becoming increasingly involved in product safety and additives in foods.

---

Activity 2.4
(a) Look through your local newspapers and identify issues that involve the actions of pressure groups.
(b) In each case note down the main issues involved and the arguments that are presented by both sides.
(c) Which side would you support? Give your reasons.

---

Activity 2.5
Analyse the objectives and effectiveness of a pressure group you know about, e.g. a trade union, a political group or an environmentalist group. Present your findings in the form of a newspaper article.

---

Activity 2.6
Keep a scrapbook of newspaper articles relating to a pressure group that is concerned with either employees, employers or consumers. In a 500-word report make an assessment of the relative success or failure of the group in achieving its objectives.

---

## FROM BRIGHT IDEA TO ACT OF PARLIAMENT

Fig. 2.6 shows how an idea can mature into party policy and then become the law of the land. It is just an example; it does not indicate the only way in which this could be achieved.

## Fig. 2.6: From bright idea to act of parliament

A group of individuals discuss over dinner that the motorways should be privatised

They introduce the idea at a Ward Party meeting which sends it to the Constituency Management Committee

The Constituency Management Committee discusses it and decides to promote it

A motion is prepared for Party Conference | It is raised with the MP or Parliamentary Candidate

The motion is discussed and debated at Conference

The motion receives a lot of support, and the Party managers promise to consider it and produce a policy brief

The policy brief is widely distributed for Party discussion

Support for the idea gathers in the constituencies

It becomes a major discussion point at the next Party Conference

The support is now overwhelming

The Cabinet takes it up and develops the idea

A Minister is handed the project and he takes the responsibility with his civil servants for framing a policy

The Cabinet receives regular reports on progress

The Cabinet is satisfied and orders the publication of a White Paper

The White Paper is available and it encourages responses from lobbyists, pressure groups and the media, e.g. the Automobile Association, Royal Automobile Club, Road Haulage Association, bus operators, petrol and oil companies, major haulage and traction companies, hotel and catering companies, trade unions, political parties

The policy takes shape after consultations

The Minister, civil servants and the Cabinet produce final draft, and a Bill is a drawn up

The Bill goes through procedure in the Commons

The pressure groups are still active, MPs make amendments

The Bill goes to the Lords, where it goes through similar procedures

The Bill is passed and goes for the Royal Assent

The bright idea discussed over dinner, perhaps three or four years before, has matured into an Act of Parliament

The Motorway Privatisation Act

# 3. Government Institutions, Local Government and Business Organisations

The activities and affairs of every business organisation are influenced in some way by the institutions of government. This may be at local, national or European level. The various levels of government may have a **direct** impact on the organisation through the creation and enforcement of legislation that regulates its behaviour, or through supporting and promoting its activities, or through offering it a range of advisory services. Government institutions may also have an **indirect** effect on the organisation by affecting the economic, social and political environment in which the organisation has to function. In this chapter and the next we look at the objectives, role and effectiveness of the major institutions that have an impact on organisations. See Fig. 3.1.

**Fig. 3.1: The major institutions of government which affect business organisations**

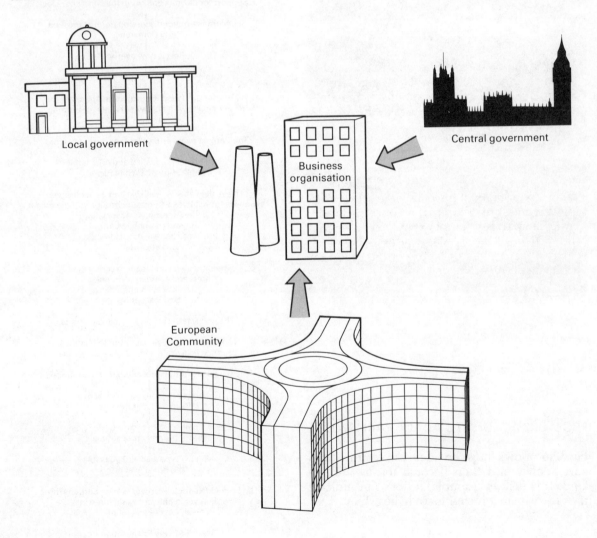

Local government

Central government

Business organisation

European Community

## THE NEED FOR INSTITUTIONS

Why is it necessary or desirable to have government institutions at all? And what determines the extent of their powers? In Book 1 it was explained that organisations in the UK operate within a **mixed economy** – that is, one made up of aspects of both a free-enterprise capitalist system and a centrally controlled one. Within such a system, the major decisions concerning the allocation of resources, methods of production, distribution of income and wealth and level of economic activity necessary to achieve stability are made by a combination of **market forces** and **government intervention**. Local and central government institutions, together with the European Community, help to make and influence these decisions.

### Limitations of market forces

The need for government institutions at all levels becomes clear if we look at what would happen if there was no intervention, as in a completely free economy.

If the allocation of resources was left entirely to free-enterprise business organisations there is a danger that certain needs of society and individuals would never be satisfied. This is because the free market system reflects only private monetary costs and benefits. Its decisions concerning the allocation of resources are based entirely upon whether they are viable in economic terms. The provision of law and order, defence, health, education and housing services cannot be considered purely in these terms. There are very few people who would refuse somebody medical treatment if they were desperately ill but could not afford the cost of treatment, or who would claim that children should be housed and educated only if their parents can afford to pay for it. Thus there are some areas where the market mechanism seems to fail and so it is generally felt to be necessary for government institutions to provide the necessary services.

The first of these areas involves the satisfaction of **'social' wants**, i.e. those which arise out of the general needs of society. They include such services as policing, the courts and defence. Market mechanisms are incapable of providing those because individuals who do not pay for the services cannot be excluded from the benefits. No one is likely to be willing to pay for an army from which everyone, including those people who have not paid for it, benefits. Therefore it is necessary for the government institutions to intervene and to satisfy such wants out of public revenue.

The second area where the market mechanism seems to have failed is over the satisfaction of **'merit' wants**. This is a controversial area of government intervention, involving wants such as housing, health and education, which could be satisfied in the private sector. However, because some individuals might be unable to afford these services, and as the services benefit both private individuals and society at large, it is felt desirable for the government to provide much of them. For example, an individual benefits from the education that he or she receives, and so does society in the sense that a better-educated individual is capable of contributing more to the general welfare.

---

Activity 3.1
(a) Study Table 3.1 which shows the government's current public expenditure plans.
(b) List four areas of expenditure which are mainly concerned with the satisfaction of **social wants** and four areas which are concerned with the **merit wants**. In each case explain why you think this is the case.
(c) Identify the trends shown by the figures and comment on what they reveal about the government's priorities.

---

If the **method by which goods and services are produced** was left entirely to free-market forces, there is a danger that employees might be forced to work in dangerous and unhealthy conditions for very long hours and might receive an extremely poor rate of pay. This is the case in some free-market-economy countries. Equally, there may be waste of resources, as the market may be divided between a large number of small competitive units all producing a similar product. These conditions may result in production inefficiencies because the small units are unable to enjoy economies of scale. The opposite problem to this might apply where one or two firms tend to dominate the market; this

**Table 3.1: Public spending in real terms by department (£ billions base year 1984–5)**

|  | 1983–4 out-turn | 1984–5 out-turn | 1985–6 estimated out-turn | 1986–7 plans | 1987–8 plans | 1988–9 plans |
|---|---|---|---|---|---|---|
| Defence | 16.2 | 17.2 | 17.4 | 16.9 | 16.6 | 16.2 |
| Foreign and Commonwealth Office | 1.8 | 1.8 | 1.8 | 1.8 | 1.8 | 1.8 |
| European Community | 0.9 | 0.9 | 0.8 | 0.6 | 1.0 | 0.8 |
| Ministry of Agriculture, Fisheries and Food | 2.2 | 2.1 | 2.4 | 2.0 | 2.0 | 2.0 |
| Trade and Industry | 2.0 | 2.1 | 1.9 | 1.4 | 1.1 | 0.9 |
| Energy | 1.2 | 2.6 | 1.0 | 0.1 | −0.5 | −0.2 |
| Employment | 3.0 | 3.1 | 3.2 | 3.4 | 3.3 | 3.4 |
| Transport | 4.5 | 4.6 | 4.4 | 4.4 | 4.3 | 4.1 |
| DOE – Housing | 3.2 | 3.2 | 2.6 | 2.5 | 2.5 | 2.5 |
| DOE – Other environmental services | 3.9 | 4.0 | 3.8 | 3.3 | 3.1 | 3.0 |
| Home Office | 4.7 | 5.0 | 5.1 | 5.1 | 4.9 | 4.9 |
| Education and Science | 14.0 | 14.0 | 13.8 | 13.0 | 12.7 | 12.4 |
| Arts and Libraries | 0.7 | 0.7 | 0.7 | 0.7 | 0.7 | 0.6 |
| DHSS – Health and personal social services | 15.4 | 15.8 | 15.9 | 16.2 | 16.2 | 16.4 |
| DHSS – Social security | 36.7 | 38.1 | 39.3 | 39.1 | 39.1 | 39.2 |
| Scotland | 7.0 | 7.0 | 7.0 | 6.9 | 6.5 | 6.4 |
| Wales | 2.7 | 2.6 | 2.6 | 2.6 | 2.6 | 2.6 |
| Northern Ireland | 3.9 | 4.0 | 4.1 | 4.1 | 4.1 | 4.1 |
| Chancellor's Departments | 1.7 | 1.7 | 1.7 | 1.8 | 1.8 | 1.8 |
| Other Departments | 1.0 | 1.2 | 1.3 | 1.4 | 1.5 | 1.5 |
| Reserve |  |  |  | 4.1 | 5.5 | 6.8 |
| Central privatisation proceeds | −1.2 | −2.1 | −2.5 | −4.3 | −4.2 | −4.1 |
| Adjustments |  |  | −0.1 | −0.4 |  |  |
| **Planning total** | 125.7 | 129.6 | 127.8 | 126.7 | 126.7 | 127.1 |

Source: *The Government's Expenditure Plans, 1986–7 to 1988–9,* HMSO.

might create a threat to consumer choice, a wastage of resources on advertising and a barrier to the entry of new firms into the market.

Within a mixed economy government institutions have some influence over how goods and services are produced. The purpose is to protect employees in their working environment, to ensure the efficient use of resources and to protect the consumer against unfair trading practices.

**The distribution of income and wealth** in a completely free-market economy would depend almost entirely upon such factors as the laws of inheritance, the chance acquisition of skills, the availability of educational opportunities, the power of money to breed money, social mobility and the structure of markets. However, such a

distribution will often be unacceptable to the bulk of the population. The majority of the members of any society would agree with some form of redistribution if it was found that a small minority of the population was living in splendour while the vast majority was poor.

To achieve what is considered to be a fair distribution of wealth, governments use a number of devices. First, the **tax system** is used to level down incomes, wealth and capital. Secondly, some of the income which has been collected in taxes is transferred to other sectors of the economy through **transfer payments**, such as grants, social benefits and the provision of free services.

Under an unregulated free-market system, fluctuations are likely to appear in the **level of** economic activity. The economy may pitch violently from boom to depression, with disastrous effects on employment, growth, prices and the balance of payments. Government institutions try to check these tendencies by direct intervention in the economy. This may be undertaken by operating policies to direct the behaviour of business organisations, by adjusting government spending or taxation and by influencing the financial and monetary system in order to create a level of activity which maintains full employment, stabilises prices, encourages economic growth and creates a healthy balance of payments.

## THE CHANGING ROLE OF INSTITUTIONS

The role and powers of government institutions are in a constant state of gradual change. This change arises from developments within the mixed economy, together with political, economic, demographic and social factors. See Fig. 3.2

### Developments within the mixed economy

*Free enterprise*
The UK mixed economy developed from what was essentially a free-enterprise system which

**Fig. 3.2: The changing role of institutions**

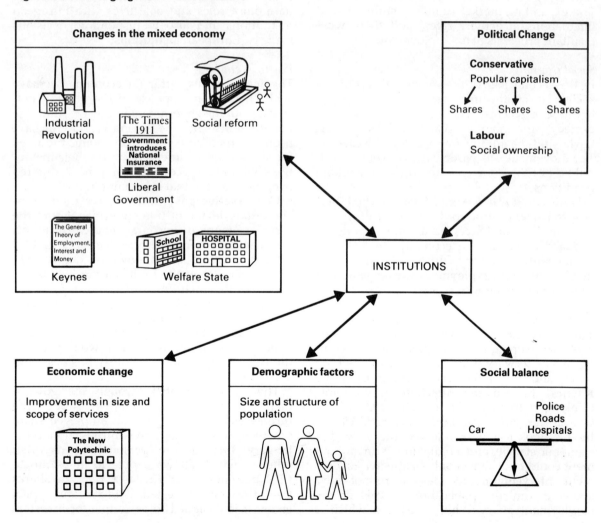

had been in operation between the seventeenth and the nineteenth centuries. During this period the main function of government institutions had been to provide law and order and defence on a national basis, and locally it had concerned itself just with the administration of justice and the relief of the poor.

The **Industrial Revolution** of 1760–1830 resulted in the development of an **urbanised society**, in which most people worked in the factories rather than on the land. This led to the creation of social and economic problems which could be handled only by central government action and institutions. The newly created urban society lived under terrible conditions in towns whose growth had been totally unplanned and which lacked basic amenities such as sewerage, health care and recreation facilities. The expanding market economy suffered wild fluctuations in activity rates, and there were resultant problems of unemployment.

*Social reform*
In the second half of the nineteenth century a **social reform** movement developed in response to these problems. The movement was supported by the enlightened factory owner **Robert Owen** and the administrator **Edwin Chadwick**. The movement was particularly concerned with public health, Poor Law reform and working conditions.

However, it was not until 1906 that the **Liberal government** introduced a number of important measures and accepted a more responsible and active role in the economy. In 1908 the Liberals introduced the **Old Age Pensions Act**, in 1910 the first **Employment exchange** and in 1911 **national insurance**.

*J. M. Keynes*
The role of the government and its institutions in the developing mixed economy took a significant leap forward during the depression of the 1920s and the 1930s. The economist **J. M. Keynes** changed the direction of economic thinking with the publication in 1936 of his *General Theory of Employment, Interest and Money*. In this book Keynes poineered the view that economic stability and a reduction of unemployment could be achieved only by greater government intervention. His ideas were not fully accepted until the publication in 1944 of the employment policy White Paper, in which it

was acknowledged that it was the government's responsibility to intervene in the economy in order to achieve full employment.

*Welfare State*
The mixed economy as the UK knows it today was finally established in 1945 when the Labour government introduced the **Welfare State** and nationalised the railways, coal, steel, the power industries and the Bank of England. Many government institutions were set up which are still with us today. Since that time their role and powers have responded to general fluctuations in the degree of mix within the economy, which is largely determined by the political views of the government in power. The institutions have also been influenced by Britain joining the European Community in 1973; there is now a need to harmonise roles and objectives with European institutions and also to respond to decisions made by European institutions.

**Political change**
The degree of mix within the economy, we have said, changes in response to the political persuasions of the government in power. Although governments since the Second World War have been in broad agreement concerning the need for some form of intervention by their institutions within the economy, they have differed over the extent of that intervention.

**Conservative governments** have tried to increase the degree of free enterprise within the mixed ecomony by encouraging the private sector. The Thatcher government elected in 1979 set out to create a **'share-owning democracy'**. The Chancellor of the Exchequer in his Budget speech of 18 March 1986 said:

'It is the long-term ambition of this government to make the British people a nation of shareholders; to create **popular capitalism**, in which more and more men and women have a direct personal stake in British business and industry.'

This was attempted through the government's **privatisation** programme, through the **incentives** that were given to employee share schemes and through the introduction on 1 January 1987 of the **personal equity plan** scheme, which allows people to invest up to £200 per month, or £2,400 a year, in shares free of tax on reinvested dividents and capital gains. It is designed to be simple for investors and especially to attract small savers and people who have never previously invested in shares. The Thatcher government has tried to give a further boost to the private sector by simplifying part of the tax system and reducing government rules and regulations concerning the employment of labour, the setting up of new businesses and the expansion of existing ones.

**Labour governments** since the Second World War, on the other hand, have promoted an expansion of **state control** and have increased the role and scope of state institutions. For example, when in 1986 the Conservative Chancellor was talking of 'popular capitalism', the Labour opposition was advocating the need for greater **'social ownership'** and an expansion of government institutions' activities, both nationally and locally, concerning health, welfare, housing, employment and education.

### Economic change

As the economy develops, people expect government institutions to provide better services, and so the scale and complexity of their operations will increase. Consider the growth of the educational system since the Second World War. Compulsory full-time education has been extended to the age of 16. The universities have been expanded. The polytechnics have been formed, and further and adult education facilities extended. The Manpower Services Commission now offers pre-vocational training through the Youth Training Scheme to all young people after they have completed their compulsory secondary education. Schools and colleges now also offer pre-vocational courses. All of these changes were made to meet the **needs of the economy** and the higher standards expected by a more affluent society.

### Demographic factors

Changes in the **size and structure of the population** mean that government institutions have to adjust their role and activities accordingly. For example, since the Second World War there has been an increase of about 4 million in the number of people over the age of 65. This change has made greater demands on the institutions providing health, social and housing facilities.

### Social balance

The economist J. K. Galbraith took the view in his book *The Affluent Society* that **public sector** services and hence the role of institutions must keep pace and be 'in balance' with changes in the **private sector**. Otherwise, he said, social disorder will result, and economic performance will be impaired. Galbraith quotes the example of cities in the United States where the level of private wealth is very high and yet there are vast areas of public squalor with poor roads, sanitation, disposal systems and hospitals. High levels of crime are a probable result. The point of balance is constantly shifting; government institutions need to be aware of developments within the private sector and then to match their activities accordingly. For example, the increase in the number of private cars on our roads has demanded vast public expenditure on the roads and policies to reduce dangers for road users and pedestrians and to check pollution.

## LOCAL GOVERNMENT

Local government provides an opportunity for local people to take part in the government of their own community. This means becoming involved in the decisions that influence the environment in which they live and the type and level of public services available. Local government also moulds the environment in which many businesses operate, providing many services for those businesses and controlling many of their activities.

### Powers and responsibilities

Local government is responsible for the administration of a variety of services including housing, planning, transport, education, the social services, the fire service, the police, consumer protection, environmental health, libraries, museums and the arts, recreational facilities, the encouragement of tourism, cemeteries and crematoria, footpaths, smallholdings and allotments. Some of these services are **mandatory**, which means that councils must provide them by law – for example, education, the fire service and refuse collection. Other services are **discretionary**, which means that the council may provide them if it wishes – for example, certain recreational facilities.

The local authority's administration of these services is controlled by three central bodies. **Parliament** exerts its influence through the statutory powers which it confers on them, either in public general Acts or by local legislation promoted by the local authority itself. **Central government departments** have an administrative influence. For example, in England the Department of the Environment is largely responsible for local government, although other departments are also concerned with various local government functions. In Scotland the Scottish Office and in Wales the Welsh Office take responsibility for local government. In Northern Ireland the Department of the Environment for Northern Ireland has responsibility.

The **courts of law** exercise a judicial control. They have the power to award damages to an individual who has been mistreated by a local authority. They may also ensure that local authorities perform their statutory duties, and restrain them from acting outside their jurisdiction. For example, under the 1944 Education Act the local authorities have to provide schools in their areas; failure to do so would result in prosecution through the courts.

### The structure of local government

The basic pattern of local government is constantly under review. Structural modifications are often necessary as the functions and responsibilities of the different authorities change. The present system of local government is based on a series of reorganisations which started in 1965 with Greater London. The rest of England and Wales was then reorganised in 1974, and a similar reorganisation took place in Scotland in 1975. Changes in the structure and functions of local government in Northern Ireland had taken place in 1973; these left the Ulster local authorities with fewer functions than those in the rest in Britain. The most recent changes took place in 1986 when an entire level or tier of local government was removed in Greater London and the English metropolitan areas.

*England and Wales*

**England and Wales** (apart from Greater London and the metropolitan areas) are organised into a **two-tier system**, as shown in Fig. 3.3. It is divided into 47 **counties**, which are further divided into 333 **district authorities**

As Table 3.2 shows, functions requiring planning and supervision over a large geographical area are undertaken by the county authorities. The second-tier district authorities provide those services that meet more immediate local needs, such as refuse collection, recreation and amenities.

**Table 3.2: Allocation of local government functions in non-metropolitan areas of England and Wales**

| Function | County council | District council |
|---|:---:|:---:|
| **Planning** | | |
| structure plans | • | |
| local plans | | • |
| development control | | • |
| country parks | • | • |
| national parks | • | |
| derelict land | • | • |
| **Transport** | | |
| transport planning | • | |
| highways | • | |
| traffic regulation | • | |
| road safety | • | |
| parking | • | |
| public transport | • | |
| **Education** | • | |
| **Social services** | • | |
| **Housing** | | • |
| **Fire service** | • | |
| **Police service** | • | |
| **Consumer protection** | • | |
| **Environmental health** | | |
| building regulations | | • |
| clean air | | • |
| control of disease | | • |
| food hygiene | | • |
| refuse collection | | • |
| refuse disposal | • | |
| street cleansing | | • |
| **Libraries** | • | |
| **Museums and the arts** | • | • |
| **Recreational facilities** | • | • |
| **Encouragement of tourism** | • | • |
| **Cemeteries and crematoria** | | • |
| **Footpaths** | • | • |
| **Smallholdings** | • | |
| **Allotments** | | • |

Source: *Local Government in Britain*, Central Office of Information Reference Pamphlet 1, HMSO 1980.

**Fig. 3.3: Counties in England and Wales**

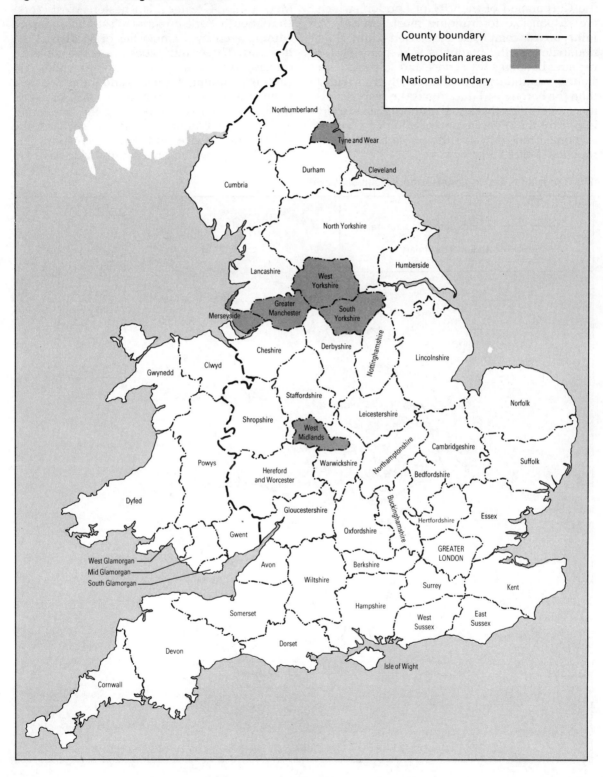

**Greater London** is divided into 32 **boroughs** and the Corporation of the City of London, which are responsible for running most services. **A joint board** composed of elected councillors nominated by the boroughs is responsible for running London's fire service and so provides a statutory authority over an area which is wider than the boroughs. Education is the responsibility of a new directly elected authority. Transport is run by the separate organisation of London Regional Transport, and the police by the Metropolitan Police Force.

The **metropolitan areas** (Tyne and Wear, Merseyside, Greater Manchester, West Yorkshire, South Yorkshire and West Midlands) are administered by a single tier of 36 **district authorities**. These authorities are responsible for carrying out most of the major functions, including planning, highways and traffic management, waste regulation and disposal, housing, trading standards, support for the arts, sport and historic buildings. Services such as the police, fire service and public transport that need to be provided on a county-wide basis are

**Fig. 3.4: Islands and regional authorities in Scotland**

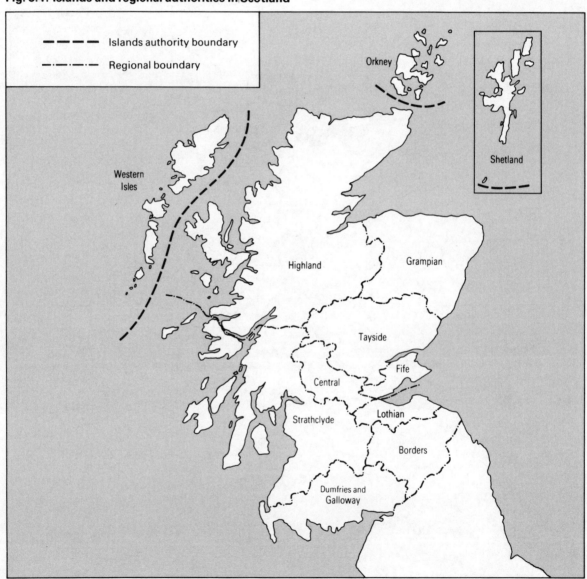

administered by joint boards composed of elected members from the districts.

Within the rural areas of England there is a minor tier of authorities know as **parish councils**. They deal with the provision of very local services, such as allotments, arts and crafts, community halls, bus shelters and car-parks. **Community councils** have a similar function in Wales.

*Scotland*

**Scotland** is organised into nine **regional authorities:** Highland, Grampian, Tayside, Central, Fife, Strathclyde, Lothian, Borders, Dumfries and Galloway. They are divided into 53 **district authorities**.Orkney, Shetland and the Western Islands are designated as **all-purpose authorities**, as shown in Fig. 3.4.

There is a similar division of functions between the regional and district authorities in Scotland as between the non-metropolitan counties and

districts in England. The regional authorities are responsible for strategic planning and related services, and the districts for everything else. The Local Government and Planning (Scotland) Act 1982, which was fully implemented in April 1983, helped to clarify the allocation of functions between the regions and the districts so that they are carried out by one or other level of local government.

*Northern Ireland*

**Northern Ireland** is organised into a single-tier structure of 26 **district authorities** based on main towns and centres, as shown in Fig. 3.5. The authorities are responsible for local public health services, entertainment, recreation, cleansing and sanitation, some regulatory services, cemeteries and crematoria, gas undertakings, markets and abattoirs. There are also five **area boards** covering Northern Ireland which administer, on a local basis, education and the

**Fig. 3.5: District councils in Northern Ireland**

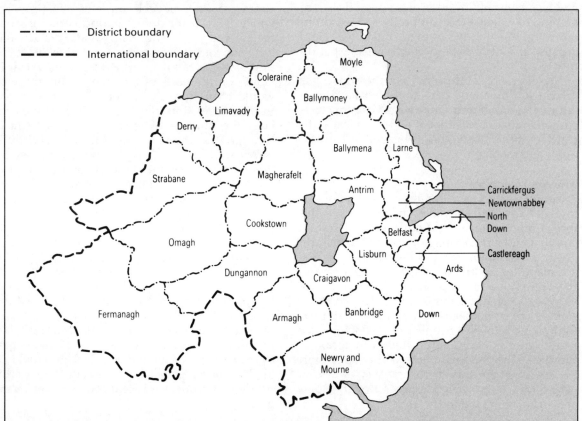

library and youth services. They combine with the districts to provide recreational, social, physical and cultural facilities. Local offices of the central government department concerned administer the health and social services, housing, the fire services and electricity.

### The organisation of local authorities

Local authorities are left to create their own internal form of organisation. Major policy decisions are generally handled by the **full council**, and the administration of the different services is put in the hands of **special committees**; this enables councillors to specialise in particular areas.

Individual **councillors** generally have to stand for re-election every four years. They are unpaid but may claim a flat-rate attendance allowance or a financial loss allowance for carrying out council business; they are also entitled to subsistence and travelling allowances. In England and Wales parish and community councillors cannot claim expenses for carrying out duties in their own areas. The work of the councillor involves contributing to broad policy decision, helping to manage local authority services, representing the interests of their constituents and exercising control over local authority expenditure.

The operation and running of the services is carried out by about $2\frac{1}{2}$ million paid **local government officers and employers**. They include administrative, professional and technical staff, teachers, fire officers, those engaged in law and order and manual workers.

### The complaints system

A **complaints system** for local government in England and Wales involves independent statutory **Commissions for Local Administration** comprising local commissioners known as **local government ombudsmen**. English commissions are made up of three local commissioners, and the Welsh of one. In Scotland the statute provides for a single commissioner. The commissioners are responsible in their particular areas for looking into local people's claims of injustice resulting from poor administration by local authorities. The commissioners will usually start an investigation only at the request of a local councillor. A similar complaints system operates in Northern Ireland.

### Financing local government

In 1984–5 expenditure by local government in the UK was about £34,100 million, which represented 26 per cent of total public expenditure. **Current expenditure** totalled £29,100 million, and **capital projects** took the remaining £5000 million. The largest single area of expenditure was education, which took one-third. Housing, transport, police, fire, social and environmental services were the other major areas of expenditure.

This expenditure is financed by local authorities from the following four major **sources**.

*Rents and charges for services*

Most of this money comes from **rents** on council properties. Some additional income comes from **direct charges** the authorities might make for services such as swimming-pools, leisure centres and theatres.

*Rates*

**Rates** are taxes payable on land and property which is used for domestic, industrial or commercial purposes. The District Valuer (an Inland Revenue official) assesses the value of every property for rating purposes, i.e. its **rateable value**, on the basis of the income the property would bring in if it were let. This is reassessed from time to time. Each local authority calculates the amount of money it needs to raise through the rates to pay for the services it provides. This is its total expenditure less all other types of income. District councils and the London boroughs collect rates for their own expenditure and where appropriate, through what are called **precepts**, on behalf of the county councils and local parish councils.

The total amount required from ratepayers is expressed as a rate payable on each £1 of rateable value, called the **general rate poundage**. This is calculated by dividing the total income required by the amount which will be raised by each 1p levied. For example, if the income to be raised from the rates was £500,000 and the yield of a penny rate were £10,000, then the rate poundage would be 50p. The actual rate in the pound payable in residential or partly residential properties is reduced by **government grant**.

The total rate payable on any property is calculated by multiplying together the rate in the £ payable and the rateable value of the property. For example, if the rateable value was £300 and the rate poundage 50p, then the total rate payable would be £150 (300 × 50p).

In Northern Ireland the rates are determined in two parts; first a regional rate is determined at a uniform level throughout Northern Ireland by the Department of Finance and Personnel; and second the district council fixes its own level of rates which reflects its needs.

From 1989 the rating system in Britain is to be replaced by a community charge. This is a domestic poll tax which falls on all members of a household who are over the age of 18. A separate business charge is made on local industry.

*Central government grants*

**Grants** from central government help to finance about half of the total spending of local authorities. A small proportion of the grant money goes towards the cost of specific services, such as the police, housing, transport and the Urban Programme.

The majority of the money comes through the **rate support grant**. This is designed to compensate for differences in the needs which local authorities have to satisfy and the resources they may be able to raise in local rates. The rate support grant is calculated so that every local authority can provide a similar level of service to that of other authorities while at the same time charging the same rate level. The authority's need to provide services is assessed on the basis of demographic trends and the general characteristics of the area. For the 1986–7 financial year the national average for rate support grant was 36 per cent. This meant that for every £100 million to be spent by a council, the government would give it £36 million. Slightly different arrangements exist in Scotland and Northern Ireland.

*Loans*

Local authorities have to borrow money in order to finance large-scale or long-term projects, such as building a new housing estate. Each year they receive a **borrowing approval** which allows them to raise **loans** up to an approved limit. In Northern Ireland long-term borrowing by district councils is subject to central approval, and in Scotland central approval is granted to capital expenditure rather than the actual loan. Local authorities may borrow from central government or may raise long-term loans through private mortgages, issuing stock on the Stock Exchange or bonds which may or may not be quoted on the Stock Exchange.

**Controls over local government finance**

The payments of **rates** represents a fixed cost to local industrial and commercial organisations, and so any increase may have a significant effect on the profitability of such organisations. Governments have recognised the possible burden that the rates may impose on such organisations and have introduced a number of measures either to control any increases or in some cases to set them at zero in order to attract some business organisations into areas requiring industrial and commercial regeneration. For example, since 1981 certain depressed areas have been designated as **enterprise zones**, where commercial and industrial properties are exempt from paying rates for ten years. In Scotland industrial premises, together with freight transport, are rated at 60 per cent of net annual value. In Northern Ireland all industrial premises are fully de-rated, as are commercial premises in enterprise zones.

The Thatcher government first elected in 1979 tried to go a stage further to redress the balance between the public and private sectors of the economy by controlling and reducing the overall level of public spending. Part of the strategy for achieving this was the reduction in real terms of central government financial support to local authorities. To prevent the local authorities from merely making up the shortfall by pushing up the rates on households and businesses, the government introduced a number of measures to make local authorities more accountable to the electorate:

- **Holding back rate support grant** from those authorities which exceeded the spending targets specified for them by central government.
- Setting up in England and Wales an **Independent Audit Commission** to audit local authorities' accounts and to ensure the economic use of resources and the publication of staffing figures.

- Reducing costs by **contracting out** those services which might be undertaken more cheaply in the **private sector**.
- In 1984 the government acquired the power to fix upper limits on the rates and spending of certain authorities whose expenditure was considered excessive. This became known as **rate-capping**. In 1985–6 eighteen local authorities had upper limits set on their rate levels.

---

Activity 3.2

(a) Mr and Mrs Miles have no children. They both work and they live in a detached house in the new town of Monkfields in Westfordshire. The rateable value of their house is £372. For the year 1986–7 the general rate poundage is 215.30p. Because the Mileses' house is a residential property, domestic relief is allowed at 18.50p. Calculate the Mileses' rate demand for the year 1986–7.

(b) Compare the Mileses' rate demand with that of Mr and Mrs Williams, who have three children of school age and live in a terraced house on the other side of Monkfields. The rateable value of their house is £198.

(c) Use your findings in (b) as the basis for a discussion about the fairness of the rating system.

---

## Local authority activities which directly affect the organisation

Many of the activities of local authorities have the indirect effect of helping to create a favourable environment for the operation of the organisation. However, some have a more direct influence on the operations of business organisations, as illustrated in Fig. 3.6.

*Environmental health*
The **environmental health department** tries to control the effects of the business organisation on various aspects of the environment. It has the power to inspect an organisation for the detection of **statutory nuisances** – for example, the carrying on of offensive trades or the making of excessive noise. It may serve an **abatement notice** in order to stop the nuisance. If the organisation does not comply with this, then legal proceedings may be taken by the authority.

The department **regulates standards** of space, light, ventilation, sanitation and drainage for buildings. It has the power to investigate unsound food and drink and to take samples for analysis. Organisations selling food which is deficient or injurious to health may be prosecuted. Local authorities, with the sanction of the Secretary of State for the Environment, may set up **smoke-control areas** and then take action against those who pollute the atmosphere.

*Town and country planning*
**The town and country planning authorities** are concerned with trying to ensure that **land** is put to the best use from the point of view of the community. This involves seeing that the area's industry, commerce and agriculture have adequate opportunities to thrive and that the demands for houses, leisure and other facilities are met. The planning process is shared between the different tiers of local government and very often involves the management of the countryside through a **green belt policy** and the official designation of **conservation areas** to protect historic towns and villages.

To maintain control over the use of land, town and country planning authorities require an application before any development is undertaken, whether it is for an organisation's factory or office block or just for a family home extension. If a business organisation wishes to appeal against the authority's decision, it must go to the Secretary of State for the Environment.

The need for adequate controls over land use was recognised more fully by the 1980 **Local Government, Planning and Land Act**. This Act gave councils in England and Wales more responsibility for planning and development control. It also clarified the roles of counties and districts in order to provide a more efficient and quicker service in planning matters.

*Trading standards and consumer protection*
In the field of **trading standards and consumer protection**, the authorities carry out **weights and measures inspections**. This involves controlling the accuracy and use of all weighing and measuring equipment for buying and selling, and checking the correctness of the weight or measure of the contents of packets, cans, jars and bottles. Local authority officers also ex-

**Fig. 3.6: Local authority activities directly affecting business organisations**

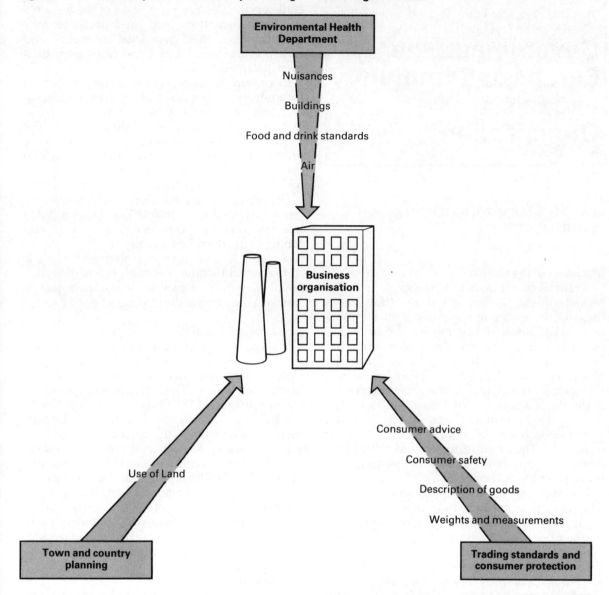

amine and test many thousands of items of foodstuffs for **purity** and both the **description** and **price** of many goods – from motor-car mileometer readings to price markings. Officers also check domestic electrical appliances, toys and goods like pots and pans on sale in shops to ensure that they comply with the various **consumer safety laws**. The local authorities have the right to set up **consumer advice centres**, which may provide pre-shopping advice and information and handle consumer complaints.

Activity 3.3
Outline the involvement which particular local authority departments might have with:

(a) the activities of a pig farmer;
(b) a dry-cleaner's shop;
(c) an indoor food market;
(d) the expansion plans of a firm concerned with the production of cosmetics;
(e) a second-hand car dealer.

# 4. Central Government, the European Community and Business Organisations

## CENTRAL GOVERNMENT AND ITS DEPARTMENTS

### Ministers of the Crown

The central government is made up of the **Prime Minister**, who is appointed by **the Crown** (usually the leader of the party with the most seats in the House of Commons), and his or her **ministers**, who are mostly drawn from the Commons, with the remainder coming from the House of Lords. All government appointments are made by the Crown on the recommendation of the Prime Minister. The Prime Minister is the head of the government, and this position depends upon having a **majority** in the House of Commons. The Prime Minister works through a personally selected **Cabinet** of ministers to formulate national policy.

The ministers in the Cabinet, in conjunction with the other ministers, are held responsible for the activities of particular **government departments**. After Parliament has passed the necessary legislation it is the government departments – operating through and with local authorities, statutory boards and other sponsored government bodies – which are the main channel for putting government policy into effect. So the activities of these departments have a considerable impact upon business organisations.

### Government departments

*Organisation*

Government departments are generally organised under a **secretary of state** or **minister**. The departments are financed by money provided by Parliament, and are run by members of the **civil service**. A large proportion of the information on which they base their decisions may emanate from their own legal, economic and statistical advisers or in some cases from their own information division.

In certain cases departments may be helped by advisory bodies, such as councils or committees, whose function is to provide the information on which a decision might be based. The majority of these committees are formed on the orders of the minister concerned, although in some cases there may be a statutory obligation for him or her to consult a standing committee.

Departments may also derive information about a particular issue from a Royal Commission like the one that considered the siting and timing of the third London airport.

If there is a change in government, this is unlikely to affect the role of a particular department. However, it may influence its **organisation** and the general direction of its **policy**.

*Functions and activities*

The **activities** of some government departments cover the whole of the UK. The Ministry of Defence falls into this category. Other departments – such as the Department of Employment – cover just Great Britain (i.e. excluding Northern Ireland). Others – for instance, the Department of Education and Science – cover just England and Wales. The activities of yet others – such as the Department of the Environment – are restricted to England. This apparent gap in the coverage of some departments is bridged by the existence in Scotland and Northern Ireland of their own government departments, and in Wales by the Welsh Office. The areas of responsibility are likely to be further influenced by the possible development of devolution for Scotland and Wales.

The **administrative work** of the various central government departments embraces every aspect of national affairs. It covers **economic issues** like inflation, unemployment, the balance of payments, economic growth and the distribution of income and wealth; **industrial relations** problems between employers and trade unions; **social issues** involving poverty, living standards, housing, education, general health and welfare; **environmental questions** concerning the use of land, pollution and the destruction of the countryside; **legal matters** embracing the rights of the individual, the employer and the business organisation. It also includes Britain's **international role** in terms of giving development aid to the Third World countries, influencing world political opinion and trying to ensure stability and peace.

All these activities have an impact on the business organisation, either by directly regulating, aiding or promoting its affairs or by indirectly affecting the social, political, economic and legal environment in which it operates.

## THE IMPACT OF GOVERNMENT DEPARTMENTS ON ORGANISATIONS

### Departments with an indirect impact

Table 4.1 summarises the **indirect** impact of the main government departments on the business environment.

### Departments with a direct impact

The seven central government departments which directly influence business organisations

**Table 4.1: Main government departments' indirect effects on business organisations**

| Department | Function |
| --- | --- |
| Management and Personnel Office | Deals with all aspects of the employment of civil servants. Responsible for ensuring that high standards of administration and management exist in government departments. |
| Home Office | Concerned with the administration of justice, criminal law, the police, prison and probation services, fire and civil defence services, race relations, immigration, public morals and safety, and the control of explosives, fire arms, dangerous drugs and gambling. |
| Lord Chancellor's Department | Concerned with the administration of the courts and of the law. Responsible for law reform. |
| Law Officers' Department | Through the Attorney-General and Solicitor-General represents the Crown in major civil, criminal and international legal proceedings. Provides legal advice for the government and is ultimately responsible for the enforcement of criminal law. |
| Foreign and Commonwealth Office | Through its diplomatic service maintains relationships with foreign countries and represents British political and commercial interests abroad. |
| Overseas Development Administration | Administers the financial and technical aid programme to the developing world. |
| Ministry of Defence | Administers and controls the army, navy and air force. |
| Department of Education and Science | Promotes and supports schools and further and higher education establishments and fosters civil science in Britain and internationally. |
| Department of Health and Social Security | Administers the National Health Service and the social services provided by local authorities. Responsible for the administration of social security payments and benefits. |

**Fig. 4.1: Central government activities directly affecting business organisations**

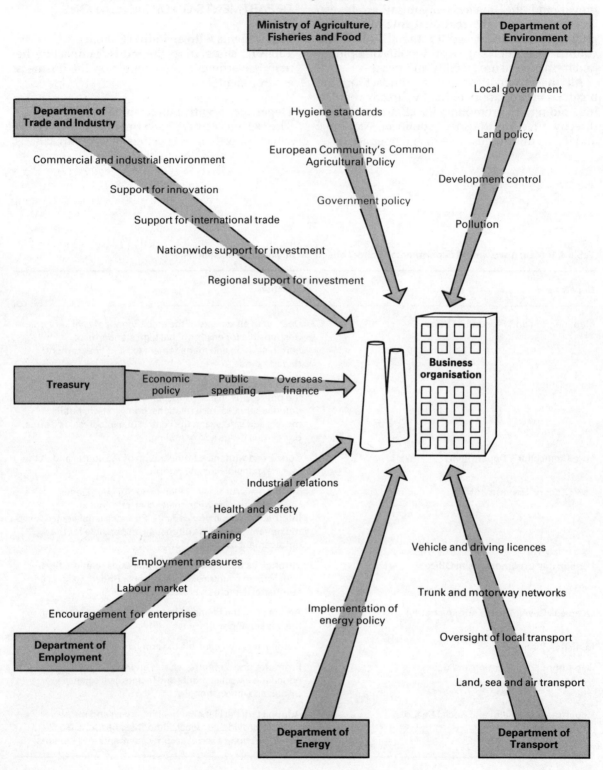

are illustrated in Fig. 4.1. In this section we consider the **role** and **objectives** of these departments and how they are involved in framing and implementing particular **policies** which directly influence business organisations, such as those relating to employment, information technology and the regions. Specific policies relating to the economy and consumer protection are looked at in more detail in Chapters 6, 7, 9, 10, 12 and 13 respectively.

### Ministry of Agriculture, Fisheries and Food
The **Ministry of Agriculture, Fisheries and Food** is responsible for the administration of government policy for the agriculture, horticulture and fishing industries. It exercises control over the business organisations which make up these industries. In the field of agriculture its responsibilities include the administration of market support schemes and the European Community's **Common Agricultural Policy**. It also encourages research aimed at improving farming techniques and eliminating animal and plant diseases.

From the point of view of food, the ministry is particularly concerned with hygiene standards, the composition of food, the use of additives, labelling and advertising.

### Department of the Environment
The **Department of the Environment** (DoE) is responsible for a variety of different issues relating to the physical environment in which people live and work and in which business organisations operate. These issues include local government, development control and general land policy, the problems of the inner cities, new towns, commercial housing and construction, and environmental pollution. The DoE is also responsible for guarding and administering historic buildings and ancient monuments.

### Department of Transport
The **Department of Transport** directly assists business organisations by taking responsibility for land, sea and air transport. It is responsible for trunk and motorway networks; the general oversight of local authority transport plans, including the payment of any central government grants; and sponsoring the nationalised transport industries. It also administers vehicle and driving licences and safety. All the department's activities should contribute towards the more efficient transportation of business organisations' products and raw materials.

### Department of Energy
The **Department of Energy** is responsible for government policy relating to all sources of energy. This involves encouraging the maximum economic exploitation of the nation's energy resources and promoting the national interest in international relations in the energy field. It acts for the government in its dealings with the nationalised energy industries and the Atomic Energy Authority. It is the sponsoring department for the nuclear power industry and has overall responsibility for the development and exploitation of gas and oil off the British coastline. It also sponsors the government's energy conservation policy and so is likely to be instrumental in determining the type of energy that business organisations may use in the future.

### Treasury
The **Treasury** is officially headed by the Lord Commissioners, with the Prime Minister as the First Lord, aided by the Chancellor of the Exchequer and five junior lords. In practice the Chancellor controls the management of the Treasury and is assisted by the Chief Secretary, the Financial Secretary, the Economic Secretary and the Minister of State.

Treasury ministers and officials are in control of all the money which Parliament allows the government to collect and spend and of any borrowing the government undertakes. Changes in these activities have a significant effect on the business environment and on the position of organisations operating within it. The Treasury has to try to tailor such changes so that they help the government's financial strategy and the achievement of its fiscal, monetary and overall economic policy.

The Treasury carries out *four major activities:*

1. It prepares **forecasts** regarding the present state of the economy, where it seems to be heading and what the effects of policy moves or present economic developments seem likely to be. Under the 1975 Industry Act it has to publish two forecasts formally each year, usually at the time of the Budget and then later as an Autumn Statement on the condition of the economy.

2. The Budget involves the Treasury in at

least one **Finance Bill** each year, which has to get through Parliament, in order to provide the government with the tax revenue it needs to finance its activities.

3. The Treasury helps to control the overall **level of public spending**. It has to lay estimates before the House of Commons each year of all proposed government spending; this includes the spending activities of central government departments and local authorities, together with any borrowing undertaken by the nationalised industries and other public corporations. Treasury controls involve checking departments' programmes, monitoring how expenditure is going during the year and making sure that the departments take corrective action when necessary. As part of its control over public spending the Treasury provides through the Chessington Computer Centre a payroll service covering the civil servants employed in more than sixty government departments. The Treasury also takes a close interest in the financial affairs of the nationalised industries.

4. The Treasury **monitors world economic events** and Britain's **balance of payments** and maintains the country's financial relations abroad.

These activities affect business organisations in a number of ways. Changes in overall **economic policy** are usually announced as part of the government's Budget. These directly influence levels of consumer demand, business confidence and the availability of capital finance. Business organisations' investment plans, pricing, profitability, wages policies and employment prospects are all influenced as a result.

Treasury ministers are responsible for two other institutions which have a direct impact on business organisation: the Inland Revenue and Customs and Excise.

*Inland Revenue*
The **Inland Revenue Department** is responsible for the administration and collection of direct taxes on income, profits, capital gains, oil and land. It operates stamp duty and also collects national insurance contributions and recovers the cost of doing so from the National Insurance Fund. It works with the Chancellor of the Exchequer and the Treasury on the implementation of any tax changes emanating from the Budget.

The Inland Revenue handles all business organisations' tax affairs. It may have further dealings with business organisations through its duties concerning the valuation of real property for local authority rating and compensation for compulsory purchase.

*Customs and Excise*
The **Customs and Excise Department** is responsible for the collection and administration of VAT (value added tax), car tax, excise duties (on hydro-carbon oils, tobacco products, alcoholic drinks and betting and gaming) and customs duties and levies on imported goods. Like the Inland Revenue it has to work closely with the Treasury on all these matters and comes into direct contact with business organisations when establishing their tax liability. The department is also responsible for import licensing and the drawing up of UK overseas trade statistics.

**Department of Employment**
The main objectives of the **Department of Employment** were set out in a government paper issued in March 1985 entitled *Employment: The Challenge for the Nation*. These objectives are:

- to promote enterprise, job creation and the reduction of administrative burdens on business, especially small firms;
- to help the labour market to work efficiently, effectively and fairly;
- to help unemployed people, particularly through measures to improve their employment prospects;
- to promote training to meet the needs of the economy and individuals;
- to help to maintain and improve industrial health and safety;
- to help to improve industrial relations and safeguard essential employment rights.

These objectives are in direct response to the fundamental problem faced by the government and highlighted in Fig. 4.2. Fig. 4.2 shows that the overall trend since 1973 has been for the working population (comprising employees, the unemployed, the self-employed and HM Forces) to expand and for **unemployment** to rise, even though in recent years the numbers in work have actually increased. This problem has been caused by a **combination of factors** over this period, including a slump in world trade, efforts to make industry more competitive which have led to a slimming down of the

**Fig. 4.2: Working population and employed labour force in Britain, 1973–86**

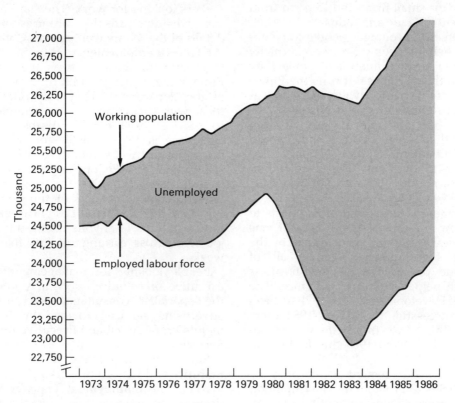

Source: *Employment Gazette*, September 1986,
HMSO.

work-force, government anti-inflation policies which have led to cuts in public expenditure, technological change which has made many jobs obsolete, an increase in the number of people of working age and an increase in the number of women wishing to work.

The objectives and the problems behind them involve the Department of Employment in six areas of work: encouragement of enterprise, the labour market, employment measures, training, health and safety and industrial relations. Some of these areas of work come directly under the department. Others are carried out by public agencies reporting to the Secretary of State for Employment, as is the case with the Manpower Services Commission and the Health and Safety Commission. In this section we look at what is done in these six areas.

Activity 4.1
(a) Study the most recent copy of the Department of Employment's *Employment Gazette* (HMSO).
(b) Find out the percentage level of unemployment for your area.
(c) Compare this percentage with the average for the whole of the country.
(d) Give reasons for any difference in the percentages.

*Encouragement of enterprise*
One of the department's top priorities is the **encouragement of enterprise**. It is felt that helping people to turn their ideas into business ventures should result in the creation of jobs. The department has accepted these responsibilities since it took over the Enterprise and Dereg-

ulation Unit from the Cabinet Office in 1985 and responsibility for small firms and tourism from the Department of Trade and Industry.

The department encourages people to be enterprising by helping people who were formally unemployed to survive financially while they are setting up their business. It runs the **Enterprise Allowance Scheme**, which is aimed at unemployed people who have a business venture in mind but who may be put off from working for themselves because they would lose their entitlement to state benefits. The scheme helps to overcome this problem by paying them a regular allowance for one year, which in 1986 was £40 per week.

The department is supported in its efforts to encourage new enterprises by the **Small Firms Service**, by **local enterprise agencies** and by the **Co-operative Development Agency**, all of which provide prospective or new business ventures with help, advice and guidance. The Co-operative Development Agency has been particularly successful, in that in 1982 there were fewer than five hundred worker co-operatives but by March 1985 this figure had grown to 1200.

As part of its encouragement to enterprise the department helps to promote the development, growth and international competitiveness of **tourism**. Tourism is potentially one of the fastest growing and most enterprising sectors of the economy and hence a good source of new employment opportunities. The department provides grants-in-aid to the British Tourist Authority and English Tourist Board. These bodies then provide help, advice and financial support for all types of tourism ventures, including hotel improvements, visitor attractions, leisure amenities, self-catering and tourism support projects.

Through the **Deregulation Unit** the department attempts to reduce the burden of rules and regulations on businesses. This has led to the simplification of VAT returns, employment protection and planning procedures.

*The labour market*
The Department of Employment tries to improve the general working of the **labour market** both by helping to bring the demand and supply sides together through Job Centres and also by improving the mobility of the work-force.

Britain's 1000 **Job Centres** help to bring

together employers with vacancies and job seekers looking for work. The staff at Job Centres give advice, display vacancies and provide details of the Manpower Services Commission's (MSC) own employment and training schemes, together with those such as the Community Programme, which the MSC operates on behalf of the department. They also offer help for those with special needs – for example, specialist services exist for the disabled. Specialist assistance is also available for the long-term unemployed (twelve months or more) through such schemes as the Job Start Allowance, which is a financial incentive for long-term unemployed people to get back on the job market. In July 1986 this was set at £20 per week, payable for six months to anyone taking on a full-time job with gross earnings of less than £80 per week.

People looking for management, scientific, executive or technical work may benefit from the specialist consultancy, recruitment and advertising service provided by the department's **Professional and Executive Recruitment Service**.

Efforts are also made to improve **labour mobility** and hence the workings of the labour market. The **Employment Transfer Scheme** is designed to improve the geographical mobility of the work-force. Under the scheme, grants, allowances and removal expenses are payable to encourage people to move to new areas for work in order to fill vacancies where no suitable local candidate may exist.

The department also works to promote **equal opportunities** by giving advice and developing policies on equal pay and on sex and race discrimination in employment. The department's **Race Relations Employment Advisory Service** promotes fair treatment and equal opportunities in employment within the terms of the Race Relations Act 1976.

*Employment measures*
The Department of Employment administers a number of schemes which are aimed at increasing the opportunities for unemployed people to find jobs while assisting the working of the labour market. The main areas are as follows.

1. The **Community Project**. This provides temporary work and training opportunities for long-term unemployed adults on projects of benefit to the community, such as clearing up

derelict land and canals or gardening and decorating for the elderly and disabled people. People who join the scheme are paid at the local rate for the job, and projects combine full and part-time opportunities.

2. The **New Workers Scheme**. This is designed to help employers take on more young people who are no longer eligible or able to continue on YTS. The employer receives a subsidy towards the pay of a young worker, and it is hoped that such a scheme will result in more full-time jobs being created.

3. Under the **Job Release Scheme** an older worker may retire early with an allowance which covers the period until the state pension starts. This then releases a job which may become available to an unemployed person.

4. The **Job Splitting Scheme**. This provides an incentive to employers to create part-time jobs for unemployed people. A grant is available where a job is split into two part-time ones, or where regular overtime is combined into a part-time job and an unemployed person is then recruited, or where two new part-time jobs are created for those leaving government schemes such as the Community Project or YTS.

*Training*
The work in this area has been influenced by the two White Papers entitled *Training for Jobs* (January 1984) and *Education and Training for Young People* (April 1985). The general objective is the need to reform skills training, to equip young people for the transition from school to work, to open up wider training opportunities for adults and to make vocational training more relevant to the needs of industry.

**Young people** have been helped through both the **Technical and Vocational Educational Initiative** (TVEI) and the **Youth Training Scheme** (YTS). The TVEI involves trying to widen the curriculum for 14–18-year-olds to include more technical and vocational subjects. The YTS provides two years of training for 16-year-old school-leavers and one year for 17-year-olds. The first year involves twenty weeks of off-the-job training (in a college or training centre) in addition to on-the-job training and planned work experience. The second year provides specific skills training, leading to vocational qualifications.

**Adult training** has been tackled through three main schemes:

- The **Job Training Scheme** provides a choice of training for unemployed people which can add to the skills they already have or, equally important, develop the new skills that local employers need.
- The **Wider Opportunities Training Programme** helps people get back to work with a range of modular full- and part-time courses at various levels, linked to employment and local needs.
- The **Open Tech. Programme** is aimed at adults wanting to achieve technician and supervisory management levels of skills. They may study at home or at work.

*Health and safety*
Through the **Health and Safety Commission and Executive** efforts are made to improve the health, safety and welfare of people at work and to protect the general public against risks arising out of the activities of people at work.

*Industrial relations*
The **Advisory, Conciliation and Arbitration Service** (ACAS) is concerned with trying to improve industrial relations. It does this by performing its basic statutory functions of:

- conciliating in industrial disputes;
- arranging independent arbitration;
- advising employers and councils on industrial relations matters;
- conciliating on complaints made by individuals under employee rights legislation.

The Department of Employment also provides administrative support for **industrial tribunals** and **employment appeal tribunals** which deal with problems relating to individual employment rights. In 1984–5 the industrial tribunals received 39,000 applications and employment appeal tribunals 776.

**Department of Trade and Industry**
The department which has the greatest influence on business organisations is the **Department of Trade and Industry** (DTI). It was formed in June 1983 following the re-election of the Conservative government. The department combined the functions of the previously separate Department of Industry with the commercial relations and trade functions of the Department of Trade. This means that it takes responsibility for general industrial strategy and the

industrial aspects of regional policy. The Scottish and Welsh Offices exercise certain regional industrial policy functions in Scotland and Wales.

The overall aims of the DTI were specified in June 1984 by the then Secretary of State for Trade and Industry, Norman Tebbitt. They are summarised in Fig. 4.3. This shows that the DTI believes that the achievement of its central aim (**the regulation and growth of trade**) depends on three factors: first, creating a **climate** for British industry and commerce which is as conducive to enterprise and competition as that in any other industrialised country; second, encouraging the **international competitiveness** of British firms through increased efficiency and

**Fig. 4.3: Department of Trade and Industry, stated aims**

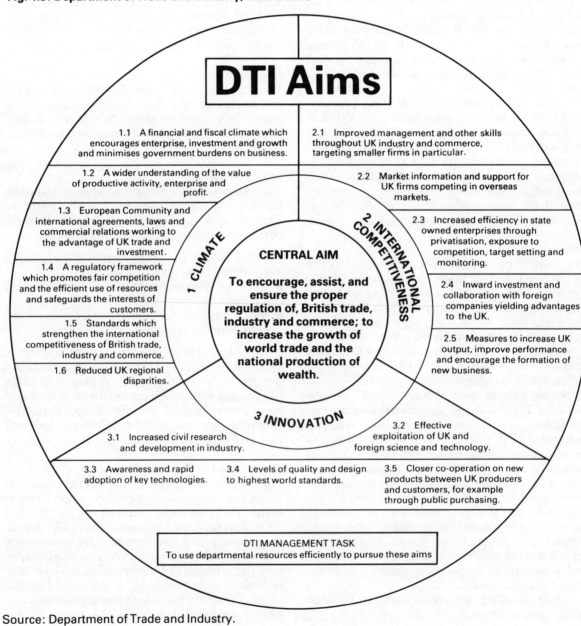

Source: Department of Trade and Industry.

adaptability; third, by **innovation**, improving the products, processes and services that British industry can offer the world.

To achieve these objectives, the DTI works to influence the environment in which business organisations operate and then to provide support for innovation, international trade and investment.

*The commercial and industrial environment*
The DTI is responsible for administering the **legal framework** within which business organisations operate, including the provisions of the 1985 Companies Act. It also represents the interests of British Companies in this field by dealing with developments in European Community companies legislation. The department's responsibility for patents and the registration of industrial design and trade-marks provides legal protection for business interests.

The DTI promotes the **interests of consumers** by taking responsibility for competition policy and consumer protection. This work includes liaison with the Office of Fair Trading and the consumer protection provisions of the Fair Trading Act and working with the Monopolies and Mergers Commission.

On a broader front the DTI monitors and deals with the industrial and commercial implications of domestic, economic, fiscal and financial policies. It also directly sponsors a large number of manufacturing industries, ranging from paper, timber and board to machine tools and mechanical engineering.

*Support for innovation*
The DTI gives support to industrial **research and development** ('R and D'). The aim is to increase the UK's international competitiveness by improving the country's technological base and by helping industry ensure that new products and processes reach the market quickly. Business organisations are encouraged to undertake innovative research and development projects which will lead to new products or processes. Support is normally in the form of a grant; in 1986 this was to cover up to 25 per cent of the eligible costs of the R and D project.

Eligible projects were usually those costing not more than £5 million or less than £100,000, although projects costing less than this could be considered from small firms. Support would be granted only if the business organisation was

able to satisfy the following criteria:

- the project was innovative and represented a significant advance for the UK industry or sector concerned;
- the market prospects for the project were good;
- the business organisation had the technical and managerial capability and commitment to carry the project through and exploit the results sucessfully;
- the project would not go ahead in the form or time-scale intended without public sector funding.

*Support for international trade*
The DTI takes responsibility for the UK's **international trade policy**, including the promotion of UK trade interests in the European Community, the General Agreement on Tariffs and Trade (GATT), the Organisation for Economic Co-operation and Development (OECD) and other international organisations.

Business organisations engaged in or about to enter export markets may receive support from the DTI through the **British Overseas Trade Board** (BOTB). The BOTB is made up of business people with practical knowledge of exporting, and its support may come in four ways:

1. Free **information and advice** may be given on specific markets and also on how to finance trade. In 1986 this was supported by a 50 per cent **grant** towards the cost of export market research.

2. Business organisations may be helped to break into overseas markets by being given **grants** or the **professional help** of embassy staff abroad. This may go as far as helping a firm to find a suitable local export representative, providing reports on market prospects or the position of a foreign company, offering travel grants towards the cost of any trade mission abroad and helping and giving grants to organisations involved in overseas trade fairs, seminars and trade missions. The BOTB also runs an Export **Intelligence Service** which identifies possible export opportunities for British firms. Loans may also be available under the **Market Entry Guarantee Scheme** for organisations thinking of setting up abroad.

3. **Specialist advice** on the particular requirements of an overseas market may be offered to business organisations. This could cover details

relating to tariffs and regulations in overseas markets, help in understanding any special technical requirements for products going abroad and help with export documentation.

4. **Grants** may be made available to help firms with major overseas projects where the UK involvement is considered to be significant. In 1986 the total was £50 million.

*Support for investment*
The DTI tries to stimulate **investment** through financial support in order to achieve a higher rate of economic growth and hence improve job prospects and the UK's industrial competitiveness. The other motive for trying to influence investment is to redress the imbalance that exists between the different geographical regions in terms of job prospects, average earnings, the standard of living and general state of the environment. Such **regional disparities** are shown in Table 4.2.

**Table 4.2: Regional unemployment (July 1986)**

| Region | Percentage of working population unemployed |
|---|---|
| South East | 8.7 |
| East Anglia | 8.9 |
| South West | 9.9 |
| North | 16.9 |
| Wales | 14.2 |
| Scotland | 14.3 |
| Northern Ireland | 19.1 |
| West Midlands | 14.0 |
| East Midlands | 11.3 |
| Yorkshire and Humberside | 13.8 |
| North West | 14.5 |

Source: *Employment Gazette*, September, 1986, HMSO.

Several factors contribute to the problem of regional disparities, tending to make the existing wealthy regions richer and the deprived areas poorer:

1. Many business organisations go against traditional market forces in deciding where to locate. Rather than setting up in depressed areas where labour, rent and rates are cheaper, they tend to be more influenced by **the need to be near other successful companies** with all the associated external economies and ancillary services they create. Such business organisations tend to be located in wealthier parts of the country.

2. Membership of the European Community has tended to strengthen the forces making for a **concentration of industry** in the wealthy areas such as London, the South East and East Anglia.

3. Labour is generally unable to react to market forces by moving to where jobs and higher wages are available in wealthy areas. This **immobility of labour** is due to social and family ties, to the cost of housing (in particular) and living (in general) and to the need to retrain if a job change is involved.

4. The relative sizes of the different regional multipliers also tend to worsen the situation by influencing the wealth of particular areas. This is because any additional spending that takes place in a particular region will tend to have a more-than-proportionate multiplier effect. However, these **multiplier effects** are likely to be enjoyed more in prosperous rather than depressed regions. Additional spending in a depressed region generates more income in the form of wages, rent, interest and profits; but most of this is likely to be earned by the owners of the factors of production, and such owners will probably live outside the region. Also, additional spending will tend to be on goods and services which have been produced outside the region. This means that depressed regions usually have smaller multipliers than more wealthy regions, thus worsening regional differences.

5. The **decline of the staple industries**, such as textiles, shipbuilding, coal and steel, has caused a gradual decline in those areas which traditionally concentrated on this type of industry. Serious localised depressions are the result.

**DTI investment schemes**
In this section we shall look at some of the schemes offered through the Department of Trade and Industry. These are aimed at improving investment both nation-wide, especially in new technologies, and also within the regions.

*Nationwide schemes*
These are to encourage investment throughout the country and are offered on a selective basis. They take into consideration the merits of the project and whether the support is essential for it to go ahead. In 1986 grants were made for

major **capital projects** of at least £500,000 which were considered to be in the national interest and would bring exceptional benefits – such as significant improvements in the performance of the company, a radically new product, a technological revolution or improvements in competitiveness. The grants were mainly given to cover fixed capital investment in buildings, plant and machinery, although some consideration was given towards other costs such as working capital, development, training and licensing.

In 1986 grants were also available for some capital investment projects which involved the production or design of advanced microelectronic, fibreoptic and opto-electronic components and related activities. In the case of microelectronics this was part of a wider programme of measures aimed at ensuring that there would be a significant UK presence in the manufacture and design of components.

*Regional investment support*

The existing system of support for **Assisted Areas** was introduced in November 1984. As Fig. 4.4 shows, it is based on a two-tier system of **Development Areas** and **Intermediate Areas**. The former are areas of greatest need, where unemployment is very high, the general standard of living and earnings is low, investment is slow and the general environment is poor. Intermediate Areas are ones which might display some of these features but to a lesser extent.

Two types of grants are available:

1. **Regional selective assistance**. This is available for commercially viable manufacturing and service projects in both types of Assisted Area. Firms applying for them need to be able to show that the project will safeguard or create employment and also bring regional and national benefits such as increases in exports or improvements in productivity. Firms are still expected to provide most of the funding for themselves; the grant essentially provides the minimum amount necessary to ensure that the project goes ahead. The grants are payable in two forms, although in some cases both may apply:

- **project grants** are based on the fixed capital costs of a project and on the number of jobs a project is expected to create;
- **training grants** may cover up to 40 per cent of

eligible training costs associated with new technology training for manufacturing and service projects; matching grants should also be available from the European Social Fund.

Some projects may also qualify for medium-term loans from the European Investment Bank or the European Coal and Steel Community.

2. **Regional development grants** are available only in Development Areas. They are calculated as the higher of:

- 15 per cent of eligible capital expenditure (capital grant); or
- £3000 for each net new job created (job grant).

Capital grants are limited to £10,000 per job for firms employing more than 200 full-time employees; otherwise the maximum grant is £75,000. Grants are available only if it can be shown that they create or expand productive capacity or result in a material change in the process of producing a product or providing a service.

Regional loans are also available from the **European Community**. The European Investment Bank provides fixed-interest-rate medium-term loans to firms investing in projects which create or safeguard employment in the Assisted Areas. The European Coal and Steel Community provides fixed-interest-rate medium-term loans for projects which create new jobs in coal and steel closure areas for redundant workers from these industries. The European Development Fund provides grants to firms employing up to 200 people and those entering business in steel, shipbuilding and textile closure areas.

---

**Activity 4.2**

Outline the assistance which particular central government departments might provide to:

(a) A large insurance company relocating in a market town forty miles from London and requiring to expand its work-force at the clerical, secretarial and junior managerial levels. ·

(b) The newly formed export department of a medium-sized private company engaged in the manufacture of children's cuddly toys. The company has traditionally sold only in the UK market but now wishes to expand its activities abroad.

**Fig. 4.4:**

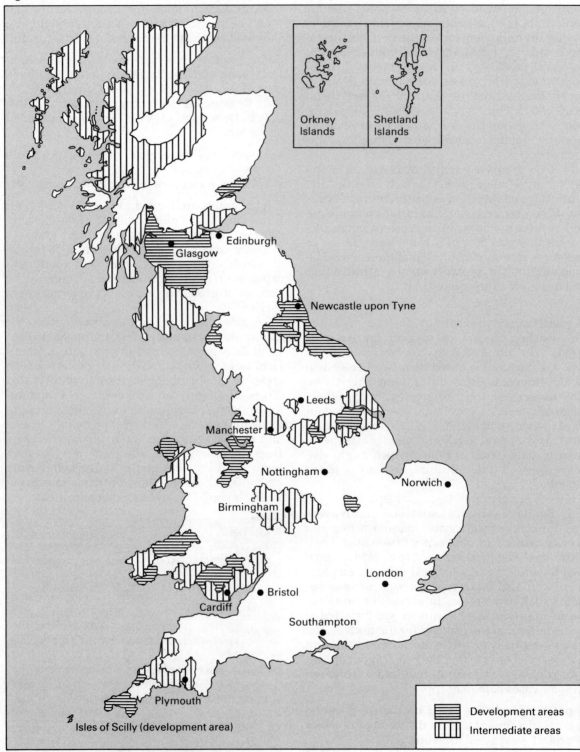

Orkney
Islands

Shetland
Islands

Edinburgh

Glasgow

Newcastle upon Tyne

Leeds

Manchester

Nottingham

Norwich

Birmingham

Bristol

London

Cardiff

Southampton

Plymouth

Isles of Scilly (development area)

Development areas

Intermediate areas

Source: Department of Trade and Industry.

Activity 4.2 (continued)
(c) Mr Fillit, who has developed a new method of filling cavity walls and wishes to set up some sort of business organisation in order to exploit it.

## THE EUROPEAN COMMUNITY AND ITS INSTITUTIONS

Membership of the European Community has allowed the UK to be part of an economic, political and social organisation which embraces the twelve European countries shown in Fig. 4.5. They have a total population of 319 million and represent the world's largest trading bloc, accounting for about a third of world trade. This has considerable significance for UK business organisations in terms of trade, investment, jobs, the role and structure of government and the structure of society.

### Growth of the Community

The thinking behind the formation of the European Community goes back to the period immediately following the Second World War. There was a common feeling at that time that to prevent war from occurring again there should be a linking of European countries economically, which might then develop in the long term into political and social ties. Winston Churchill declared in 1945: 'We must build a kind of United States of Europe.'

The first steps towards achieving this objective were taken in 1951 with the signing of the treaty establishing the European Coal and Steel Community (ECSC). This was followed in 1957 by the **Treaty of Rome** establishing the European Economic Community (EEC), and the European Atomic Energy Community (Euratom). The institutions of the three communities – the ECSC, EEC and Euratom – were merged in 1967 and became known as the European Community.

**Fig. 4.5: The European Community**

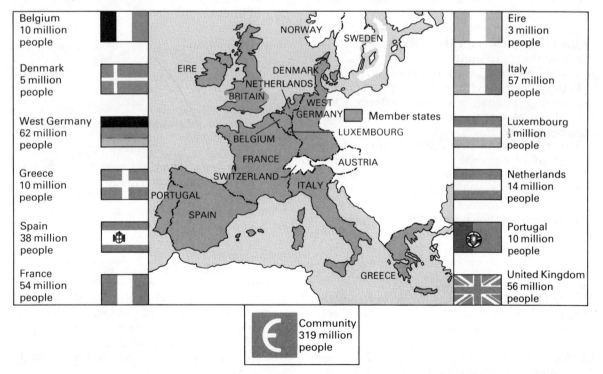

The six founder members of the community were Belgium, France, West Germany, Italy, Luxembourg and the Netherlands. The UK had tended to stay on the sidelines but then tried unsuccessfully to join in 1961 and 1967. On both occasions the French prevented the UK's membership. The UK eventually joined, together with Denmark and Ireland, in 1973. UK membership was endorsed in a national referendum in 1975. The Community was further expanded in 1981 when Greece became a member. Then Spain and Portugal formally joined the Community in January 1986.

## Objectives

The basic objective of the European Community is to promote economic, social and political union so that Europe may be strong enough to influence world affairs. The treaties on which it is founded laid down a number of channels through which overall union was to be achieved. These included:

- The creation of a **customs union** and the phased adoption of a common external tariff against non-members.
- The creation of a situation which would facilitate the **free movement of labour and capital** within the community.
- The acceptance of a **Common Agricultural Policy** aimed at achieving an improvement in productivity, a fair income for farmers, stable markets, security of supply and reasonable prices for consumers.
- The achievement of **economic union** by the creation of common transport and trading policies and the co-ordination of financial, commercial, economic and social objectives. The Treaty forbids trading practices or arrangements which restrict free competition.
- The eventual achievement of some degree of **political union**.

## Community institutions

The following institutions have been established and developed by the European Community to achieve its objectives.

### Council of Ministers

The **Council of Ministers** takes all the major decisions concerning Community policy and allows member countries to take their own interests into consideration in the formation of

that policy. It is composed of one minister from each country representing the particular field of discussion. Broader issues are normally handled by the Foreign Ministers, while on more specific issues governments may be represented by, for example, the Minister of Transport or the Agriculture Minister. Heads of government normally meet about three times a year for a 'summit' to discuss major areas of policy.

The presidency of the Council alters every six months. Unanimous support is required from all members for any decision involving important issues. However, issues of less importance may be carried by a 'qualified majority' of weighted votes. The votes are weighted according to the population size as follows:

| | |
|---|---|
| West Germany | 10 |
| France | 10 |
| Italy | 10 |
| United Kingdom | 10 |
| Spain | 8 |
| Netherlands | 5 |
| Belgium | 5 |
| Greece | 5 |
| Portugal | 5 |
| Denmark | 3 |
| Irish Republic | 3 |
| Luxembourg | 2 |
| Total | 76 |

A qualified majority usually requires fifty-four votes.

The Council is helped by the **Committee of Permanent Representatives**, which is composed of the member states' ambassadors to the Community. They help the Council by preparing its meetings and co-ordinating the work of other serving bodies.

### The Commission

The **Commission** of the Community acts as its executive body. It guards the Community's interests, puts into practice the decisions of the Council and puts forward proposals concerning the operations of the Community. It has particular executive powers of decision-making in such areas as agriculture, trade and competition policy.

The Commission is essentially a European organisation in that the seventeen commissioners have to take an oath that they will serve the

Community first and accept no instructions from their own government or any outside body. The commissioners are chosen by agreement of the Community governments; they serve for a period of four years and can be removed only following a vote of censure from the European Parliament. They are assisted in the performance of their duties by a staff of international civil servants.

Each commissioner usually takes responsibility for a particular area of policy, such as agriculture, transport or the environment. He or she generally formulates draft proposals only after engaging in considerable discussions with officials of national governments and with producers, trade unions, employers' associations and other interested parties. Such draft proposals are then discussed by all the commissioners before they put forward a final proposal.

*European Parliament*

The **European Parliament** is consulted on and debates all major policy issues of the Community. It comments on any proposals put forward by the Commission and the Council and also acts as a forum for discussion and criticism of the Community's activities. Its powers are derived from its powers to reject in its entirety the draft annual budget as presented by the Commission and approved by the Council.

The European Parliament is strictly a political organisation in that it is made up of directly elected representatives drawn from each of the member countries, who sit according to party affiliation rather than nationality. Table 4.3 shows the composition of the Parliament.

The Parliament meets on average about once a month for a session which could extend up to a week. A lot of its work is carried out by the Euro-MPs working within **standing committees**. They consider proposals put forward by the Commission and report back on these proposals to Parliament so that debate can take place. The Parliament has the power to dismiss the Commission by a two-thirds majority vote. Any decision it makes is influential on the Council of Ministers but not binding.

*Economic and Social Committee*

The **Economic and Social Committee** is a consultative body made up of representatives from each country. It is concerned with the position and status of employers, trade unions, the pro-

**Table 4.3: Composition of the European Parliament**

| Member state | Number of seats (total 518) |
| --- | --- |
| West Germany | 81 |
| France | 81 |
| Italy | 81 |
| United Kingdom | 81 |
| Spain | 60 |
| Netherlands | 25 |
| Belgium | 24 |
| Greece | 24 |
| Portugal | 24 |
| Denmark | 16 |
| Irish Republic | 15 |
| Luxembourg | 6 |

*Main political party groups:*
Communists
European Democrats
European People's Party
European Progressive Democrats
Liberal and Democrat Group
Socialists

fessions and farmers. Like Parliament, its function is to comment on the proposals put forward by the Commission and Council. The UK is allowed to send 24 members out of a total of 156.

The four institutions described above are responsible for making **Community laws**. They combine together for this purpose as shown in Fig. 4.6.

*European Court of Justice*

The **European Court of Justice** is one of the most important institutions of the Community. The Treaty of Rome defines the Court of Justice's task as that of ensuring 'the observance of law and justice in the interpretation and application of the Treaty'. This involves ensuring that the Community's treaties and legislation are complied with. This may require the court to deal with a complaint from the Commission against a member state or to handle a dispute between member states, firms or Community institutions. The court sits in Luxembourg and is made up of thirteen judges including one

## Fig. 4.6: Making Community laws

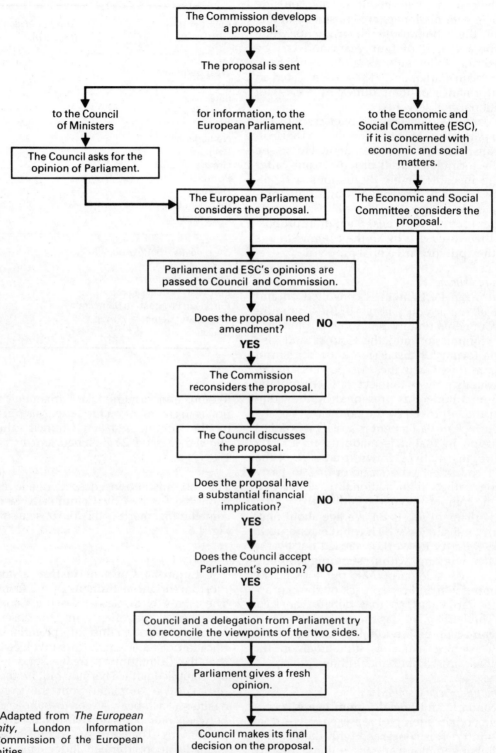

The Commission develops a proposal.

The proposal is sent

to the Council of Ministers

for information, to the European Parliament.

to the Economic and Social Committee (ESC), if it is concerned with economic and social matters.

The Council asks for the opinion of Parliament.

The European Parliament considers the proposal.

The Economic and Social Committee considers the proposal.

Parliament and ESC's opinions are passed to Council and Commission.

Does the proposal need amendment?   NO

YES

The Commission reconsiders the proposal.

The Council discusses the proposal.

Does the proposal have a substantial financial implication?   NO

YES

Does the Council accept Parliament's opinion?   NO

YES

Council and a delegation from Parliament try to reconcile the viewpoints of the two sides.

Parliament gives a fresh opinion.

Council makes its final decision on the proposal.

Source: Adapted from *The European Community*, London Information Office, Commission of the European Communities.

drawn from each member state. The judges are reappointed every six weeks.

The Court of Justice is the Community's highest court. However, because it has no enforcement agency its judgements have to be carried out through the national courts. The Treaty limits it to dealing with constitutional and commercial matters. It has no jurisdiction over criminal or civil issues.

Issues are often raised in the national courts involving Community law. Under these circumstances the issue may be referred to the European Court of Justice for a preliminary ruling. By the end of 1983 around 5000 decisions taken by national courts dealing with Community law in the Community context were considered by the court. Such referrals are requests to the court for it to rule on the interpretation or to assess the validity of particular portions of Community law. Links between the national and European courts have grown closer.

A great deal of international law has little direct effect on firms and individuals. Community law ruled through the Court of Justice, however, often has a very significant impact on their actions.

## HOW COMMUNITY MEMBERSHIP AFFECTS UK ORGANISATIONS

In trying to fulfil their objectives, Community institutions have introduced policies and passed legislation which have had a direct impact on UK residents and business organisations. What has been the impact on organisations of working within a European rather than a national environment?

### Advantages of membership
Membership of the European Community has produced the following positive advantages.

*Business environment*
It has placed business organisations in a more **dynamic, faster-growing environment**, experiencing a higher standard of living and higher wages than the UK. This has resulted in some beneficial spin-offs to UK organisations, especially those with initiative that have been able to expand and develop to their full potential.

*Markets*
Europe offers the business organisation a **larger potential market** of over 319 million people. This is almost six times the size of the UK domestic market. Through association and trade agreements the Community is linked with more than half the countries in the world. Entry into this larger market has helped to stimulate the growth of those organisations that have the potential to benefit from economies of scale from larger operations.

*Free trade*
The **removal of trade barriers**, and in particular tariffs, has helped to create this larger potential home market. This could in the long term create a wider range of cheaper goods, which in itself would result in a **better standard of living** for community citizens. The existence of such a **large internal market** provides a certain amount of security for European business organisations. They are also helped by the fact that the Community is the world's largest trader, which gives it considerable **bargaining power** when negotiating on trading matters with other countries or trading groups.

*Investment incentives*
European membership has helped to provide **incentives** for businesses to invest. This is because the free movement of factors of production within Western Europe, in particular of capital, has facilitated better investment opportunities, which may then bring the benefits of technological and managerial improvements.

Business organisations have benefited from the **collaboration** between member states on investment in technological, industrial and research projects. For example, the ESPRIT programme has linked many of the Community's computer companies in research and development into information technology. Similar joint projects have been established in aerospace and telecommunications.

European membership has also encouraged non-European **foreign investment** in the UK. In particular United States and Japanese firms have invested in the UK as a result of the access this provides them to Community markets, which are then free to them from tariff and other trade barriers. The UK has benefited considerably from this. In 1984 the UK received more than half of United States investment in

Community countries, whereas in 1971 (two years before we joined the Community) the UK's share was only one-quarter.

*Job mobility*
The free movement of factors of production throughout the Community has given Britons **free access to jobs** anywhere within the Community. All citizens of the Community are free to seek jobs in any member country, on equal terms with nationals of that country. Work permits are not required, and there is no loss of social security rights.

*Institutional help*
Business organisations may also benefit from the activities of, and sources of finance made available by, the European Investment Bank, the Regional Development Fund and the European Social Fund.

The **European Investment Bank** was set up under the Treaty of Rome in 1958. Its basic function is to provide finance for projects which benefit less developed regions, are outside the scope of individual member states or are of common interest to a number of member states. The bank is controlled by a board of governors drawn from the member states. By January 1985 the UK had received £3374 million from the bank.

The **Regional Development Fund** was set up in 1975 to help member states with their regional problems. Its financial assistance is allocated on a quota basis, with the quota reflecting the Community's assessment of the nation's needs. By January 1985 the UK had received £1621 million.

The **European Social Fund** was set up in 1957 to help with the problems of redeploying redundant workers. It performs this function, for example, by providing assistance with retraining programmes. Up to January 1985 the UK had received £1254 million from the fund to retrain workers and teach job skills to young people.

*Collective problem-solving*
One of the major advantages of European membership has been the opportunity for member states to be part of a collective European effort to tackle particular economic, social or political problems. This has been particularly true with respect to European efforts to achieving **monetary stability** and to **influence world affairs**.

The **European Monetary System** (EMS) was established in 1979 to promote monetary stability within the Community. It was intended to prevent a repeat of the disarray caused by the breakdown of the world monetary system based on the dollar in the 1970s. The EMS has three aspects:

- an **exchange-rate mechanism** which limits the amount by which member states' exchange rates may vary;
- a **European Currency Unit** which reflects movements in national currencies and is used within the Community for budgetary and other purposes;
- Community short- and medium-term **credit facilities**.

By 1986 the UK was making use of the second and third aspects but had yet to join in the first, although this was the aim of the UK government.

In the case of world affairs, the twelve countries of the Community attempt to work together and take up a common position. This is true of talks within the **United Nations** on matters relating to international trade. In the case of the **General Agreement on Tariffs and Trade** (GATT), the Commission negotiates on behalf of all the Community countries.

A collective community stance is also taken towards the developing countries. For instance, under the **Lomé Convention**, signed for the third time in 1984, the Community helps sixty-six developing countries in Africa, the Caribbean and the Pacific with aid, trade and co-operation. The Community is pledged to provide more than £5 billion in aid for the period of 1985–90, together with technical and industrial co-operation, free access to European markets and a guarantee of export earnings.

**Disadvantages of membership**
Membership of the European Community has produced the following disadvantages.

*Competition*
The benefits listed above can be realised only if UK business organisations respond quickly enough to the larger potential markets. Failure to do this will mean the UK businesses are in danger of being swamped by **competition** from

European firms. The resulting **increase in imports** will have an extremely adverse effect on the UK balance of payments. In fact the UK has been running a **balance of trade deficit** with Europe since 1980.

*Legislation*
Business organisations operating in Europe have the problem of dealing with new and different **legislation** concerning policy, transport standards and technical requirements.

*Loss of sovereignty*
There is a danger that, if complete economic, social and political union were to be finally achieved, it might result in a **sacrifice of national sovereignty**. This in turn could lead to the national government not truly or effectively being able to represent the interests of UK business organisations. Some people are already concerned about the fact that under the Community treaties policies are decided, rules made, laws enacted and taxes raised not by our own Parliament but by the European Parliament. The UK law can be changed by British people whereas changes in Community laws need the agreement of the other members of the Community.

*Food production and pricing problems*
The **Common Agricultural Policy** (CAP) has the objective of trying to ensure that food supplies are set at a reasonable price for consumers and that a fair standard of living is achieved by farmers. To achieve this objective charges are placed on imported food and the level of prices within Europe is maintained by a system of internal support buying.

This system has produced a number of problems. First, it is very expensive, taking about two-thirds of the Community budget. Second, it has led to the creation of food mountains, which are stored in warehouses and then later destroyed or sold to the Soviet Union or elsewhere at knock-down prices. Food prices in the UK are said to be 10 per cent higher as a result of the Common Agricultural Policy than they would have been outside the system.

---

**Activity 4.3**
By the end of 1986 the European Community's Common Agricultural Policy (CAP) had helped to create the following accumulated intervention stocks or mountains:

Butter:    1,500,000 tonnes
Grain:    16,780,000 tonnes
Beef:    620,000 tonnes
Milk powder:    1,100,000 tonnes
Wine:    15,000,000 hectolitres.

Is there any justification for this situation? Present your answer as a series of points for and against the CAP.

---

**Activity 4.4**
Carry out a survey using a suitably designed questionnaire to discover the effect European Community membership has had on local industry. Choose the representative sample to be investigated according to relative payroll strength, turnover and the type of activity in which the business is engaged. (Part-time students may be able to include the firms for which they work.) Analyse your findings and present them in the form of a report.

# 5. The National Economy

ment can also use much broader policies as a means of influencing the total **level of economic activity** and hence the total **level of output and employment** in the economy.

To appreciate how the economy reacts to such policies it is important first of all to see how the economy would operate in the *absence* of government intervention. The following sections therefore gradually build up a simple model of the economy, which can then be used to demonstrate how certain economic forces interact and eventually determine the total level of output and employment in the economy.

In Chapter 3 we saw how the government can encourage business activity. Possible measures include those designed to stimulate investment and those that encourage the development of a better trained and more mobile work-force. In addition to these specific measures, the govern-

## THE CIRCULAR FLOW OF INCOME

The first stage in building up a model of the economy involves dividing it up into two very broad sectors. These are the **households** and the **business organisations** which form the basis of Fig. 5.1.

**Fig. 5.1: The circular flow of income**

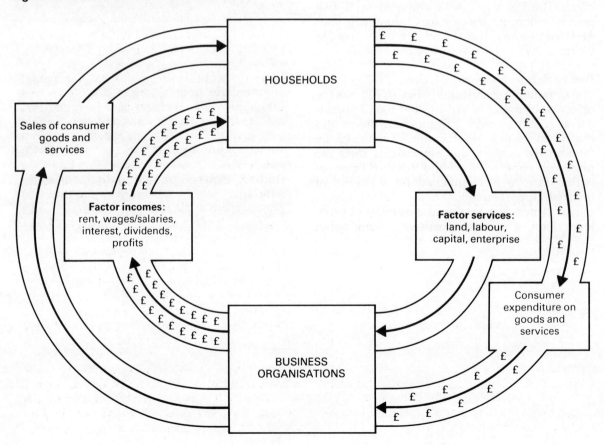

HOUSEHOLDS

Sales of consumer goods and services

Factor incomes: rent, wages/salaries, interest, dividends, profits

Factor services: land, labour, capital, enterprise

Consumer expenditure on goods and services

BUSINESS ORGANISATIONS

## Factor services and factor incomes

The term 'households' is used not in the context of family units but rather to describe those who earn an income from supplying business organisations with a factor service of some kind. Households are the source of the **factors of production** required by business organisations. These factors of production are the **land, labour** and **capital** which are essential for the output of all goods and services. Households are also a source of the factor of production known as **enterprise**. This refers to the entrepreneurial skills required to assess the various market opportunities and to organise and combine the other factors of production in order to achieve the desired output of a particular good or service.

In return for providing their respective factor services households receive **factor incomes**. Those that supply land receive **rent**, while those that provide labour are paid a **wage** or **salary**. In the case of households which supply business organisations with capital in the form of loans, their income will be derived from the **interest payments** which the business organisation makes to attract the necessary loan capital. The income earned by the households that supply entrepreneurial skills will come from the **profits** made by their respective business organisations where they have used their skills and risked their personal capital. If these entrepreneurs have also obtained risk capital from households willing to take a direct stake in their business, then some of this profit will also be paid out in the form of **dividends** to those households holding shares in the business.

The interrelationship between households and business organisations is shown in Fig. 5.1. The figure illustrates the flow of factor services from households to business organisations and the flow of factor incomes in the opposite direction.

## Why output = expenditure = national income

It is assumed that all the money flowing into households in the form of factor incomes paid out by business organisations is spent on the consumption of the goods and services produced by business organisations. This may seem a very extreme assumption to make, but it will soon be relaxed as the real world is gradually introduced into our model of the economy.

The assumption does not of course suggest that all those households supplying factor services to a factory that manufactures shoes, for example, will then spend all their factor income on the shoes they have helped to make! The assumption simply refers to a situation whereby the **total output** of consumer goods and services in the economy as a whole is absorbed by the **total level of household expenditure**. In other words, the total level of spending in Fig. 5.1 is exactly equal to the total value of goods/services produced in the economy.

The value of total output must also be the same as the **total level of income** earned by households. This is because the prices charged for various goods and services must be sufficient to cover the amounts paid out by business organisations to households which supply them with factor services. Assume, for example, that an entrepreneur incurs costs of £20 for each pair of jeans produced and then adds £4 as a profit on each pair of jeans sold. Thus each pair of jeans produced contributes £24 to the total output of the economy and also £24 to the total level of household income.

In our model of the economy the entrepreneur is treated just like any other household supplying a factor service. So all their profits are spent on the various goods and services produced in the economy. As far as the economy in Fig. 5.1 is concerned, we have now established that the value of total output is the same as total income and this in turn is the same as total spending.

## Equilibrium

An economy is said to be in a **state of equilibrium** when there is no tendency for the total level of output and hence employment and income to change. This is the case with the economy in Fig. 5.1, because there is no reason why the total level of output should change. The total level of consumer expenditure flowing into business organisations is just sufficient to absorb the total output of goods and services. Total output will therefore remain unchanged, and business organisations in general will have no reason either to expand or to reduce their employment of factor services. Since the total level of employment remains unchanged, the total level of income also remains unchanged. We can take this a stage further by saying that because the total level of income remains unchanged the total level of household expendi-

**Fig. 5.2: Withdrawals from the circular flow**

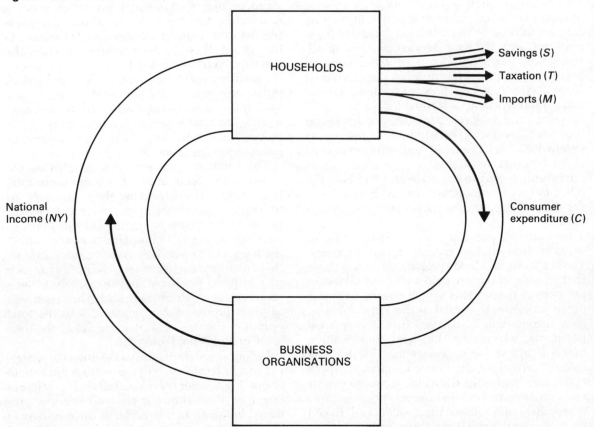

## WITHDRAWALS FROM THE CIRCULAR FLOW

Let us now relax the earlier assumption that all the money flowing into households in the form

ture remains unchanged. Our analysis of the economy in Fig. 5.1 now comes full circle, because if the total level of household expenditure remains unchanged then total output in the economy remains unchanged.

We can conclude that equilibrium in an economy is reached when **total expenditure is equal to total income**. When this is the case the total amount of money flowing into business organisations via expenditure is exactly equal to the total amount of money they are paying out in the form of incomes. Since total income also reflects the value of total output, this is another way of saying that the flow of spending is just enough to absorb the level of output produced by business organisations.

of income is returned to business organisations via consumer expenditure. In the real world there are leakages or **withdrawals** from the circular flow of income, so that some of the money flowing into households does not flow back to become the income of business organisations. There are three withdrawals from the circular flow of income: **savings, taxation** and **imports**.

### Savings

There are a wide range of financial institutions competing for **household savings**. These include building societies, banks, life assurance companies, investment trusts, unit trusts and the various national savings schemes. Business organisations may also save. This is the case when a company retains some of its profits rather than paying it all out to shareholders in the form of dividends. In Fig. 5.2 the savings withdrawal also includes business savings, because business organisations in effect save on behalf of those households that have supplied capital funds that earn them profits or dividends.

## The distinction between savings and investment

You may be tempted to say that household savings are only a temporary withdrawal from the circular flow of income, since they will soon flow back into the economy when such funds are used by business organisations to finance their investment in plant, machinery and premises. But this will not necessarily be the case. The factors which influence the level of household savings are not the same as those which influence the level of investment expenditure by business organisations. Savings and investment decisions are taken by different groups of people for different reasons, and any developments in the economy which encourage the level of household savings will not automatically guarantee that such an increase in the supply of 'loanable' funds will lead to an immediate and comparable increase in the level of investment expenditure by business organisations.

This tendency to assume that any change in the level of savings will immediately be balanced by an equal change in investment expenditure is possibly based upon a failure to distinguish correctly between savings and investment. If you have put some money into a bank or building society account then you may well claim that you have 'invested' your money, but strictly you have only saved your money in such institutions. Money is **invested** only when it is used by business organisations to finance **expenditure on capital projects**, for example as part of expansion or modernisation programmes. Households therefore are responsible for savings and not investment, even though investment may be financed by funds saved by households, which financial institutions then make available to business organisations.

*Business savings*
There is a much closer link between the savings and investment decisions of business organisations themselves. But once again there is no guarantee that the savings which they undertake on behalf of the suppliers of capital will all be spent on investment projects. The general economic climate and developments in the markets where they sell their goods or services may

lead to a business strategy which involves using some of the undistributed profits to build up their **reserves**. A part of business savings may therefore be used to acquire a range of **financial assets** that provide them with interest and varying degrees of liquidity.

*The level of national income*
The most important long-term influence upon the total level of savings in an economy is the level of **national income**. As households become better off they can afford to engage in savings plans as a means of protecting their post-retirement living standards. Apart from such long-term savings plans, households can also afford to save on a short- or medium-term basis as a means of financing the future purchase of expensive consumer durables. Similarly in the case of business organisations a rise in profits will allow them to increase the level of retained profits while still providing their suppliers of risk capital with a return which at least compensates them for the risks they take.

*The level of interest rates*
As far as the general level of **interest rates** is concerned, there is no clear-cut evidence that it plays a major part in determining the total level of savings. The households that save part of their income do so because it is a general characteristic of such people to plan for their future. Having reached a certain standard of living, they are willing to save part of any increase in their income, knowing that their future living standards are more secure, rather than maximising their current standard of living when measured in material terms. Because so many households attach such importance to saving it is doubtful if a general fall in interest rates would cause a significant reduction in the total level of savings. Similarly a general rise in interest rates will not necessarily lead to a significant increase in total savings if the majority of savers believe that their current savings plans adequately safeguard their future living standards.

A general rise in interest rates is brought about by financial institutions having to compete more fiercely among themselves on occasions in order to protect or increase their share of the total savings market. Such a rise in interest rates therefore causes a **redistribution** to some extent of total savings between the various financial institutions. Some households may hold part of their savings in a form which makes them readily accessible and they incur little or no penalty if they are withdrawn and placed with another institution which offers more attractive terms with no significant loss of liquidity.

### The marginal propensity to save

Total savings, then, as a withdrawal from the circular flow of income, are largely determined in the long run by the level of national income. Fig. 5.3 depicts a total savings schedule (S) which slopes upward from left to right. As national income increases, so does the level of total savings. The actual slope of S depends upon the **marginal propensity to save** (MPS), defined as the proportion of an increase in income which is saved. If, for example, an economy in general displays an MPS of 0.08, this means that the average household will save 8p of every extra £ of income. In this case a rise in national income of £100 million will lead to an increase in total savings of £8 million.

The higher the MPS, the steeper will be the slope of S. Thus if the MPS is 0.12, a rise in national income of £100 million will generate extra savings of £12 million. Similarly the lower the MPS, the less steep will be the slope of S. If the MPS is only 0.05, a rise in national income of £100 million will generate extra savings of only £5 million.

Because the savings schedule in Fig. 5.3 is a straight line, this indicates that the economy displays a constant MPS, and the value of the MPS itself is not influenced by the level of national income. The savings schedule in Fig. 5.4, however, shows an economy which displays a rising MPS. The gradual increase in the slope of S means that as households become better off they tend to save an increasing proportion of their extra income. This can be seen in Fig. 5.4 by comparing the extra savings generated by equal increases in income occurring at different levels of national income.

The savings schedule in Fig. 5.4 is more realistic than the one in Fig. 5.3, because as national income rises some households are able to save for the first time, while others will reach a position whereby they can afford to save more in a wider range of savings schemes. As their incomes continue to rise and more of their needs are satisfied, some households become increasingly confident that they can also put some money into much longer-term savings schemes such as those offered by life assurance companies or unit trusts. They can do this because any unforeseen need for cash can be met by drawing upon their existing savings in schemes that give them ready access to their money.

If households save an increasing proportion of increases in income, this also indicates that they spend a decreasing proportion of this extra income on goods and services. Even so, a rising MPS does not mean a fall in total consumer expenditure but rather a gradual fall in the **rate of increase** of total consumer expenditure. As household incomes rise they can both spend and save more money than before, but the

**Fig. 5.3**

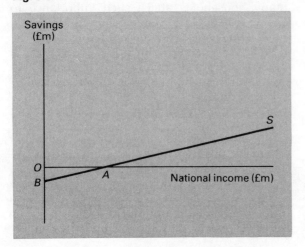

**Fig. 5.4**

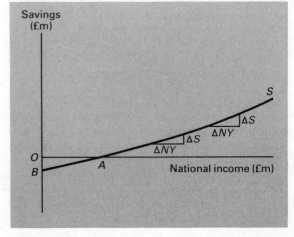

rising MPS means that households are expressing an increasing preference in favour of savings rather than consumption.

Although the savings schedule in Fig. 5.4 is closer to the real world than the one depicted in Fig. 5.3, we will use Fig. 5.3 to help build a simple model of how the economy works. The use of this straight-line savings schedule does not affect the essential characteristics of such a model or your ability to analyse how an economy is likely to react to various governmental economic policies.

*Autonomous consumption*
In both Figs. 5.3 and 5.4 the savings schedules start below the origin. This is described by economists as representing the level of **autonomous consumption**: a level of consumer expenditure which is not induced by national income and exists even when national income is zero. The level of autonomous consumption in both diagrams is equivalent to *OB*. Even though national income has fallen to zero, this amount of consumption is possible because households are using past savings to finance their purchase of goods produced in an earlier period. When

households use up their savings they are said to be **dissaving**. At zero national income the level of dissavings is *OB*, the level of autonomous consumption. As national income increases the level of dissavings gradually falls, but households in general are still spending more than their income. Once national income reaches *OA*, however, total expenditure is equal to total income, and there is neither saving nor dissaving. Increases in national income beyond *OA* start to generate savings according to the value of the MPS.

In 1985 the national income of the UK economy was approximately £3000 billion, and about 11 per cent of disposable income was saved. As far as our model of the national economy is concerned, the lower parts of the savings schedule are of little significance. But the above comments concerning autonomous consumption and dissavings will help you appreciate the main characteristics of a savings schedule.

Activity 5.1
(a) Account for the relationship between the retail price index (RPI) and the personal sector savings ratio in Fig. 5.5. Note that the personal savings ratio is defined as the proportion of disposable income allocated to savings.
(b) Describe any other factors that may have contributed to the decline in the savings ratio since 1980.

**Fig. 5.5: Personal saving ratio and RPI (percentages)**

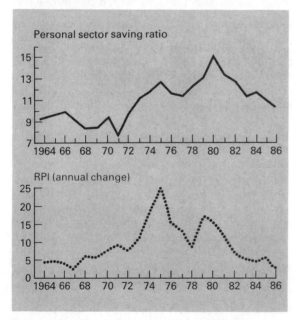

Source: *Economic Progress Report*, Nov./Dec. 1986, HMSO.

**Taxation**
Taxation is a withdrawal from the circular flow of income because some of the money earned by households is taken by the government in the form of direct and indirect taxes. **Income tax** is deducted on wages, salaries and interest and dividend payments. Business organisations also have to pay **corporation tax** on their profits, and this is a withdrawal because it affects the amount of money received by those households which have supplied risk capital

**Indirect taxes** such as VAT and excise duties are also withdrawals and arise when households spend their income. These taxes are collected by business organisations on behalf of the government because they are levied on the goods and services which business organisations sell to households. These taxes are then passed on to consumers by business organisations because they set their prices at levels which enable them to recoup the taxes they have to pay to the government.

The government finds this a very convenient way of collecting its indirect taxes. It is far easier to tax the manufacturer of electrical appliances on each of the units it produces than to allocate a tax collector to every single electrical shop in order to collect the tax as the customers leave the shop with their new purchases.

*The marginal rate of taxation*
The taxation schedule in Fig. 5.6 slopes upwards from left to right. This shows that as national income increases so does the total amount taken by the government in taxes. The actual slope of *T* depends upon the **marginal rate of taxation** (MRT), i.e. the proportion of an increase in income which is withdrawn from the circular flow of income in taxes. Since the taxation schedule in Fig. 5.6 is a straight line, this indicates that each of the various types of direct taxes take a fixed proportion of income. In the case of households paying income tax, the same rate is paid regardless of the income levels they reach. This schedule also indicates that the government does not levy different rates of indirect taxes by charging higher rates on those goods and services which could be classified as luxuries, for example, because they are generally in demand when incomes reach much higher levels.

*A progressive taxation system*
The taxation schedule in Fig. 5.7 depicts an economy with a rising MRT. This indicates a **progressive taxation system**. In the case of income tax it means that as households earn more money they may move into a tax bracket whereby the extra income is taxed at a higher rate than their previous income. Someone earning £8000 a year may pay income tax at 30 per cent, and this rate may apply up to an income of £15,000. The next £4000 of income may then be taxed at 40 per cent, with progressively higher rates being charged as income rises beyond certain levels.

A rising MRT may also reflect a system of indirect taxation which is designed to be progressive. The basic necessities which account

**Fig. 5.6**

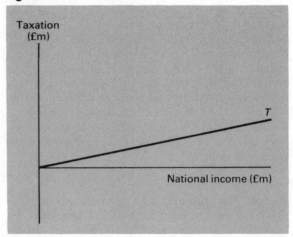

for a large part of the expenditure of households when they are on low incomes may be zero-rated, while other goods and services may then carry progressively higher taxes according to the government's interpretation of the degree of necessity or luxury attached to them. Thus as the total level of income rises in the economy the pattern of consumer expenditure will produce a progressively larger withdrawal in the form of indirect taxes. Households will tend to spend a larger proportion of extra income on those goods and services which are subject to the higher VAT or excise duties.

Once again you may say that, although taxation is a withdrawal from the circular flow of income, this will soon be balanced by the government when it spends all of its tax revenues on social and welfare services, for example. As was described in *Business Organisations and Environments* Book 1, Chapter 5, however, governments have been prepared to borrow money to finance some of their spending on capital projects. This means that the government spends more than it receives in the way of tax revenues. The extent to which a government is willing to spend more or less without a compensating change in tax revenues depends upon its overall social, political and economic objectives and the degree to which it wishes to intervene in the economy.

**Imports**
Some of the money spent by households is destined to flow out of the economy to business organisations abroad. Where goods have been

**Fig. 5.7**

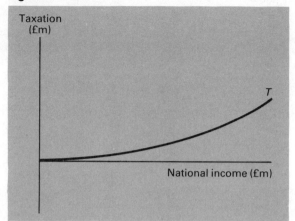

**Fig. 5.8**

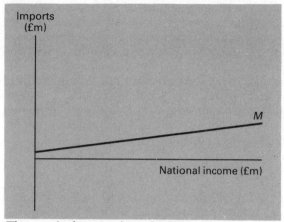

made abroad, for example, a Japanese video-recorder, the purchase is obviously a withdrawal from our circular flow of income, because a proportion of the price paid in the shop goes abroad to the manufacturer. However, not all the money that is paid for goods made abroad represents a withdrawal. The retail price of the video-recorder also has to cover the costs incurred by business organisations in the UK that were involved for example in its transport, storage, wholesaling and retailing.

Even with UK manufacturers, part of the price that organisations charge for their output is used to help meet their import costs. Business organisations may import raw materials, energy components and items of plant and equipment. As with the costs incurred in using domestic resources, these costs must be recouped in the prices they charge for their goods and services.

It is in fact very difficult to imagine a good or service which has not incurred an import cost somewhere along the line. You may suggest that the price you pay for locally grown vegetables must represent a 100 per cent home cost. But perhaps the grower used an imported weedkiller or pesticide, storage facilities built partly from imported materials and sacks made from an imported fibre, driving the vegetables to the wholesalers in a Volvo lorry. All these import costs will be passed on, so the final retail price for locally grown vegetables will include an amount to cover import costs. A bank, for example, may use an imported computer. A hotel or catering establishment may serve dishes made partly from imported ingredients, and some of its furnishings and fittings could have been manufactured abroad.

*The marginal propensity to import*

The import schedule in Fig. 5.9 shows that total imports rise along with national income. The slope of *M* depends upon the **marginal propensity to import** (MPM) and this is defined as the proportion of an increase in income which is withdrawn from the circular flow via the import elements of consumer expenditure. The import schedule in Fig. 5.8 displays a constant MPM, and this means that as households become better off they do not express an increasing preference for imported goods and services. A constant MPM must also imply that business organisations themselves do not alter the import element of their output as they expand production to meet the growing demand for goods and services as households spend part of their extra income.

It is possible, however, that a sudden and large rise in the level of national income may produce a rise in the MPM. If domestic producers cannot cope with the resulting increase in the level of consumer expenditure then more households may choose to buy imported goods rather than accept extended delivery dates. Producers themselves may also experience shortages of materials and components because domestic suppliers do not have the spare capacity to satisfy a significant increase in the demand for their output. Producers therefore will need to import an increasing part of their materials and components, and so a larger proportion of consumer expenditure will be accounted for by the import content. If an economy displays a rising MPM as national income increases, then this would be reflected in an import schedule with a rising curve.

Both Figs. 5.3 and 5.4 showed savings schedules starting below the origin because there is a certain amount of autonomous consumption. A proportion of this autonomous consumption is accounted for by imports, and this is why the import schedule in Fig. 5.8 starts above the origin: there will be a withdrawal in the form of imports even if national income falls to zero. Once again for the sake of simplicity our model of the economy will use an import schedule displaying a constant MPM.

### The total withdrawals schedule (W)

The three kinds of withdrawal schedule in Figs. 5.3, 5.6 and 5.8 are now combined to produce the **total withdrawals schedule** (*W*) in Fig. 5.9. This shows the level of total withdrawals at various levels of national income. Since we have used individual schedules which display a constant MPS, MRT and MPM *W* is also a straight line.

The slope of *W* depends upon the **marginal propensity to withdraw** (MPW). This refers to the proportion of an increase in income which is withdrawn from the circular flow of income in the form of savings, taxation and imports. If, for example, the MPS = 0.08, the MRT = 0.020 and the MPM = 0.12:

then MPW = 0.08 + 0.20 + 0.12 = 0.40.

This means that a rise in national income of, say, £100 million will generate total withdrawals of £40 million. If the slope of *W* changed and became steeper as national income rose, this would show that at least one of the three withdrawals tended to account for a progressively larger proportion of an increase in household income.

### The marginal propensity to consume

The numerical example above shows that 0.40 of an increase in national income is withdrawn from the circular flow. This means that 0.60 of the increase stays in the circular flow and is returned to business organisations to become their income. This 0.60 represents what is known as the **marginal propensity to consume** (MPC) and in our analysis this is the proportion of an increase in income which is spent by households and remains the income of business organisations. Since we have already accounted for imports in the MPW, this MPC refers only to the **home cost element** of consumer expenditure

**Fig. 5.9**

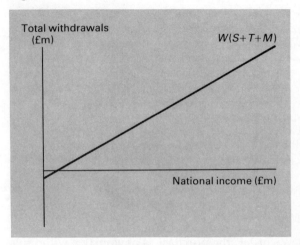

and is therefore the income of business organisations after having met their import costs. Later on in this chapter we will return to the MPC, as it has a role to play in understanding how the economy works.

### The effect of withdrawals upon the circular flow of income

To demonstrate the pressures which withdrawals exert upon the level of total output, employment and income, the following analysis assumes that they are not offset by any other form of expenditure being added to the consumer expenditure of households.

In Fig. 5.2 the withdrawals from the circular flow of income mean that less money is now flowing back to business organisations via consumer expenditure than they are paying out in the form of incomes. Since total income reflects the value of total output, this means that total household expenditure is not large enough to absorb all the goods and services currently being produced in the economy. Business organisations will in general therefore reduce their output, which means that they will employ fewer factor services. The rise in unemployment will produce a fall in national income, and this in turn will lead to a fall in consumer expenditure. The fall in consumer expenditure means that business organisations are still faced with a situation whereby the money flowing back to them from households is less than the money they are paying out in incomes. Total consumer expenditure is still not enough to absorb even their reduced output of goods and services.

**Fig. 5.10: Injections into the circular flow**

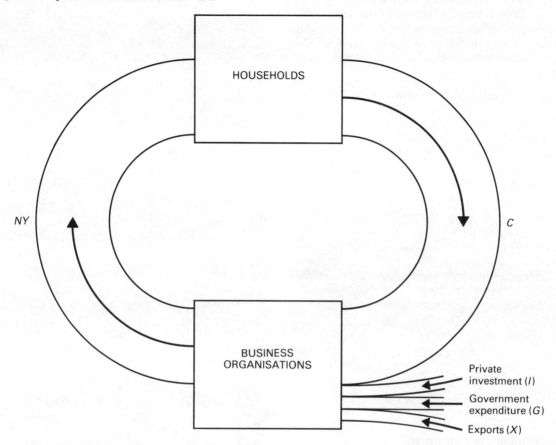

Thus since business organisations are still left with unsold goods and services they will react by cutting their output yet again. This leads to yet more unemployment and a further fall in national income and hence consumer expenditure.

By now you will have realised that withdrawals cause business organisations to react in a way which leads to a **cumulative decline** in total output, employment and national income. In other words, withdrawals exert a **downward pressure** upon the overall level of economic activity.

## INJECTIONS INTO THE CIRCULAR FLOW

The next stage in building up a simple model of the economy involves introducing other forms of expenditure into the circular flow of income. So far we have assumed that the only form of

expenditure experienced by business organisations is the money flowing into them in the form of consumer expenditure by households. There are however **injections into the circular flow of income** representing expenditure which does not originate directly from households. Households are directly responsible only for consumer expenditure. There are three injections into the circular flow of income: **private investment, government expenditure** and **exports**. These are shown in Fig. 5.10.

### Private investment (*I*)

Private investment leads to a demand for a wide range of capital goods by business organisations which wish to expand their operations and introduce new technology into their production processes and techniques. This type of expenditure also covers capital spending programmes on factories and other premises where goods and services are produced.

The private investment schedule (*I*) in Fig. 5.11 is based on the assumption that such spending is independent of the level of national income. The following are just some of the factors which could cause *I* to shift up or down:

- the level of **business confidence** and **expectations** concerning developments in both the economy as a whole and particular market sectors;
- current and anticipated **levels of profitability**;
- movements in the general level of **interest rates** and the extent to which **external capital** is readily available.

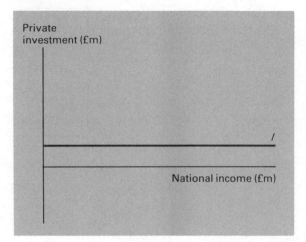

**Fig. 5.11**

Private investment (£m)

National income (£m)

*I*

Activity 5.2
Look through some recent editions of both national and local newspapers and identify articles that describe various kinds of capital investment projects. Report upon the projects from the following points of view:

(a) the organisation responsible for the project and the amount of money involved;
(b) the kinds of business organisation that are likely to receive contracts or orders during the various phases of the projects.

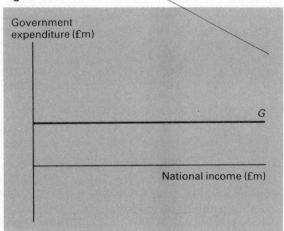

**Fig. 5.12**

Government expenditure (£m)

National income (£m)

*G*

### Government expenditure (*G*)

Government expenditure includes both the **current** and the **capital expenditure** of a government in such areas as those shown in Table 6.4 (page 96). The government expenditure schedule in Fig. 5.12 assumes that this injection into the circular flow of income is also independent of the level of national income. The government's spending plans are determined by its social and political objectives and by the costs of financing government measures aimed at promoting specific aspects of economic activity such as investment in high-technology projects and improved training programmes in the private sector. Since the government can exert a direct control over the capital expenditure programmes of the nationalised industries this type of spending is also included in the schedule shown in Fig. 5.12

### Exports (*X*)

This injection into the circular flow of income arises from the overseas demand for the goods

and services produced by business organisations in the UK. The export schedule in Fig. 5.13 is also independent of the level of national income.

The major influences upon the demand for exports are as follows:

- the rate at which the **prices** of UK goods and services rise or fall relative to those charged by business organisations in competing economies;
- the extent to which UK business organisations can compete in overseas markets with respect to **non-price factors** such as quality, reliability, design, delivery dates and after-sales service;

**Fig. 5.13**

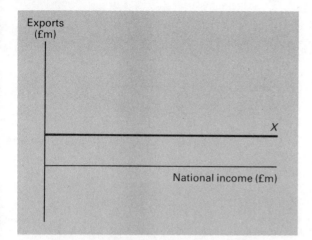

**Fig. 5.14**

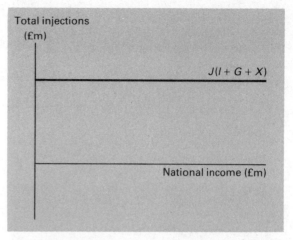

- the **rate of economic growth** in overseas economies and how this is likely to effect the UK's existing sales to such countries;
- **exchange rate movements**;
- measures introduced in other countries which make their markets either more or less accessible to UK business organisations, e.g. the removal or introduction of **import restrictions**.

### The total injections schedule (*J*)

The three kinds of injection are now combined to produce the total injections schedule (*J*) in Fig. 5.14.

Activity 5.3
Select a group of firms in your area and establish their respective product ranges. Investigate and report upon the firms from the following points of view:

(a) the extent to which they rely either directly or indirectly upon
    (i) consumer demand for goods and services;
    (ii) private investment expenditure;
    (iii) central or local government expenditure;
    (iv) export markets;
(b) the extent to which they use imported raw materials, semi-processed goods, components, machinery and equipment;
(c) their contribution to local employment.

### The effect of injections upon the circular flow of income

To discover the effect which injections exert upon total output, employment and national income, the following analysis is based upon the assumption that there are no withdrawals from the circular flow of income.

In Fig. 5.10 the introduction of injections means that more money is now flowing into business organisations via all types of expenditure than they are paying out in the form of incomes. The total output of various kinds of goods and services is therefore not large enough to satisfy the total demand, and some business organisations have to increase their output, which means that they will employ more factor services. This rise in employment will produce a rise in national income, and this in turn will lead to a rise in consumer expenditure. This rise in consumer expenditure means that some of those business organisations producing consumer goods and services still face a situation in which the money flowing back into them from households is greater than the money they are paying out in incomes. Output will be expanded in an attempt to meet this increase in consumer expenditure, and this will lead to yet more employment and a further rise in national income and hence consumer expenditure

This sequence of events will continue. We can conclude that injections will exert an **upward pressure** upon the level of total output, employment and national income. This is in contrast to the downward pressure exerted by the withdrawals in Fig. 5.2.

Activity 5.4
Which of the following would be classified as either a withdrawal or an injection in terms of the circular flow of income? In each case give reasons for your answer.

(a) British Telecom laying more fibre-optic cables.
(b) A road haulier buying a fleet of Volvo lorries.
(c) An increase in local authority house-building programmes.
(d) The privatisation of British Airways.
(e) The extension of VAT to books, newspapers and periodicals.
(f) The sale of Rolls-Royce aero-engines to the Boeing Corporation.
(g) The interest earned on building society deposits.
(h) The building of the Channel tunnel.
(i) The spending of overseas students in the UK.
(j) An increase in the motor vehicle road-fund licence.

## THE DETERMINATION OF EQUILIBRIUM

### The injections/withdrawals approach

The **total injections schedule** and the **total withdrawals schedule** can be combined to produce a simple diagrammatic model of how an economy works and of the forces that determine the equilibrium level of total output, employment and national income. When dealing with the economy in Fig. 5.1 (page 64), which had neither withdrawals nor injections, we saw that when total expenditure was equal to total income then the economy would be in a state of equilibrium. This was because total household expenditure was just sufficient to absorb the total output in the economy. Business organisations in general would have no reason to alter their output, and thus employment and national income would show no tendency to change.

Let us now re-examine the condition for equilibrium by dealing with an economy which is a closer reflection of the real world. We will now take account of the existence of both withdrawals and injections. Assume that the economy in Fig. 5.15 has currently reached a level

**Fig. 5.15**

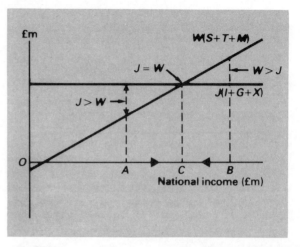

of national income of *OA*. However, this does not reflect an equilibrium level of national income, output and employment, because forces are at work which will lead to an increase in the overall level of economic activity. At *OA* the forces which tend to depress the level of national income (i.e. withdrawals – *W*) are more than outweighed by the forces that tend to increase the level of national income (i.e. injections *I*). From the point of view of the circular flow of income and the economy as a whole, the total amount of money flowing into the business organisations via total expenditure (i.e. *C + I + G + X*) is greater than the total amount of money they are currently paying out in the form of income. Since the level of national income *OA* reflects the value of total output, the economy in general is not able to satisfy the current level of total expenditure. To satisfy the various types of expenditure, some business organisations will have to increase their output, and this will lead to an increase in employment and hence national income. The level of national income will therefore continue to rise.

A level of national income such as *OA* does not therefore reflect an economy in a state of equilibrium, because forces are at work which stimulate the overall level of economic activity. In fact as long as the amount of money flowing into business organisations via total expenditure is greater than the amount of money which they are paying out in the form of incomes (as shown by the gap between *J* and *W*), then output, employment and hence national income will continue to rise.

**Fig. 5.16: Equilibrium**

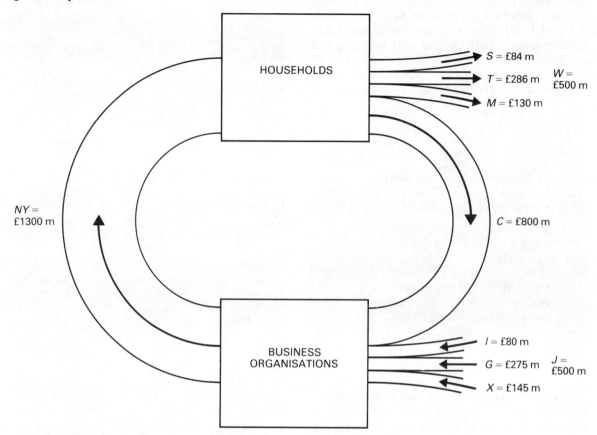

In Fig. 5.15 as national income rises the gap between $J$ and $W$ is gradually closed. This must mean a corresponding reduction in the extent to which the money flowing into business organisations exceeds the money they are paying out. The gap between $J$ and $W$ closes because the rise in national income generates additional withdrawals in the form of savings, taxation and imports.

The economy in Fig. 5.15 will cease to expand when a level of national income of $OC$ is reached. At this point the injections of spending into the circular flow of income are now matched by the withdrawals. Equilibrium exists at $OC$ because $J = W$: the amount of money flowing into business organisations via total expenditure is equal to the amount of money they are paying out in the form of incomes. In other words, total spending in the economy is just sufficient to absorb the total output produced by business organisations.

The equilibrium situation in Fig. 5.15 is also shown in Fig. 5.16, where some possible values have been added as an illustration of the previous analysis.

Before leaving Fig. 5.15, however, it will be useful to consider a level of national income such as $OB$, where total withdrawals from the circular flow of income are greater than the injections of additional spending into the circular flow of income. Because withdrawals outweigh injections, the level of total spending in the economy is not large enough to absorb the total output. Some business organisations are therefore obliged to cut back their output, and this leads to a fall in national income. This decline in the overall level of economic activity will continue as long as withdrawals exceed injections. The fall in the level of national income will, however, gradually reduce the level of savings, taxation and imports, and this will close the gap between withdrawals and injections. Thus if the economy in Fig. 5.15 were currently producing a level of national income such as *OB*, this would not represent an equilibrium situation. Total output and employment would continue to fall until the level of national income *OC* was reached, where once again withdrawals match injections.

**Activity 5.5**
Make six copies of Fig. 5.17. Use each of them as a basis for showing the effect of the following developments upon the level of national income, output and employment by indicating the new equilibrium position.

(a) the building of more hospitals;
(b) a fall in the MPS;
(c) a rise in the level of regional development grants;
(d) a fall in the world price of raw materials;
(e) a rise in the MPC;
(f) a reduction in the level of VAT.

**The expenditure/income approach**
As an alternative to the injections/withdrawals approach to examining the forces which determine equilibrium in an economy it is also possible to use the **expenditure/income** method. This particular diagrammatic model uses a total expenditure schedule and what is known as a '45° line'.

The first step in building up a **total expenditure schedule** involves consumption. In Fig. 5.18 the consumer expenditure schedule (*C*) slopes upwards from left to right, and this indicates that as national income rises so does the level of consumer expenditure. The slope of *C* depends upon the **marginal propensity to consume** (MPC). Our earlier definition of the MPC on page 72 referred only to that part of an increase in income which is spent by households and remains the income of business organisations in the UK. The import element of household expenditure is therefore not included in our consumer expenditure schedule in Fig. 5.18.

*C* is a straight line, which indicates that this economy displays a constant MPC, and the MPW therefore does not vary with the level of national income. In Fig. 5.3 we also recognised the possibility of **autonomous consumption**,

**Fig. 5.17**

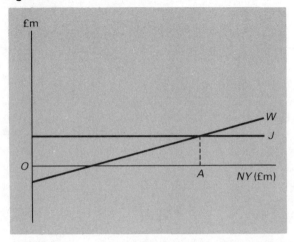

**Fig. 5.18**

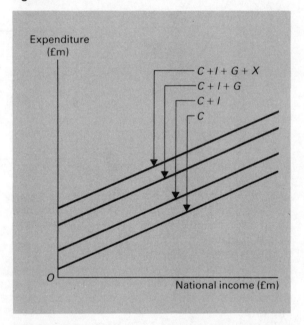

and this explains why the consumer expenditure schedule in Fig. 5.18 starts above the origin.

If this economy displayed a rising MPW (because of increases in the MPS, the MRT or the MPM), this would be reflected in a declining MPC. The use of a constant MPC, however, does not detract from the conclusions which we can draw from this alternative approach to the determination of equilibrium in an economy.

The various types of expenditure which represent injections into the circular flow of income

**Fig. 5.19**

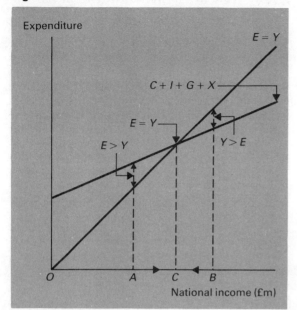

are now added to *C* to arrive at a total expenditure schedule (i.e. *C + I + G + X*). As each of these components is added to *C*, the new schedule can be shown by an upward parallel shift, since each of the injections is assumed to be independent of the level of national income.

The total expenditure schedule is now combined in Fig. 5.19 with a 45° line. Any point on this 45° line must indicate a position where total expenditure in the economy is equal to national income.

Let us now assume, as we did in our approach to Fig. 5.15 (page 76), that this economy is currently at a level of national income of *OA*. This does not represent the equilibrium position, however, because the level of economic activity will tend to expand. At *OA* total expenditure in the economy exceeds the level of national income (i.e. the value of total output). If looked at from the point of view of injections and withdrawals, this means that injections currently exceed withdrawals. Business organisations react by expanding their output, and we now have the familar sequence of developments which produce a rise in employment and national income. As long as total expenditure is greater than national income, the level of economic activity continues to expand. The rise in national income will gradually close the gap between total expenditure and national income,

because income will rise faster than expenditure. The reason for this is that some of the extra income will be withdrawn in the form of savings, taxation and imports. The equilibrium level of national income is therefore at *OC*, where total expenditure is equal to national income, and injections match withdrawals.

## UNEMPLOYMENT AND INFLATION

Having seen how an economy works and the factors that help to determine the overall level of economic activity, we can now examine some of the problems that may arise when an economy is left to operate solely in response to market forces.

### The unpredictable nature of an unregulated economy

There is no automatic mechanism whereby an economy will always expand so that it eventually reaches an equilibrium level of output and national income which reflects a position of full employment, and where the only people not working are those in the process of changing jobs rather than being out of work because of a lack of employment opportunities. The economy shown in Fig. 5.20, for example, has reached an equilibrium which has left a significant margin of spare capacity. This is because the level of output and national income which could be produced if full employment were reached is £10,000 million. There is no reason why this economy will then automatically expand towards this full employment situation, as total expenditure is not large enough to encourage the total output and national income that a fully employed economy is capable of producing. It would be a complete coincidence if the millions of independent spending decisions in this economy added up to an amount that would produce full employment. This economy therefore is suffering from unemployment because of a general lack of demand for the additional output which the economy as a whole is capable of producing. Some of its business organisations are operating well below capacity and may even have plant and machinery lying completely idle, while at the same time there are unemployed people who could be taken on to operate it if there was only the extra demand to warrant the higher output.

**Fig. 5.20**

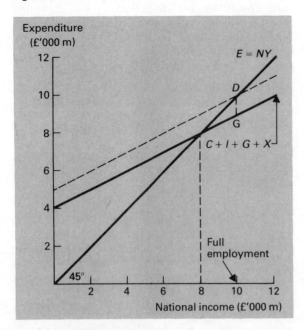

Economists describe this unemployment as being caused by **demand deficiency**. In terms of Fig. 5.20 it is reflected in the existence of a **deflationary gap**. This is defined as the amount of additional expenditure required to produce full employment; in Fig. 5.20 this is equivalent to *DG*. If total expenditure were to rise by this amount, the deflationary gap would be removed, and the economy would expand to a position of full employment.

### The classical view on unemployment

The situation in Fig. 5.20 is similar to the one that existed in the UK economy during the inter-war years, when unemployment reached 22 per cent at times and rarely fell below 10 per cent. This severe and prolonged recession was not in accordance with the traditional theories which formed the basis of the most popular economic thinking during those years, because it was generally thought that an economy would always show a tendency to move towards a full employment level of national income. Any unemployment that arose would be a purely temporary phenomenon. Accepted economic theory was centred on economic mechanisms operating in a free market economy that would soon overcome any tendency

for the economy to move away from full employment.

### The classical view on the labour market

If unemployment did exist, this would prove to be only temporary because of its impact upon the **labour market**. The supporters of traditional economic theories believed that the resulting excess supply of labour would produce the same kind of result that they expected to occur in a product market where excess supply existed: namely, a fall in price or, where labour was concerned, a **fall in the general level of wages**. Lower wage rates would then reduce unit costs of production so that business organisations could afford to lower their prices as a means of stimulating the demand for their output.

Particular attention was paid to the effect of these lower prices upon both **exports** and **imports**. The general improvement in competitiveness would encourage the overseas demand for UK output while also reducing the demand for imports as some households and business organisations switched their expenditure to the more competitively priced goods and services available in the domestic economy. This rise in total expenditure combined with lower wages would then encourage business organisations to take on more labour. This downward flexibility in wages and prices was an important aspect of classical economic thought, which relied heavily upon **market developments** as part of the automatic corrective mechanism that would always restore full employment.

### The classical link between savings and investment

A further example of such an automatic adjustment would be if at full employment there was an increase in savings. According to our circular flow of income analysis, this would cause a fall in total expenditure and a rise in unemployment. The classical school of economists, however, believed that an increase in savings would cause interest rates to fall because more money would be chasing potential borrowers; business organisations could therefore attract external capital by offering lower rates of interest. Some investment projects that had previously been shelved because their anticipated return on the capital involved and the cost of raising the necessary funds had made them unattractive now become more viable. The fall in the cost of raising external capital would improve the net return on such projects and compensate for the risks involved. The fall in interest rates would therefore stimulate investment expenditure and help restore full employment by compensating for the original fall in consumer expenditure. This corrective mechanism relied heavily upon investment expenditure being sensitive to what may prove to be relatively small reductions in interest rates, while also assuming that there would be no decline in the general level of business confidence.

### Traditional explanations of the failure of the unregulated economy

Traditional economists therefore attributed the prolonged and severe unemployment of the inter-war period to the growth of activities in the economy which led to imperfections in the working of the economic system. Such imperfections were said to be largely the fault of trade unions which attempted to resist a fall in wage rates, thus preventing prices from falling. The government of the time also believed that its own spending was too high, and this not only kept wages up but also absorbed funds which should have been left in the economy as savings to help push interest rates down. These funds would also be released to help finance the anticipated increase in investment expenditure.

Following this traditional line of economic thinking led the government to tackle the unemployment of the inter-war period by adopting policies which sought to cut wages and reduce public spending, including plans to cut unemployment benefits. Again, according to our earlier analysis, this would lead to even lower levels of demand in the economy and would worsen unemployment, hardly creating an economic climate to stimulate private investment expenditure.

### The need for government intervention

The work of John Maynard Keynes, and in particular his book *The General Theory of Employment, Interest and Money*, published in 1936, showed that the workings of an unregulated economy could persistently produce a level of national income and output which fell short of a full employment position, and that full employment would be the exception rather than the general rule. Keynes recognised that govern-

ment policies were aggravating the situation. The correct approach required the government to stimulate the level of demand by cutting taxes and increasing government expenditure. This would have involved the government in running a **budget deficit** and borrowing money but this was a complete break from the long-standing obligation of the government to balance its expenditure with its tax revenues. The proposals Keynes put forward were not fully accepted. It was the arms build-up and increased spending on defence as the threat of war increased which helped to reduce unemployment.

Not until the post-war period was serious attention paid to Keynesian techniques of influencing the overall level of economic activity by managing total demand. The importance attached to the breakthrough in economic thinking which Keynes made was reflected in a White Paper produced in 1944 expressing the government's intention to avoid the return of mass unemployment. The government's confidence in the new measures available led to a commitment to secure 'a high and stable level of employment'. It sought to achieve this using economic policies designed to ensure that total demand in the economy was always sufficient to produce full employment.

### Keynesian economics and demand-pull inflation

Although the development of **demand management policies** was promoted to avoid the possibility of large-scale unemployment, they also helped to deal with another situation which Keynes recognised could arise if the economy were left to its own devices. The situation could arise where the level of total expenditure was such that it was running in excess of the productive capabilities of the economy. The threat always existed in an unregulated economy that the total demand for the output of business organisations could more than outweigh their ability to meet this demand. This position would arise if the economy had already attained a state of full employment because total spending had reached a level sufficient to provide employment for all those seeking work. Keynes demonstrated that there were a virtually infinite number of less-than-full-employment equilibrium positions, but he also investigated the likely repercussions for the economy of this full

**Fig. 5.21**

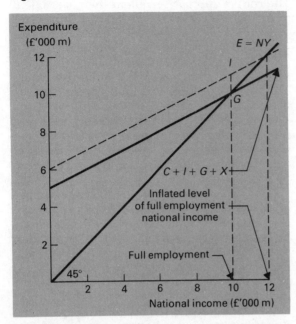

employment ceiling being reached.

Fig. 5.21 illustrates an economy that has reached a full employment equilibrium and has given rise to a national income of £10,000 million. Until this full employment position was reached, Keynes believed that any increase in total expenditure could be met by an increase in output, since use could be made of existing unemployed labour to meet any such increase in demand, without any significant impact upon the general level of prices. Thus increases in national income and output up to £10,000 million would be in real terms, in that such movements represented an actual increase in the output of goods and services, and a corresponding rise in real income for the economy as a whole. More output was being produced, and the incomes were being generated to allow this output to be purchased by households providing the factor services to those business organisations expanding their output.

**Increased spending at full employment**
It is now assumed that the total expenditure schedule in Fig. 5.21 shifts upwards because of an increase in one of its components or a combination of them. If, for example, private investment expenditure increased, this would

lead to a condition of excess demand in the economy and higher prices. According to the classical school of economists, however, this would not be the case, because it was believed that such an increase in injections would automatically be balanced by a comparable increase in withdrawals in the form of savings. The classical view claimed that an increase in the demand for investment funds would raise interest rates and thus lead to an increase in savings. This meant a fall in consumer expenditure by an amount which made room for the increase in investment expenditure. Full employment was therefore preserved without inflation, and the pattern of output had moved in favour of investment goods at the expense of consumer goods and services.

This kind of thinking was based upon savings being very sensitive to changes in the rate of interest, but this proved to be an unreliable assumption. There was no guarantee that consumer expenditure would fall to release resources to meet the increased demand for investment goods.

**The emergence of excess demand**
The Keynesian view of full employment was that any excess demand, produced by a further rise in total expenditure, would persist and be reflected in an excess demand for labour, because there was no automatic mechanism whereby an increase in one of the components of total expenditure would automatically be offset by a fall in any of the other types of expenditure. The developments outlined in Fig. 5.22 show how a condition of excess demand in the economy will affect the labour market and 'pull' up wages and salaries.

This **demand-pull** theory of the cause of inflation was very popular among economists for much of the 1960s. The post-war policy of maintaining full employment (unemployment was rarely allowed to rise above 2.5 per cent) was seen as being partly responsible for the higher rates of inflation that were experienced during those years. Until then inflation had averaged about 2 per cent, but the periodic emergence of excess demand and the subsequent shortage of labour were blamed for the gradual rise in inflation, which reached over 5 per cent by 1970. Such a level of inflation was of increasing concern to the government; before then even a rate of 3 per cent was considered to

**Fig. 5.22: Demand-pull inflation**

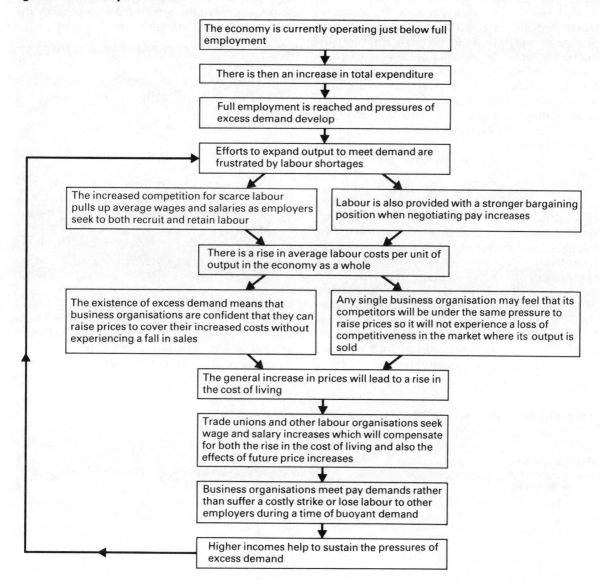

have very serious implications for the overall competitiveness of the UK economy.

### Excess demand before full employment

It is possible for an economy to suffer from demand-pull inflation before full employment is reached. The growth of total expenditure in the economy may be concentrated mainly on the output of a narrow range of goods and services. The manufacturers of consumer durables, for example, may experience a significant increase in the demand for their products; despite the existence of a relatively high level of unemployment in the economy as a whole, these manufacturers may soon experience labour shortages. This is because unemployment is not evenly distributed on a geographical basis throughout the country.

Some parts of the country may suffer from exceptionally high levels of unemployment due to the decline of traditional industries that had previously been the main source of employment. The growth industries, however, may be located mainly in other parts of the country where the growing level of economic activity has produced full employment in their labour catchment area. If the manufacturers of consumer durables are located in such areas, they may face labour shortages and seek to fill their vacancies by offering higher wages and salaries in an attempt to recruit the skills they require. Even if there is a certain amount of unemployment in the local area, there is also the problem that very few of the unemployed may possess the necessary skills and abilities to fill the vacancies. The manufacturers who supply the consumer durables industry with capital goods may also suffer from labour shortages as they seek to expand their output to meet the growing demand for the necessary plant, machinery and equipment.

Pressures of excess demand may therefore begin to develop at an early stage in the growth of the economy, as employers compete more strongly in those parts of the country where there is a growing shortage of the necessary skills. The uneven **geographical and occupational distribution of unemployment** explains why the wages and prices spiral can start to gather momentum well before the economy reaches full employment.

Activity 5.6
(a) Use the information contained in Fig. 5.23 to describe the kind of problem that might arise in the economy if there was a significant increase in the level of total demand.
(b) Collect information on the various schemes which have been introduced by the government in the last few years to deal with the problem of unfilled vacancies. Produce a report outlining the main features of such schemes and the extent to which you believe they need to be supported by additional measures.

### Accelerating inflation

The continued existence of excess demand in an economy can lead to the creation of an **inflationary spiral** as prices and wages continue to rise. Thus the increased level of national income of

**Fig. 5.23: Labour shortages, unfilled vacancies and unemployment**

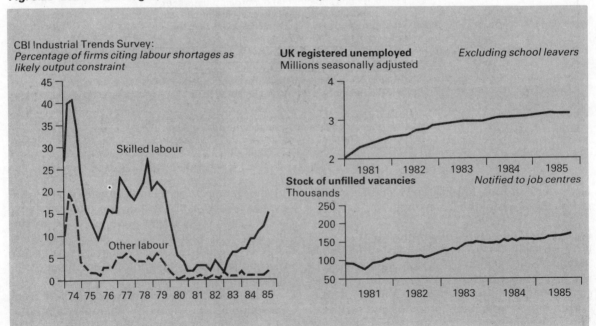

Source: *Economic Progress Report*, Aug. and Nov./ Dec. 1985, HMSO.

£2000 million in Fig. 5.21 is solely a movement in money terms, in that it is the same total output of goods and services as occurred at full employment but now expressed at higher prices. Similarly the money value of national income has increased, but, because this does not reflect an increase in actual output, average **real incomes** have remained unchanged. The chain of events in Fig. 5.22 was due to the creation of an **inflationary gap** in the economy; this can be defined as the extent to which total expenditure at full employment exceeds the full employment level of national income and output. This is equivalent to *IG* in Fig. 5.21.

An inflationary situation is potentially very unstable. The **rate of inflation** can gather momentum as both sides seek to protect themselves from both earlier and anticipated increases in prices and costs. If inflation is believed to be on a rising trend, both trade unions and employers will take this into account during the next round of pay claims and when introducing price increases. Such action will then help to fuel inflation and lead to the realisation of their expectations concerning future rates of inflation. This makes both sides even more determined to try to keep ahead of inflation, which will lead to a further acceleration in the inflationary spiral.

Under these circumstances the money value of national income and output will continue to rise at an increasing rate. Thus the level of national income of £12,000 million in Fig. 5.21 will not represent an equilibrium situation but rather the money value of national income and output at the end of a particular period of time during which prices rose by 20 per cent. If this economy then experiences inflation of 25 per cent the following year, the level of national income in money terms will be £15,000 million.

**A fall in demand and the return of unemployment**
Because of the unpredictable nature of an unregulated free market economy, the internal position could be rapidly reversed if total expenditure were suddenly to slacken. This **downturn** in the overall level of economic activity might, for example, be triggered off by business organisations reviewing their investment plans and then cutting back on their capital expenditure programmes. Because wages and prices are not very flexible in a

downward direction, this reduction in total expenditure will produce unemployment rather than a fall in the general level of prices from their inflated levels.

Wages and prices tend to operate with a ratchet effect in that they are very sticky in a downward direction. The end result of a sudden fall in total demand is unemployment, accompanied by prices and incomes at the inflated levels for the remaining output and employment. For example, suppose the continued existence of excess demand in the economy shown in Fig. 5.21 leads to a level of national income of £15,000 million. This will act as our starting-point in Fig. 5.24, which can be used to analyse the effects of a sudden downturn in total expenditure after a period of rapid inflation.

As far as this same economy is concerned, the monetary value of the full employment level of total output and national income is now £15,000 million. This shows that prices and incomes have risen by an average of 50 per cent as a result of the initial excess demand. A fall in total expenditure will not only remove inflation (inflation is the process of **rising prices**, not simply high prices) but also lead to a fall in total output and employment. This is because total expenditure in the economy is no longer high enough to absorb total output. In Fig. 5.24 this is reflected in a downward shift of the total expenditure schedule; the new level of total output and national income is now £13,500 million.

The sequence of developments (i) unemployment, (ii) the expansion of output until full employment is reached, (iii) the emergence of excess demand and inflation and (iv) the return of unemployment is also illustrated in Fig. 5.25. The parcel represents the actual output of the economy; the price-tag gives the monetary value of the output and national income; and each figure represents the employment of 100,000 workers. At stage 1 the economy is suffering from unemployment of 20 per cent and is operating well below its productive capacity. An increase in total expenditure then produces a growth in total output until the full employment level of national income of £10,000 million is reached at stage 2. Excess demand occurs during stage 3 and continues during stage 4, and the resulting inflation is reflected in the higher price-tags. The size of the parcel has remained unchanged at stages 3 and 4, how-

**Fig. 5.24**

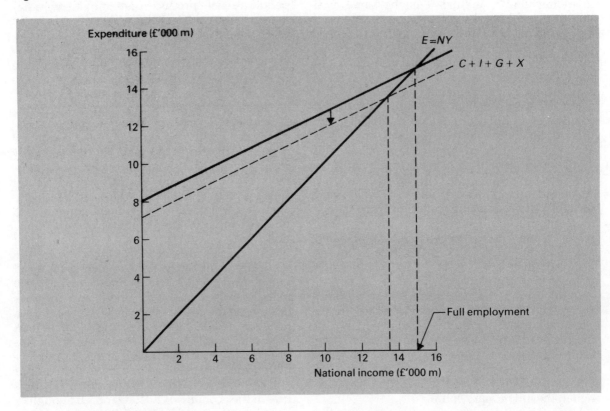

**Fig. 5.25: From unemployment to expansion to inflation and the return of unemployment**

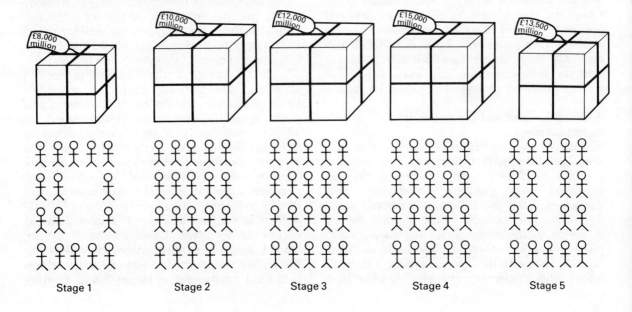

ever. The fall in total expenditure during stage 5 leads to a reduction in the size of the box, and this is reflected in the level of unemployment.

### Cost-push inflation

So far we have assumed that the presence of excess demand in an economy and growing labour shortages have been the cause of the developments which give rise to inflation. In the late 1960s and early 1970s, however, the UK began to experience both growing unemployment and rising inflation. Under these circumstances the cause of inflation could hardly be attributable to pressures of excess demand in the economy, and this led to increasing support for the view that inflation could also be triggered off by **cost-push** factors.

This view on the cause of inflation placed particular emphasis upon the role of trade unions and other labour organisations using their collective bargaining power to push up wages and salaries at rates in excess of improvements in productivity. This is in contrast to the earlier view on inflation, where excess demand in the economy led to wages and salaries being 'pulled' up by competition for scarce labour. Cost-push supporters saw excessive pay awards being granted by reluctant employers as the initial cause of inflation. They also believed that such developments did not depend upon the existence of excess demand pressures in the economy.

Cost-push inflation is the result of business organisations granting pay increases in excess of productivity improvements. If, for example, the negotiations between an employer and employees eventually produce a pay settlement of 10 per cent, while productivity is expected to rise by only 4 per cent, this will lead to a rise in unit labour costs of nearly 6 per cent. This can be confirmed by the use of a simple numerical example:

|  | Before pay award | After pay award |
|---|---|---|
| Total labour costs per year | £500,000 | £550,000 |
| Total output per year | 50,000 units | 52,000 units |
| Labour cost per unit | £10 | £10.57 |

To protect its profit margin this particular business organisation will then be obliged to raise its selling price.

If pay increases in excess of productivity improvements are a general feature of the economy, then the producer in our example is

also likely to experience a rise in its other costs, because suppliers of materials and components are also obliged to charge higher prices to recoup their increased costs. In this case our producer will then introduce further price increases to cover the general rise in the costs of production. The developments which contribute to a cost-push inflationary spiral in the economy as a whole are outlined in Fig. 5.26.

*Increases in the price of energy and raw materials*
Apart from a rise in the price of labour, cost-push inflation may also be caused by an increase in the costs of other important inputs. In the early 1970s many business organisations in the UK, along with those in other major manufacturing economies, experienced very large increases in the world price of oil, which raised their **energy costs**. At about the same time there was also a significant rise in the world price of many major **raw materials** because of a sudden upturn in the demand as manufacturing economies in general experienced a period of rapid growth. When such cost-push factors work their way through the economy in the form of higher prices, this will raise the cost of living and lead to higher pay claims, which then contribute to additional cost and price increases.

### The monetarist view of inflation

Since the late 1970s a great deal of attention has been paid to the **monetarist** view of the cause of inflation. Many of the economists who belong to this school of thought claim that there is only one possible cause of persistent inflation and that is an excessive growth in the **money supply**. They do not accept that excess demand or cost-push are the basic causes of inflation but believe rather that such developments are the direct and inevitable result of an uncontrolled and excessive growth in the money supply. The monetarists therefore emphasise the amount of money which is lent by **financial institutions** in general and banks in particular. If loans and overdrafts are more readily available to both households and business organisations, this can contribute to a substantial and sudden increase in the amount of money that can be used to finance additional expenditure.

Monetarists stress the need to ensure that the money supply does not grow faster than the rate of growth of total output. If, for example, output is expected to grow by 4 per cent the

**Fig. 5.26: Cost-push inflation**

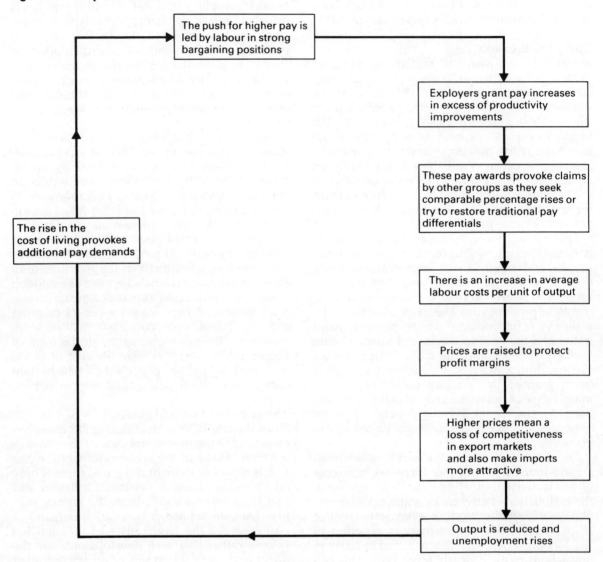

The push for higher pay is led by labour in strong bargaining positions

Explorers grant pay increases in excess of productivity improvements

These pay awards provoke claims by other groups as they seek comparable percentage rises or try to restore traditional pay differentials

The rise in the cost of living provokes additional pay demands

There is an increase in average labour costs per unit of output

Prices are raised to protect profit margins

Higher prices mean a loss of competitiveness in export markets and also make imports more attractive

Output is reduced and unemployment rises

resulting increase in the volume of transactions can be financed without inflationary pressures if the growth in the money supply is restricted to 4 per cent. In this case the extra borrowing is used solely to support increases in output. Total spending in the economy will be matched by a comparable increase in the supply of various goods and services.

If, however, the expansion of various kinds of credit facilities leads to an increase in the money supply of 10 per cent, while output grows only by 4 per cent, then according to the monetarists this will eventually produce inflation of 6 per cent. Some of the developments that arise from an excessive increase in the money supply and exert inflationary pressures upon the economy are outlined in Fig. 5.27.

The increase in the money supply caused by too much lending not only stimulates consumer spending but also allows business organisations to obtain the money to finance pay increases in excess of anticipated increases in productivity. Total expenditure in the economy will therefore increase more rapidly than the rate at which

**Fig. 5.27: Money supply and inflation**

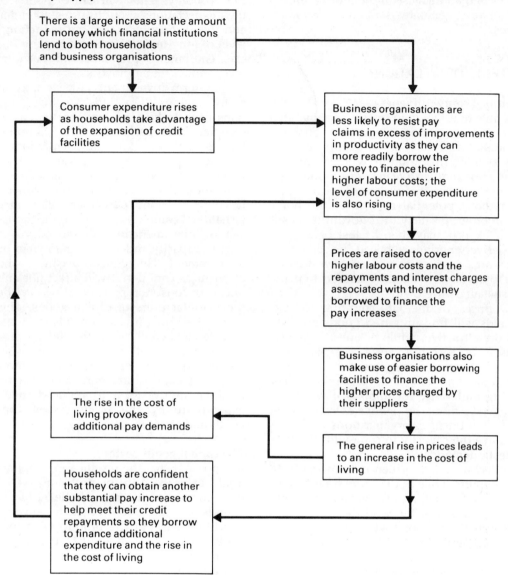

output can be increased. In their efforts to meet this demand, employers will not want any disruptions to their output by industrial action that stems from resisting further pay increases. Nor will they want to lose key workers by failing to pay the going rate for certain skills. As long as there is plenty of money available to borrow they will continue to meet pay demands, while the continued expansion of **consumer credit facilities** helps to sustain a rise in household expenditure.

The monetarists see both excess-demand and cost-push inflation as the result of an excessive growth in the money supply and not as separate causes of inflation. This view of inflation is also used to explain why inflation can increase even with a relatively high rate of unemployment, since it depends solely upon the money supply increasing faster than the rate at which output can be increased. If the economy is close to full employment, however, even a relatively small increase in output will be increasingly difficult to achieve and an increase in the money supply will therefore generate serious inflationary pressures.

## THE EFFECTS OF INFLATION

### International competitiveness
1. If the rate of inflation in the UK is above that in other manufacturing economies, business organisations which rely upon exporting a significant part of their output will become increasingly **less competitive** in overseas markets.

2. Some business organisations may be tempted to redirect potential exports to the home market in order to satisfy the buoyant domestic demand. Exports may then be lost because of **longer delivery periods**, while at the same time business organisations in general have **less incentive** to develop new export markets to maintain or sustain their growth.

3. As prices in the UK continue to rise, households will find imported goods and services more attractive, while business organisations may also turn to overseas suppliers who can offer materials, components, machinery and equipment at more competitive prices. The **increasing preference for imports** may also be encouraged by more competitive delivery dates, particularly if business organisations in the UK do not have the capacity to cope with the level of domestic demand.

The effect of inflation then is to increase the level of imports while at the same time making the UK less competitive in overseas markets. The UK's position in the world economy may then deteriorate to a point where it is no longer able to earn sufficient foreign currency to pay for its imports. This deterioration in the **balance of payments** is one of the major reasons why the government may seek to manage the economy when the rate of inflation threatens to reach an unacceptable level.

### Private investment
As the rate of inflation rises, business organisations may also scale down their investment programmes as they may become increasingly uncertain about the future. They will be particularly concerned about the prospect of the government eventually being obliged to introduce anti-inflation policies which have the effect of depressing the level of consumer expenditure in the economy. This will cause them to revise their expectations about future market demand, and this in turn will lead to a **reduction in the level of long-term investment** in plant, machinery, equipment, premises and even training programmes for employees.

Long-term investment projects may involve many millions of pounds. Business organisations need to be confident that when they are completed the market demand will remain at a high enough level for a sufficiently long period of time to provide an acceptable return on the money they have invested. As inflation gathers momentum, the competitive position of business organisations, particularly those facing international competition, will be threatened by a lack of investment in new and improved productive capacity and a slowing down in product development. This general decline in the level of business confidence will affect not only producers of consumer goods and services but also the manufacturers of capital goods. They will revise their own investment plans in response both to the actual fall in the demand for their output and in anticipation of fewer orders, as the effects of government policy upon total consumer expenditure gradually filter through to them in the form of reduced investment expenditure by the producers of consumer goods and services.

### The capital goods sector
It is possible that the producers of capital goods might experience major problems even before the general downturn in the level of business confidence. The initial boom in consumer expenditure will put the producers of consumer goods and services in a much stronger position when competing for those skills which are in increasingly short supply. They can offer more competitive wages and salaries as a means of overcoming any shortage of labour, and this may be at the expense of producers of capital goods whose current financial position may not be so strong and who are therefore in a weaker position when **competing for scarce** skills in various parts of the labour market.

The producers of consumer goods and services are also likely to be in a stronger position when seeking to raise **short-term finance**. Their buoyant markets and higher profits will make them an attractive proposition from the point of view of financial institutions looking for secure, profitable, short-term outlets for their funds. The producers of capital goods may find it increasingly difficult to raise finance unless they are able to offer higher rates of interest and meet more demanding repayment conditions.

Financial institutions will also find a ready outlet for their funds in the form of **consumer credit**. The general rise in employment along with large pay awards makes households more confident that they can use various kinds of credit facilities to bring forward their purchases of consumer durables, for example, and still be able to meet the necessary interest charges and repayment conditions.

A period of rising inflation also tends to mean exceptionally large **increases in property prices**. The producers of capital goods will have to compete for finance with property companies and home-buyers, especially if banks move into the market for mortgages.

The capital goods industry is therefore likely to be one of the first casualties of rapid inflation. The government will be concerned that an increasing proportion of the nation's resources of labour and capital is being devoted to consumption at the expense of the private investment which is so vital to protect the future competitiveness of the economy as a whole.

### Government expenditure
Growing inflation will also oblige the government to raise extra money to pay for the **increased costs of providing social and welfare services**, for example. It has either to accept the political consequences of large **tax increases** or to be willing to borrow more money in order to maintain its expenditure in real terms. If it increases taxes, particularly indirect taxes, this will further add to the rise in the cost of living and help to provoke even larger pay claims. If the government seeks to borrow more, it will add to the competition for funds and bid up interest rates in trying to attract the necessary extra finance. This upward pressure upon **interest rates** will then raise the borrowing costs of the private sector. This so-called 'crowding-out' effect of increased government borrowing may then depress the level of private sector investment.

### The distribution of income
Some groups of workers will not be in a strong bargaining position. Their lack of industrial muscle means they will not be able to secure pay increases which protect them from the rise in the cost of living. This will produce a shift of real purchasing power in favour of the more powerful groups of workers who are able to secure pay increases which more than compensate for the rise in the cost of living. In the longer term, therefore, the erosion of real incomes in certain types of employment may lead to a **lack of new recruits** in sectors which have a crucial role to play in the future growth of the economy and in the general level of welfare. This may be the case if the pay of skilled engineers or nurses, say, falls progressively behind the rate of inflation.

### The value of savings
The government will also be concerned about the effect of inflation upon the **value of savings** and the **real purchasing power** of the income which households derive in the form of interest. Although a period of growing inflation is also one of rising interest rates, some households may hold their savings in a form where the higher interest payments do not keep up with the rate of inflation. Under these circumstances such households will experience a fall in the real value of their savings.

# 6. Fiscal Policy

## FISCAL THEORY

Fiscal policy is the use of the government's powers in the fields of **taxation** and **expenditure** to influence the **total level of demand** in the economy. Our initial approach to the possible use of such powers will assume that the government is adopting what is mainly a Keynesian view, in that the total level of demand in the economy is the major cause of either unemployment or inflation. This Keynesian approach to such problems will then be re-examined in the light of other views on the possible causes of unemployment and inflation.

### Economic forecasting

The government's annual and interim budgets are constructed after a detailed consideration has been given to the existing and predicted state of the economy as a whole. A great variety of economic data is collected and analysed to discover what is currently happening to key factors in the economy. This information is then used to produce **forecasts** about the direction in which these factors are moving the economy and the likely pace of these movements. If, for example, the forecasts provide evidence that the future level of total demand in the economy is likely to be excessive and produce an unacceptable rate of inflation, the government will budget to achieve a surplus. A **budget surplus** means that more money is withdrawn from the economy via taxation than is injected through government expenditure. The net effect of such a policy is to reduce the total level of demand in the economy to a level where it is more in line with its productive capacity and thus to avoid the inflationary pressures exerted by a condition of excess demand.

Similarly the budget can be used to deal with a situation which forecasts suggest is likely to produce a level of demand in the economy that will leave an unacceptable level of unemployment. In this event the government will aim for a **budget deficit** so that the net effect is to increase total demand in the economy. Such a policy will stimulate total output and promote employment. The difference between the government's income from taxation and its spending will be financed by borrowing through the sale of **government securities**.

## TAXATION

### Direct taxes

The manipulation of **direct taxes** is a means of altering the net incomes and hence the spending power of both households and business organisations.

#### Income tax

**Income tax** is paid by individuals according to the bands within which their **taxable income** falls. A certain amount of income is free of tax, depending upon the individual's domestic and personal circumstances. The tax rates and allowances for the financial year 1987–8 are given in Fig. 6.1.

Table 6.1 shows that income tax accounted for about 64 per cent of the money collected by the Inland Revenue in the financial year 1985–6. Changes to the rates of this tax, in particular to the basic rate, are therefore likely to have a

Table 6.1: Net receipts by Inland Revenue, 1985–6

| Item | £ million |
|---|---|
| Income tax | 35,418 |
| Corporation tax | 10,699 |
| Capital gains tax | 916 |
| Capital transfer tax | 888 |
| Stamp duties | 1230 |
| Petroleum revenue tax | 6380 |
| Other | 69 |
| Total | 55,600 |

Source: *Financial Statistics*, July 1986, HMSO.

Sorry for handing in
late but on monday was
due to be a witness
in court.

Anthony Neale.


Handed in by J. Miles. 3/3/92

_____

Hello from 2024, 08/11/24
T. Phelps, G. Reynolds, E. Perrior

**Fig. 6.1: Tax rates and allowances, 1986–7 and 1987–8**

### Rates of tax

The basic rate of income tax was reduced from 29% to 27% from 6 April 1987.

The higher rates of tax (40% to 60%) remained unchanged. The starting point for the 40% rate was increased from £17,201 to £17,901 taxable income. The starting point for the 45% rate was also increased – from £20,201 to £20,401. The other higher rates remained unchanged. The following table shows the 1986–7 and 1987–8 taxable income bands:

|  |  | *1986–7* | *1987–8* |
|---|---|---|---|
| *Basic rate* | 27% | £1–17,200 | £1–17,900 |
| *Higher rates* | 40% | £17,201–20,200 | £17,901–20,400 |
|  | 45% | £20,201–25,400 | £20,401–25,400 |
|  | 50% | £25,401–33,300 | £25,401–33,300 |
|  | 55% | £33,301–41,200 | £33,301–41,200 |
|  | 60% | over £41,201 | over £41,200 |

### Personal allowances

| *Allowance* | *1986–7* | *1987–8* |
|---|---|---|
| Single person | £2,335 | £2,425 |
| Married man | £3,655 | £3,795 |
| Wife's earned income | £2,335 | £2,425 |
| Age* – single person | £2,850 | £2,960/£3,070** |
|      – married man | £4,505 | £4,675/£4,845** |
| Additional personal | £1,320 | £1,370 |
| Widow's bereavement | £1,320 | £1,370 |

\* Income limit £9,800 in 1987–8, previously £9,400.
\*\* In 1987–8 the age allowance was divided into those aged 65–79 and those aged 80 or over.

significant impact upon the total level of consumer expenditure. If, for example, the government wishes to stimulate demand, a cut in the basic rate (at which the bulk of those paying tax contribute) will have a much larger effect than if a reduction was made in the higher rates of income tax. Also, those paying tax only at the basic rate will tend to spend a much larger proportion of the increase in their disposable incomes compared with those on higher incomes. This is because the latter will display a higher **marginal propensity to save** than those on lower incomes. If, however, the government wishes to cut consumer expenditure it will need to increase the basic rate of income tax, because those people who are subject only to this rate will have a higher **marginal propensity to consume**. Thus a fall in their disposable income will produce a significant reduction in consumer expenditure.

The government can also influence the level of disposable incomes by altering **allowances**. It is generally accepted that these allowances will be raised in line with the Retail Price Index in order to protect their real values. However, if the allowances are raised by more than the rate of inflation, this will increase the real purchasing power of that part of income which is tax free. Similarly the government may decide to increase certain allowances by less than the rate of inflation. This will have the effect of reducing the real value of tax-free incomes and is a method of reducing demand in the economy.

*Corporation tax*
**Corporation tax** is levied on a company's profits. A cut in the rate of corporation tax will raise net profits and may therefore enable the company to pass on some of the benefits to its shareholders in the form of higher dividend

payments. This may then make it easier for the company to secure additional external finance through the issue of new shares, because the improved return will help to make the company more attractive to potential investors.

The most important effect of a cut in corporation tax is the resulting increase in the funds available to the company for investment from its internal sources. The extent to which business organisations will increase their investment expenditure, however, depends on the ability of the government to raise the general level of business confidence and to create an economic climate which is conducive to investment expenditure. Such investment will not be undertaken if those responsible for investment decisions are not confident about the strength and duration of their future market demand.

**Stimulating the level of private investment expenditure** is perhaps the most difficult task that faces any government, yet it is the ideal way of leading an economy out of recession and promoting employment. A rise in private investment expenditure along with selective increases in government expenditure on certain aspects of the economic and social infrastructure will raise employment in those business organisations involved in the manufacture of investment goods and in construction projects. Not only will investment, particularly in the manufacturing sector, help to raise the productive capacity of the economy; also the resulting improvements in productivity will strengthen

**Table 6.2: Net receipts by HM Customs and Excise, 1985–6**

| Item | £ million |
|---|---|
| Value added tax | 19,328 |
| Car tax (new vehicles) | 836 |
| Hydrocarbon oils | 6395 |
| Tobacco | 4459 |
| Spirits | 1504 |
| Beer | 1957 |
| Wines and other alcohol | 737 |
| Betting and gaming | 745 |
| Customs duties | 1239 |
| Other | 158 |
| Total | 37,358 |

Source: *Financial Statistics*, July 1986, HMSO

the position of business organisations in both export and home markets where they face intense competition from overseas producers. A combination of higher exports and lower imports will then lead to a further rise in total demand and more employment in the economy.

The amount of corporation tax paid by a company and hence its net profits can also be influenced by changes in tax **allowances** such as those associated with the acquisition of new capital assets and their subsequent depreciation. In 1986–7 the main rate of corporation tax was 35 per cent, and 29 per cent for small companies.

**Indirect taxes**
Total demand in the economy can also be influenced by changes in **indirect taxes**. Table 6.2 gives an indication of the revenue derived from the different indirect taxes in the financial year 1985–6.

*Value added tax*
**VAT** is broadly based and is less concentrated than other indirect taxes. Certain categories of products such as food, basic household items, children's clothing and footwear, and books and newspapers are exempt from VAT.

Changes in the level of VAT can alter the amount of money which a consumer has left after making a purchase. If VAT were lowered, this would release more money to finance extra consumer expenditure. An increase in VAT, or its extension to include certain goods and services which are currently 'zero rated', will withdraw purchasing power from the economy and deflate the total level of demand. The government also has the option of introducing different rates of VAT, such as a higher rate for certain types of consumer durables or personal services which it regards as luxuries.

*Excise duties*
**Excise duties** are taxes on home-produced goods, as distinct from customs duties, which are levied on imports. As Table 6.2 indicates, the main sources of excise duties are alcohol, tobacco and petrol. The demand for these products is very inelastic with respect to increases in their prices, so higher duties can have a very significant impact upon the amount of spending power withdrawn from the economy.

*Customs duties*
**Customs duties** do make a contribution to government revenue but are primarily intended to discourage the purchase of imported goods. An increase in such duties can encourage the demand for domestic output; imports will become relatively less competitive, and this will reduce the withdrawal from the economy in the form of expenditure on imports. This will help to close a deflationary gap and promote employment in business organisations whose products replace imports in the home market.

**Taxation and consumer demand**
These then are the main areas where taxes can be adjusted to regulate total spending in the economy. When seeking to reflate the level of consumer demand in the economy, however, it is highly unlikely that the government would resort to a cut in the excise duties on tobacco and alcohol, say. Any such changes in indirect taxes are likely to be concentrated upon lowering VAT. If a government uses lower direct taxes to encourage consumer spending, a cut in the standard rate of income tax may be combined with increases in allowances in excess of the rate of inflation. This is because a cut in the standard rate of income tax alone will have only a marginal effect upon the disposable income of those who are on low incomes.

Assume, for example, that an individual claims a married persons' allowance of £3655 and after national insurance and pension contributions has a taxable income of £1500 a year. A reduction in the standard rate of tax from 29 per cent to 27 per cent will raise the person's disposable income by approximately 60p a week. But if this tax cut is combined with an increase in the married persons' allowance to £4000, then the disposable income will rise by approximately £2.37 a week. If the increase in the allowance more than compensated for inflation, this policy on direct taxation would be of greater benefit to the lower-paid compared with a policy which concentrated the scope for tax cuts mainly upon larger reductions in the standard rate of income tax.

## GOVERNMENT EXPENDITURE

In the financial year 1985–6 the ratio of *total public expenditure* to gross domestic product was estimated at roughly 44 per cent. Table 6.3 shows the scale and variety of this expenditure and the ability of the government to exert a major influence upon total demand in the economy by altering the level of its expenditure in various areas.

If it is the aim of the government to reflate the level of demand to reduce unemployment, this can be achieved by **increased spending** on health, education, housing and roads, for example, and by encouraging the nationalised industries to bring forward their **investment programmes** such as the building of new power-stations or the modernisation of the railways. The government can also seek to encourage investment expenditure in the private sector by both increasing and widening the scope of its **investment grants**. The government may also take the opportunity to concentrate part of any such increase in its expenditure upon those parts of the country where unemployment is much higher than the national average; this is done by increasing the **financial incentives** for business organisations to locate or expand in the Assisted Areas or where they make a contribution to the regeneration of the inner cities.

The government can also stimulate total demand in the economy by taking advantage of the opportunity to increase **unemployment benefits** and **pensions**, for example. This is a means of raising the spending power of those who do not benefit from cuts in direct taxes.

**Government expenditure in real terms**
In describing the effects of changes in government expenditure it is important that such changes are viewed in **real terms**. If, for example, the rate of inflation is expected to be 4 per cent, then government expenditure will have to increase by the same amount just to maintain the **real value** of its existing expenditure.

The government is faced with exactly the same situation as households when they experience a rise in the cost of living. If inflation is running at 4 per cent and some households are able to increase their expenditure by only 3 per cent, they will not be able to purchase as many goods and services as before. Similarly if the government increases its expenditure by only 3 per cent, this will not cover the increase in costs associated with just maintaining its existing provision of services, for example. If this is the

Table 6.3: Public spending (£ billion)[1]

| Department | 1983–84 out-turn | 1984–5 out-turn | 1985–6 out-turn[2] | 1986–7 plans[3] | 1987–8 plans | 1988–9 plans |
|---|---|---|---|---|---|---|
| Defence | 15.5 | 17.2 | 18.2 | 18.5 | 18.8 | 19.0 |
| Foreign and Commonwealth Office | 1.7 | 1.8 | 1.9 | 2.0 | 2.0 | 2.1 |
| European Community | 0.9 | 0.9 | 0.8 | 0.7 | 1.1 | 1.0 |
| Ministry of Agriculture, Fisheries and Food | 2.1 | 2.1 | 2.5 | 2.2 | 2.2 | 2.3 |
| Trade and Indutstry | 1.9 | 2.1 | 2.0 | 1.6 | 1.3 | 1.0 |
| Energy | 1.1 | 2.6 | 1.0 | 0.1 | –0.5 | –0.3 |
| Employment | 2.9 | 3.1 | 3.3 | 3.7 | 3.8 | 4.0 |
| Transport | 4.3 | 4.6 | 4.6 | 4.8 | 4.8 | 4.8 |
| Department of Environment: housing | 3.1 | 3.2 | 2.7 | 2.8 | 2.8 | 2.9 |
| Department of Environment: other environmental services | 3.8 | 4.0 | 3.9 | 3.6 | 3.5 | 3.6 |
| Home Office | 4.5 | 5.0 | 5.3 | 5.5 | 5.6 | 5.7 |
| Education and Science | 13.4 | 14.0 | 14.5 | 14.3 | 14.4 | 14.5 |
| Arts and Libraries | 0.6 | 0.7 | 0.7 | 0.7 | 0.7 | 0.8 |
| Department of Health and Social Security: health and personal social services | 14.7 | 15.8 | 16.7 | 17.7 | 18.4 | 19.1 |
| Department of Health and Social Security: social security | 35.2 | 38.1 | 41.2 | 42.9 | 44.4 | 45.9 |
| Scotland | 6.7 | 7.0 | 7.4 | 7.6 | 7.4 | 7.4 |
| Wales | 2.6 | 2.6 | 2.8 | 2.9 | 2.9 | 3.0 |
| Northern Ireland | 3.7 | 4.0 | 4.3 | 4.5 | 4.7 | 4.8 |
| Chancellor's department's | 1.6 | 1.7 | 1.8 | 2.0 | 2.0 | 2.1 |
| Other departments | 1.0 | 1.2 | 1.3 | 1.5 | 1.7 | 1.8 |
| Reserve | — | — | — | 4.5 | 6.3 | 8.0 |
| Central privatisation proceeds | –1.1 | –2.1 | –2.6 | –4.7 | –4.7 | –4.7 |
| Adjustments | — | — | –0.2 | –0.4 | — | — |
| Planning total | 120.3 | 129.6 | 134.2 | 139.1 | 143.9 | 148.7 |
| % change on previous year | +6.1 | +7.8 | +3.5 | +3.6 | +3.5 | +3.3 |
| General government gross debt interest | 14.5 | 16.1 | 18.0 | 18.5 | 18.5 | 19.0 |

[1] Cash terms; figures are rounded.
[2] The 1985–6 estimated out-turn figures includes an allowance for shortfall.
[3] The 1986–7 plan figure includes external finance of –£400 million for nationalised industries to be privatised that year.

Source: *Economic Progress Report*, Jan./Feb. 1986, HMSO.

case then an increase in government expenditure of 3 per cent will actually have a **deflationary** effect, because it amounts to a cut in real terms. So a government which is seeking to reduce unemployment will have to raise its expenditure by more than the rate of inflation in order to achieve an increase in real terms and ensure that more jobs are created in various parts of the economy.

Activity 6.1
Suppose that the Chancellor wishes to cut the size of the **public sector borrowing requirement**.

(a) Which goods and services would you be in favour of being taxed more highly or of being subject to taxation for the first time?

(b) How should the Chancellor use direct taxes to reduce the level of disposable incomes?
(c) Where would you be prepared to see cuts in government expenditure?

Organise a discussion session during which each person has the opportunity of defending their recommendations.

## THE MULTIPLIER EFFECT

Whether the net effect of budgetary changes is designed to reflate or deflate total expenditure, the Chancellor will have to take account of the **multiplier effect** of any such initial changes upon the level of national income. For example, if the government leaves taxes unchanged and at the same time raises its capital expenditure on roads and housing by £800 million a year, the eventual increase in national income will be a **multiple** of this increase in the level of injections. This results from the following chain of events.

The increased expenditure on roads and housing will become the income of all those business organisations and their employees involved in the new construction projects. The initial rise in national income is thus £800 million, but this will then give rise to further expenditure and create income elsewhere in the economy. Each time money is spent it creates incomes. So business organisations that were in no way involved either directly or indirectly in the new road-building programmes will eventually experience an increase in the demand for their goods and services.

### The size of the multiplier

When building up our model of how the economy works we recognised that only a part of the money received by households will remain within the circular flow of income and be returned to business organisations via consumer expenditure. The amount of money withdrawn at each stage of income depended upon the MPW. Suppose, for example, the MPW = 0.4. In this case only £480 million will be passed on by those who originally derived incomes from the initial expenditure of £800 million. This

£480 million will then create income for those households who provide factor services to the business organisations experiencing a higher demand for their goods and services. The process of income creation will continue as shown in Table 6.4.

**Table 6.4: The multiplier effect**

| Increase in total expenditure | Increase in national income | Increase in total withdrawals |
|---|---|---|
| £800 m. | £800 m. | £320 m. |
| £480 m. | £480 m. | £192 m. |
| £288 m. | £288 m. | £115.2 m. |
| £172.8 m. | £172.8 m. | £69.1 m. |
| £103.7 m. | £103.7 m. | £41.5 m. |

Table 6.4 shows that the initial rise in government expenditure of £800 million a year has already produced an increasing national income of £1844.5 million. Assuming that the economy was in a state of equilibrium before the government increased its annual expenditure, the rise in national income and employment will come to an end when a new equilibrium position has been reached. From an initial situation where $J = W$ the increase in government expenditure now means that $J$ exceeds $W$ by £800 million. The subsequent rise in national income will continue until once again $J = W$. To generate additional withdrawals of £800 million to match the increase in injections and establish a new equilibrium, national income will rise by £2000 million. So an increase in government spending of £800 million in this case produces a rise in national income of £2000 million and the value of the multiplier is 2.5.

If the MPW had been 0.5, the extra withdrawals necessary to establish a new equilibrium would have required that national income increase by only £1600 million, and in this case the value of the multiplier would have been 2.0. The **value of the multiplier** ($M$) is determined as follows:

$$M = \frac{1}{MPW}$$

The multiplier effect exerted by the increase in government expenditure is also shown in Fig. 6.2, where the $J$ shifts upwards by £800 million. This means that the level of national income of

**Fig. 6.2**

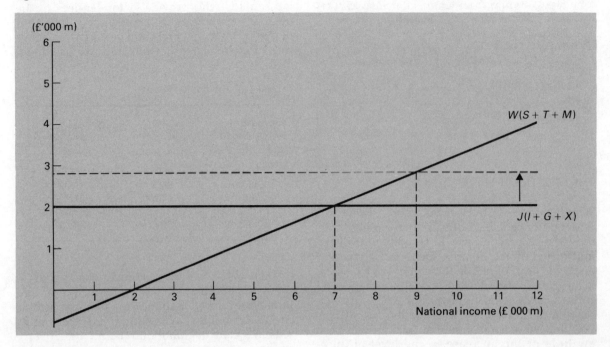

£7000 million no longer represents an equilibrium position, because *J* now exceeds *W*, and the economy will expand. The new equilibrium level of national income is £9000 million, where *J* is again equal to *W*.

Any developments in the economy which lowers the MPS, the MRT or the MPM will increase the value of the multiplier. Similarly a rise in any of the components of the MPW will reduce the size of the multiplier. If, for example, the total withdrawals schedule in Fig. 6.2 rose less steeply (meaning a lower MPW), then the rise in government expenditure would have produced a larger multiplier effect. But if the total withdrawals schedule had been steeper (meaning a higher MPW), then the multiplier effect would have been smaller.

**Importance of the multiplier**

This multiplier effect is of particular importance to the Chancellor if the economy has a relatively low level of unemployment. An excessive increase in government spending may then contribute to a level of inflation which seriously weakens the position of business organisations when competing with overseas producers.

So far the importance of the multiplier for fiscal policy has been described only within the context of the government seeking to increase the total level of demand in the economy. Of equal importance is that the multiplier will exaggerate the impact upon national income and employment of a reduction in injections. If the government had cut its annual expenditure by £800 million, then *W* would exceed *J* by £800 million, and national income would start to fall. If the MPW = 0.4 then national income would have to fall by £2000 million in order to reduce *W* by £800 million, so that once again *J* = *W* and an equilibrium position is reached. This multiplier effect in a downward direction will be of particular importance to a government taking action to remove any excess demand which is developing in the economy.

**Other causes of a multiplier effect**

A multiplier effect can also be set in motion by a change in any other component(s) of total expenditure. A lower rate of income tax, for example, will increase disposable incomes and raise the level of consumer expenditure. Assuming that this cut in taxation is not offset by a reduction in government expenditure, the increase in consumer expenditure will work its way through the economy, creating additional incomes and more consumer expenditure. The original cut in taxation means that *J* now exceeds *W*, and the level of national income will continue to rise until *W* has reached a level where once again *J* = *W*.

Similarly an upturn in the general level of business confidence, perhaps supported by increased financial assistance from the government, may produce a rise in the level of private investment. Not only will this lead to a multiplier effect, but the subsequent increase in the output of some goods and services will reflect the improvements in productivity associated with such investment expenditure.

Government policies that are successful in reducing the rate of inflation to a level which is below that ruling in other manufacturing economies may help to stimulate the demand for exports and reduce the level of imports. Apart from the general improvement in the UK's trading position, both the rise in exports and the fall in imports will increase the level of total expenditure in the economy. The multiplier effect means that a range of business organisations will experience a rise in the demand for their output – not just those which are increasing their exports or raising their output to meet the growing preference for home-produced goods and services.

A fall in consumer expenditure, private investment or exports and a rise in imports will exert a multiplier effect in a downward direction.

Activity 6.2
Assume that private investment expenditure is expected to rise by £3500 million and that the MPS = 0.10, the MRT = 0.25 and the MPM = 0.18. Calculate the anticipated increase in the level of national income.

Activity 6.3
The following information concerns the various types of expenditure in a particular economy.

When the level of national income is zero, the level on consumer expenditure is £1500 million; and when national income is £10,000 million, consumer expenditure is £7500 million. The economy displays a constant MPW.

The level of government expenditure is £900 million; private investment is £400 million; exports are £700 million. These three types of expenditure remain constant regardless of the level of national income.

(a) Calculate the value of the multiplier.
(b) With the aid of graph paper, determine the equilibrium level of national income, using the expenditure/income method and a 45° line.
(c) If the full employment level of national income is £6500 million, by how much should the government increase its own expenditure in order to produce full employment without generating demand-pull inflation?

## UNEMPLOYMENT, INFLATION AND FISCAL POLICY IN PRACTICE

### Limitations of economic forecasting

In recent years economic research and improvements in the collection of a wider range of data have been combined with advances in computers to produce sophisticated models of the economy. Economics is not an exact science, however, and such models are continually being reviewed and improved upon. Establishing relationships between various developments in both the UK and the world economy and using them as a basis for economic forecasting is a very complex business. Such models must seek to establish what motivates the actions of people as consumers, savers, workers, employers and investors. Unfortunately human behaviour is often unpredictable. A particular group of people cannot always be relied upon to react in the same way even when faced with circumstances they have experienced before.

Recognising that economic forecasting has its limitations, the following sections describe some of the other problems that governments have encountered in their use of fiscal measures as a means of managing the economy. The initial sections examine the weaknesses of such measures from the point of view of a government which regards unemployment or inflation as being caused primarily by demand deficiency or excess demand. The later sections describe the implications for the traditional use of fiscal policies of other possible causes of inflation and unemployment.

## Time-lags

The use of fiscal measures is complicated by the existence of **time-lags**, not only between the **collection of data**, their **interpretation** and the production of **economic forecasts** but also between **constructing the Budget** itself, the **implementation** of budgetary changes and the eventual **impact** of these changes upon the economy.

As far as changes in direct and indirect taxation are concerned, changes can be implemented without much delay and will therefore have an effect upon total demand after a relatively short period of time. It is with changes in government expenditure that the existence of time-lags can give rise to problems at a later date. For example, if the government wishes to reflate the economy by increasing its capital expenditure, it will obviously take time to get such projects as the building of hospitals and roads off the ground. The money allocated to such programmes will be spent over a long period of time as various phases are completed. The initial phases may account for only a small part of the total costs, and major payments to contractors may occur only when the projects are well under way.

A government seeking to deflate total demand by cutting its capital expenditure is also likely to encounter difficulties. Many earlier projects may still be in the course of completion, while others which are about to be started may play a major role in improving the economic and social infrastructure. Whatever cuts the government decides upon, it will take some time before the effects of such measures are reflected in the level of total demand in the economy.

Because of these time-lags there is a possibility that between the diagnosis of the problem and the impact of fiscal measures the economy may not only be moving at a different pace but may even be changing direction and giving rise to new problems. For example, the Budget may have been designed to deflate demand because inflation was seriously threatening the competitiveness of the economy. However, because of the unpredictable nature of a complex economy,

well before such measures have an effect the level of private investment expenditure, say, may have started to fall. The level of total demand and hence employment may also be affected by a sudden downturn in the level of world trade, because of slowing down in the growth rates in other manufacturing economies. Thus by the time the fiscal measures introduced in the earlier period start to have an effect they may no longer be appropriate. Unemployment rather than inflation presents the most serious problem. The lagged effect of cuts in government expenditure may then worsen the recession already developing in the economy.

## Uncertainty

The frequent use of fiscal measures tends to increase the **uncertainty** surrounding the timing and degree of government intervention with the level of total demand.

Because of the dynamic nature of the economy and the problems of economic forecasting, it may be better to wait in order to identify the underlying movements in the economy and the action which is needed rather than deal with a situation that may be clouded by time-lags. Sudden fiscal changes may result only in a more confused situation at a later date. Frequent and perhaps unpredictable changes will depress the level of **business confidence**. Those business organisations directly affected by possible cuts in government expenditure will be increasingly reluctant to expand or even maintain their own investment programmes.

Some business organisations rely heavily upon contracts placed with them by the government for much of their work; others may derive a significant part of their business from the orders placed with them by the main contractors. The construction industry in particular and those that supply it with materials, equipment and plant are very susceptible to cuts in government expenditure. Similarly business organisations which supply equipment and materials to the health and education services may experience the problem associated with an **unstable demand** for their output.

This uncertainty may also affect those industries which rely upon orders arising out of the investment programmes of the nationalised industries. This will be the case, for example, if the government reduces its financial support for those projects which the nationalised industries would find difficulty in financing from their own resources. Even if the government increased its expenditure in such areas, the business organisations most affected may hesitate to expand their own investment programmes. Experience has perhaps told them that such an upturn in the demand for output is not likely to be sustained, and that they will feel the brunt of any future cuts if inflationary pressures develop in the economy.

## The need for fine tuning

The uncertainty that affects the level of business confidence is mainly due to the defects of fiscal policies where developments in the economy call only for **fine tuning**. If the main objective is to tackle a high level of unemployment, the necessary adjustment for a directional change of this magnitude can be achieved by large increases in government expenditure with perhaps some cuts in direct taxation. For much of the post-war period governments did in fact use fiscal measures to maintain a high and stable level of employment, but this often meant that the economy was precariously close to spilling over into inflation if total demand expanded any further. Under these circumstances a degree of fine tuning was needed to achieve the desired adjustment in total demand so that greater price stability could be achieved without sacrificing the commitment to maintain full employment. At the same time governments generally accepted that they should also seek to maintain a healthy balance of payments, a strong currency and a rate of economic growth that would ensure a rise in real incomes and hence an improvement in the standard of living. Unfortunately, attempts to secure these objectives simultaneously exposed some of the limitations of fiscal measures, as they proved to suffer from some of the problems described in the previous sections.

Seeking to make small **directional changes** with little room for error led to fiscal measures being labelled as 'blunt weapons' where fine tuning was required or likened to 'heavy artillery' in that they were slow to manoeuvre and cumbersome in effect. The result is that some of the government's objectives may be achieved, but others may have to be sacrificed along the way.

*Conflicting objectives*

Some examples will illustrate the problems arising out of **conflicting economic objectives**. Remember that during the years when such problems became evident, an unemployment figure approaching 3 per cent was considered to be politically unacceptable; governments sought to keep unemployment well below this figure.

1. Assume that the government is concerned about rising unemployment and deals with the situation by introducing a budget deficit to reflate total demand. Its aim is to reduce unemployment from, say, 3 per cent to about 2.2 per cent. The inappropriate nature of fiscal policies as a means of achieving a relatively small increase in demand and hence employment pushes the economy towards full employment, and pressures of excess demand start to develop. There is no significant increase in private investment, because business organisations in general fear that any inflation during this 'go' phase will cause the government to reverse its fiscal policies and deflate the level of demand.

The lack of upturn in the level of private investment means that there is no significant increase in the productive capacity of the economy, and full employment output is soon reached. Excess demand leads to shortages and bottlenecks, and the resulting demand-pull inflation will cause a deterioration in the balance of payments (see page 90).

It is also doubtful if much improvement in the average level of real incomes has occurred during this 'go' phase, because of the effect of increasing uncertainty upon those responsible for investment decisions. This will also have implications for the competitiveness of the economy in the long run.

2. Now assume that the government is eventually obliged to tackle the inflation and improve the balance of payments by deflating the level of demand. This is achieved by introducing a budget surplus. This will cause a fall in output and a rise in unemployment. During this 'stop' phase the balance of payments will eventually start to improve, as shown in Fig. 6.3.

The depressed home market, however, will not have produced an economic climate in which business organisations will invest in additional or improved productive capacity. So the rate of economic growth will suffer. Thus both current and future living standards will be affected by the deflationary policy. This 'stop'

**Fig. 6.3: How deflation will improve the balance of payments**

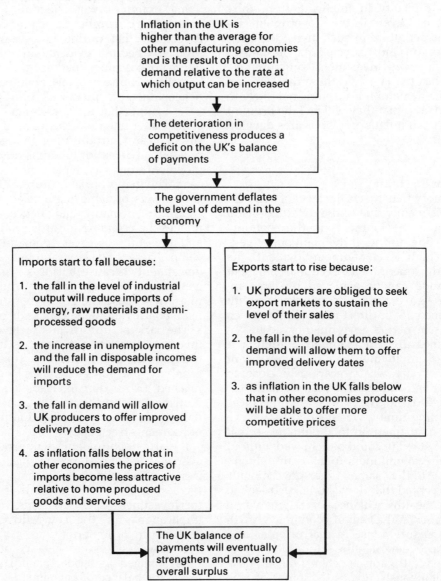

phase will also confirm the earlier expectations of business organisations, and during any future 'go' phase they will be even more convinced that any expansion of demand is likely to be short-lived.

Once again the major economic objectives have proved incompatible. Greater price stability and a stronger balance of payments have been achieved, but at the expense of higher unemployment and a lower rate of economic growth. These examples demonstrate the kind of problem that has been encountered by governments seeking to fine-tune the economy and to achieve objectives far removed from the first and single objective of preventing mass unemployment. This **'stop–go'** nature of the economy for much of the post-war period was to a large extent responsible for the lack of long-term investment in the UK. This in turn was a major reason why the economy did not match the economic growth rates and improvements in competitiveness achieved in other manufacturing economies.

### Fiscal policy and cost-push inflation

The deflation of demand using fiscal measures is a means of tackling inflation if it is caused by excess demand but it has definite limitations if the inflation is caused by other factors. In the late 1960s and early 1970s when there was a great deal of support for the **cost-** (i.e. **wage-**) **push theory of inflation**, it was suggested that increases in government expenditure actually helped to maintain the cause of such inflation. Fig. 5.26 (page 88) shows that one of the effects of excessive pay increases and the resulting inflation is to produce higher unemployment. If governments were prepared to deal with the higher unemployment by reflating demand, then it was argued that trade unions would have no incentive to moderate their pay claims. They would be confident that the political repercussions of any increase in unemployment would always ensure that the government would increase its own expenditure to help reduce unemployment.

Under these circumstances the view developed that trade unions would eventually moderate their pay claims if the government refused to increase its own expenditure. For the resulting rise in unemployment would be seen as the price which had to be paid for the higher wages and salaries earned by those who remained in work. It was also suggested that the refusal of the government to sustain the level of demand and the resulting decline in markets would eventually force employers to resist excessive pay demands because of a growing need to remain competitive when faced with a smaller domestic market, fewer export orders and increased import penetration. At the time when this method of tackling inflation was put forward, however, there was no clear indication of how far unemployment would have to rise before a growing resistance from employers and a greater awareness by trade unions that the government was not going to relent produced more moderate pay increases. A level of unemployment of up to 5 per cent was often suggested, but since this was far above the post-war average it was considered political suicide for a government to pursue such a policy.

### Fiscal policy and the monetarist view on inflation

If the government is prepared to use budget deficits to prevent further rises in unemployment, and at the same time is faced with rising inflation, it will have to borrow increasingly larger amounts each year in order to maintain or increase the level of its expenditure in real terms. The government will have to borrow not only to support the expenditure undertaken by central government departments but also to maintain the financial assistance it provides to local authorities.

The total amount of money which the government has to borrow each year is known as the **public sector borrowing requirement** (PSBR). The rapid growth in the PSBR in the 1970s was criticised by the monetarists as being partly responsible for the very high rates of inflation experienced during those years. They believed that the problem of an excessive growth in the money supply caused by too much lending to households and business organisations was made worse by the level of government borrowing. The resulting inflation would then lead to higher unemployment because of the further loss of international competitiveness. This in turn would lead to yet another rise in the PSBR as the government increased its expenditure in order to deal with the growing unemployment.

The **monetarist view of inflation** therefore calls for a cut in government expenditure and/or an increase in taxation in order to reduce the PSBR and help slow down the growth in the money supply. The anticipated fall in inflation would eventually restore international competitiveness. Unemployment would be expected to fall as business organisations in the UK experienced an increase in the demand for their output. The monetarist policy for tackling unemployment therefore points to cuts in government expenditure and/or higher taxes. This is in stark contrast to the Keynesian view, which sees a deficiency of demand rather than inflation as being the essential cause of unemployment and therefore requires the government to borrow money to finance increases in its expenditure as a means of stimulating demand. A further explanation of the monetarist approach to tackling inflation is given in Chaper 7, which deals with monetary policy.

# 7. Monetary Policy and Income Controls

## MONETARY THEORY

### The importance of credit

A major part of the expenditure of both households and business organisations is financed by various kinds of **credit** facilities such as **loans** and **overdrafts**. Monetary policy is aimed at influencing the level of such expenditure by measures which are designed to control the demand for credit and/or the supply of credit from banks and other lending institutions. If, for example, the government wishes to reduce the total level of expenditure in the economy because of growing inflation, then it will seek to achieve a rise in interest rates in order to curb the demand for credit. This may also be supported by measures which have the effect of reducing the amount of money which banks are able to lend. Thus money becomes not only more expensive to borrow but also more difficult to get hold of because of a 'squeeze' on the banks that means a period of 'tight' credit. If, however, the government feels that there is scope for allowing an increase in total expenditure, since the most pressing problem is unemployment, then it may initiate a fall in interest rates and a period of relatively 'easy' credit.

The importance of credit can be seen in Table 7.1, which deals with advances by banks in the UK. There are other sources of credit, such as hire purchase and instalment-payment arrangements; in 1986 the total amount of such credit outstanding to finance houses and retailers was more than £18 billion.

**Table 7.1: Outstanding loans and advances to UK residents in sterling and other currencies (£ million)**

| Sector of economy | May 1985 | May 1986 |
|---|---|---|
| **Manufacturing:** | | |
| Extractive industries and mineral products | 1371 | 1444 |
| Metal manufacturing | 1035 | 859 |
| Chemical industry | 1479 | 1543 |
| Mechanical engineering | 1717 | 1805 |
| Electrical and electronic engineering | 2363 | 2510 |
| Motor vehicles and parts | 571 | 671 |
| Other transport equipment | 1204 | 1395 |
| Other engineering and metal goods | 1668 | 1821 |
| Food, drink and tobacco | 3474 | 3679 |
| Textiles, leather, footwear and clothing | 1573 | 1567 |
| Other manufacturing | 4409 | 5084 |
| **Other production:** | | |
| Agriculture, forestry and fishing | 5542 | 5963 |
| Oil and extraction of natural gas | 3002 | 2399 |
| Other energy industries and water | 2612 | 1652 |
| Construction | 4792 | 5442 |
| **Services:** | | |
| Wholesale distribution | 8088 | 7980 |
| Retail motor trade | 2024 | 2269 |
| Other retail distribution | 5227 | 6180 |
| Hotels and catering | 3295 | 3666 |
| Transport and communications | 3874 | 3860 |
| Central and local government services | 2492 | 1509 |
| Property companies | 5902 | 7687 |
| Business and other services | 14,289 | 19,603 |
| **Financial:** | | |
| Building societies | 1818 | 2428 |
| Investment and unit trusts | 2859 | 3785 |
| Insurance companies, pension funds | 2676 | 2664 |
| Leasing companies | 5315 | 6253 |
| Other financial | 20,319 | 18,311 |
| **Personal:** | | |
| House purchase | 17,755 | 22,068 |
| Other | 18,180 | 21,681 |
| **Total loans and advances** | **150,925** | **167,748** |
| Of which sterling | 111,114 | 129,399 |
| Other currencies | 39,811 | 38,349 |

Source: *Financial Statistics*, July 1986, HMSO.

## CREDIT AND THE BANKING SYSTEM

Before examining how monetary measures can influence the price and availability of credit, it is necessary first of all to understand how the **banking system** can create or reduce credit.

### Credit creation

Over a period of time, every bank is aware that although some customers will be withdrawing some of the money which they have deposited with it, others will also be making new deposits. There is, nevertheless, always the possibility that during a particular period of time the withdrawals may exceed the deposits. To ensure that they can deal with such an eventuality, banks maintain a reserve of cash.

Assume, for example, that Bank A receives a deposit of £2000 and that it is generally considered prudent for all banks to maintain a cash reserve of 10 per cent against their liabilities. Bank A will therefore retain £200 of this new deposit as part of its cash reserve and then put the remaining £1800 to work to earn a return. This £1800 may be advanced to a customer in the form of a loan to finance the purchase of a second-hand car, for example. Table 7.2 shows the items that would then be added to Bank A's balance sheet.

Now assume that the car dealer making the sale deposits the £1800 in Bank B. This bank will add £180 to its cash reserve and lend out the remaining £1620. When this money is spent, it may find its way into Bank C. Bank C in turn will respond in just the same way as the other banks, retaining £162 and lending out £1458. Thus the banking system as a whole has so far increased the total amount of credit by £4878 as a result of an initial deposit of only £2000. The process of credit creation will finally come to an end when all of the £2000 is acting as a cash reserve of 10 per cent against the increase in deposits. This situation is shown in Table 7.3.

### The contraction of credit

Whereas a new deposit leads to the multiple **creation of credit**, the withdrawal of a deposit will lead to the multiple **contraction of credit.** Assume, for example, that Bank A is currently in the situation shown in Table 7.4.

The balance sheet of Bank A shows that it is currently following the need to maintain a cash reserve of 10 per cent. A withdrawal of £2000

**Table 7.2**

| Assets | | Liabilities | |
|---|---|---|---|
| Cash | £200 | Deposits | £2000 |
| Advances | £1800 | | |
| Total | £2000 | Total | £2000 |

**Table 7.3**

| | Assets | | Liabilities |
|---|---|---|---|
| | Cash | Advances | Deposits |
| Bank A | £200 | £1800 | £2000 |
| Bank B | £180 | £1620 | £1800 |
| Bank C | £162 | £1458 | £1620 |
| Sum for an indefinite number of banks | £1458 | £13,122 | £14,580 |
| Totals | £2000 | £18,000 | £20,000 |

**Table 7.4**

| Assets | | Liabilities | |
|---|---|---|---|
| Cash | £20,000 | Deposits | £200,000 |
| Advances | £180,000 | | |
| Total | £200,000 | Total | £200,000 |

**Table 7.5**

| Assets | | Liabilities | |
|---|---|---|---|
| Cash | £18,000 | Deposits | £198,000 |
| Advances | £180,000 | | |
| Total | £198,000 | Total | £198,000 |

from this bank will leave it with the balance sheet shown in Table 7.5.

This means that Bank A is now in a position where its cash reserve is only just over 9 per cent. To replenish its cash, this bank will not relend all of the money which is receives when some of its earlier advances are repaid. Instead, it will use this money to restore its cash reserve

**Table 7.6**

| Assets | | Liabilities | |
|---|---|---|---|
| Cash | £19,800 | Deposits | £198,000 |
| Advances | £178,200 | | |
| Total | £198,000 | Total | £198,000 |

to 10 per cent. To do this, it will have to cut its lending by £1800. Table 7.6 shows the balance sheet of Bank A after it has made the necessary adjustment to its cash position and level of advances.

The reduction in lending by Bank A will mean a comparable fall in the level of expenditure which is financed by credit. This in turn will lead to a fall in income for those who normally benefited from such an expenditure and a net reduction in the level of bank deposits. Suppose that this effect is felt by Bank B, which experiences a fall in deposits of £1800. It will now be the turn of Bank B to deal with a cash reserve which has fallen below 10 per cent. This will require that it reduces the level of its advances by £1620, and the result will be a further reduction in the level of expenditure financed by credit by £1620. This contraction in the level of advances caused by the initial withdrawal of £2000 will continue until the banking system as a whole has reduced its lending by a total of £18,000.

Thus for the banking system as a whole to create credit, there must be a **net increase** in the level of total deposits rather than simply a redistribution of existing deposits between the banks. The process of credit creation therefore, shown in Table 7.3, will take place only if the original £2000 represented a new deposit and was not the result of a transaction whereby, for example, Bank A received this deposit at the expense of Bank B, which experienced net withdrawals of £2000. If this was the case, then the extra lending by Bank A would be matched by a reduction in the level of lending by Bank B. Similarly, the process that leads to a multiple contraction of credit requires that there is a **net reduction** in the level of deposits, because money is withdrawn from the banking system as a whole.

**Activity 7.1**
(a) Assume that there is a net deposit of money into the banking system of £100 million. What would be the increase in the total level of bank lending if the banks were required to maintain a cash reserve of 15 per cent?
(b) What would be the effect upon the total level of bank lending if the cash reserve was $12\frac{1}{2}$ per cent and there was a net withdrawal of £200 million from the banking system?

## LIQUIDITY AND PROFITABILITY

The examples used to demonstrate the process of credit creation and contraction dealt with banks which were solely concerned with maintaining a **cash reserve** against their liabilities. The remaining cash was used to earn interest by providing their customers with **advances** in the form of loans and overdrafts. It was assumed that all of a bank's assets were accounted for by cash and advances. In practice, however, a bank will hold a range of **interest-bearing assets**. The distribution of these assets must work within the constraint of keeping an acceptable balance between **liquidity** and **profitability** – two factors that pull in opposite directions.

**Liquid assets**
The degree of liquidity associated with an asset depends upon the relative ease with which it can be turned into cash and the extent to which a capital loss may be incurred on any transaction involved. The more liquid an asset, the less profitable it generally proves in terms of earning a rate of interest. An asset that represents a very short-term loan to a well-established and financially secure organisation will be regarded as highly liquid, because the loan will be repaid in a very short period of time, and there is little risk of the borrower defaulting on the payment.

A bank will therefore be willing to accept a relatively low return on such assets, while the borrower will be willing to pay only such a return. After all, the organisation receiving the loan is committed to repayment in a short period of time, and this may prove to be far less convenient when compared with raising a loan on a longer-term basis. A financially secure organisation will also be aware that it represents an attractive proposition from the point of view of banks and other lending institutions seeking to acquire liquid assets via the provision of short-term loans.

### Illiquid assets

An asset will be considered much less liquid if a bank has to accept a much longer repayment period or if it is some time before it matures at its face value and the full amount is repaid. This also raises the possibility of having to sell a longer-term asset before its maturity date. Such a sale at an inopportune time can result in a capital loss, or in such a small capital gain that the bank may have earned a disappointingly low return on the asset during the period in which it was held. Banks will be tempted to acquire such assets only if they are compensated by a relatively high return. Those organisations seeking to obtain longer-term loans will also be more willing to pay a higher return when compared with borrowing short term, because they do not have to meet demanding repayment conditions.

Some assets may be exceptionally illiquid if there is no ready market for them. Profitability will in this case depend heavily upon the creditworthiness of the borrowers and their ability to meet their financial repayments at the agreed times. Such risks will be associated with an even higher rate of interest, since the possibility of default of payment is combined with the absence of a ready market where the asset can be sold. There is, in fact, a very wide range of financial assets; the returns which they yield will reflect the market's assessment of such assets from the point of view of their liquidity and risk.

## BANK ASSETS

The following section describes the kinds of assets which are held by the banks. This is a necessary step in appreciating how the government can influence the price and availability of credit.

*Notes and coins ('till money')*

**Notes and coins** are the money banks use for their everyday banking activities in terms of meeting the cash withdrawals of their customers. Since this cash cannot be put out to earn a rate of interest, the banks seek to keep such holdings of notes and coins to a minimum, while still allowing them to operate efficiently.

*Balances at the Bank of England*

Banks and other financial institutions that make up the 'monetary sector' are required to retain 0.5 per cent of their **eligible liabilities** (comprising mainly customers' deposits) in the form of **cash balances at the Bank of England**. This money is held in 'non-operational' accounts in that banks do not have ready access to such funds, nor do they earn them a rate of interest.

Banks also maintain additional balances at the Bank of England in order to settle **inter-bank debts**. This reflects the role of the Bank of England as the bankers' bank and is the means by which the banks settle their transactions with each other at the end of the day.

*Market loans*

Banks lend money on a very short-term basis to the institutions and individuals who make up the **London money market**. Money may be lent for anything from one day to three months. An important part of the money market from the point of view of the government's monetary policy is the **London Discount Market Association** (LDMA). The banks lend money 'at call' or 'very short notice' to the **discount houses** which make up the LDMA. The discount houses in turn lend to the government and other organisations through the purchase of UK **Treasury Bills** and commercial **bills of exchange**. These bills have a maturity period of 91 days. The activities of the money market also include the very short loans which banks make to each other, often only on an overnight basis, to meet their immediate needs to even out their cash flows.

Banks regard the money market as a very important source of the liquid assets which reflect prudent banking practices. Regardless of this, every bank is required by the government to keep an average of 5 per cent of its eligible liabilities in certain parts of the money market, and never less than $2\frac{1}{2}$ per cent with the LDMA.

*UK Treasury Bills*
**Treasury Bills** are initially bought by the discount houses with the money placed with them. When they have just a few weeks left to maturity, they are often then acquired by the banks as liquid assets.

*Local authority bills and commercial bills of exchange*
These bills are also acquired on the money market and become attractive to banks when they have just a few weeks to run before their maturity date is reached.

Although all the above assets give the banks a relatively low return, they provide the liquidity which is so important for dealing with sudden large net withdrawals of customers' deposits. Banks can readily call in their money from the discount houses, for example, while some bills will generally be in the process of maturing. These holdings of liquid assets also allow banks to be more confident in the acquisition of the more illiquid but more profitable assets listed below.

*Investments*
**Investments** are the banks' holdings of British **government stocks** as well as those issued by foreign governments. A bank will hold a range of such stock to ensure that some is always near the point of maturing. The money can then be used to support the level of liquid assets or to buy additional stock. Banks prefer to hold such stock until its maturity date and therefore seek to maintain a position which reduces the risk of an enforced sale at an unsuitable time. A detailed description of British government stock and the factors that determine the return on such assets is given in *Business Organisations and Environments* Book 1, Chapter 5.

*Advances*
**Advances** are the most illiquid of a bank's assets, representing the loans and overdraft facilities granted to its customers. Advances cannot readily be recalled, and there is a risk, depending upon the bank's judgement, that the arrangements for repayment cannot be adhered to by the customer to whom the advance was made. The illiquid nature of advances and the element of risk are reflected in interest charges that make them the most profitable of all a

bank's assets. The rate of interest charged on an advance will depend upon the bank's estimation of the creditworthiness of the borrower and the security which is offered by the borrower. Advances usually account for more than 50 per cent of a bank's sterling assets.

## MONETARY MEASURES TO CONTROL CREDIT

Although monetary policy is used to influence the lending activities of all the financial institutions that make up the monetary sector, the following section concentrates upon how such measures effect the banks. The measures described are all available to the government, but the choice of measures and the degree of emphasis may differ, not only between governments, but also over the lifetime of any one government. The measures are considered in the context of a decision by the government to deflate the level of demand in the economy.

**Making money tight**
Since the ability of the banks to lend money is determined by the level of their deposits, a **net withdrawal of deposits** from the banking system as a whole will bring about a **multiple contraction in the level of credit.** In particular, the government will be seeking to reduce the level of bank advances. This can be achieved by putting pressure on the level of banks' liquid assets. In the earlier description of the banks' assets, we saw that they must maintain a cash ratio of 0.5 per cent against their eligible liabilities. In addition, they must keep a certain percentage of their assets in a highly liquid form, i.e. very short-term loans to certain parts of the money market. These requirements provide the government with the leverage it needs to exert pressure upon the level of their advances.

*Open-market operations*
Besides its usual sales of Treasury Bills to the discount houses to obtain short-term finance for the government, the Bank of England also sells Treasury Bills on the **open market.** These are offered at a price which makes them particularly attractive to a wide range of organisations and individuals seeking a secure and short-term outlet for their funds. Buyers pay for them by

cheques drawn upon their accounts at the banks, which will result in some of the money which banks hold as balances at the Bank of England being transferred to the government's account.

The banks will now find that their cash ratios have slipped below 0.5 per cent. To restore their positions and obtain the necessary cash, they will call in some of their money from the discount houses. Having dealt with the immediate problem posed by their cash ratios, the banks now face the new problem of keeping less than $2\frac{1}{2}$ per cent of their eligible liabilities with the discount houses. Assuming that the banks will not obtain sufficient cash from any government stock currently maturing, they will now have to reduce the level of their advances. They do this by not relending some of the money they receive from customers repaying earlier advances. Instead, they use this money to replenish their liquid assets in the money market.

So the effect of **open-market operations** is to cause a net withdrawal of deposits from the banking system. This will begin a chain of events that leads to a reduction in the level of bank advances. The resulting contraction in the level of credit will be a multiple of the initial drain of deposits. This will have the desired effect of reducing the total level of expenditure in the economy.

*Funding*

**Funding** involves a lengthening of the **National Debt** whereby the government converts some of its short-term debt into longer-term debt. If the banks are well endowed with very liquid assets, this may frustrate the government's open-market operations designed to cause a drain of cash from the banking system. This is because the banks can call in some of their short-term loans to the discount houses, for example, use the money to purchase large quantities of Treasury Bills and still meet the requirements concerning their cash ratios and holdings of liquid assets. The government would then have to continue its open-market operations until the banks were no longer in a position to run down their market loans any further, and the Treasury Bills were increasingly bought by the banks' customers. Only then would the banks begin to feel the effects of a loss of deposits upon their cash and liquidity positions and be obliged to reduce the level of

their advances. Such large-scale sales of Treasury Bills, however, may cause short-term interest rates to rise to much higher levels than the government is prepared to accept (see pages 112–13).

However, if the government conducts its open-market operations in longer-term securities, then such illiquid assets are more likely to be acquired by non-bank financial institutions. This will hasten the process whereby the banks experience a loss of deposits. Since funding involves the increased sale of government stock, the banks are less likely to sell any of their existing holdings of stocks to help restore their levels of cash and liquid assets, because their current market prices are likely to be depressed by the new issue of stocks. Thus the brunt of the banks' adjustment to the loss of deposits will be borne by a reduction in advances.

*Special deposits*

**Special deposits** are a more direct way of reducing the level of bank advances. The Bank of England will call upon the banks to place with it a certain percentage of their eligible liabilities in cash. This cash is effectively frozen by the Bank of England and will be returned to the banks only when the government is willing to relax its monetary policy. Since these special deposits cannot now be counted as part of their cash ratios of 0.5, they will have the same effect upon the banks as open-market operations. The banks will be obliged to reduce the level of their advances.

*Directives*

The Bank of England can issue directives to the lending banks to keep the level of their advances within an agreed ceiling or rate of growth. These **'quantitative' directives** may also be reinforced by **'qualitative' directives** whereby the Bank of England seeks to influence the type of expenditure financed by bank advances. It may, for example, direct the banks to show restraint in making advances to finance consumer expenditure or speculative investment in property. Greater priority will be directed to business organisations that are investing in new and improved productive capacity, particularly if this is likely to give rise to exports or import substitutes.

In the past, these directives have not generally proved very successful. Governments have usually had to resort to those monetary measures which reduce the level of bank advances by putting their cash and liquidity levels under pressure.

*Hire purchase controls*
This particular monetary measure is aimed at the finance houses rather than the banks. A large part of consumer expenditure on consumer durables is financed by **hire purchase agreements**. The government can curb such expenditure by regulations which both require a **minimum deposit** and stipulate a **maximum repayment period**. If the minimum deposit was, say, 40 per cent, the outstanding amount including interest charges had to be repaid over a maximum of three years, then this would be likely to have a significant impact upon the level of consumer expenditure financed via hire purchase agreements. The level of consumer expenditure financed by the use of credit cards can also be influenced by the government if it raises the minimum monthly repayments made by credit-card users.

These, then, are the monetary measures available to the government if it wishes to deflate the level of demand in the economy. If, however, the government was prepared to ease credit restrictions, then it would take steps which allowed the banks to increase the level of their advances. The reader should now trace through the effects upon the cash and overall liquidity positions of banks of open-market operations which involved the purchase of Treasury Bills from existing holders or the return of special deposits to the banks.

**Raising the cost of borrowing**
The process of credit creation depends not only upon the ability of the banks to make advances but also upon the willingness of people to use such advances. Open-market operations, funding and special deposits seek to reduce the supply of credit by forcing the banks to reduce the level of their advances. We will now examine how these particular measures also tend to produce a rise in interest rates that may reduce the demand for bank advances. This will help the government achieve its aim of deflating the level of demand.

*Short-term interest rates*
Assume that Treasury Bills with a maturity value of £10,000 are currently being bought by the discount houses for £9800. If these bills are then held until their maturity date in 91 days' time, they will earn a rate of interest equivalent to approximately 8.2 per cent per annum, i.e.

$$\frac{£200}{£9800} \times \frac{100}{1} \times 4.$$

Open-market operations however, designed to produce a net withdrawal of deposits from the banking system, will involve the sale of additional Treasury Bills. This increase in their supply will depress their market price, because they must compete with other short-term assets that attract potential buyers by providing them with a higher rate of interest. If, for example, their price falls to £9750, then they will provide their holders with a rate of interest equivalent to 10.25 per cent per annum.

This rise in the rate of interest earned on Treasury Bills will then produce a general rise in other **short-term interest rates.** This is because Treasury Bills have become more attractive for those organisations and individuals seeking a short-term outlet for their money. Those business organisations seeking to raise short-term finance by selling commercial bills of exchange, for example, will have to accept prices which provide their holders with a higher rate of interest than before, in order to compete with Treasury Bills. Such developments will then oblige the banks to raise the rates of interest that they pay to their depositors, so that they can compete with these other assets and continue to attract funds. To protect their profits the banks will then have to increase the interest charges on their advances. Thus open-market operations will mean not only a period of tight money but also a rise in borrowing costs, which may help to reduce the demand for advances.

*The Bank of England's lending rate*
There is a further way by which open-market operations and other measures that squeeze the cash and liquidity positions of the banks can exert an upward pressure upon interest rates in the economy as a whole. This is based upon the Bank of England in its role as **lender of last resort**, whereby it is always willing to lend to the discount houses but at a penal rate of

interest. When the government's monetary measures cause the banks to experience a loss of deposits, they restore their cash position by calling in some of their money from the discount houses. The discount houses then need to restore their own cash positions and they will turn to the Bank of England for assistance. The Bank of England will lend to the discount houses but at a higher rate of interest than they are currently earning on their holdings of Treasury Bills.

Alternatively, the Bank of England will provide the discount houses with money in exchange for bills. But it will accept (i.e. rediscount) these bills only at a rate which provides the discount houses with a lower return than they might otherwise have received had they not been forced to sell them at this time.

Having been forced to obtain money from the Bank of England on unfavourable terms, the discount houses will take this into account when they tender for the next issue of Treasury Bills and buy commercial bills of exchange. They will therefore tender prices which are lower than before, in an effort to earn a return that goes some way towards protecting themselves in the event of being forced to go to the Bank of England again for assistance. The discount houses will also be obliged to raise the interest which they pay on money at call and short notice, in order to deal with the position they find themselves in after the banks have withdrawn their money to support their cash ratios.

So, because of the rise in the interest earned on Treasury Bills, commercial bills and very short-term deposits, there will now be a general rise in other rates of interest. This will add to the upward pressure exerted upon interest rates as a result of the original measure that involved open-market operations.

Although open-market operations have the effect of both reducing the level of advances and raising the level of interest rates, the government can achieve the latter without necessarily resorting to such measures. If the Bank of England wishes to see a rise in interest rates, then it can increase the rate at which it is *prepared* to assist the discount houses as lender of last resort. Even if the discount houses are not in need of such assistance, because the banks are still maintaining a healthy level of money at call and short notice, they are still

likely to react by offering lower prices for new bills in order to earn a higher rate of interest. They do this to protect themselves from the possibility of being in a position of having to turn to the Bank of England for assistance.

If the discount houses fail to respond to this signal from the government that it wishes to see a rise in interest rates, then they are always aware that it can engage in open-market operations or funding or make a call for special deposits that will oblige the banks to call in some of their money. If this happens, the discount houses will be forced to borrow from the Bank of England or have bills rediscounted on even less favourable terms.

Therefore, not only is the rate charged by the Bank of England as lender of last resort always above the rate which the discount houses earn on Treasury Bills, but the discount houses will always follow any increases in the Bank of England's lending rate in order to keep the difference between the two rates to the minimum permitted by the Bank of England. A rise in the Bank of England's lending rate can generally be relied upon to cause a similar increase in both short-term interest rates and the rates which banks charge on their advances.

*Long-term interest rates*
The funding of a larger part of the National Debt will not only put the banks' cash and overall liquidity positions under pressure but also push up **long-term rates of interest**. The increased supply of government stock coming on to the market will have to compete with existing long-term securities such as earlier issues of government stock and those representing longer-term borrowing by the private sector. To attract potential investors the government will, therefore, have to accept a price for its new issue which provides the holders with a higher yield than could be earned on similar assets. This will then have a knock-on effect in the overall market for longer-term securities, because the fall in demand for them will eventually lower their prices until anyone acquiring such assets is able to earn a yield higher than its previous level. Business organisations seeking to borrow on a longer-term basis will then be obliged to offer higher rates of interest to attract extra funds. The higher cost of borrowing may force some business organisations to reduce their expenditure.

## Activity 7.2

Assume that the government applies monetary measures aimed at reducing the level of consumer expenditure financed by bank loans and other forms of consumer credit.

(a) Give examples of retail outlets in your area which are most likely to be affected by such a policy, and suggest reasons for those outlets which you have selected.

(b) Using examples where possible, explain why the policy might also affect other employers in your area.

(c) Explain why the policy may also have a significant impact upon the level of imports.

## Activity 7.3

(a) Look through both local and national newspapers for examples of advertisements that seek to attract sales by offering customers or clients credit facilities.

(b) Describe how they try to make their credit facilities attractive.

(c) Do you feel that there is a case for the government introducing stricter controls on advertisements offering credit, to support its monetary measures?

## Activity 7.4

Use a flow chart to demonstrate how open-market operations will eventually force both banks and building societies to raise the interest which they charge on their advances.

## MONETARY POLICY IN PRACTICE

The use of monetary measures as a means of either deflating or reflating demand will contribute to the same kind of uncertainty that is produced by sudden and frequent changes in fiscal measures. Once again the level of investment expenditure is likely to be a casualty if a combination of higher interest rates and a credit squeeze is used to cut total spending in the economy. The government would hope that its monetary measures would reduce the amount of consumer credit and the borrowing by business organisations to finance excessive pay increases; but the level of investment expenditure may also fall, because such measures may contribute to the 'stop–go' pattern of the economy.

### Business confidence and productive capacity

The fall in consumer demand will depress the level of **business confidence**, particularly among the producers of **consumer durable goods.** Any future reflation of demand using a policy of easier credit and lower interest rates will soon lead to inflationary pressures developing in those sectors of the economy which produce the very goods that will be in greater demand when there is a rise in the average level of household income. This is because consumer durables have in general a relatively high income elasticity of demand. A lack of investment in new and improved capacity is therefore likely to hasten the reintroduction of deflationary monetary measures, because of the inflationary pressures that arise when increases in output cannot keep up with increases in consumer expenditure.

This lack of investment by the consumer durables industry will also affect the future prospects of business organisations which produce capital goods, for example those supplying plant, machinery and equipment to the motor-vehicle manufacturing industry. This may slow down the development and application of new technology, because neither business's profits nor their future expectations support the very large sums of money which are involved in such long-term projects. Thus the reduction in the scale of major industries and the subsequent cut-back in their investment programmes may leave them in a position of not being able to respond to an upturn in the level of world trade. So, if inflation does fall to very low levels but high unemployment persists, the government may hesitate to use large scale reflationary measures to assist the expansion of the economy because of the potential effects of a lack of productive capacity upon the **balance of payments.** The high unemployment may now be the result of demand deficiency rather than inflation. Any tax cuts and easy credit facilities to stimulate the demand may lead to more spending on imports – not only because UK producers have cut back their capacity, but because overseas producers may have maintained their investment programmes and can therefore offer new and improved products at even more competitive prices.

### Long-term investment

Even if the overall level of business confidence is not too severely damaged by what is believed to be only a temporary slowing down of the economy, the level of **long-term investment** may still be affected by a significant rise in interest rates. This is because a larger proportion of the total costs of such projects are accounted for by interest payments when compared with the borrowing costs associated with short-term projects.

### Small business organisations

A credit squeeze and higher interest rates will tend to have a particularly severe effect upon small- and medium-sized business organisations which have borrowed either to set themselves up in business for the first time or to expand their operations. Large business organisations will have the financial resources to survive a temporary decline in their markets, but smaller concerns, relying heavily upon loan capital, may find it increasingly difficult to meet their interest charges and loan repayments. Some of them may be forced to close down or drastically curtail their expansion programmes.

### The problem of measuring the money supply

If a government follows the monetarist view that the sole cause of inflation is an excessive growth in the money supply, then it is hardly surprising that it will concentrate upon using monetary measures to control the growth of credit in the economy. Readers should refer back to the section on 'Credit and the banking system – credit creation' (page 105) to remind them how a rise in bank lending will lead to an increase in the amount of money in the economy.

To decide upon the direction and magnitude of monetary measures, the government needs to know the current **rate of growth of the money supply.** This information is needed to predict the extent to which future levels of expenditure will exceed the anticipated increases in total output. But this raises the problem of what should be regarded as money and

therefore included in defining and then measuring changes in the money supply. Such a definition of the money supply should include only the money which people are likely to use to finance their transactions – obviously this means the notes and coins currently in circulation, but what else? From this point on, there has been much debate concerning what else should be counted as money in terms of it helping to forecast the future level of expenditure.

It was commonly accepted that a definition of money supply should also include **sight deposits in banks** (i.e. money available on demand in current accounts). This would seem to produce an acceptable measurement as it covers the two most frequently used means of payment: cash, and cheques drawn on bank accounts. In practice, however, there are also some **interest-bearing deposits** in banks and building societies which many people are prepared to use for transaction purposes, since such money is readily accessible with little or no penalty in terms of lost interest. In the case of **time deposits**, however, a period of notice must be given before money can be withdrawn; although these deposits are generally held for savings purposes rather than to finance transactions, they nevertheless hold money which is potential purchasing power.

### M0 and £M3

The Conservative government which came to power in 1979 followed the monetarist approach to tackling inflation. It eventually settled for two measurements of the money supply. One was known as **M0** (M 'zero') and covered notes and coins in circulation with the public, plus banks' holdings of cash (till money) and their operational balances at the Bank of England (i.e. excluding their cash reserve). The government selected M0 as its guide to what was happening in general to those money balances which are readily available to finance current spending, i.e. for transactions purposes. The second measurement was sterling **£M3** and covered notes and coins in circulation with the public, plus all private sterling deposits (sight and time) held by UK residents in UK banks. This was used to measure money held for transaction purposes and money held as a form of savings. It provided an indicator of the private sector's holdings of relatively liquid assets, i.e. assets which could be converted with relative ease and without capital loss into spending on goods and services.

There are several other ways of measuring the money supply. The one selected as the basis for monetary policy will depend upon the evidence put forward to support the claim that it is the most reliable indicator of future levels of spending in the economy.

*Which indicator to use?*

If a great deal of emphasis is placed upon controlling the growth in the money supply as a way of tackling inflation, then the government must be very concerned about selecting the 'correct' indicator of money supply, i.e. the one most closely linked to the level of spending and hence the future rate of inflation.

For example, suppose that M0 and £M3 are currently increasing at annual rates of 10 per cent and 16 per cent respectively, and the government is concerned that such developments in the money supply will lead to a much higher rate of inflation in the future. The government may then set initial targets for the rate of growth of M0 and £M3 of 6 per cent and 12 per cent respectively and introduce stricter monetary measures to achieve its first objectives. After a while a credit squeeze and higher interest rates result in both M0 and £M3 expanding more slowly at 8 per cent and 14 per cent and the government is hopeful that it will soon achieve its initial targets. However, say that at the end of the next period M0 is expanding at 6 per cent, but £M3 is now increasing at an annual rate of 17 per cent. This is possible because they are different ways of measuring the money supply.

The government is now faced with the dilemma of which of the two measurements is the most reliable indicator of future developments in the economy in terms of the level of spending. If it decides to use £M3, it will have to introduce even more severe monetary measures. Suppose that the government does this, and after a while M0 is expanding at 4 per cent and £M3 at 14 per cent. The tougher monetary measures may have caused a very sharp downturn in the economy, however, which the government did not anticipate when putting its faith in £M3 as the indicator to be followed. The government then relaxes its monetary measures to some extent because of the deepening recession and rapidly rising unemployment and does

so on the basis of the performance of M0. Very soon M0 is expanding at only 5 per cent but £M3 is growing at a rate of 18 per cent, while the rate of inflation starts to rise once more. The government may then be tempted to revert back to £M3 as the most reliable guide to the future level of spending in the economy.

If a government sees an excessive growth in the money supply as the root cause of inflation, at first sight the solution may seem relatively simple. But the above example illustrates the kind of problem facing a government when different measurements not only change at different rates but move in different directions.

Also, if the government periodically swaps between different measurements of the money supply and then adjusts its money supply targets and monetary measures as a result, this will add to the problem of uncertainty in the economy.

Fig. 7.1 shows how M0 and £M3 have tended to move in different directions and shows the high interest rates which have played a major role in the government's monetarist policy. Although interest rates fell from their initial very high level, they still reflected a policy that sought to deter borrowing, because the gradual reduction in the rate of inflation still left real rates of interest at relatively high levels. If, for

**Fig. 7.1: Money supply indicators, 1982–6**

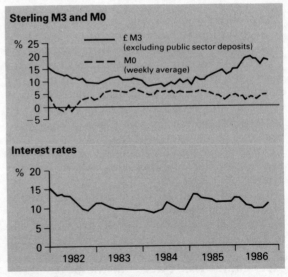

Source: *Economic Progress Report*, Nov./Dec. 1986, HMSO.

example, the interest charged on a bank loan is 18 per cent while the rate of inflation is 10 per cent, then the real rate of interest is 8 per cent. Thus a fall in the rate of interest to 14 per cent with inflation at 5 per cent will mean a rise in the real rate of interest to 9 per cent.

---

Activity 7.5
Collect leaflets from local banks, building societies and a post office which describe how they seek to attract deposits and savings from the general public.

(a) Draw up a chart which outlines the essential features of such schemes in terms of the extent to which households would be able to call upon such assets to finance an increase in their expenditure.
(b) Argue the case for not including some of the assets in the measurement of the money supply.

---

**The effect of the PSBR upon the money supply**
If a government believes that a high level of unemployment is the result of a lack of demand in the economy, it may follow the traditional Keynesian policy of selective increases in its own capital expenditure programmes to pull the economy out of recession. This approach to reducing unemployment will involve an increase in the **public sector borrowing requirement** (PSBR). But the monetarists claim that such a policy will be inflationary because of the effect of the PSBR upon the money supply.

Suppose, for example, the government sells Treasury Bills as a way of raising money and that the banks are in a position to buy them. The banks have lent money to the government and in return are holding very liquid assets; they will therefore not be forced to reduce the level of their advances. Total lending has now increased, however, because the banks have lent money to the government, and when this money is spent it will give rise to incomes and additional bank deposits. Government borrowing from the banks will therefore contribute to the creation of credit and an increase in the money supply.

If a government uses increased spending on capital projects to encourage the expansion of the economy, it can seek to minimise the effect upon the money supply by borrowing directly from the public. It can, for example, raise the rate of interest on the various schemes offered by the Department of National Savings to attract funds from the public that might otherwise have been deposited in the banks. Or the increase in the PSBR may be financed by the sale of government stock to the non-bank financial institutions which attract household savings. If the government can avoid the need to borrow from the banks, the increase in its expenditure will be financed by the transfer of purchasing power rather than an increase in the money supply.

The monetarists are sceptical that a government will be able to expand its expenditure by a significant amount without being obliged to borrow from the banks and thus generating inflation through an increase in the money supply. They regard any such policy as self-defeating, because the increase in employment generated by the higher government expenditure will eventually be offset by the loss of jobs produced by the effects of the higher inflation upon both exports and imports. If a government follows the monetarist line that unemployment is the result of inflation and this in turn is caused by an excessive increase in the money supply, then its monetary measures designed to achieve a credit squeeze and higher interest rates will have to be supported by tax increases and/or cuts in public spending in order to reduce the PSBR. This is considered necessary to ensure that any success in reducing the level of borrowing by the private sector is not offset by an increase in borrowing by the public sector. If, at the same time, the government is seeking to reduce direct taxes in order to stimulate 'initiative' and 'enterprise', even larger cuts in public expenditure will be needed to achieve the desired reduction in the PSBR. If the government is also engaged in a policy of **privatisation**, the proceeds derived from the sale of any public sector assets will also help to reduce the PSBR in any particular year.

The cuts in government spending aimed at reducing the PSBR will increase the level of unemployment. But the monetarist view is that the reduction in the rate of growth of the money supply will produce a fall in inflation. A combination of higher exports and lower imports will then contribute to a net reduction in the level of unemployment. Such a policy is also supported on the grounds that the jobs created will be more secure in the long run because the stricter financial climate will have forced firms to reduce their unit labour costs, and the general improvement in competitiveness will have produced a stronger foundation for future growth.

### The effect of the PSBR upon interest rates

On pages 112–13 a description was given of the possible effects upon private investment of deflationary monetary measures that involved increases in interest rates. An increase in the PSBR as a means of reflating demand to reduce unemployment may also produce higher interest rates. This is because such a policy may oblige the government to offer significantly higher rates of interest in order to attract households to its savings schemes or to sell its new issues of stock. It is said that this will produce a 'crowding-out' effect; the private sector will find it increasingly more expensive to raise external funds to finance its own investment programmes. However, those who support an increase in the PSBR as a means of stimulating the economy accept that modest increases in government spending financed by higher borrowing can be introduced without a major rise in interest rates, particularly if the recession has already depressed the level of private investment.

Thus rather than a very large and sudden increase in government spending, such a policy will have to rely upon a series of more modest increases that will gradually help to stimulate the overall level of economic activity and reduce the level of unemployment. As the economy expands it is also anticipated that the resulting increase in tax revenues and reduced expenditure on unemployment benefits will contribute to a gradual reduction in the size of the PSBR. This will not only ease any pressure on the level of interest rates but also help to avoid a significant increase in the money supply.

Activity 7.6

Divide yourselves into two groups each of which will support one the following views concerning the management of the economy:

(a) A significant fall in unemployment and an increase in investment in the manufacturing sector require the government to increase its own expenditure to encourage the expansion of the economy.

(b) A reduction in unemployment requires that government to exert a tight control over the rate of growth of the money supply and to continue to reduce the real level of government expenditure.

Each group should meet to prepare the various points it will use to support its view and to argue against the opposing view during a class discussion.

## INCOMES POLICIES

In analysing how inflationary pressures develop in an economy, frequent references have been made to the effects upon **costs of production** and hence on **prices** of excessive **pay increases.** The word 'excessive' was used to describe pay increases which were greater than increases in productivity. The analysis of cost-push inflation on page 87 and Fig. 5.26 (page 88), for example, described how such excessive pay increases would contribute to the creation of an inflationary spiral. Similarly, the investigation into money supply inflation as in Fig. 5.27 (page 89) showed how excessive pay increases are made possible if business organisations find it relatively easy to secure the advances required to finance the higher labour costs.

We also saw how monetary measures can be used to produce a financial environment in which it is increasingly more difficult and expensive to grant excessive pay increases, because of a credit squeeze and higher interest rates. The impact of such deflationary measures upon markets also forced business organisations to pay more attention to their labour costs, to improve their competitive positions. The effect of a strict financial climate and high unemployment upon **labour costs** is shown in Fig. 7.2.

## Why incomes policies are used

Both monetary and fiscal measures may eventually succeed in reducing the rate of inflation but only at the cost of higher unemployment and a fall in investment that makes economic growth all the more difficult to achieve. In an effort to avoid the serious side-effects of deflationary measures, various governments have in the past attempted to use **incomes policies** as a more direct means of influencing pay increases and getting them down to less inflationary levels. Between 1974 and 1978 the government used incomes policies as an important part of its anti-inflationary measures.

*Unit labour costs*

The logic behind an incomes policy is relatively simple: greater price stability can be secured if incomes are not allowed to rise faster than the anticipated rise in **productivity**. If an employer grants employees an increase of 5 per cent, say, and productivity is raised by the same amount, the increased labour costs are absorbed by the increased output; the result is that the labour costs per unit of output are left unchanged. If this method of determining pay increases is widely adopted by other employers, then any single business organisation may find that its other costs of production – such as materials and components – are also stabilised, because domestic suppliers will avoid an increase in their **unit labour costs.**

Under such a scheme, the increases in money incomes may be relatively small but are far greater in real terms compared with very large pay rises which simply allow employees to keep up with increases in the cost of living due to rapid inflation. An incomes policy linked in some way to productivity will stabilise unit costs and hence prices. Pay increases will then represent a comparable improvement in real purchasing power. An increase in real income of 4 per cent a year for a period of twenty years, for example, will more than double the level of real purchasing power. If investment is stimulated by an economic climate that is not periodically affected by 'stop–go' policies, and productivity rises by 7 per cent then real incomes would double in only ten years.

**Fig. 7.2: Percentage change in labour costs per unit of output, 1979–85**

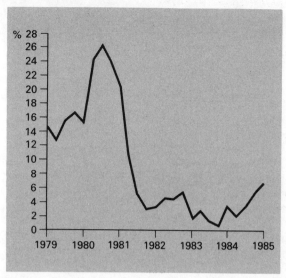

Source: *Economic Progress Report*, June/July 1985, HMSO.

Activity 7.7
Answer the following questions based on Fig. 7.3.

(a) During which period did the average employee experience the most rapid improvement in their standard of living?
(b) Describe those developments that may have contributed to the periods during which there were significant falls in the rate of inflation.
(c) Obtain a copy of a publication that includes various kinds of economic data, and produce an updated version of Fig. 7.3. Calculate what has happened to the average level of earnings in real terms over the period covered by your chart.

## Problems associated with an incomes policy

Reaching the stage where incomes are linked to productivity is a very difficult task. If a government is faced with rapid inflation and very high pay settlements, then its income policy may consist of several stages whereby it aims to reduce pay settlements gradually to a level which then makes it possible to link them with productivity.

**Fig. 7.3:**

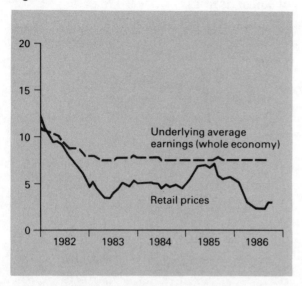

Source: *Economic Progress Report*, Nov./Dec. 1986, HMSO.

*Securing agreement to an incomes policy*

**Trade unions** may be willing to give up well-established collective bargaining techniques and to moderate pay claims only if inflation is already on a downward trend and real incomes are rising at an acceptable rate. The ideal time to introduce an incomes policy is when inflation is very low and economic growth is producing a general rise in living standards. In this case it may be easier to secure agreement to an incomes policy, because trade unions will be less concerned about demanding the large percentage pay increases which are a feature of their negotiations when inflation is rising rapidly.

Even when governments' fiscal and monetary measures have successfully got inflation down to a low level, they have generally shied away from an incomes policy as a way of preventing the re-emergence of inflation. This perhaps reflects the kind of problem associated with such a policy. Governments have generally resorted to incomes policies only when very inflationary pay settlements have forced them to exert a more direct control over wages and salaries; but it is during such a period of high inflation that the government is likely to encounter a great deal of resistance to its incomes policy. This is because different groups in the economy – depending upon relative bargaining

positions – will seek to use their power to obtain a greater share of the current output of the economy by keeping as far as possible ahead of the rate of inflation.

To reduce inflation and eventually produce an economic climate more conducive to investment, and thus succeed in raising living standards, the government needs union agreement to an incomes policy. But trade unions are unlikely to support such a policy unless the government can first of all get the rate of inflation down, but this in turn depends upon union support for an incomes policy! This problem in securing the initial agreement to an incomes policy is shown in Fig. 7.4.

The government may in fact need to support the earlier stages of its incomes policy with legislation in order to ensure that pay limits are not exceeded. All those subject to the policy must feel confident that the pay limit is not going to be breached and that, if they settle within the agreed limit, they will not witness exceptional pay awards at a later date.

*The cut-off point*

The government may have great difficulty in deciding upon the **cut-off point** from previous periods of pay negotiations that did not involve an incomes policy. If pay increases are currently running at 12 per cent, the first stage of the government's policy may set a maximum of 8 per cent. But there may be some groups of workers still attempting to obtain an increase based upon the previous average of 12 per cent. Others may be in the process of negotiating an increase of more than 12 per cent on the basis that in previous rounds of pay awards they were obliged to settle for increases well below the rate of inflation; they may now be seeking a large increase just to catch up with the increase in the cost of living. If these groups are then allowed to negotiate an increase of more than 8 per cent, this will immediately put the policy under pressure, because other workers will seek comparable increases.

*The lower paid*

If the maximum increase permissible under the incomes policy is 8 per cent this will discriminate in favour of those on high incomes. Those people earning £15,000 a year will receive an increase of about £20 per week, whereas

**Fig. 7.4: Problems of securing agreement to an incomes policy**

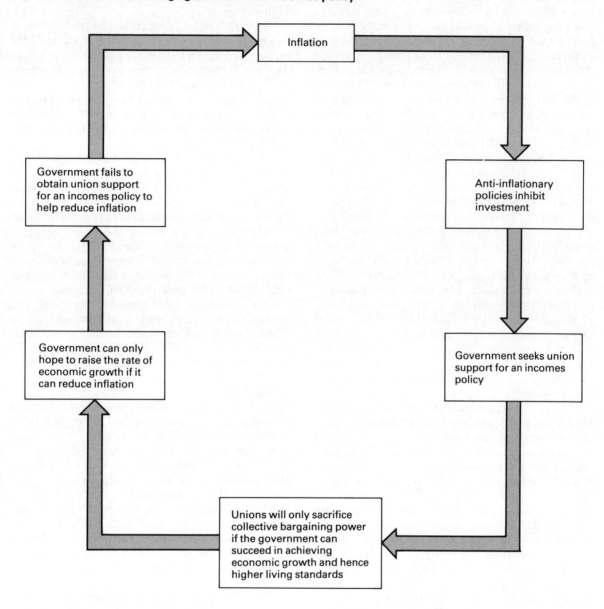

those on £6000 a year will get only an extra £8 per week. The gap between the two income groups has actually widened, and this is also based on the assumption that the lower paid are in a position to negotiate an increase of 8 per cent. The **lower paid** are often in the type of employment where they have little collective bargaining power or where the use of strike action may be ruled out on humanitarian grounds. Many of the lower paid are employed in the public sector in health and social services departments, and the government may use its influence there to encourage settlements below the norm of 8 per cent. The government may do this to avoid further large increases in taxes and local authority rates, in the hope that such action will help to slow down the rise in the cost of living and thus enable it to introduce the next stage of its incomes policy that involves setting a maximum pay increase of perhaps 5 per cent.

*Traditional differentials*

Trade unions and other labour organisations have traditionally conducted their negotiations on the basis of maintaining well-established **pay differentials** between different groups of workers. These differentials are based on such factors as the nature and level of their skills, the sector of the economy in which they are employed and the physical environment in which they work. A maximum pay increase of 8 per cent may lead to the erosion of these differentials. Suppose that a particular group of skilled workers earn a basic wage of £200 a week, while those who are semi-skilled earn £160 a week. The skilled workers earn £40 more than the semi-skilled, and this may reflect the well-established and generally accepted pay differential between the two groups. If both are granted a pay increase of 8 per cent their respective rates of pay are now £216 and £173 a week, and the differential has widened to £43. If the government continues to establish a series of maximum percentage pay increases, pay differentials will widen even further. The incomes policy will then be under increasing pressure as various groups of workers attempt to restore previous differentials through claims that exceed the current limit on pay increases.

The problems associated with differentials also arise if the government eventually introduces a stage in its income policy whereby it seeks to discriminate in favour of the lower paid and other groups of workers that qualify as special cases. The latter may involve work which is of a particularly dangerous or unpleasant nature, or where unsocial hours are concerned. This may then provoke large pay claims by other groups on the basis of the further erosion or widening of traditional differentials. Care must also be taken that special cases are clearly defined. Too much flexibility in response to other claims on the basis of comparability will seriously weaken the government's incomes policy.

*The need for simplicity*

The success of the policy may well depend upon its **simplicity**. If the government initially sets out to control in too much detail by vetting pay increases and considering the case behind every such claim, it may end up controlling nothing. If the government concentrates upon controlling wage settlements in key sectors which tend to act as wage leaders, this will assist the policy at a later stage.

The problem of competing claims and 'leapfrogging' can also be tackled if the unions concerned can be persuaded to settle on a single date with a minimum period of a year between such settlements. This will remove the fears of strong unions which might otherwise have settled earlier but do not want to see themselves left behind when larger increases are negotiated later by other unions.

An additional advantage of a settlement day for key unions is that it will help to improve the accuracy of economic forecasts and avoid sudden changes in fiscal and monetary measures. This is because, for example, tax revenues can be more readily estimated, the data for future wage costs per unit of output will be more reliable, and the relative competitive position of the economy can be estimated with greater confidence. This will allow the government to adopt a more certain approach to fiscal and monetary measures and so contribute to the restoration of confidence in the business world. Sudden and possibly destabilising changes in government economic measures are less likely.

*'Wage drift'*

The government will also have to take account of **'wage drift'**, as unions and other groups of workers negotiate bonus schemes, for example, which are not justified on the basis of productivity. Employers may also agree to a reduction in the number of working hours whereby employees still work the same number of hours as before but are automatically paid at the overtime rate for the last half-hour of the day, say. Such payments mean that earnings exceed what they should be according to the maximum pay increase laid down in the government's incomes policy.

Once this practice is communicated to other groups of workers, this total increase in earnings may then be regarded as the norm. Claims may then be submitted on the basis of differentials and comparability, because it appears that the policy has been breached by some groups. The opportunity for employees to benefit from wage drift or other allowances with a monetary value is unevenly spread. The incomes policy will then be under increasing attack for being unfair and for discriminating in favour of certain groups of workers.

## The effect upon growth sectors

In placing progressively lower limits on pay increases before it reaches a stage where they can be linked to productivity, the government's incomes policy may **inhibit the growth** of those business organisations which are seeking to expand their operations. They may need certain skills which are in relatively short supply and are therefore willing to offer higher wages and salaries to attract the necessary labour. These business organisations may be highly profitable, their growth being based upon substantial improvements in productivity. Even though they are in a position to pay higher wages and salaries without experiencing a rise in unit costs and a loss of competitiveness, they will still have to conform to the current limit imposed upon pay increases.

The future growth of efficient business organisations may therefore be frustrated by labour shortages. They will not be able to realise their full potential in both domestic and overseas markets. This may provide foreign competitors with an opportunity to increase their market share and undertake the necessary investment which along with additional economies of scale will allow them to widen the competitive gap between themselves and UK producers. Thus an incomes policy which sets a relatively low limit to pay increases in the interest of reducing inflation may slow down the reallocation of labour from those sectors which are in the process of decline to those which can make a more efficient use of such skills as they expand to meet growing demand.

## The link with productivity

Having used a series of progressively lower pay limits to overcome inflation, the next stage of the government's incomes policy may allow greater flexibility in pay increases by linking them to **productivity**. At this stage the government's incomes policy will find itself under renewed pressure. Business organisations with impressive improvements in productivity are able to grant their employees pay increases far in excess of the norm that characterised the previous stage of the incomes policy. Trade unions will no longer negotiate pay increases on a nationwide basis but according to productivity at company or plant level. This will give rise to new pay differentials that conflict with those that had become well established under the traditional methods of collective bargaining. More employers may also introduce profit-sharing schemes as a means of linking part of pay to the overall performance of their organisation. The flexibility provided by an incomes policy linked to productivity or profits will also stimulate the movement of labour into the growth sectors of the economy. These sectors will be in a position to offer particularly attractive rates of pay to those with the skills in greatest demand.

## Measuring productivity

In the case of business organisations involved in manufacturing, for example, **measuring improvements in productivity** does not normally present too many problems. If a motor-vehicle manufacturer introduces new production methods which, along with changes in working practices, produce a 10 per cent rise in output with only a 2 per cent increase in the input of labour, then this shows a rise in productivity of approximately 8 per cent.

It is often suggested that in the case of business organisations providing services it is much more difficult to measure productivity, but there is no reason why this should be so. In the case of a bank, the number of financial transactions it deals with may increase more rapidly than the number of its employees. Similarly, a hotel or catering business may be able to deal with a larger number of guests and customers without a corresponding increase in the number of employees.

The problems associated with measuring productivity are most acute in those areas of employment where the quality of the service may deteriorate as a result of attempts to make savings through greater efficiency. If a hotel or restaurant achieves savings through a more efficient use of labour, but this is at the expense of deterioration in the standard of its services, then the penalty is a loss of business. In the case of the public sector – health and education, for example – the vast majority of the 'customers' cannot turn to alternatives in order to register their disapproval of what they believe to be a decline in the quality of a service.

Suppose that the government seeks to raise the pay of nurses, say, by using the money obtained by the introduction of cost-saving programmes. There is then the risk that the standard of patient care may suffer as the nurses and other medical staff find it increasingly difficult to look after a larger number of patients without a comparable increase in staffing levels. The government will therefore, have to find some other formula for pay increases for those involved in the provision of social and welfare services.

However, if the incomes policy contributes to a more favourable economic climate, and this is reflected in more investment and economic growth, then the rise in real incomes will generate more tax revenue for the government without the need to increase tax rates. This will provide the government with the resources to increase both the scope and the level of social and welfare services. It will be able to grant pay increases to public sector employees that not only allow them to benefit from some of the fruits of economic growth but also ensure that the services provided do not suffer from a labour shortage because of unattractive rates of pay.

*The need to control price increases*

If the government believes that not all productivity deals are entirely genuine and that employers are engaging in 'wage drift' to retain or recruit labour, and this is reflected in a round of price increases that may put its incomes policy under pressure, then it may establish a **Prices Board** to investigate such price rises. If a price increase is the result of an excessive pay increase or of 'wage drift', the government can prohibit the price increase. It may be more lenient where a producer's costs have been seriously affected by the prices of imported raw materials. Yet even then the government may sanction only a price rise which allows the producer to recoup just a part of the higher costs. The government may take this approach in the hope that the producer will then be obliged to pay more attention to other possible ways of absorbing such costs, by using production methods that make more efficient use of energy and raw materials or by seeking to reduce unit labour costs by improved productivity.

Activity 7.8

(a) Collect information concerning a recent pay dispute which has attracted the attention of the media.

(b) Produce a report on the dispute covering the following issues:
   (i) the parties involved;
   (ii) the pay offer made by the employer and the extent to which it was linked to a productivity agreement;
   (iii) how the employer sought to achieve an improvement in productivity;
   (iv) the pay claim submitted by the trade union and the points which the union raised to support its case;
   (v) the view of the trade union concerning the productivity agreement;
   (vi) any opinions expressed by an employers' association, the Confederation of British Industry, the Trades Union Congress or leading politicians;
   (vii) the final settlement and any conditions attached to it;
   (viii) your own opinion on whether the final settlement was fair and reasonable;
   (ix) describe the possible effects of the settlement upon other pay claims and the rate of inflation.

Activity 7.9

A company that manufactures components for the motor-vehicle industry is seeking to introduce an agreement aimed at achieving a greater degree of flexibility in its workforce. This agreement will involve the removal of demarcation lines between one craft and another, between skilled and unskilled workers, between supervisors and supervised and between staff and shop-floor workers. The company is especially keen to implement working practices whereby production-line workers, for example, will undertake basic maintenance such as lubrication, cleaning and minor repairs on the machines they operate, instead of having to stop work and wait for an engineer. It is also hoped to remove barriers between skilled workers with different crafts by combining jobs that had previously been done by two or more craftsmen with different skills, so that a wider range of maintenance and repair work can be carried out by a single worker.

Such changes will also involve a reduction in the number of grades and job titles, to simplify the system of pay bargaining. The distinction between supervisors and supervised will also become less rigid, as supervisors will be required to help directly with the work of their teams when the need arises. The introduction of multi-skilled craftsmen will lead to the phasing out of separate supervisors for each of the traditional crafts.

The company estimates that the new working practices will raise productivity by 5 per cent during the course of the first year, and an improvement of 10 per cent is expected the following year.

(a) Describe the advantages to the company of the flexibility agreement.
(b) Outline the points which the company could raise to secure the agreement of the workforce to the proposed changes.

# 8. The International Economy

In 1973 the level of unemployment in the UK was 2.9 per cent but by 1986 it had reached more than 13 per cent. During these years pressure was often exerted upon governments to curb the level of imports of manufactured goods. This, it was said, would both protect existing jobs and create additional employment in those industries which have lost market shares to foreign producers. Before discussing the reasons why the UK government, like those of other manufacturing economies, has not resorted to large-scale protectionism, it is essential to consider the advantages to countries of participating in an **international trading system** which is free from government intervention.

## TRADE AND COMPARATIVE ADVANTAGE

**Comparative advantage**
The main economic forces that encourage different countries to specialise in the output of various goods and services stem from what economists refer to as the **theory of comparative advantage.** This theory points to countries concentrating upon those lines of output where they have a comparative advantage, which arises from being able to supply a product at a lower **opportunity cost** than other countries.

Perhaps we could grow cotton and oranges in the UK by using acres of heated glass-houses, artificial sunlight, special soil additives and various other sophisticated growing methods. But the cost in terms of land, labour, capital and entrepreneurial skills consumed in the process of growing such crops would be very high indeed. The prices that would have to be paid to attract large quantities of resources into cotton and orange growing, and away from a wide range of valuable alternative uses, would mean very high prices having to be charged for home-grown cotton and oranges.

The theory of comparative advantage is demonstrated in Table 8.1, which involves two countries, Enterprise and Tardis, indicating the output of labour in each of them in two lines of production: wheat and chemicals.

**Table 8.1**

| | Annual output of wheat per worker | Annual output of chemicals per worker |
|---|---|---|
| Enterprise | 400 tons | 200 tons |
| Tardis | 300 tons | 100 tons |

From the information in Table 8.1 an additional chart can be drawn to determine where each country's comparative advantage lies. The opportunity cost of producing wheat and chemicals in the two countries is shown in Table 8.2.

**Table 8.2**

| | Opportunity cost of a ton of wheat | Opportunity cost of a ton of chemicals |
|---|---|---|
| Enterprise | $\frac{1}{2}$ ton of chemicals | 2 tons of wheat |
| Tardis | $\frac{1}{3}$ ton of chemicals | 3 tons of wheat |

For example, if a worker in Enterprise is producing wheat, the opportunity cost of obtaining every 400 tons of wheat is the 200 tons of chemicals which he or she could have produced in that alternative employment. So the opportunity cost of 1 ton of wheat is $\frac{1}{2}$ ton of chemicals. Similarly in Enterprise, the opportunity cost of every 200 tons of chemicals is the alternative output of 400 tons of wheat sacrificed to obtain the chemicals. There the opportunity cost of each ton of chemicals is therefore 2 tons of wheat. Thus Enterprise has a comparative advantage in chemicals, because the opportunity cost of each ton of chemicals is 2 tons of wheat, compared with 3 tons in Tardis.

Tardis, however, has a comparative advantage in wheat production. Its opportunity cost of each ton of wheat is $\frac{1}{3}$ ton of chemicals, compared with $\frac{1}{2}$ ton of chemicals in Enterprise.

These lower opportunity costs will be reflected in having to pay a lower price to attract resources into those areas where each has a comparative advantage. These lower cost prices will in turn be reflected in lower selling prices, in that Enterprise can produce and sell chemicals more cheaply, while wheat can be produced and sold more cheaply in Tardis. These competitive strengths will attract demand for their respective products, causing a shift of resources that leads to a greater degree of specialisation between the two countries.

Suppose that, when the two countries first start to trade with each other, market forces bring about a situation where Enterprise is willing to exchange 2000 tons of chemicals for 4800 tons of wheat from Tardis. The rate at which chemicals will be exchanged (i.e. traded) for wheat is therefore 1 ton of chemicals for 2.4 tons of wheat. This ratio of 1:2.4 is known as the **external terms of trade** and is the basis upon which Enterprise and Tardis conduct their business with each other. Table 8.3 shows that as the two countries start to specialise, by shifting more workers into the production in which they have a comparative advantage, the total output of both wheat and chemicals starts to rise from its previous levels without either country experiencing an increase in the size of its workforce.

**Table 8.3**

| Reallocation of workers | Effect upon total output of wheat | Effect upon total output of chemicals |
|---|---|---|
| Enterprise: 10 workers moved from wheat to chemicals | − 4000 tons | +2000 tons |
| Tardis: 16 workers moved from chemicals to wheat | +4800 tons | −1600 tons |
| | + 800 tons | + 400 tons |

The reallocation of resources within each country will continue to promote the growth of international trade as long as the external terms of trade are more advantageous than their respective 'internal' terms of trade. In the case of Enterprise, the country can obtain 4800 tons of wheat by giving up (i.e. exporting) 2000 tons of chemicals; whereas if it sought to obtain the same amount of wheat by using its own resources, it would have to give up 2400 tons of chemicals. This is because Enterprise faces internal terms of trade whereby chemicals and wheat are given up for each other on the basis of ratio of 1:2. Tardis can acquire 2000 tons of chemicals by giving up (i.e. exporting) 4800 tons of wheat, rather than attempting to obtain the same amount of chemicals from its own resources, because its internal terms of trade ratio of 1:3 would involve giving up 6000 tons of wheat.

Both countries are clearly better off trading with each other, because market force will always produce external terms of trade which lie between their respective internal terms of trade.

*Changes in the terms of trade*
Although our example has demonstrated that both countries have benefited from trading with each other, the gains accruing to a particular country will not remain unchanged. Changes in the external terms of trade will bring about a redistribution of the total gains from trade. Assume, for example, that developments in Enterprise lead to a greater demand for wheat. Market forces produce a situation in which Enterprise is now willing to export 2100 tons of chemicals for every 4800 tons of wheat from Tardis. The external terms of trade which govern the exchange of chemicals for wheat are now approximately 1:2.3. This means that Tardis has experienced a favourable movement in its terms of trade, because the same quantity of chemicals exports will now buy more wheat than before. Enterprise, on the other hand, has experienced an unfavourable movement in its external terms of trade. It now has to export more chemicals to pay for the same quantity of wheat imports.

There has therefore been a redistribution of the gains from trade in favour of Tardis. But even with the now less favourable terms of trade, Enterprise is still better off importing chemicals from Tardis rather than shifting its own resources into the production of chemicals.

Although the theory of comparative advantage demonstrates the gains from free trade, the degree of specialisation and hence the **pattern** of **international trade** is influenced by factors that artificially distort the relative competitive positions of business organisations in different parts of the world.

## GOVERNMENT INTERVENTION IN INTERNATIONAL TRADE

There are several ways in which a government can control the **level of imports** coming into a country. The government can either introduce measures which provide home producers with an artificial price advantage over otherwise competitive foreign suppliers; or it can take action which restricts the supply of imports on to the home market. The government can also assist the **level of exports** by measures which improve the competitive position of home producers in overseas markets.

### Import duties
**Import duties** have the effect of raising the prices of imports so that domestic products become more attractive. In some cases these import duties may have to be very high – for example, if the overseas producers have a very strong price advantage because of lower production costs, or if they are exceptionally attractive because of the value which potential buyers place upon their non-price features such as quality, design, delivery and after-sales service. Import duties are also known as import **levies** or **tariffs**.

### Subsidies
The government may provide home producers with financial help that acts as a **subsidy** so that they can afford to charge more competitive prices and obtain a larger share of the home market. The financial assistance may take the form of a loan at a heavily subsidised rate of interest or a generous investment grant.

A subsidy may also keep down the costs of other home producers. If the steel industry receives a subsidy, for example, this will both help to curb the level of steel imports and also provide the users of steel, such as motor-vehicle manufacturers and their suppliers, with subsidised materials and components.

If government subsidies allow home producers to retain or increase their share of the domestic market, this may also be reflected in a larger share of export markets where they face competition from the same overseas producers.

### Import quotas
**Import quotas** distort not the prices of imports but their **availability** by imposing a limit on the amount that can be imported over a period of time. Some of the demand will therefore be redirected to home-produced products. In some cases overseas producers may agree to voluntary, unofficial quotas in the knowledge that, if they are exceeded, the government may introduce more restrictive official quotas. In recent years, for example, a voluntary agreement has restricted Japan to 10.8 per cent of the British car market, with each Japanese car maker given its individual quota. Nissan has been allocated 110,000 cars a year; Toyota has been restricted to just 40,000.

### Foreign-exchange controls
In the UK there are no government controls on individuals or business organisations wishing to exchange sterling for foreign currencies to pay for imports of goods and services. **Foreign-exchange controls** are most commonly found in East European countries and in those developing countries where foreign currency earnings from exports are generally in short supply and the government has to ensure that they are used only to pay for essential imports. To administer foreign-currency controls, the government can establish a system whereby exports must pass through certain agencies so that it receives all foreign currencies, and exporters are then paid in the local currency. By this arrangement the government can exert control over the use of foreign currency to pay for imports. Other countries' foreign-exchange controls can therefore be a barrier making it more difficult for some UK business organisations to export to certain parts of the world.

### Import deposit schemes
Some importers may be able to conduct their business on the basis of credit provided by their overseas suppliers. They will be required to pay for the goods only at a much later date, when they have earned sufficient revenue from their sales. The government may introduce an **import deposit scheme** to moderate the growth of this kind of import business. The importer will be required to place with the customs authorities a

deposit of, say, 50 per cent of the total value of the imports. This may be an effective way of stifling the growth of new import businesses, which may find great difficulty in securing the money to finance the deposit from either internal or external sources.

*'Hidden' protection*

The adverse international opinion aroused against import restrictions has led to the development of more subtle methods of controlling imports. These are generally designed to deter imports by making it much more difficult for potential foreign exporters to sell their goods in the home country. The government may, for example, require importers to apply for a **licence** to buy certain goods from abroad, and these may be granted or renewed only after a great deal of bureaucratic procedure and conditions have been adhered to. There may also be regulations in force that restrict the import of various items to certain **points of entry**. The government may say that it has very limited administrative capacity and cannot therefore effectively staff all the customs posts at sea ports, airports and border crossings. The government may also stipulate that each point of entry is reserved for a certain kind of import, since it is staffed by specialist officials who are trained to deal with the necessary documentation relating to duties and quotas, for example, and to carry out inspection or testing procedures.

A foreign exporter of a range of electronics products, for example, may then discover that there are different points of entry for video recorders, colour TVs and hi-fi systems. These places may also be several hundreds of miles apart, in remote areas well away from the goods' final destination and with insufficient staff to cope with the work. This will not only add to transport costs but also mean long delays before the goods are released from warehouses, which will affect delivery dates of both finished products and spare parts.

Legislation dealing with **safety features** and **environmental protection** may be constructed so that it has the effect of discriminating against imported products. The government may identify certain features of the imported products that are not commonly found in the equivalent goods sold by home producers. Having isolated such differences, the government can then impose stringent regulations that will not affect domestic products because they do not incorporate the same features as the imports.

For example, large executive-type cars have high-capacity engines, and the government may impose unusually strict regulations governing exhaust emissions and safety features. This may raise the exporter's production costs, and the situation may be aggravated by a regulation that inspection and testing are carried out in the country of destination but that any resulting deficiencies must be rectified in the factory where the car was made.

Such measures will tend to make it very difficult for a manufacturer to penetrate foreign markets, especially if each foreign country makes different requirements concerning safety and environmental factors, permitted materials, ingredients and design features, and if these involve costly alterations to the manufacturing methods or processes. The manufacturer will lose potential economies of scale. The home producer in the overseas market will have cost advantage, since its scale of output of the acceptable product wil be that much larger.

Hidden protection may also involve a government putting pressure upon its own departments and the industries in the public sector to **favour home producers** when they are spending money on materials, plant, machinery and equipment. Pressure may be exerted upon a national airline, for example, to buy aircraft from the home industry or at least to ensure that they are fitted with engines from domestic producers. The government may insist that both central and local government departments favour the home industry when buying computers and other items of office technology.

## PROTECTIONISM: FOR AND AGAINST

Having described the measures a government can use to protect home producers from imports or to assist them in export markets, let us consider the arguments generally used by governments to justify such intervention in international trade, as well as the problems that may result.

### In favour of protection

Our analysis of the theory of comparative advantage demonstrated that free trade allows an economy to obtain goods and services from overseas suppliers at a lower opportunity cost than if they were produced from domestic resources. From the point of view of consumers this was reflected in either lower prices or better value for money. Free trade allows consumers to maximise the level of their real incomes.

The pattern of international trade, however, is continually changing. Over a period of time, new suppliers enter the market, or existing suppliers gain a competitive advantage in the output of a wider range of goods and services. A government may be concerned about the effect of **increased foreign competition** upon its own producers, particularly if the decline of some domestic industries is not balanced by the growth of exports to create new employment opportunities and to earn the foreign currency to pay for the increased volume of imports. The effect of a **loss of international competitiveness** upon employment and the balance of payments is a central factor that motivates a government to try to protect its domestic industries in the home and export markets.

*To promote the development of 'infant industries'*
The removal of trade barriers which distort the relative competitive positions of producers in different countries will help to stimulate the growth of those business organisations whose goods and services are seen as offering the best value for money. A movement towards free trade may, however, prevent the entry of a new and potentially very competitive producer into an existing market. A new supplier will find it very difficult to break into a market which is dominated by well-established producers operating on such a large scale that their low unit costs allow them to offer highly competitive prices. Their competitive positions will also be continually strengthened by the financial resources and expertise which they can devote to their investment programmes, marketing and product development. An existing supplier will therefore be able to widen the competitive gap between itself and any other supplier seeking to enter the same market for the first time.

When a new supplier is setting up in production, the technology involved may require a minimum capital investment programme of vast sums of money. A large market share may be needed before unit costs approach those of the existing suppliers. In the early stages of development, the output of a new producer will be highly uncompetitive, but the **growth of an infant industry** can be fostered if the government implements measures to restrict imports and provide the infant industry with a protected home market. However, if the home market on its own is not sufficiently large to generate a demand which brings about a significant reduction in unit costs and other economies of scale, then the government may provide financial assistance so that the industry can also compete in overseas markets.

In recent years, for example, some governments of the industrialised countries have been concerned about getting a foothold in the new markets associated with computer technology, microelectronics, space communications and biotechnology. Certain countries – Japan, the United States – are already beginning to dominate such industries.

The 'infant industry' case for protection is often used in developing countries where governments hope to establish a manufacturing sector that will both save on imports and also increase foreign-exchange earnings from exports. These industries are likely to take advantage of the abundant supply of labour and will therefore employ labour-intensive methods of production. The small use of plant and machinery and low wage rates mean that only a relatively small output is required to achieve low unit costs. Such industries may nevertheless need protection from imports until they have managed to develop some of the non-price features that will make them more competitive and better value for money, and thus allow them to compete more successfully in overseas markets.

Governments in the developing countries may also assist new industries which are designed to raise the value of their exports. Many of them rely heavily upon the export of a single primary product for their foreign-currency earnings; the government will seek both to provide employment and to earn more foreign exchange by refining the raw material and undertaking some of the manufacturing stages normally carried out in the user countries. A developing country that exports a basic food or beverage crop may establish its own processing, blending, packaging and canning operations to raise the value of its exports.

*To promote the regeneration of key industries*
Protection can be used to provide a 'breathing-space' for **the regeneration of 'middle-aged' industries**. If an economy is slow to adapt to the changing patterns of world demand and the growth of new and more competitive foreign producers, the competitive gap will continue to widen. A failure to recognise that key industries in their current form can no longer survive without adjusting the level, method and type of output will make it increasingly difficult for that economy to sustain employment and to earn foreign exchange to pay for imports. The government may feel that a point has been reached where certain industries have failed to respond to market developments and foreign competition and are in danger of total collapse.

In identifying the industries which it is prepared to help through temporary import controls or financial assistance, the government must ensure that it selects those with a viable future once the necessary adjustments have been made. These industries must use the opportunity provided by the breathing-space to resolve their problems by investing in new technology, product development and training, for example.

*To sustain a technological base*
The government may be prepared to assist certain parts of the high-technology sector if they are threatened by imports or find it difficult to retain their share of export markets. Investment in high technology, such as aero-engines, may mean many years before the projects are completed; vast sums of money will be involved. If, in the meantime, the industry finds itself in financial difficulties with the rest of its operations and is in danger of losing its position in both the domestic and world markets, the government may provide it with temporary financial assistance until its new generation of products is ready for the market.

The government will be concerned that the **momentum of technological advance** is not lost. Once research and development are halted, it may be virtually impossible to re-enter the same field at a later date. Teams of scientists and engineers would have been broken up and perhaps lost to companies abroad, and technology will meanwhile have progressed to a stage that provides other countries with a competitive advantage that they will never lose. Mergers and take-overs may then lead to just a few overseas producers dominating the market, and the country will become totally dependent upon imports of high-technology products. The decline of its own high-technology sector will also mean that other industries will no longer benefit from spin-offs from the mainstream of technological research and development.

*To prevent 'dumping'*
The government may take action to protect its own producers from imports which are being 'dumped' on the home market. **'Dumping'** refers to goods being sold at prices below those charged in the country of origin and perhaps at prices which do not even cover their costs. The country responsible for the dumping will protect itself from the possibility of the same products finding their way back into its own market by imposing import duties on them.

A government may be a party to the dumping of agricultural and dairy products, for example, where its price support schemes have given rise to large surpluses which would depress prices if released on to its own market. A detailed description of why and how a government can protect the incomes of its farming community was given in Book One of *Business Organisations and Environments*. Book 1, Chapter 9 (pp. 147–51).

Each year the government may be under pressure from a large number of small-scale, high-cost producers to raise the guaranteed price which they receive for their annual output. This will lead to over-production by the large-scale, capital-intensive producers which are able to take advantage of new technology, pesticides, fertilisers and other developments allowing them to improve their yields. The government will therefore be obliged to buy up increasingly larger surpluses, and these 'mountains' and 'lakes' will become a drain upon government expenditure.

In addition to the purchase of surpluses, the government will have to finance the construction of more storage facilities. These may have to be especially designed to prevent the stocks from deteriorating.

The government may eventually decide that its price support schemes are proving so costly that it has to reduce the size of its food 'mountains' and 'lakes'. It may set up its own agency to dump some of its stocks in overseas markets, and also instruct producers to sell their surpluses abroad for whatever price they can get, while agreeing to make up the difference between their dumped price and the guaranteed price. This dumping will be welcomed by those countries which rely heavily upon food imports but it is likely to provoke a call for protection from genuine low-cost producers in other parts of the world, which find both their home and overseas markets seriously affected by such dumping. Faced with the prospect of their own producers not earning enough to invest in next year's output, other governments may then use a combination of import restrictions and subsidies to guarantee the future of their own agricultural sector.

Dumping may also involve consumer goods and industrial products such as machinery, chemicals and steel. This is most likely to occur when lower growth rates in the major manufacturing economies are reflected in a slowing down in the rate of growth of world trade. Highly capital-intensive industries may seek to maintain the demand for their products by selling at prices below cost but which still allow them to earn sufficient revenue to cover their very high fixed costs. Such a strategy may be pursued in order to maintain as large a share of the market as possible and avoid a run-down in capacity that would prevent them from being in the strongest position to take full advantage of an upturn in world demand. A shipbuilder or chemical producer, for example, may also secure financial support from its government that will allow it to grab a larger share of a depressed world market; this may also contribute to the collapse of some of its major competitors in other countries. A government may therefore be under pressure to protect its own producers from dumping, by restricting imports or granting them financial assistance.

Dumping has also been associated with imports from East European countries. Eastern bloc governments are often faced with a very acute shortage of foreign exchange and are therefore willing to sell abroad at prices well below cost, in order to get a foothold in the rich markets of Western Europe.

**Fig. 8.1**

Source: *British Business.*

Activity 8.1
(a) Find some recent editions of the weekly magazine *British Business* (published by the Department of Trade and Industry) and refer to those sections dealing with government measures that control certain types of imports (see Fig. 8.1). Use this information to give an assessment of the range of consumer goods and industrial products which are subject to import controls and their countries of origin.
(b) Give examples of companies in your local area that would be most affected, directly or indirectly, if such import controls were relaxed.

## Some problems with protection

Despite a high level of unemployment and/or a balance of payments deficit, a government may hesitate to resort to protectionist measures to tackle such problems. This is because import restrictions and government subsidies may give rise to other developments that reduce their effectiveness.

*Retaliation*

Import restrictions or subsidies will affect the level of employment and the balance of payments positions of other countries. If many of the world's major manufacturing economies are also suffering from high levels of unemployment and trade deficits, they may react by implementing their own protectionist measures. The government which initiated the move towards protectionism will then find the gains soon wiped out by a loss of employment and foreign-exchange earnings as a result of a fall in its exports.

In recent years there has been a growing concern that world trade is increasingly being threatened by a shift towards protectionism to preserve jobs and to protect balance of payments positions. This could lead to a series of retaliatory measures and a cumulative decline in the level of world trade.

*Complacency*

Protection to promote infant industries or the regeneration of key industries may lead to **complacency** and further inefficiency, because such industries will be insulated from the competition which is said to act as a spur to greater efficiency. A protected industry may also develop a product with a home market bias rather than an international appeal, because it has not been forced to respond to the non-price features which overseas producers are continually updating in order to create a worldwide market for their products. Thus, when the home industry has reached a stage where its prices are competitive and the import restrictions are lifted, foreign products may again penetrate the home market, and exports may not materialise. This is because the industry has failed to recognise and incorporate recent trends and developments into its product with respect to style, design, quality and performance, say, and overseas producers will still have a strong competitive advantage.

In an effort both to protect and to stimulate greater competitiveness, the government may use a subsidy rather than import controls. The amount of the subsidy may be just enough to ensure that the industry can avoid any further decline and provide it with the opportunity to embark upon cost-saving programmes, investment in new technology and the development of new and improved products. The total amount of financial assistance which the government is willing to provide can be allocated on an annual basis, with the payments becoming progressively smaller. As long as the government has made a firm decision that no more money will be available at the end of this period, the industry may take more urgent steps to improve its competitive position. The subsidy will also allow the industry to enter export markets, where it will be obliged to take account of non-price factors in making its product more competitive. Any use of the financial assistance from the government to meet excessive pay demands will lead to the further penetration of its home market by foreign suppliers.

*Import controls are inflationary*

Restrictions on imports oblige consumers to buy higher-priced goods from home producers. If the goods in question form a significant part of household expenditure, this will contribute to a rise in the cost of living that may provoke pay claims and add to any existing **inflationary pressures** in the economy.

Import controls designed to protect one industry can also raise the costs of production of another industry. If, for example, a motor-vehicle manufacturer imports certain materials and components, its competitive position will be undermined if the government imposes import controls to protect the home suppliers of these materials and components. Its production costs will increase, while the quality of its motor vehicles may suffer by not having access to materials and components which it regards as being superior to those supplied by domestic producers. There is also the possibility that these suppliers, due to a lack of investment in an earlier period, cannot cope with a sudden increase in demand; any such lack of up-to-date productive capacity may also be aggravated by a shortage of skilled labour, which in turn may contribute to inflationary developments in certain parts of the labour market. The motor-vehicle manufacturer may therefore be less competitive in overseas markets and also suffer from a decline in its share of the home market. An increase in the number of imported motor vehicles will then reduce the demand for home-produced materials and components. The government will then be faced with an even more serious situation than before, because it will also find itself under pressure to protect the motor-vehicle manufacturer from imports.

*Measuring the costs of protection*
A subsidy may be preferable to import controls as a form of protection, because the government can more accurately **measure the costs of the protection** and compare them with the benefit. The annual subsidy will be debated by Parliament. If the industry is continually asking for larger amounts, this is likely to promote a review of how the money is being used and whether or not the costs of protection are reaching levels where the money could be more effectively spent on other projects.

If an import duty is used to protect the industry, it is much more difficult to measure the costs involved and to decide if they are reaching unacceptable levels. The costs will be borne by consumers or other producers who no longer have access to the lower-priced imports, which may also represent better value for money in terms of non-price factors. These hidden costs of protection will be difficult to measure. If the import controls remain in force for a long period of time, such costs will also rise if the competitive gap between the protected industry and foreign suppliers continues to widen.

In the case of textiles, for example, the UK government, like those in other manufacturing economies, places quotas on imports of textiles and clothing from the developing countries. These quotas are intended to bring about a gradual rationalisation of the home industry, rather than risk the dislocation that would be caused by a sudden rush of uncontrolled imports. It is argued, however, that the extra amount of money which consumers have had to pay for textiles and clothing as a result of these quotas on cheap imports may be greater than the amount of money the government may have needed to help promote the development of other sources of employment in those parts of the country which have traditionally relied upon jobs in textiles and clothing.

*European Community membership*
If the UK government wished to restrict imports to reduce unemployment or deal with a balance of payments deficit, such a move would be contrary to the Treaty of Rome, which governs UK **membership of the European Community**. Under very exceptional circumstances a member of the Community may be permitted to introduce some form of temporary protection if the situation has reached crisis proportions and the remaining members have relatively strong economies that can absorb a temporary loss of certain export markets.

The European Community accounts for more than 48 per cent of the UK's total imports, and these are comprised largely of manufactured goods. Thus although the Community is a major source of imports the UK government is not in a position to introduce controls on such products even if it believed that they would help to regenerate certain sectors of the economy. Other members of the Community have, like the UK, also been suffering from very high levels of unemployment, and this is likely to provoke retaliatory measures.

Although UK imports from Community countries are over nine times greater than those from Japan, it is often the latter country which is the source of debate concerning import controls. This is largely because imports of consumer durables from Japan, such as cars and home electronics products, tend to gain a great deal more attention than, say, machine tools from West Germany or chemicals from the Benelux countries. The case for restricting imports from Japan is also usually based on the fact that the UK's trading deficit with that country is generally much larger than the trading deficits it has with some of the individual members of the European Community. It is claimed that, if Japan retaliates against any protectionist measures taken by the UK then, since our exports to Japan are much lower than our imports, in the long term the jobs gained by reduced imports will exceed jobs lost through lower exports. However, if consumers in the UK are not able to buy Japanese products, they will not necessarily turn to home-produced suppliers, because many of them may then express a preference for European products.

If, for example, the UK government places very severe import controls on Nissan and Toyota cars, some people might then buy a Renault or a Fiat. Also, the UK government would have to gain the support of the rest of the Community for such action, since it would involve raising the common external tariff that is placed upon goods coming into the Community from non-members.

*Import controls may be regressive*

We have seen that protective duties give rise to costs in the form of the higher prices that must be paid by consumers. An individual's contribution to the costs of protection will be determined by the quantity purchased and the difference in price between the home products and the imports previously bought. Thus the costs of protection will not be related to an individual's income, and this may have a regressive effect. This will be the case, for example, with food and cheaper items of clothing and footwear. These products are likely to form a larger percentage of the total expenditure of the lower income groups when compared to that of the higher income groups.

If the government decides that it is in the national interest to protect an industry, then the population as a whole should contribute to the costs of protection according to their ability to do so. This means that an individual's contribution to such costs should be related to their income rather than to how much they spend on the protected products. This **regressive effect**

**Fig. 8.2**

# US hits back at EEC on exports

**From Peter Pringle**
**in Washington**

THE REAGAN Administration yesterday announced a variety of restrictions on imports from European Community countries, including gin from Britain, brandy and bulk white wine from France, and cheese from the Netherlands.

The restrictions, some of which will amount to a 200 per cent import duty, are in retaliation for tariff increases on US corn sales to Spain after Spain joined the EEC in January. The US claims its exports of seed grains would drop between $400m to $500m because of the new tariffs.

US trade representative Clayton Yeutter said the retaliatory duties on French brandy and wine would account for $250m of US imports a year, and the gin from Britain for $70m (£48.6m). "The intent is to stop the trade dead in its tracks," said Mr Yeutter.

The Community has argued that the net loss to the US because of Spain's EEC membership would be far less, because American manufacturers will benefit from reduced Spanish tariffs on industrial goods.

However, in an effort to avert an immediate trade war, the Administration said there was still a possibility for further negotiations for at least 30 days — the period before the new restrictions could take effect.

"We'll keep trying," said a White House official, "It will take at least a month before anything will happen, but at this point it doesn't appear as if the Europeans are willing to make compromises."

The US restrictions came after protracted negotiations during which the Europeans indicated they would retaliate against any new US restrictions by imposing counter measures against the import of wheat, rice and animal feed made from American corn.

The Administration announced the new restrictions under Section 301 of the 1974 Trade Act, which authorises the President to "take action against foreign trade practices that violate international trade agreements or burden or restrict US commerce in an unjustifiable, unreasonable or discriminatory fashion."

Source: *The Independent*, 31 December 1986.

can be avoided if the government uses a subsidy rather than an import duty to protect home producers. The subsidy will come out of taxation, and since the taxation system is designed to be progressive, then the amount of tax which an individual contributes to the subsidy will be more closely related to their income. This means that some people buying the subsidised product do not contribute to the cost of the subsidy because they are on low incomes and do not pay income tax. The argument for exempting such people from making a contribution to the costs of protection is the same as that applying to other areas of government expenditure which are undertaken in the national interest, such as hospitals; the lower income groups' use of hospital services may be disproportionately higher than the taxes they contribute to their financing.

Activity 8.2
Read the article in Fig. 8.2, then complete the following:

(a) Explain why Spain's entry into the European Community obliged that country to place a tariff on US corn while at the same time reducing its tariffs on industrial goods.
(b) Explain why the agricultural policies of both the European Community and the USA are likely to spark off a trade war that may also spread to industrial goods.
(c) Discuss the following ways of dealing with their respective agricultural problems:
   (i) stimulating domestic consumption of agricultural products;
   (ii) seeking other overseas markets;
   (iii) increased food aid to the Third World;
   (iv) cutting back on the output of their agricultural sectors.

## THE GENERAL AGREEMENT ON TARIFFS AND TRADE

The **General Agreement on Tariffs and Trade** (GATT) came into force in 1947 and is the main forum for global negotiations designed to reduce trade barriers. The ninety-two signatories to GATT account for about 80 per cent of world trade. The major non-signatories are the USSR, China and Taiwan. There have been seven rounds of trade negotiations since GATT was established. Fig. 8.3 illustrates the results of the talks held in Tokyo between 1973 and 1979. The **'Tokyo round'** also led to greater GATT intervention to free trade from **technical barriers** and other forms of **hidden protection** such as government spending that discriminated in favour of domestic industries. GATT rules have also been introduced that ban **quota restrictions** on trade, but members are allowed to take action to protect their economies from dumping and the unfair subsidisation of goods.

### The principle of non-discrimination
A major principle of the negotiations conducted under GATT is that there must be **no discrimination between member countries**. If a member agrees to give another greater access to its domestic market, this offer must also be made to all other member countries producing the same kinds of goods. Another principle of GATT is that the country that was part of the original negotiations that allowed it greater access to the market of another must then agree to some kind of reciprocal arrangement, whereby it grants that country greater access for some of its exports.

The principle of non-discrimination means these concessions must then be granted to other members of GATT. The fact that there must be no 'most favoured nation' helps to ensure that the benefits and the costs that arise from a more open trading system, in terms of greater exports and imports, are relatively fairly distributed between the members of GATT.

This emphasis upon non-discrimination will also prevent a government from imposing restrictions upon the imports from just one particular country with which it has a large trade deficit. If it wishes to restrict certain categories of imports it would be obliged to impose the same controls upon similar goods from other members of GATT. This may upset its trading relationships with other countries which are valuable export markets, and may lead to a series of reciprocal arrangements that restrict certain kinds of imports from the country that initiated the original move towards protectionism.

**Fig. 8.3: GATT Tokyo round, 1973–9**

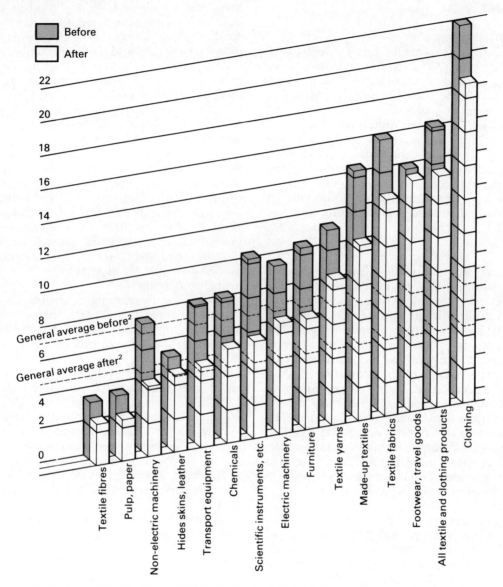

1. US, EEC9, Canada, Japan, Austria, Switzerland, Finland, Norway, Sweden.
2. All industrial products except petroleum.
Note: Tariff averages are weighted according to total imports of the 17 countries.

Source: *OECD Observer*, May 1985.

## RECENT TRENDS IN THE INTERNATIONAL ECONOMY

### New forms of protectionism

Although GATT has made valuable progress in the reduction of quotas and import duties, there is still a great deal of concern about the growing trend towards the use of **voluntary export restraint agreements, subsidies** to exporters and new methods of **hidden protection**. The world recession, rapid technological change and the growth of newly industrialising countries have severely affected key industries in some of the manufacturing economies. This has led to pressure upon governments for some kind of protection and produced more subtle forms of protection.

### Agreements with multinationals

The pattern of world trade is also being affected by the distortions that can arise when a government offers generous financial assistance to attract a **multinational corporation** to set up a factory in an area of high unemployment. The government may then reach an informal agreement whereby the company has to ensure that a minimum percentage of the value of its finished product is accounted for by local inputs of materials and components, rather than importing them from some of its other factories. The company may also have to agree that a certain percentage of its output is exported, rather than taking a larger share of the market of the host country, because the government will wish to protect the interests of its own industry.

### The service sector

In recent years there has been very rapid growth in **services** which are traded internationally, and it is estimated that they now account for about 25 per cent of all trade. This has led to governments devising ways of protecting the interests of their own sectors supplying such services as banking, insurance, travel and tourism.

### Agricultural protectionism

There is a growing recognition of the need for GATT to secure an agreement that will help to remove the distortions that affect **agriculture**. Most of the major manufacturing economies use subsidies or intervention prices and import restrictions to protect their agricultural sectors. If agricultural protection was lifted in these countries, the needs of both the food-processing industry and consumers would be met from the most efficient sources of supply; this would mean lower prices and reduced taxation.

At present, the costs of protecting inefficient home producers is borne by consumers, in the form of higher prices or increased taxes to pay for subsidies or to buy up surpluses. Agricultural protection is particularly damaging to many developing countries, which are potentially very low-cost suppliers of basic foodstuffs. If the rich manufacturing economies opened their markets to food exports from the developing countries, the latter countries could then earn more of the valuable foreign exchange they need to develop their own economies. Improved rates of economic growth in the developing countries would then increase the market potential for exports from the manufacturing economies.

Where the developing countries do find a market for their food exports, they often face a system of import controls which is more severe the greater the stage of processing. Raw sugar cane, for example, may be allowed into an industrial economy under a quota system that still leaves most of that economy's domestic market for its sugar-beet producers. If the cane is refined into sugar, however, it is likely to face import duties, because the government of the industrial economy wishes to protect its own sugar refineries from low-cost imports.

This kind of protection inhibits the attempts of a developing economy to increase the value of its exports and to create employment in its rural areas by undertaking processing, refining and packaging, for example.

A new round of GATT negotiations was launched in September 1986 in Uruguay and was expected to last four years. It is hoped that GATT will be able to tackle the kind of problem just described. The world urgently needs to reverse the trend towards protectionism which has been a feature of the last few years. The increasing impact of the newly industrialised countries upon the pattern of world trade also needs to be more evenly spread among the members of GATT.

# 9. The Balance of Payments and the Exchange Rate

All those transactions between UK residents and overseas residents which give rise to either an inflow or an outflow of foreign currency are collectively known as the **balance of payments**. We will shortly look at how a government can try to improve its **trading performance**. First, let us consider what makes up the balance of payments, including the terminology used when discussing **international trade** and other international transactions.

## VISIBLE AND INVISIBLE TRADE

### The visible balance

The **visible balance** deals with trade in the various categories of products shown in Table 9.1. It is also known as the **balance of trade**.

Until the development of North Sea oil, the UK constantly had a deficit on its visible trade

Table 9.1: UK visible trade (£ million)

| | Exports (f.o.b.) 1985 | 1986 | Imports (c.i.f.) 1985 | 1986 |
|---|---|---|---|---|
| **Food and live animals chiefly for food** | 3252.4 | 3740.1 | 8106.5 | 8719.9 |
| Live animals chiefly for food | 262.0 | 299.89 | 238.3 | 293.4 |
| Meat and meat preparations | 497.4 | 521.9 | 1400.9 | 1465.5 |
| Dairy products and birds' eggs | 281.3 | 331.5 | 606.3 | 653.3 |
| Fish, crustaceans and molluscs, and preparations thereof | 260.3 | 323.6 | 600.4 | 748.7 |
| Cereals and cereal preparations | 833.0 | 1177.1 | 713.2 | 769.3 |
| Vegetables and fruit | 205.3 | 251.7 | 2037.1 | 2184.4 |
| Sugar, sugar preparations and honey | 220.8 | 170.4 | 508.1 | 530.3 |
| Coffee, tea, cocoa, spices and manufactures thereof | 390.8 | 364.0 | 1205.7 | 1220.8 |
| Feeding stuff for animals (not including unmilled cereals) | 121.8 | 139.3 | 487.4 | 527.3 |
| Miscellaneous edible products and preparations | 179.7 | 160.6 | 309.0 | 326.9 |
| **Beverages and tobacco** | 1719.1 | 1737.9 | 1230.8 | 1347.0 |
| Beverages | 1253.7 | 1331.7 | 843.6 | 1008.3 |
| Tobacco and tobacco manufactures | 465.4 | 406.3 | 387.2 | 338.8 |
| **Crude materials, inedible, except fuels** | 2032.1 | 1940.9 | 4856.8 | 4622.7 |
| Hides, skins and fur skins, raw | 288.5 | 260.2 | 238.9 | 216.4 |
| Oil seeds and oleaginous fruit | 90.4 | 155.5 | 238.8 | 271.3 |
| Crude rubber (including synthetic and reclaimed) | 173.9 | 183.0 | 228.3 | 206.3 |
| Cork and wood | 25.7 | 22.9 | 895.3 | 1000.4 |
| Pulp and waste paper | 24.7 | 25.0 | 505.9 | 523.3 |
| Textile fibres (other than wool tops) and their wastes (not manufactured into yarn or fabric) | 419.4 | 373.0 | 662.8 | 546.9 |
| Crude fertilisers and crude minerals (excluding coal, petroleum and precious stones) | 269.2 | 272.3 | 354.1 | 217.0 |
| Metalliferous ores and metal scrap | 645.8 | 538.6 | 1371.8 | 1139.8 |
| Crude animal and vegetable materials | 94.3 | 110.4 | 361.0 | 404.2 |
| **Mineral fuels, lubricants and related materials** | 16,795.5 | 8683.4 | 10,663.6 | 6294.1 |
| Petroleum, petroleum products and related materials | 16,133.9 | 8221.2 | 8316.2 | 4393.5 |
| Coal, coke, gas and electric current | 661.8 | 462.1 | 2347.4 | 1900.5 |
| **Animal and vegetable oils, fats and waxes** | 95.9 | 105.3 | 531.5 | 365.1 |

| | Exports (f.o.b.) 1985 | 1986 | Imports (c.i.f.) 1985 | 1986 |
|---|---|---|---|---|
| **Chemicals and related products** | 9411.7 | 9691.8 | 6900.8 | 7345.7 |
| Organic chemicals | 2742.8 | 2585.3 | 1893.8 | 1830.9 |
| Inorganic chemicals | 979.6 | 1123.5 | 897.0 | 952.5 |
| Dyeing, tanning and colouring materials | 692.0 | 763.3 | 310.9 | 396.5 |
| Medicinal and pharmaceutical products | 1427.0 | 1532.8 | 590.4 | 679.7 |
| Essential oils and perfume materials; toilet, polishing and cleansing materials | 767.9 | 807.8 | 443.3 | 480.3 |
| Fertilisers manufactured | 74.8 | 67.4 | 217.3 | 212.7 |
| Explosives and pyrotechnic products | 45.7 | 42.8 | 20.0 | 21.2 |
| Artificial resins and plastic materials, and cellulose esters and ethers | 1330.7 | 1401.4 | 1763.5 | 1985.8 |
| Chemical materials and products, not elsewhere specified | 1351.3 | 1367.5 | 764.6 | 786.3 |
| **Manufactured goods classified chiefly by material** | 10,430.2 | 10,979.0 | 14,342.3 | 15,327.9 |
| Leather, leather manufactures n.e.s., and dressed fur skins | 295.2 | 321.6 | 250.3 | 247.9 |
| Rubber manufactures n.e.s. | 554.4 | 611.9 | 527.4 | 589.8 |
| Cork and wood manufactures (excluding furniture) | 84.1 | 77.2 | 632.0 | 686.6 |
| Paper, paperboard and articles of paper pulp, of paper or of paperboard | 767.6 | 824.3 | 2532.0 | 2703.0 |
| Textile yarn, fabrics, made-up articles n.e.s., and related products | 1709.1 | 1711.5 | 3032.0 | 3162.6 |
| Non-metallic mineral manufactures n.e.s. | 2164.5 | 2549.2 | 2242.6 | 2661.7 |
| Iron and steel | 1856.2 | 1866.7 | 1715.5 | 1796.3 |
| Non-ferrous metals | 1379.6 | 1551.5 | 1903.4 | 1836.2 |
| Manufactures of metal n.e.s. | 1619.6 | 1465.0 | 1507.2 | 1643.9 |
| **Machinery and transport equipment** | 24,667.5 | 25,348.9 | 26,937.5 | 28,769.2 |
| Power generating machinery and equipment | 3061.3 | 3248.6 | 1997.5 | 2238.0 |
| Machinery specialised for particular industries | 3077.6 | 3101.5 | 2327.3 | 2362.2 |
| Metalworking machinery | 521.1 | 581.2 | 525.1 | 645.7 |
| General industrial machinery and equipment n.e.s., and machine parts n.e.s. | 2937.5 | 3035.2 | 2603.9 | 2755.4 |
| Office machines and automatic data processing equipment | 3746.7 | 3561.7 | 4510.0 | 4545.1 |
| Telecommunications and sound recording and reproducing apparatus and equipment | 1295.1 | 1402.3 | 2130.6 | 2402.3 |
| Electrical machinery, apparatus and appliances n.e.s., and electrical parts thereof (including non-electrical counterparts n.e.s., of electrical household type equipment) | 3380.1 | 3383.0 | 4276.9 | 4446.4 |
| Road vehicles (including air cushion vehicles) | 3910.6 | 3954.4 | 6800.6 | 7939.7 |
| Other transport equipment | 2737.4 | 3080.9 | 1765.6 | 1434.4 |
| **Miscellaneous manufactured articles** | 7996.8 | 8575.5 | 10,131.6 | 11,391.0 |
| Sanitary, plumbing, heating and lighting fixtures and fittings n.e.s. | 135.0 | 126.3 | 177.2 | 216.7 |
| Furniture and parts thereof | 357.7 | 356.4 | 662.8 | 776.0 |
| Travel goods, handbags and similar containers | 29.4 | 30.6 | 174.9 | 199.9 |
| Articles of apparel and clothing accessories | 1171.7 | 1228.6 | 2090.1 | 2386.7 |
| Footwear | 159.2 | 167.2 | 671.1 | 735.0 |
| Professional, scientific and controlling instruments and apparatus n.e.s. | 2151.7 | 2284.2 | 1761.5 | 1792.5 |
| Photographic apparatus, equipment and supplies and optical goods n.e.s., watches and clocks | 817.3 | 843.5 | 1173.0 | 1285.3 |
| Miscellaneous manufactured articles n.e.s. | 3174.9 | 3539.1 | 3420.9 | 3998.9 |
| **Manufactured goods** | 52,506.1 | 54,595.2 | 53,010.7 | 58,288.0 |
| **Commodities and transactions not classified elsewhere** | 1990.7 | 2206.2 | 1325.7 | 1884.0 |
| **Total** | 78,391.8 | 73,009.0 | 85,027.0 | 86,066.7 |

Source: *Monthly Digest of Statistics,* February 1987, HMSO.

because of the level of its **food, raw materials** and **energy imports.** In 1979, for example, the UK's visible trade deficit was £3449 million, but by 1981 the country had a visible surplus of £3360 million. The UK had become a net exporter of oil at a time when there was also a very large increase in the world price of oil. At the same time, however, the surplus which the UK always managed to earn on its visible trade in **manufactures** has gradually declined; and in recent years the UK has had a deficit on its trade in manufactures. Thus the visible balance moved back into a deficit in 1983.

Table 9.2 shows the UK's **trading partners** – its export markets and the sources of its imports.

**Table 9.2: UK exports and imports by countries (£ million)**

| | Exports (f.o.b.) 1985 | 1986 | Imports (c.i.f.) 1985 | 1986 |
|---|---|---|---|---|
| **Total trade** | **78,391.8** | **73,009.0** | **85,027.0** | **86,066.7** |
| **European Community: total** | 36,233.8 | 35,003.5 | 39,004.8 | 44,505.9 |
| France | 7771.4 | 6210.2 | 6635.8 | 7348.6 |
| Belgium and Luxembourg | 3347.7 | 3832.6 | 4015.2 | 4083.9 |
| Netherlands | 7344.8 | 5442.5 | 6553.2 | 6615.9 |
| Germany, Federal Republic | 8966.1 | 8542.2 | 12,655.3 | 14,139.1 |
| Italy | 3466.2 | 3472.4 | 4293.1 | 4658.0 |
| Irish Republic | 3631.1 | 3558.4 | 2817.2 | 3053.8 |
| Denmark | 1371.1 | 1211.6 | 1714.8 | 1752.2 |
| Greece | 335.4 | 356.0 | 320.1 | 308.6 |
| Portugal | 439.6 | 472.1 | 695.7 | 768.5 |
| Spain | 1552.6 | 1905.5 | 1773.4 | 1777.3 |
| **Rest of Western Europe total** | 9430.6 | 6962.2 | 14,571.5 | 11,864.2 |
| Norway | 1140.7 | 1147.8 | 4444.3 | 3265.2 |
| Sweden | 3025.3 | 2307.9 | 2467.4 | 2765.5 |
| Finland | 705.4 | 664.5 | 1324.0 | 1346.1 |
| Switzerland | 1306.6 | 1575.2 | 2370.9 | 2989.1 |
| Austria | 381.0 | 403.0 | 630.2 | 705.7 |
| Yugoslavia | 177.5 | 188.4 | 122.2 | 145.1 |
| Turkey | 459.8 | 433.8 | 538.5 | 406.6 |
| Other countries | 242.1 | 241.7 | 205.0 | 249.9 |
| **North America: total** | 13,331.5 | 12,128.4 | 11,709.1 | 10,054.2 |
| Canada | 1693.6 | 1698.4 | 1653.0 | 1499.6 |
| United States | 11,519.4 | 10,379.6 | 9925.5 | 8468.2 |
| Other countries | 118.6 | 50.4 | 130.6 | 86.4 |
| **Other developed countries: total** | 3791.1 | 3614.3 | 6379.3 | 6860.7 |
| South Africa | 1009.2 | 849.6 | 989.8 | 829.3 |
| Japan | 1012.3 | 1193.9 | 4115.5 | 4932.5 |
| Australia | 1373.0 | 1227.9 | 741.0 | 643.2 |
| New Zealand | 396.6 | 343.1 | 533.0 | 455.7 |

| | Exports (f.o.b.) 1985 | 1986 | Imports (c.i.f.) 1985 | 1986 |
|---|---|---|---|---|
| **Oil exporting countries: total** | 5952.1 | 5495.0 | 2814.7 | 1876.5 |
| Algeria | 176.6 | 129.6 | 262.1 | 140.9 |
| Libya | 237.2 | 260.5 | 311.8 | 136.4 |
| Nigeria | 961.0 | 566.2 | 663.0 | 329.0 |
| Gabon | 30.7 | 16.6 | 48.3 | 36.6 |
| Saudi Arabia | 1249.0 | 1507.1 | 496.3 | 435.9 |
| Kuwait | 347.9 | 300.6 | 161.5 | 58.5 |
| Bahrain | 161.5 | 131.0 | 45.1 | 19.7 |
| Qatar | 142.1 | 112.1 | 32.6 | 29.6 |
| Abu Dhabi | 246.7 | 168.1 | 25.2 | 14.6 |
| Dubai | 345.3 | 379.5 | 44.4 | 56.2 |
| Sharjah etc | 29.3 | 34.2 | 27.3 | 3.3 |
| Oman | 489.9 | 399.6 | 68.4 | 87.2 |
| Iraq | 444.7 | 443.9 | 44.1 | 66.1 |
| Iran | 525.6 | 399.4 | 63.3 | 100.3 |
| Brunei | 71.5 | 154.1 | 23.3 | 71.6 |
| Indonesia | 175.3 | 196.6 | 156.5 | 141.2 |
| Trinidad and Tobago | 93.9 | 79.0 | 83.7 | 41.6 |
| Venezuela | 165.3 | 170.1 | 238.9 | 96.3 |
| Ecuador | 58.6 | 46.7 | 19.0 | 11.3 |
| **Other developing countries: total** | 7923.5 | 7643.7 | 8512.0 | 8637.3 |
| Egypt | 470.5 | 371.0 | 162.0 | 328.1 |
| Ghana | 116.9 | 113.2 | 99.4 | 103.5 |
| Kenya | 160.6 | 170.7 | 185.6 | 163.7 |
| Tanzania | 88.6 | 62.9 | 46.6 | 40.3 |
| Zambia | 85.9 | 77.8 | 27.9 | 27.3 |
| Cyprus | 151.2 | 140.4 | 93.7 | 124.2 |
| Lebanon | 52.8 | 55.9 | 7.9 | 9.8 |
| Israel | 434.5 | 462.4 | 404.0 | 385.2 |
| Pakistan | 255.4 | 227.1 | 119.0 | 131.3 |
| India | 895.1 | 941.2 | 431.8 | 440.7 |
| Thailand | 157.7 | 158.2 | 131.8 | 182.8 |
| Malaysia | 281.7 | 226.9 | 383.9 | 350.1 |
| Singapore | 612.9 | 547.4 | 441.3 | 462.9 |
| Taiwan | 164.8 | 192.5 | 582.9 | 705.8 |
| Hong Kong | 949.2 | 961.0 | 1176.0 | 1530.8 |
| South Korea | 247.8 | 288.4 | 480.4 | 662.0 |
| Philippines | 94.4 | 79.8 | 180.0 | 182.9 |
| Jamaica | 44.3 | 43.4 | 89.7 | 87.4 |
| Mexico | 203.4 | 162.3 | 236.8 | 116.1 |
| Chile | 73.9 | 67.5 | 134.8 | 128.0 |
| Brazil | 211.5 | 295.2 | 610.9 | 552.3 |
| Argentina | 3.8 | 10.1 | 2.0 | 28.6 |
| Other countries | 2166.5 | 1988.6 | 2422.7 | 1893.8 |
| **Centrally planned economies: total** | 1587.2 | 1720.9 | 1893.6 | 1856.2 |
| Soviet Union | 536.5 | 539.4 | 724.5 | 694.6 |
| German Democratic Republic | 63.8 | 81.3 | 204.3 | 195.5 |
| Poland | 184.2 | 182.8 | 320.3 | 309.7 |
| Czechoslovakia | 100.5 | 108.8 | 120.0 | 125.4 |
| Romania | 78.5 | 82.0 | 102.9 | 86.7 |
| Other countries | 623.8 | 726.5 | 421.6 | 444.2 |
| Low value trade[1] | 141.9 | 441.1 | 142.5 | 411.7 |

[1] Prior to January 1986 items valued at less than £200 have not been allocated to specific countries and areas. With effect from 1 January 1986 the threshold was raised to £475.

Source: *Monthly Digest of Statistics*, February 1987, HMSO.

Activity 9.1
(a) Make a list of all the consumer durables, especially electrical appliances, that you have at home.
(b) Identify their country of origin.
(c) Combine your results with the rest of the group to produce a chart which shows the most important sources of imports.
(d) Discuss the significance of your chart for UK manufacturers and the extent to which either price or non-price factors have been the most important determinant of competitiveness.

## The invisible balance

The **invisible balance** covers **services** and other **transactions** that are not included among the tangible items covered by the visible trade statistics. The UK's invisible transactions overseas are shown in Table 9.3. The regular surplus which the UK achieves in invisibles has often been large enough to compensate for the deficit incurred on its visible trade. In 1985, for example, the visible trade deficit was £2068 million but the **current account** (visible plus invisibles) was kept in the black by an invisible surplus of £5713 million.

The following invisible trade headings in Fig. 9.3 need some explanation and comment.

### General government services

This item covers the amount spent by the **government** in staffing and maintaining its embassies, consulates and diplomatic missions around the world. The largest single debit item is the cost of maintaining the UK military forces overseas, which in 1985 amounted to nearly £1500 million.

### Sea transport

The demand for UK **shipping services** is influenced by the level of world trade and by the extent to which UK operators can offer competitive freight rates. The recent world recession has left many countries with excess shipping capacity, and there has been fierce competition between shipping lines. This has provided an advantage to those overseas lines which have been able to make full use of an abundant supply of relatively cheap labour to crew their vessels. Both UK importers and exporters have increasingly opted to use overseas shipping operators, and the size of the UK merchant fleet has also shrunk dramatically because shipowners have preferred to register their companies in other countries.

The data under this heading also cover the payments made by UK shipping lines to various overseas organisations in connection with their port, handling and repair charges, for example. Their vessels will also need to purchase fuel and other supplies while they are in foreign ports. Similar payments by overseas shipping companies while their ships are visiting the UK represent credit items; but ports such as Rotterdam and Hamburg have increased their importance at the expense of such UK ports as London and Liverpool. Passenger ships such as cross-Channel ferries are also included under this heading.

### Civil aviation

Credit items under this heading include receipts by UK airlines from overseas residents for **passenger fares** and for the **movement of freight**. Approximately 20 per cent of the value of the UK's imports and exports is conducted using air transport. Competition between airlines is restricted to some extent by the need to obtain a licence to fly certain routes, while international agreements often regulate the fares which are charged. An upturn in the level of economic activity will increase the demand for business travel, while higher real incomes will increase the demand for foreign holidays. Other payments and receipts under this heading involve **landing charges, servicing** and **fuel**. Heathrow Airport, which handles a very large number of international flights, earns a substantial amount of foreign exchange from overseas airlines.

### Travel

This covers all kinds of expenditure by **UK residents travelling abroad** and similar expenditure by **overseas visitors** to the UK. The rate of inflation in the UK and movements in the exchange rate are important factors in determining the extent to which the UK can remain an attractive travel and conference destination. The travel account is also assisted by the fact that overseas visitors tend to spend much more during their visits to the UK than UK residents do when they are abroad. In 1984, for example,

**Table 9.3: The UK's invisible trade (£ million)**

| | 1975 | 1976 | 1977 | 1978 | 1979 | 1980 | 1981 | 1982 | 1983 | 1984 | 1985 |
|---|---|---|---|---|---|---|---|---|---|---|---|
| **CREDITS** | | | | | | | | | | | |
| Services | | | | | | | | | | | |
| General government | 140 | 215 | 241 | 254 | 268 | 317 | 407 | 407 | 473 | 474 | 490 |
| Private sector and public corporations | | | | | | | | | | | |
| Sea transport | 2651 | 3233 | 3433 | 3149 | 3804 | 3816 | 3784 | 3267 | 3054 | 3254 | 3272 |
| Civil aviation | 780 | 1049 | 1203 | 1455 | 1755 | 2210 | 2359 | 2471 | 2665 | 2931 | 3188 |
| Travel | 1218 | 1768 | 2352 | 2507 | 2797 | 2961 | 2970 | 3188 | 4003 | 4614 | 5451 |
| Financial and other services | 2888 | 3754 | 4396 | 5075 | 5726 | 6371 | 7364 | 8162 | 9428 | 10,110 | 11,852 |
| | | | | | | | | | | | |
| Interest, profits and dividends | | | | | | | | | | | |
| General government | 266 | 253 | 384 | 691 | 816 | 943 | 948 | 816 | 616 | 606 | 554 |
| Private sector and public corporations | 6297 | 8126 | 8405 | 10,504 | 16,707 | 22,590 | 36,189 | 42,990 | 41,449 | 50,950 | 52,478 |
| Transfers | | | | | | | | | | | |
| General government | 366 | 253 | 298 | 439 | 550 | 958 | 1658 | 2157 | 2221 | 2370 | 1812 |
| Private sector | 393 | 537 | 614 | 774 | 801 | 842 | 956 | 1134 | 1315 | 1428 | 1511 |
| **Total invisibles** | 14,999 | 19,188 | 21,326 | 24,848 | 33,224 | 41,008 | 56,635 | 64,592 | 65,224 | 76,737 | 80,608 |
| **DEBITS** | | | | | | | | | | | |
| Services | | | | | | | | | | | |
| General government | 709 | 867 | 941 | 987 | 1074 | 1166 | 1266 | 1756 | 1523 | 1655 | 1775 |
| Private sector and public corporations | | | | | | | | | | | |
| See transport | 2562 | 3155 | 3345 | 3162 | 3677 | 3675 | 3944 | 3890 | 4067 | 4386 | 4429 |
| Civil aviation | 675 | 840 | 984 | 1176 | 1467 | 1815 | 1922 | 2146 | 2354 | 2683 | 2835 |
| Travel | 917 | 1068 | 1186 | 1549 | 2109 | 2738 | 3271 | 3640 | 4090 | 4664 | 4877 |
| Financial and other services | 1478 | 1844 | 2131 | 2088 | 2205 | 2413 | 2655 | 3456 | 3937 | 4251 | 4525 |
| | | | | | | | | | | | |
| Interest, profits and dividends | | | | | | | | | | | |
| General government | 491 | 478 | 565 | 650 | 681 | 895 | 938 | 1091 | 1189 | 1329 | 1507 |
| Private sector and public corporations | 5182 | 6351 | 7986 | 9725 | 15,649 | 22,860 | 35,250 | 41,755 | 38,455 | 46,070 | 48,125 |
| Transfers | | | | | | | | | | | |
| General government | 703 | 1029 | 1381 | 2103 | 2568 | 2740 | 3292 | 3958 | 4177 | 4499 | 5174 |
| Private sector | 531 | 547 | 659 | 901 | 1062 | 1138 | 1298 | 1294 | 1463 | 1604 | 1648 |
| **Total invisibles** | 13,248 | 16,179 | 19,178 | 22,341 | 30,492 | 39,440 | 53,836 | 62,986 | 61,255 | 71,141 | 74,895 |
| **BALANCES** | | | | | | | | | | | |
| Services | | | | | | | | | | | |
| General government | −569 | −652 | −700 | −733 | −806 | −849 | −859 | −1349 | −1050 | −1181 | −1285 |
| Private sector and public corporations | | | | | | | | | | | |
| Sea transport | 89 | 78 | 88 | −13 | 127 | 141 | −160 | −623 | −1013 | −1132 | −1157 |
| Civil aviation | 105 | 209 | 219 | 279 | 288 | 395 | 437 | 325 | 311 | 248 | 353 |
| Travel | 301 | 700 | 1166 | 958 | 688 | 223 | −301 | −452 | −87 | −50 | 574 |
| Financial and other services | 1410 | 1910 | 2265 | 2987 | 3521 | 3958 | 4709 | 4706 | 5491 | 5859 | 7327 |
| | | | | | | | | | | | |
| Interest, profits and dividends (i.p.d.) | | | | | | | | | | | |
| General government | −225 | −225 | −181 | 41 | 135 | 48 | 10 | −275 | −573 | −723 | −953 |
| Private sector and public corporations | 1115 | 1775 | 419 | 779 | 1058 | −270 | 939 | 1235 | 2994 | 4880 | 4353 |
| Transfers | | | | | | | | | | | |
| General government | −337 | −776 | −1083 | −1664 | −2018 | −1782 | −1634 | −1801 | −1956 | −2129 | −3362 |
| Private sector | −138 | −10 | −45 | −127 | −261 | −296 | −342 | −160 | −148 | −176 | −137 |
| **Invisibles balance** | 1751 | 3009 | 2148 | 2507 | 2732 | 1568 | 2799 | 1606 | 3969 | 5596 | 5713 |

Source: *Central Statistical Office Pink Book,* HMSO, 1986.

overseas residents made nearly 14 million visits to the UK while UK residents made more than 22 million visits to other countries, yet the travel account still managed to achieve a surplus.

*Financial services*

The earnings under this heading stem from the highly developed services provided by the **City of London,** where the financial and allied institutions display an expertise which is recognised throughout the world. These services earn fees and commissions and include banking, brokerage, commodity trading, merchanting, underwriting of capital issues, risk underwriting and other insurance.

*Other services*

Other services provided to overseas residents include **telecommunications and postal services, royalties** from films and television, **consultancies,** such as those connected with the construction industry and engineering, **road hauliers, advertising** and the income of UK **entertainers** and **sports people** performing overseas. This heading also includes the expenditure of **overseas students** in the UK, the personal expenditure of overseas **military personnel** and **embassy officials** stationed in the UK and also the money spent by their establishments on goods and services supplied by UK business organisations.

*Interest, profits and dividends (i.p.d.)*

I.p.d. credits and debits are the result of payments which arise out of **investment** and other capital flows, either out of or into the UK economy. The following transactions will, for example, give rise to debit items as far as i.p.d. is concerned:

- An overseas company builds a factory in the UK, and some of the profits are then repatriated to the country where its headquarters are located.
- Overseas financial institutions buy UK stocks and shares, or deposit some of their money in the UK banking system or in the London money market. Such dealing will then produce outflows in the form of interest and divident payments.
- Overseas governments hold part of their foreign-currency reserves in sterling assets such as UK government stock, as well as more liquid assets.
- The UK government borrows from other central banks to support its foreign-currency reserves.
- Overseas banks lend to business organisations in the UK.

When such transactions occur in the opposite direction, in that investment and capital flow out of the UK, this will eventually produce credit items as far as i.p.d. is concerned. The factors which help to determine the relative size and direction of these flows and hence the total credits and debits under this heading on the invisible account are outlined on page 143.

*Transfers*

These refer to transactions in which one of the parties does not receive anything in return. Government transfers include the **grants** and the value of **technical assistance** which it provides to Third World countries as part of its overseas aid and development programmes; in 1985 this amounted to just over £600 million. The largest single debit item, however, is the government's contribution to the **European Community budget**; in 1985 this amounted to £3800 million. The 1985 credit item of £1812 million represents the money which the UK government receives from the European Community to assist with its part of the Common Agricultural Policy and with projects in the UK which qualify for support from the Community's Social and Regional Development Funds.

**Private transfers** include the money which immigrants sent back to their families overseas and the relief and development work financed by such charitable organisations as Oxfam, Christian Aid and Band Aid. Private credits include the money sent back to their families by UK residents working abroad for foreign companies.

**Investments and other capital transactions**

Although the interest, profit and dividends (i.p.d.) associated with investments and other such capital flows will eventually produce debits and credits on the invisible balance, the **capital movements** themselves are included under a separate heading in the balance of payments. The capital flows into the UK which eventually produce debit items in the form of i.p.d. are credit items as far as this component of the balance of payments is concerned.

*Direct investment*

When an overseas company builds a factory in the UK this is known as **direct investment.** In order to finance its capital investment programme, the company will need to exchange its own currency for sterling, which means an inflow of foreign currency and therefore a credit item in the UK's balance of payments. This is because the overseas company will place orders with UK business organisations involved in the construction of the factory and perhaps also with the manufacturer of plant and machinery. The UK has therefore earned foreign exchange by selling a variety of services and products to an overseas buyer; these amount to 'exports' despite the fact that the plant and machinery, for example, have not left the country.

If a UK company engages in **direct investment overseas**, it will require foreign exchange to finance its capital projects. This gives rise to a currency outflow and hence a debit item in the UK's balance of payments.

The flow of overseas direct investment into the UK will depend upon the following factors:

- The prospect of economic growth in the UK and the extent to which this is likely to provide an overseas company with a sufficiently large and sustained market for its goods or services.
- The level and scope of financial assistance which the UK government provides as part of its policy of promoting regional development and/or the development and application of new technology in the manufacturing sector, for example.
- An adequate supply of labour with the appropriate skills and wage levels that will contribute to a competitively priced output.
- An exchange rate that is stabilised at a level that will allow the company to compete in export markets.

These factors are particularly important to US and Japanese companies, for example, wishing to locate in a European Community country in order to get behind the common external tariff and sell in the large European market.

The multiplier effect of overseas investment upon the region in which the company is located, and upon the UK economy as a whole, will depend upon the ability of home producers to supply materials and components which meet its specifications in terms of quality, performance, cost and delivery. If these needs are not met, the overseas company will tend to import supplies from one of its other factories.

As Table 9.4 indicates, there has been a substantial amount of overseas direct investment by UK companies. Such organisations seek to take advantage of locations in countries where the market potential is greater than in the UK and where their costs of production allow them to be more competitive when exporting to other markets. These outflows of capital also include overseas investment by oil companies. The large inflows in the last half of the 1970s and the early 1980s reflect overseas investment in North Sea oil.

*Portfolio investment*
In addition to direct investment, Table 9.4 includes what is known as **portfolio investment**. This covers capital flows which represent purchases of **shares** and both private and public sector **stock**. If, for example, an overseas institution buys shares in a UK company or British government stock, this will also involve dealings whereby foreign exchange is converted into sterling, which means an inflow of foreign currency, because the UK has 'exported' securities of some kind. Portfolio investment in the UK by overseas institutions will depend upon the anticipated returns which can be earned on such assets compared with those which can be earned in other parts of the world.

Table 9.4: Capital flows arising out of direct investment and portfolio investment (£ million)

| | 1975 | 1976 | 1977 | 1978 | 1979 | 1980 | 1981 | 1982 | 1983 | 1984 | 1985 |
|---|---|---|---|---|---|---|---|---|---|---|---|
| Investment overseas by UK residents[1] | | | | | | | | | | | |
| Direct | −1324 | −2420 | −2399 | −3520 | −5889 | −4926 | −6094 | −4322 | −5301 | −5957 | −7307 |
| Portfolio | −59 | 90 | 12 | −1073 | −909 | −3230 | −4300 | −6720 | −6520 | −9550 | −18,220 |
| Total UK investment overseas | −1383 | −2330 | −2387 | −4593 | −6798 | −8156 | −10,394 | −11,042 | −11,821 | −15,507 | −25,527 |
| Investment in the United Kingdom by overseas residents[1] | | | | | | | | | | | |
| Direct | 1518 | 1653 | 2546 | 1962 | 3030 | 4355 | 2932 | 2964 | 3438 | 425 | 3370 |
| Portfolio | 194 | 1032 | 1910 | −139 | 1549 | 1499 | 323 | 225 | 1888 | 1419 | 7065 |
| Total overseas investment in the UK | 1712 | 2685 | 4456 | 1823 | 4579 | 5854 | 3255 | 3189 | 5326 | 1844 | 10,435 |

[1] Assets: increase−/decrease+. Liabilities: increase+/decrease−.
Source: *Central Statistical Office Pink Book*, HMSO, 1986.

*Speculation and capital flows*

A highly volatile element of this component of the balance of payments is 'hot money'. This is a description given to **short-term capital movements** from one country to another, seeking to take advantage of movements in the exchange rate. When such funds are deposited in the UK banks or in the money market, this will produce a credit item, because foreign exchange is converted into sterling in order to earn the rates of interest that are paid on sterling assets.

An actual or rumoured fall in the value of the pound may cause an outflow of short-term capital from the UK and into overseas assets in countries where the currencies are considered stronger and more likely to appreciate in value. Suppose that an organisation is currently holding short-term assets in the UK amounting to £1 million and the exchange rate is £1 = $1.50. There is then growing speculation that the pound is going to fall in value against other major currencies such as the dollar. The £1 million is then converted into $1.5 million and placed in a short-term deposit in the USA. This currency outflow will represent a debit item in the UK's balance of payments. Now assume that, after a period of three months, the pound falls to what is generally regarded as a more realistic level of £1 = $1.25 . The $1.5 million may now have increased to $1.53 million because of the interest earned on the deposit in the USA. When this is then brought back to the UK at the new exchange rate and placed in a short-term deposit, it will be worth £1.224 million.

When the funds returned to the UK this represented a currency inflow and thus a credit item in the balance of payments. But from the point of view of the economy as a whole, there was an outflow of $1.50 for each pound that was exchanged when the funds were transferred abroad, but an inflow of only $1.25 for each pound when the funds were deposited back in the UK. These sudden and large-scale flows of 'hot money', in response to real or anticipated movements in the exchange rate, can have a very destabilising effect upon the economy. They will exaggerate the eventual movement in the exchange rate which was the initial cause of the original inflow or outflow of capital.

Activity 9.2

Explain whether the following activities produce either credits or debits and where each of them would be recorded in the UK's balance of payments.

(a) The sale of Nelson's Column to a Californian theme-park.
(b) Nissan building a motor-vehicle assembly plant in the UK.
(c) The export of cars from a Nissan factory in the UK.
(d) Elton John giving a concert in New York.
(e) The export of natural gas to Holland.
(f) The subsidiary of a US oil company operating in the North Sea repatriates its profits to its parent company in the USA. *[debit]*
(g) A UK importer paying interest on trade credit received from an overseas supplier. *[debit]*
(h) A UK life-assurance company buys some of the new shares issued by an Australian brewing company, which uses the money which it has raised to finance the export and distribution of its products in the UK.
(i) A multinational corporation uses the conference facilities of a London hotel to hold a sales meeting for the heads of its European subsidiaries.
(j) Manchester United FC accept an invitation to play an exhibition match in Saudi Arabia.

## BALANCE OF PAYMENTS PROBLEMS AND THE EXCHANGE RATE

If the economy fails to produce goods and services at competitive prices, and neglects the importance of the various non-price factors that attract customers, this will lead not only to a **loss of export orders** but also a **rise in imports**. Both consumers and business organisations will turn to overseas suppliers to satisfy their needs. The resulting deficit in the balance of payments will then produce developments in the foreign-exchange markets that exert a downward pressure upon the **value of sterling**.

To appreciate why this happens it is necessary to look at the market for pounds and how the forces of demand and supply determine the price of pounds in terms of other currencies, i.e. the **exchange rate**. We will consider the exchange rate in terms of that part of the foreign-exchange market which reflects international transactions between the UK and the USA and other countries that conduct their overseas business in dollars.

### Supply and demand and the price of sterling

The **supply** of pounds on to the foreign-exchange market comes from all those UK residents who wish to exchange them for dollars in order to pay for imports of goods and services or to undertake overseas investment. The **demand** for pounds comes from all those who wish to buy UK exports of goods and services and to invest in the UK. For the moment we will leave out those who buy or sell pounds as a speculative activity rather than for purposes of paying for exports, imports or other international transactions not associated with 'hot money' flows.

Just like in any other free market, the forces of demand and supply eventually produce a price for pounds (in terms of dollars). This represents an **equilibrium** position in that the demand for pounds is equal to the supply of pounds. We have seen that the supply of pounds on to the foreign-exchange market must represent the total value of UK imports and overseas investment, while the demand for pounds represents the total value of UK exports and overseas investment in the UK. So if the supply of pounds is equal to the demand for pounds the UK has neither a deficit nor a surplus on its balance of payments.

Assume, for example, that the equilibrium price for pounds is $1.50, i.e. the exchange rate is £1 = $1.50. Suppose that the UK then experiences a period of inflation causing a serious loss of competiveness. This will then reduce the demand for UK exports while also increasing the demand for imports. The resulting balance of payments deficit will mean that the supply of pounds is now greater than the demand for pounds. If the forces of supply and demand are allowed to operate freely, just as in any other market the excess supply of pounds will depress the price until once again the supply and demand are equal and an equilibrium price is re-established.

If, for example, the new market price for pounds is $1.25, this means that the new exchange rate is £1 = $1.25. Another way of describing this fall in the price of pounds is to say that the pound has gone down in value (i.e. **depreciated**), since a pound will now buy $1.25 compared to the original amount of $1.50. Looked at from the point of view of anyone buying pounds, they are much cheaper than before; each pound now costs only $1.25 rather than $1.50.

### Supporting the exchange rate

For various reasons, however (see page 148), the government may not be willing to accept a fall in the exchange rate and will therefore intervene in the foreign exchange markets to protect the value of the pound. As with any other price support scheme, this will involve the government in buying up the excess supply of pounds which is threatening to depress its value. In other words, the government adds its demand to the now lower market demand in order to raise the total demand to a level that will absorb the supply of pounds at the original price of $1.50. This **support buying** will be conducted on behalf of the government by the Bank of England 'stepping into the market'. Just like any other buyer of pounds, the Bank of England will have to sell dollars in exchange for pounds, and this involves calling upon the country's **official reserves** of gold and foreign currencies.

*Use of official reserves*
These reserves will have been accumulated during those periods when the economy was running a balance of payments surplus, i.e. when exports and overseas investment into the UK exceeded imports and UK investment overseas. During these periods of a UK balance of payment surplus the demand for pounds exceeded the supply of pounds. In the absence of any government intervention in the foreign-exchange market this would have produced a rise in the price of the pound to perhaps $1.65, i.e. a rise in the exchange rate to £1 = $1.65. Just as we have assumed that the government wishes to avoid a fall in the exchange rate, let us also assume that during such times it wanted to prevent a rise. It would therefore deal with this shortage of pounds in the foreign-exchange market by adding to the supply, i.e. selling pounds in exchange for dollars.

The government can use these dollars to buy

gold to hold as a reserve. But because gold does not give a return in the form of a rate of interest, the dollars would have been used to acquire assets in the USA such as US government stock and more liquid assets. Some of these dollars may also have been converted into other currencies to acquire assets in other countries which generally have sound and stable currencies. All these assets represent the UK's official foreign currency reserves.

When the government is faced with a balance of payments deficit, it will convert some of these overseas assets into dollars and use them to buy pounds in the foreign-exchange market. If the balance of payments deficit proves to be more serious than the government thought, it may be obliged to support its reserve position by borrowing from the US government via its federal reserve system (the US central bank) or from the **International Monetary Fund.**

The government's reserve and borrowing facilities are limited. If the deficit widens, the position may be aggravated by speculation that the government may be eventually obliged to withdraw its support for the pound and allow it to fall to a more realistic level. As speculators move their money out of the UK this increased selling of pounds will put even greater pressure on the rapidly dwindling official reserves if the government is to continue to defend the exchange rate.

*Fiscal and monetary measures*
The government will then have to take urgent steps to stem the 'run' on the pound by implementing policies that seek to restore **international confidence** in the future value of the pound. This is likely to involve the use of the **deflationary fiscal and monetary measures** described in Chapters 6 and 7. Such measures, however, are essentially the means of tackling the immediate problem of the balance of payments deficit and are therefore aimed at the symptoms of the problem rather than the fundamental economic ills that have given rise to the persistent deficit. Deflationary measures do not themselves solve the economy's problems but simply provide a breathing-space during which the government should implement longer-term measures aimed at curing the loss of international competitiveness.

The government must seek to create an economic climate that is conducive to the develop-ment of new and improved products and the growth of new industries to replace those that are in decline. It must also pursue policies that will stimulate the development of new skills, so that overall economic growth of the economy is not frustrated by labour shortages in certain skills.

**'Pegged' currency adjustment**
We have seen that both deflationary and protective measures cannot necessarily be relied upon to create an economic climate that will help to bring about the fundamental changes needed to restore competitiveness and produce a long-term improvement in the balance of payments. Despite government intervention in the foreign-exchange market, a serious and persistent balance of payments problem may eventually force the government to accept a lower exchange rate. Such **adjustments in the exchange rate** are a means of providing a breathing-space that avoids the need for a severe deflation of the economy.

In these circumstances the government has to estimate what a more realistic exchange rate will be and then allow the rate to fall until it reaches the desired level. It will then 'peg' the exchange rate at this level by taking the necessary action to support it. The government will hope that the devaluation is large enough to stem the pressure on the pound so that it will no longer be required to call upon its reserves to support the new exchange rate.

*How a 'pegged' devaluation affects export and import prices*
Assume, for example, that an adjustable peg system is in operation, and the current exchange rate is £1 = $1.50. This means that an executive-type car priced at £16,000 in the UK will sell for $24,000 in the USA; whereas a small computer priced at $6000 in the USA will sell for £4000 in the UK. If the pound is then devalued to $1.25, the price of the car in the US market will fall to $20,000 while the price of the US computer in the UK will rise to £4800.

The devaluation has therefore made the UK motor-vehicle manufacturer and other exporters more competitive in the US market. Not only have UK exporters become more competitive when facing competition from US producers; they will also be in a stronger position when competing with other foreign producers in the

US market. The devaluation has also increased the sterling price of the US computer in the UK market, and this will strengthen the competitive position of the UK's own computer manufacturers. Since the adjustment in the exchange rate will have involved a devaluation of the pound against other currencies, this will also make UK exports in general more competitive in other parts of the world while also raising the sterling price of imports from other countries. The resulting increase in the demand for UK exports and the fall in imports will contribute to an improvement in the balance of payments.

Until 1972 the UK adhered to this adjustable peg system. In the post-war period it resorted to only two such acts of devaluation to deal with balance of payments problems. Successive governments tended to use a variety of deflationary measures to improve the balance of payments because of the disadvantages that were associated with a greater degree of flexibility in the exchange rate.

## A FLOATING EXCHANGE RATE SYSTEM

If the exchange rate is freed totally from government intervention, the value of the pound on the foreign-exchange market will be determined by the forces of demand and supply. A simple demand and supply diagram can be used to appreciate how such an exchange rate system operates. In Fig. 9.1 the vertical axis shows the price of pounds expressed in dollars (i.e. the exchange rate), and the horizontal axis measures the quantity of pounds bought and sold per period of time.

The **demand schedule** for pounds slopes downwards from left to right. A high exchange rate will make UK exports relatively more expensive than those produced by other countries, and the low demand for UK exports will therefore be reflected in a low level of demand for pounds on the foreign-exchange market. When the exchange rate is at a much lower level, however, this will make UK exports much more attractive; the greater demand for exports will mean a higher demand for pounds. The **supply schedule** for pounds slopes upwards from left to right. A high exchange rate will make imports relatively cheaper in the UK mar-

ket, and the high demand for imports will be reflected in a large supply of pounds on to the foreign-exchange market. A low exchange rate will raise the price of imports, and the lower demand will mean a smaller supply of pounds on to the foreign-exchange markets. The reader can confirm the effect of a high exchange rate upon the prices of UK exports and imports and hence the demand for them by raising the exchange rate from £1 = \$1.50 to £1 = \$1.75 in the example on page 146.

Both the demand and supply schedules in Fig. 9.1 are based on the assumption that all the other factors that are likely to affect the demand for UK exports and imports – such as relative rates of inflation in various countries and the non-price factors that influence demand – remain unchanged.

In Fig. 9.1 the market has produced an equilibrium exchange rate of £1 = \$1.60. This must also indicate that the UK has neither a deficit nor a surplus on its balance of payments. Now assume that an increase in inflation in the UK relative to that in other manufacturing economies leads to lower exports and higher imports. This will be reflected in a leftward shift of the demand schedule for pounds from $D_1$ to $D_2$

**Fig. 9.1: Floating exchange rate**

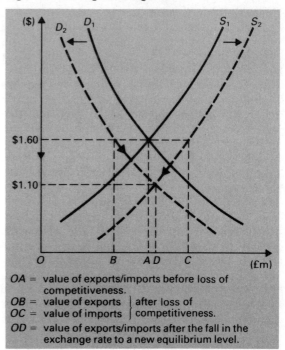

OA = value of exports/imports before loss of competitiveness.
OB = value of exports ⎫ after loss of
OC = value of imports ⎭ competitiveness.
OD = value of exports/imports after the fall in the exchange rate to a new equilibrium level.

and a rightward shift of the supply schedule from $S_1$ to $S_2$. The supply of pounds at an exchange rate of £1 = \$1.60 is now greater than the demand, and this will cause the exchange rate to fall. As the exchange rate falls, however, this will help to offset some of the initial loss of competitiveness; the demand for UK exports will start to recover, which in Fig. 9.1 is shown by a downward movement along $D_2$. Similarly, the fall in the level of imports is shown by a downward movement along $S_2$. The fall in the exchange rate will continue until it again reaches a new market equilibrium. This occurs when £1 = \$1.10 and means that the UK no longer has a balance of payments deficit.

### Some problems with a floating exchange rate
The previous demand and supply analysis of how a floating exchange rate system operates or the effects of devaluing under the adjustable peg system would seem to suggest that greater flexibility in the value of the pound can always be relied upon to deal with a balance of payments deficit. However, the following factors must be taken into account when the government decides to allow the exchange rate to float or to peg it at a lower level.

*Price elasticity of demand*
How far the exchange rate has to fall before the balance of payments deficit is removed will depend upon how sensitive the demand for both imports and exports is to changes in price. If the demand for both UK imports and exports of manufactures proves to be elastic, then only a relatively small reduction in the exchange rate will be needed to bring about the desired improvement in the balance of payments.

If, however, the demand for such UK imports and exports is relatively **inelastic**, then a very large reduction in the exchange rate may be needed before the demand proves sufficiently responsive to overcome the deficit in the balance of payments. This will be the case if the prices of manufactured goods in the UK are already well in excess of those abroad, or if they are distinctly lacking in non-price qualities such as design, reliability, after-sales services and delivery dates. In this case a very large fall in the relative prices of UK manufactures will have to occur before they reach more competitive levels or where the lower prices more than compen-

sate for their deficiencies with respect to non-price factors.

The larger the fall in the exchange rate that is needed to improve the balance of payments, the more serious are many of the problems associated with such a policy, discussed below.

*Responsiveness of UK producers*
Even if the demand for both imports and exports proves to be relatively elastic, the benefits of a fall in the exchange rate will depend upon the ability of UK producers to respond to an increase in the demand for their output. A lack of investment in an earlier period, resulting partly from the effects of 'stop–go' policies and a general lack of business confidence, may mean a **shortage of capacity**. Producers may not be able to increase their output at a rate which can satisfy the increase in demand. If the situation is further aggravated by **shortages of skills**, inflationary pressures may then be increased. So the competitive advantage provided by the fall in the exchange rate may soon be wiped out.

If the government believes that the manufacturing sector is not in a position to cope with an increase in demand, the fall in the exchange rate may have to be accompanied by deflationary measures. In deflating the total level of demand in the economy, the government will aim to make room for the effects of the fall in the exchange rate by ensuring that sufficient capacity is released to meet the increased demand for both import substitutes and exports. However, these deflationary measures may then depress the level of business confidence and threaten the very investment which is needed to achieve improvements in productivity and the development of new products.

*Worsening terms of trade*
A fall in the exchange rate will reduce the amount of foreign exchange which the UK earns per unit exported. In our examination of the theory of comparative advantage we noted how a movement in the terms of trade will lead to a redistribution of the gains from trade (see page 125). A fall in the exchange rate will in fact lead to an **unfavourable movement** in the UK's **terms of trade** because less foreign exchange will be earned per unit exported. Although the UK government will hope that the fall in the exchange rate will reduce the volume of imports, particularly in the case of manufactures,

the economy will now have to export more to pay for each item that is still imported. This amounts to an unfavourable movement in the UK's terms of trade.

When the exchange rate falls, the UK as a whole experiences a fall in its average standard of living, because it is obliged to give up a larger slice of its national 'cake' in exchange for the same slice of another country's national cake. Using the example of the car exports on page 146: prior to the fall in the exchange rate the export of 1000 cars would earn enough to pay for £24 million worth of imports. Afte the fall in the exchange rate, however, the UK would have to export 1200 cars to pay for £24 million worth of imports. If the exchange rate continued to fall because of a failure to tackle the root cause of the growing loss of competitiveness, this would mean that the UK's terms of trade would become even more unfavourable and lead to a further decline in the average standard of living in the UK.

*Rise in the cost of living*
Having established that a fall in the exchange rate does impose a cost upon the economy in terms of having to sacrifice (export) more to pay for imports, we can also trace how such a movement in the exchange rate will affect the **cost of living**. The effect is similar to that of an import duty which raises the prices of imports. If consumers continue to buy certain imports they will suffer from a rise in their cost of living. This will be the case even if they turn to home-produced goods and services, because it is the rate of inflation of prices in the domestic economy which brought about the fall in the exchange rate in the first place. Whichever way consumers turn, therefore, they will now be faced with higher prices than before, which will reduce the level of their real incomes and hence their standard of living.

The fall in the exchange rate will also raise the costs of energy and raw materials imports, while some business organisations may still import components and certain items of capital equipment, despite their higher prices, because of the competitive nature of their non-price features. This will then be reflected in higher prices and will offset part of the competitiveness advantage which the fall in the exchange rate has given to UK exporters. The general rise in the cost of living may also provoke wage in-

creases and additional inflationary pressures, and this will mean a further erosion of the initial competitive advantage.

*Short-sighted price increases*
If business organisations do not anticipate any marked improvement in the economic environment of the domestic economy and fear that the competitive advantage provided by the fall in the exchange rate is only likely to be temporary, they may not be prepared to invest their resources in consolidating their newly acquired export markets. Some business organisations may be tempted to reap higher profits in the short run by **raising their prices**.

If, for example, the UK motor-vehicle manufacturer on page 146 responded to the fall in the exchange rate by raising its prices by 10 per cent then instead of selling for $20,000 on the US market it would sell for $22,000. The car is still $2000 cheaper on the US market. Not only may the UK manufacturer sell more cars, but each one now earns £17,600 rather than £16,000. This policy may increase profits in the short run, but had the manufacturer been willing to take full advantage of the fall in the exchange rate and kept the price at £16,000 it may well have increased its sales by a much larger amount. The larger long-run profits would then allow the manufacturer to finance additional investment projects that further increase its share of export markets at the expense of its competitors.

Similarly there may be some business organisations that do not exploit the long-run opportunities by building upon the competitive edge that they have been given when facing competition from overseas suppliers in domestic markets. If business organisations raise their prices to maximise profits in the short run, this will accelerate the erosion of their initial advantage.

*Productivity and business confidence*
If the government is prepared to accept a fall in the exchange rate to compensate for the effects of inflation upon the balance of payments, then neither employers nor trade unions will refrain from price increases or excessive pay claims, because both domestic and export markets will be protected by the fall in the exchange rate. The government must therefore use the breathing-space to tackle inflation and the fundamental causes of the low levels of **productiv-**

ity. By allowing the exchange rate to depreciate, however, it should be able to avoid the serious effects upon the level of **business confidence** of the exceptionally severe deflation that would otherwise be needed to deal with a balance of payment deficit.

Those who support a more flexible exchange rate believe that the level of business confidence may actually start to improve if investment decisions are no longer influenced by the prospect that the government will immediately deflate the economy as soon as any inflationary pressures are felt on the balance of payments. If there is an upturn in investment, the resulting improvement in productivity will help to moderate the rise in unit costs, while the fall in inflation will also improve the level of real incomes. The more noticeable improvements in living standards may then help to avoid the large pay claims that would be a feature of an otherwise inflationary climate. At the same time, the improved job opportunities and more secure employment may also make it easier for business organisations to introduce changes in working practices that will make a further contribution to an improvement in productivity. The fall in the exchange rate will provide a steady and sustained stimulus to the economy, and this may further raise the level of business confidence and investment in new and improved capacity.

The overall improvement in productivity and falling inflation will allow an improvement in the UK's balance of payments without such a large fall in the exchange rate. This will moderate the unfavourable movement in the UK's terms of trade and the inflationary repercussions of a large adjustment in the exchange rate. The improvement in the UK's trading performance will no longer be the result solely of a fall in the exchange rate, whereby the UK is in effect cutting its overseas prices simply to stay in business, but the result of the greater productivity whereby the economy can now afford to offer more competitive prices for its output.

*Opportunities for speculation*

A floating exchange rate is susceptible to **speculative dealings** whereby large and sudden inflows and outflows of funds produce a period of intense instability and uncertainty in foreign-exchange markets. The speculative buying and selling of pounds will lead to unpredictable fluctuations in the exchange rate. The resulting effects upon import costs and export prices will make it very difficult for UK producers to plan their longer-term business strategies with confidence.

It may take only a rumour of adverse developments in either the UK or the world economy to trigger off such speculation. Even if the developments do materialise, the movement to a more realistic exchange rate may be preceded by a period during which the value of the pound fluctuates wildly before it eventually settles at a more stable and appropriate level. In 1985, for example, the pound–dollar exchange rate averaged £1 = $1.30, but during the course of the year the pound's value fluctuated between $1.03 and $1.44.

## THE UK ECONOMY AND INTERNATIONAL COMPETITIVENESS

Between 1980 and 1982 the benefits derived from North Sea oil meant that the UK was able to enjoy large surpluses on its visible trade. The visible balance, as shown in Table 9.5, then moved back into deficit; but the surpluses on invisible trade still allowed the UK's current account to remain in overall surplus. The rapid fall in the world price of oil, however, emphasised the urgent need to improve the competitive position of the UK's manufacturing sector. The deterioriation in the visible balance was also the result of imports of manufactures growing faster than manufactured exports. If this trend continues, the surplus on the invisible balance will no longer be able to offset the deficit on the visible balance. A position will be reached where the UK will not be earning enough from its exports of goods and services to pay for its imports.

The general **loss of competitiveness** of UK manufacturers is indicated in Table 9.6. This shows that by 1986 exports of manufactures were only 14 per cent above their 1980 level. The data also show that, although the growing recession in the UK initially reduced the volume of imports of manufactures, by 1986 they were nearly 49 per cent above their 1980 level. This rapid growth in imports occurred during a period when there was rising unemployment and when the real level of consumer expenditure increased by only 12 per cent. A particular-

**Table 9.5: UK Balance of payments current account (£ million)**

| | Seasonally adjusted | | | | | | | Not seasonally adjusted |
|---|---|---|---|---|---|---|---|---|
| | | Visible trade | | | Invisibles | | | |
| | Exports | Imports | Visible balance | Credits | Debits | Invisible balance | Current balance | Current balance |
| 1980 | 47,422 | 46,061 | 1361 | 25,934 | 23,818 | 2116 | 3477 | 3477 |
| 1981 | 50,977 | 47,617 | 3360 | 56,666 | 53,800 | 2866 | 6226 | 6226 |
| 1982 | 55,565 | 53,234 | 2331 | 64,680 | 62,979 | 1701 | 4032 | 4032 |
| 1983 | 60,776 | 61,611 | −835 | 65,225 | 61,227 | 3998 | 3163 | 3163 |
| 1984 | 70,367 | 74,758 | −4391 | 77,192 | 71,239 | 5953 | 1562 | 1562 |
| 1985 | 78,072 | 80,140 | −2068 | 81,074 | 75,243 | 5831 | 3763 | 3763 |
| 1986 | 72,842 | 81,096 | −8254 | 75,880 | 68,726 | 7154 | −1100 | −1100 |

Source: *Monthly Digest of Statistics*, April 1986, HMSO.

**Table 9.6: Export and import volume index numbers (seasonally adjusted; 1980 = 100)**

| | Total | Food beverages and tobacco | Basic materials | Fuels | Total manufactures | Manufactures excluding erratics | | | | | | | |
|---|---|---|---|---|---|---|---|---|---|---|---|---|---|
| | | | | | | Total | Semi-manufactures excluding precious stones and silver | | | Finished manufactures excluding ships, North Sea installations and aircraft | | | |
| | | | | | | | Total | Chemicals | Other | Total | Passenger motor cars | Other consumer | Intermediate | Capital |
| **Exports** | | | | | | | | | | | | | |
| (Weights) | (1000) | (69) | (31) | (136) | (735) | (658) | (252) | (112) | (141) | (406) | (18) | (71) | (170) | (147) |
| 1981 | 98.9 | 105 | 96 | 121 | 94 | 97 | 98 | 102 | 95 | 96 | 99 | 96 | 98 | 94 |
| 1982 | 101.6 | 107 | 94 | 133 | 95 | 97 | 99 | 106 | 93 | 96 | 94 | 94 | 99 | 95 |
| 1983 | 102.2 | 110 | 101 | 148 | 93 | 94 | 102 | 113 | 93 | 90 | 86 | 96 | 99 | 87 |
| 1984 | 112.8 | 117.2 | 106.3 | 160.2 | 104.4 | 107 | 112.1 | 124.3 | 102.3 | 103.8 | 82.4 | 107.8 | 105.4 | 102.6 |
| 1985 | 119.3 | 119.1 | 107 | 170.9 | 110.8 | 115.7 | 118.9 | 133.3 | 107.5 | 113.7 | 99.4 | 111.6 | 121.4 | 107.6 |
| 1986 | 123.6 | 129.6 | 117.1 | 175.5 | 114 | 116.9 | 121.9 | 139.4 | 108.1 | 113.8 | 93.2 | 117.5 | 120.4 | 106.9 |
| **Imports** | | | | | | | | | | | | | |
| (Weights) | (1000) | (124) | (81) | (138) | (626) | (543) | (217) | (63) | (154) | (326) | (42) | (94) | (96) | (94) |
| 1981 | 96.1 | 103 | 95 | 82 | 98 | 105 | 103 | 113 | 99 | 106 | 96 | 114 | 106 | 102 |
| 1982 | 100.1 | 108 | 93 | 75 | 106 | 115 | 111 | 123 | 107 | 117 | 110 | 113 | 120 | 122 |
| 1983 | 107.8 | 108 | 104 | 67 | 119 | 128 | 123 | 143 | 115 | 131 | 125 | 125 | 129 | 142 |
| 1984 | 120.2 | 112.3 | 101.7 | 86.5 | 134.1 | 146.7 | 137.2 | 164.5 | 125.9 | 153 | 119.9 | 139.6 | 161.4 | 172.9 |
| 1985 | 124.3 | 113.6 | 102.2 | 85 | 140.7 | 154.5 | 143.9 | 176.2 | 130.6 | 161.5 | 127.9 | 139.6 | 172.8 | 187.2 |
| 1986 | 132.8 | 123.5 | 108.7 | 93.4 | 148.2 | 163 | 152 | 188 | 137.2 | 171 | 131.6 | 158.3 | 187 | 183.1 |

Source: *Monthly Digest of Statistics*, May 1987, HMSO.

ly serious trend was the growth in the volume of imports of industrial products such as chemicals and capital goods which used to be major earners of foreign exchange for the UK economy. It is important, therefore, to examine the developments which contributed to the loss of competitiveness and the serious trend in the UK's trade in manufactures.

### The exchange rate

*The exchange rate index*
The information in Table 9.7 gives the pound–dollar exchange rate and what is known as the sterling **exchange rate index** (ERI). The ERI is used because it measures the overall change in

**Table 9.7: Exchange rate, US $ and sterling exchange rate index**

|      | US $ | Exchange rate index (980 = 100) |
|------|------|---------------------------------|
| 1876 | 1.81 | 89.1  |
| 1977 | 1.75 | 84.6  |
| 1978 | 1.92 | 84.9  |
| 1979 | 2.12 | 90.9  |
| 1980 | 2.33 | 100.0 |
| 1981 | 2.03 | 98.9  |
| 1982 | 1.75 | 94.2  |
| 1983 | 1.52 | 86.7  |
| 1984 | 1.34 | 81.9  |
| 1985 | 1.30 | 81.5  |
| 1986 | 1.47 | 75.9  |

Source: *National Institute Economic Review*, May 1987, National Institute of Economic and Social Research.

the value of the pound against a 'basket' of other currencies rather than just the dollar. The USA is a large market for UK exports and is also a major source of imports, while oil imports and many of the commodities from the developing countries are also priced in US dollars. The dollar exchange rate is therefore still very significant, particularly in connection with UK industries' import costs; but a floating exchange rate system means that it is important to measure the movements in the average exchange rate for the pound against other currencies as a whole.

It is possible, for example, for the dollar to strengthen or weaken against all the major currencies including the pound. To concentrate solely upon the pound–dollar rate may then give a misleading impression of how exchange rate developments affect the competitive position of the UK in the world economy. The ERI is a more reliable guide to competitiveness, because it takes account of the fact that the pound may be appreciating against some currencies while depreciating against others.

The ERI is calculated by taking a weighted average of the sterling exchange rate against seventeen other currencies ranging from the dollar to the Finnish mark. The weight allocated to each currency reflects its relative importance to the UK's trade in terms of imports and exports. The importance of the dollar is shown

by the fact that it accounts for approximately 25 per cent of the weighted index.

*Why sterling rose and fell*
Table 9.7 shows that between 1978 and 1980 there was a very large rise in the value of the pound. Although it then fell against the dollar, it still remained relatively strong when measured on the ERI. Table 9.8 indicates that, during the years covered by the table, 'factory-gate' prices in the UK rose by approximately 76 per cent, compared with 20 per cent in Japan, 33 per cent in West Germany and an average of 62 per cent for all the developed economies. Rather than an appreciation in the exchange rate, then, we might have expected it to *fall*; but it was not until 1984 that the ERI eventually fell below its 1978 level. During this period, therefore, the movement in the exchange rate did not compensate for the loss of competiveness caused by the UK's relatively high rate of inflation.

The initial rise in the exchange rate was in fact caused by the development of North Sea oil at a time of a large increase in the world price of oil. Political instability in the Middle East also made the UK an attractive place for overseas funds seeking an economy that would be better placed to withstand a second oil crisis. The government's reliance upon higher interest rates as a means of tackling inflation via control of the money supply also stimulated an inflow of funds into the UK. These developments led to a very large increase in the demand for pounds on foreign-exchange markets and produced a significant rise in the exchange rate.

The UK manufacturing sector had, as a result, to face high rates of interest and inflationary increases in costs. Many people believe that the rise in the exchange rate was largely responsible for the loss of competiveness that made it increasingly difficult for UK organisations to export, while also promoting further import penetration of their domestic markets. It is also argued that the resulting decline in the size of the UK's manufacturing sector and the effect upon the level of business confidence and investment helped prolong the adverse trend in the UK's trade in manufactures during the following years.

After 1980 the pound, along with other currencies, fell against the dollar. A period of very high interest rates in the USA caused a large shift of funds out of the UK and other manufac-

**Table 9.8: Prices in OECD industrial countries (index: 1980 = 100)**

| | | Producer prices of manufactures | | | | | | | | | Consumer prices[1] | | | | | | |
| | USA | Canada | Japan | France | West Germany | Italy | UK | OECD total | USA | Canada | Japan | France | West Germany | Italy | UK | OECD total |
|---|---|---|---|---|---|---|---|---|---|---|---|---|---|---|---|---|
| 1976 | 69.1 | 65.4 | 81.4 | 73.7 | 85.8 | 58.2 | 60.9 | 72.8 | 69.1 | 70.7 | 79.7 | 66.7 | 85.5 | 54.8 | 59.6 | 68.7 |
| 1977 | 73.6 | 70.6 | 83.7 | 77.8 | 88.2 | 68.6 | 72.0 | 77.5 | 73.5 | 76.4 | 86.1 | 72.9 | 88.6 | 64.1 | 69.0 | 74.7 |
| 1978 | 79.4 | 77.0 | 83.0 | 81.1 | 88.9 | 75.8 | 79.1 | 81.2 | 79.2 | 83.2 | 89.4 | 79.5 | 91.0 | 71.9 | 74.7 | 80.7 |
| 1979 | 88.2 | 88.2 | 87.2 | 92.0 | 93.4 | 84.9 | 87.7 | 88.8 | 88.1 | 90.8 | 92.6 | 88.1 | 94.8 | 82.5 | 84.8 | 88.6 |
| 1980 | 100.0 | 100.0 | 100.0 | 100.0 | 100.0 | 100.0 | 100.0 | 100.0 | 100.0 | 100.0 | 100.0 | 100.0 | 100.0 | 100.0 | 100.0 | 100.0 |
| 1981 | 109.3 | 110.2 | 101.1 | 113.4 | 106.0 | 117.2 | 109.5 | 108.8 | 110.4 | 112.5 | 104.9 | 113.4 | 106.3 | 117.8 | 111.9 | 110.5 |
| 1982 | 113.7 | 116.9 | 101.6 | 123.4 | 111.1 | 134.6 | 118.0 | 115.1 | 117.1 | 124.6 | 107.7 | 126.8 | 111.9 | 137.3 | 121.5 | 119.1 |
| 1983 | 115.6 | 120.9 | 100.8 | 137.0 | 112.8 | 151.1 | 124.4 | 120.2 | 120.9 | 131.9 | 109.7 | 139.0 | 115.6 | 157.3 | 127.1 | 125.4 |
| 1984 | 118.0 | 125.9 | 100.8 | 155.2 | 116.0 | 165.8 | 132.1 | 126.8 | 126.1 | 137.6 | 112.1 | 149.3 | 118.4 | 174.3 | 133.4 | 132.0 |
| 1985 | 119.1 | 129.2 | 100.0 | 161.5 | 118.4 | 179.2 | 139.4 | 131.3 | 130.6 | 143.0 | 114.4 | 158.0 | 121.0 | 190.4 | 141.5 | 138.1 |
| 1986 | 117.3 | 131.8 | 95.1 | 149.6 | 114.9 | 187.3 | 145.7 | 130.0 | 133.1 | 149.0 | 114.9 | 162.2 | 120.7 | 201.4 | 146.3 | 141.2 |

[1] The retail price index for the UK and broadly similar series for other countries.

Source: *National Institute Economic Review*, May 1987, National Institute of Economic and Social Research.

turing economies and into the USA. The value of the pound was also increasingly affected by a fall in the world price of oil. These speculative movements of capital recognised that a further fall in the oil price would seriously undermine the UK economy at a time when its manufacturing sector was not in a position to compensate for the resulting adverse effects upon the UK's trading position. The UK government was concerned that a continuing fall in the pound–dollar exchange rate would prevent it from achieving a further reduction in inflation because of the potential effects upon the costs of imported oil and commodities priced in dollars. Higher interest rates may help to stem the outflow of funds which put pressure on the exchange rate, but they will also prevent the fall in the ERI which is necessary to compensate for a rate of inflation higher than that in other manufacturing economies.

Thus by 1985 the pound was still relatively strong in terms of the ERI. Since the measurement of the ERI would have taken account of the very large fall in the pound–dollar rate, this suggests that the pound was still exceptionally high against some of the other major currencies. In fact between the beginning of 1983 and the end of 1985 the overall fall in the pound against the West German mark was less than 4 per cent while it hardly moved at all against the Netherlands' guilder and the Belgian franc. Because these are some of the UK's major export markets and sources of imports (see page 139), the exchange rate failed to provide the UK with any significant advantage by more than compensat-

ing for its loss of competitiveness in the earlier periods. Also, the fall in the value of the pound against the Japanese yen of about 20 per cent between 1983 and 1985 was much smaller than one would have expected when comparing the rates of inflation in the two countries.

**Productivity**
Since 1980 the UK has achieved improvements in the productivity of its manufacturing sector which compare more favourably with the performances of other economies – see Table 9.9.

**Table 9.9: Productivity in OECD industrial countries (seasonally adjusted; index: 1980 = 100)**

| | Output per person-hour in manufacturing | | | | | | |
| | USA | Canada | Japan | France | West Germany | Italy | UK |
|---|---|---|---|---|---|---|---|
| 1976 | 92 | 91 | 80 | 85 | 91 | 86 | 98 |
| 1977 | 94 | 94 | 84 | 88 | 94 | 85 | 100 |
| 1978 | 95 | 98 | 91 | 92 | 96 | 88 | 101 |
| 1979 | 98 | 100 | 97 | 99 | 100 | 96 | 101 |
| 1980 | 100 | 100 | 100 | 100 | 100 | 100 | 100 |
| 1981 | 103 | 101 | 100 | 101 | 102 | 104 | 105 |
| 1982 | 108 | 100 | 100 | 105 | 104 | 104 | 110 |
| 1983 | 114 | 107 | 103 | 109 | 110 | 106 | 119 |
| 1984 | 119 | 120 | 112 | 115 | 113 | 112 | 124 |
| 1985 | 124 | 121 | 116 | 119 | 119 | 115 | 128 |
| 1986 | 127 | 121 | 116 | 121 | 120 | — | 131 |

Source: *National Institute Economic Review*, May 1987, National Institute of Economic and Social Research.

The need to raise productivity has been an essential theme in our examination of the competitiveness of the economy and its ability to take advantage of any upturn in the level of world trade. The recession and high borrowing costs produced a financial climate which forced business organisations to pay more attention to their labour costs. Industries have shed labour, and this will help them not only to charge more competitive prices but also to achieve savings that will reduce the level of their borrowing at a time of high interest rates.

In the short term, changes in working practices can lead to a more efficient use of labour. Between 1980 and 1985 the total output of the UK's manufacturing sector increased by approximately 4 per cent, while total employment in this sector fell by about 20 per cent. This indicates that those manufacturing companies which survived the earlier recession had drastically cut the size of their workforces in an effort to reduce their **unit labour costs.**

In the long run, the ultimate determinant of further improvements in productivity is the **level of investment** in new plant, machinery and equipment. There is a limit to the extent to which a manufacturer can continue to rely upon changes in working practices and a reduction in the number of employees in an effort to raise productivity. Investment in new and improved capacity is vital to ensure that manufacturers can cope with an upturn in the level of demand and that future levels of productivity will help to avoid the shortages and inflationary pressures that will mean lost exports and rising imports.

*Capital expenditure and modernisation*
Between 1980 and 1982 the level of **capital expenditure** in the UK manufacturing sector fell by approximately 27 per cent. Although it then recovered, by 1985 it was still 12 per cent below its 1980 level. The recession, high interest rates and fluctuating exchange rates have inhibited the investment upon which competitiveness depends in the long run. For example, the UK's use of industrial robots and degree of modernisation are proportionately much smaller than those of its main competitors. In fact the rate of introduction of robots *fell* after 1985, whereas before then the number of firms using robots had increased at a rate of 50 per cent a year.

At the beginning of 1986 there were 3208 robots in use in the UK, but this total number was less than the number by which the robot population in West Germany increased during the course of 1985. At the beginning of 1986 there were only 740 factories in the UK using robots, i.e. only about one factory in 40. It remains to be seen whether the rate of modernisation of the manufacturing sector can help to sustain the improvements in productivity which occurred in the earlier period.

**Wage costs**
Despite improvements in productivity the potential effect upon the UK's competitive position can be more than offset by percentage **pay increases** which are higher than those in other manufacturing economies. This has been the case in recent years in the UK. Pay increases have prevented the improvements in productivity from being reflected in a comparable improvement in the competitive position of the UK in terms of unit labour costs.

The extent to which the government can reduce the rate of increase of unit labour costs depends upon its ability to create an economic environment that both encourages investment and leads to lower pay awards. In particular, any upturn in the rate of inflation will make it more difficult to secure lower pay increases. There is also the possibility that, despite very high levels of unemployment and the introduction of legislation which has reduced the threat of industrial action by trade unions in support of pay claims, there is still a shortage of certain skills. Competition in the labour market may therefore produce excessive pay increases in some parts of the economy.

Activity 9.3
Assume that the UK has total visible imports of £90 billion and visible exports of £84 billion. The elasticity of demand for imports and exports is 1.2 and 1.6 respectively.

(a) What will be the effect upon the UK's visible trade balance if the sterling exchange rate index falls by 20 per cent?
(b) What would be the effect upon the visible balance if there was the same fall in the sterling exchange rate index but the elasticity of demand for imports and exports was 0.8 and 0.6 respectively?

# 10. The Newly Industrialising Countries and World Trade in Primary Products

## THE NEWLY INDUSTRIALISING COUNTRIES

The rapid growth of imports to the industrialised world of manufactures from the developing countries of the world has attracted a great deal of attention since the early 1970s, when they became a growing source of textiles, clothing and leather, footwear and travel goods. The so-called **newly industralising countries** (NICs) have accounted for the bulk of these imports from the developing countries. The term NICs is generally used to describe the top seven countries in Fig. 10.1.

### Employment and wages in the NICs
These imports from the NICs are highly competitive. The producers in the developing countries can take advantage of a workforce which has few alternative sources of employment, and this is reflected in very **low wages**. The producers in the fully industralised manufacturing economies exert pressure upon their governments to protect their domestic markets from what they regard as unfair competition from 'sweated-labour' products. The home industries claim that they are paying a good living wage to their workers, who, in turn, are concerned about the threat to their jobs.

The difference in the wage levels between the developed economies and the NICs is a reflection of their respective **stages of economic development**. Unlike in the advanced manufacturing economies, the labour market in the NICs works completely in favour of the employers, who do not have to pay very high wages to recruit or retain their workers. The manufactures exported by the NICs tend to be the products of **labour-intensive industries**, where a great deal of **unskilled work** is done by hand, and wages are low. By contrast, the higher wages paid in the advanced manufacturing economies tend to be in **capital-intensive industries**, where the workforce is more skilled in order to handle complicated machinery. The higher wages are partly the result of **market forces**; where skills are in short supply, this also strengthens the bargaining power of groups of workers when negotiating pay increases.

### 'Sweated labour'
The term 'sweated labour' implies that the workers in the NIC are being exploited by their employers. In many instances they work long hours for very low pay, in crowded, dangerous and unhealthy working conditions. Developing countries have very few rules and regulations to govern **health and safety** at work and **employment conditions.** Their growing population, combined with a lack of employment opportunities in the agricultural sector, has driven many millions of people to move to the urban areas and to compete for the jobs that are available in manufacturing.

These economies are passing through a stage in the process of industrialisation which was experienced in the nineteenth century by the developed economies. It is occurring much more rapidly in the NICs because of the knowledge and the technology available to them and the existence of such large overseas markets for their products. So the employers in the developing countries are 'exploiting' their workers in the same way as did the employers in the UK during the Industrial Revolution. That is, they are taking full advantage of the resource which they have in abundance, namely **labour**, and which is available to them at a low price. Faced with a supply of cheap labour and a shortage of domestic capital, it is hardly surprising that such countries do not employ the capital-intensive techniques which are used in the developed economies.

If the population growth slows down in the developing countries, then, as their economies continue to grow, this will add to the competitive demand for labour. Such pressures should eventually lead to a gradual rise in wages, while also strengthening the bargaining positions of various groups of workers. Also, the gradual adoption of more capital-intensive techniques,

**Fig. 10.1: Individual countries' share of total imports of manufacturers from developing to developed countries, 1979 and 1984**

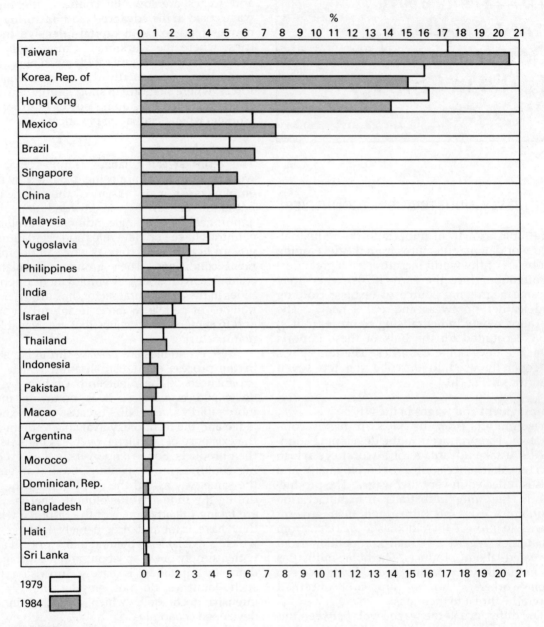

1979 ☐
1984 ▨

Source: OECD.

the need to develop their economic and social infrastructure and the rise in real incomes in these countries should increase the demand for a wide range of goods and services from the developed economies.

**The impact of the NICs**

The governments of the developed economies have had to balance the interests of consumers who wish to buy the goods that are produced by the developing countries with the interests of those workers whose jobs are lost as a result of such imports. The UK government, like those of other manufacturing economies, has used **quotas** to protect its own producers in an effort to bring about a more gradual adjustment to the impact of NIC imports upon traditional areas of employment such as textiles, clothing and leather, footwear and travel goods. In such sectors, employment in the UK fell from more than one million in 1972 to just over half a million in 1984. However, this decline is also the result of imports of these products from other manufacturing economies, such as shoes, clothing and textiles from other members of the European Community.

The UK government, like those of other manufacturing economies with high and persistent unemployment, now faces the prospect of a wider range of imports from the NICs of both finished manufactures and components which are then assembled domestically. This emphasises the need to create an economic environment which will contribute not only to the growth of new industries but also to the regeneration of existing areas of the manufacturing sector. Employment and exports can also be boosted if the UK is seen as an attractive location for more of the operations of US and Japanese **multinationals** that are seeking to increase their sales to the large European markets. A UK location would allow them to avoid the import duties imposed by the European Community on non-members. To attract such overseas investment, the government offers **regional financial incentives**; some trade unions have agreed to **'no-strike' deals** to bring jobs to areas of high unemployment.

The UK currently attracts about 36 per cent of all Japanese investment that flows into Europe, and some recent examples are shown in Fig. 10.2. There is a possibility that the governments of the European Community will increasingly compete for such investment from 'footloose' business organisations. In doing so, they may provide subsidies that distort competition between Community members. This will lead to moves by the European Commission to regulate such incentives and to ensure that they are standardised.

## THE MULTINATIONALS

In recent years the NICs have moved into motor vehicles, home electronics products, furniture and industrial products such as chemicals, steel, machinery, equipment and shipbuilding. In many cases, these developments have been the result of **multinational corporations** shifting part of their operations to the NICs. Argentina, Brazil, Hong Kong, Malaysia, Mexico and Singapore have received most of this investment. The multinationals have been attracted to the NICs for the following reasons:

*Cheap and flexible labour*
In the early part of the 1970s the **wage rates** in the manufacturing economies rose, very rapidly. At the same time, the multinationals felt that **employment laws** made it increasingly difficult for them to lay off and then rehire workers in response to changes in the demand for their products. The NICs would therefore not only be a source of **cheap labour** but could also be more **flexible** in their employment policies, because there was less unionisation and fewer employment laws.

*Labour-intensive production*
Developments in technology have allowed firms to create production methods which reduce their reliance upon skilled labour. Very little training is needed for workers to acquire the skills to perform a series of relatively simple repetitive tasks. This is the case even with a high-technology industry such as electronics; it can use **labour-intensive processes** and assembly techniques to produce finished products which are designed to be labour saving for their eventual users. This has allowed the multinationals to take advantage of the labour force in the developing countries.

*Communications*
Technological advances in **communications** means that the management of multinationals' operations can be conducted from a single base many thousands of miles away from the NICs where their factories and plants are located.

*Transport*
Improvements in both **sea and air transport** have reduced the relative importance of freight charges in total costs. The suppliers of transport

**Fig. 10.2**

# Japanese manufacturing investment* in the UK, 1981-86

Japanese investment in Europe has shown a marked increase in the past few years. Britain has been particularly successful in attracting about 36 per cent of all this investment representing almost twice as much as any other European country.

Currently there are 45 Japanese companies manufacturing in the UK and they cover a range of sectors — from zips (YKK Fasteners) to VTR's (Sanyo), from ball bearings (NSK Bearings) to cars (Nissan) — although electronics is dominant.

Significantly, Japanese firms have introduced modern, highly efficient production techniques and innovative management methods to the UK. Investment decisions made by Japanese companies setting up or expanding in the UK since 1981 are expected to involve capital expenditure of well over £550m and to create or safeguard nearly 12 000 jobs.

| Date | Company | Location | Product |
|---|---|---|---|
| Mar 81 | Yuasa Battery (UK) | Gwent | Sealed lead acid batteries (for electronics industry) |
| Apr 81 | Toshiba Consumer Products (UK) | Plymouth | CTVs VTRs and microwave ovens |
| 1981 | Dainichi-Sykes | Lancs | Final assembly of industrial robots |
| 1982 | NEC Semiconductors (UK) | Scotland | Semi-conductors |
| 1982 | J2T | East Sussex | VTRs |
| Sep 82 | Sanyo Industries (UK) | Suffolk | CTVs, VTRs and Hi-fi |
| Jun 83 | Mitsubishi Electric UK | West Lothian | Video tape recorders |
| Nov 83 | Maxell UK | Shropshire | VHS video tapes and floppy disks |
| 1983 | Ricoh UK Products | Shropshire | Photocopiers and associated products |
| Mar 84 | Sharp Manufacturing Co of UK | North Wales | VTRs microwave ovens, and electronic typewriters |
| Mar 84 | Hitachi Consumer Products (UK) | Mid Glamorgan | Colour tvs |
| Jul 84 | Yamazaki Machinery (UK) | Worcester | Numerically controlled machine tools |
| Nov 84 | Alps Electric (UK) | Milton Keynes | Turners and modulators for VCRs |
| Nov 84 | IWAX | Northern Ireland | Disposable cigarette lighters |
| Dec 84 | Tabuchi Electric (UK) | Cleveland | Transformers for CTVs, VTRs and microwave ovens |
| 1984 | S P Tyres (UK) | West midlands | Car tyres and inner tubes |
| 1984 | Shin-Etsu Handotai | West Lothian | Silicon wafers |
| 1984 | Nissan UK | Tyne and Wear | Automobiles |
| Mar 85 | Brother Industries (UK) | Clwyd | Electronic typewriters |
| Oct 85 | Ikeda — Hoover Trim Manufacturing Co | Tyne and Wear | Car seats for Nissan project |
| Oct 85 | BKL Fittings | Worcester | Pipe fittings |
| Dec 85 | DHK (UK) | Carlisle | Retractor springs for car seat belts |
| Dec 85 | Kibun Co (UK) | Lanarkshire | Frozen fish-based products |
| Dec 85 | Komatsu | Tyne and Wear | Hydraulic excavators and wheeled loaders |
| Feb 86 | Tomtin Distillers | Scotland | Whisky distillers |
| Apr 86 | Orion Electric | W Glamorgan | Video tape recorders |
| Jun 86 | Fuji Seal UK | Kent | Heat shrink PVC labels and seals |
| Aug 86 | Kyushu Matsushita Electric UK | Gwent | Typewriters and printers |

* *Recorded by Invest in Britain Bureau, August 1986.*

Source: *British Business*, 12 September 1986.

have been obliged to offer more competitive rates because the relatively slow growth in the volume of world trade has left many of them with excess capacity and high fixed costs. Many of the imports from the NICs such as those based upon microelectronics are relatively low in bulk but high in value; in many cases, this makes air transport more attractive.

### New markets

The multinationals have been attracted to those countries which are close to **large markets** or where they have **expanding internal markets.** The South American countries, for example, have fast growing internal markets, as well as being particularly well located for exporting to North America.

### Special concessions

The governments of the NICs have offered the multinationals **tax-free periods and exemption from foreign-exchange controls,** so that their profits can be repatriated. The NICs also compete among themselves to attract multinational investment by establishing special areas known as free-trade, export-processing or **enterprise zones**, with ready-built factories. They have also invested in international telecommunications and sea and air transport facilities. The import of materials and parts into these zones and the export of goods are also exempt from customs duties. It is estimated that more than fifty-five countries have now set up these special zones; a recent example is the growing importance of the zones which China has established along its border with Hong Kong.

### The 'global factory'

An increasing number of business organisations are following the example set by the multinationals by shifting part of their operations to the NICs to take advantage of the world market in labour. At one time, some of them relied upon migrant workers from the developing countries to work in their factories, but now the increased mobility of business organisations means that more of the work is taken to the workers. This is giving rise to the **'global factory'**. An increasing part of international trade reflects the movement of materials, components and other inputs between different plants or factories, contributing to the overall production process of a single business organisation.

Information technology and satellite communications are also likely to hasten the rise of the **'global office'**. The processing of data by large business organisations involved in the provision of services can increasingly be located in those countries where both office space and clerical rates of pay are lower than those in the large cities of the developed countries.

---

Activity 10.1
Read the article in Fig. 10.3 and then complete the following:

(a) Outline the factors that have stimulated the import of textiles and clothing from Hong Kong and Korea.
(b) Conduct a survey of all the different items of clothing belonging to the members of your family. Combine your results to produce a chart which shows the percentage distribution of clothing according to the country of origin (including the UK).
(c) Divide into groups which will represent the following:
  (i) UK textile and clothing manufacturers most affected by imports;
  (ii) trade-union officials from the areas where more jobs are likely to be lost because of the growth of imports;
  (iii) a consumers' association;
  (iv) UK manufacturers of 'upmarket' clothing who rely upon imported textiles to maintain their competitive position in both domestic and overseas markets;
  (v) the Department of Trade and Industry;
  (vi) textile and clothing manufacturers from other countries in the European Community.

Hold a meeting to discuss a proposal by the government to restrict imports of textiles and clothing by taking unilateral action to reduce import quotas and/or raise import duties.

**Fig. 10.3**

# Imports growth hits UK textiles

By Michael Smith and
Clive Woodcock

Britain's balance of payments in textiles and clothing has deteriorated during 1986 because of continued expansion in imported goods.

Total imports of textiles and clothing grew by 7 per cent to £4.23 billion in the first nine months of 1986 while exports of British-made products was largely unchanged at £2.28 billion.

The British Textile Confederation says that the volume of imported garments was 22 per cent higher than in the same nine months of 1985 and 17 per cent above the intake seen in the same period of 1984.

According to the confederation, the surge in imports has come mainly from producing countries like Hong Kong and Korea whose sales are governed by the Multi Fibre Arrangement.

Import volume from the MFA nations was 21 per cent higher in the opening nine months of 1986 compared with a 1 per cent rise in imports from EEC producers.

The biggest increase in sales came from the Far East, where the six major producers lifted their share of UK clothing imports from 43 to 52 per cent in the first nine months of 1986.

Ian MacArthur, the BTC director said: "It needs to be stressed that these imports came in under the terms of the Multi Fibre Arrangement bi-lateral arrangement between the EEC and the countries concerned, which shows the flexibility allowed to suppplying countries to expand their exports before coming up against limits written into the agreements."

Nevertheless, the BTC still regards the MFA as the best defence for Britain's textile industry against unrestrained imports of cheap clothing.

But Mr MacArthur said that most of the countries sending large and growing quantities of textiles and clothing imposed "intolerable" barriers when Britain tries to export to them.

"The grotesquely high tarrifs and the imports bans or tiny quotas which most of them apply are a scandal of international trade," he said.

On the plus side, there were increased UK exports to Western Europe.

Source: *Guardian*, 12 January 1987.

Activity 10.2

A Japanese company is considering the possibility of establishing a factory in the UK to manufacture or assemble computers. Senior representatives of the Japanese company have already held talks with various officials from other countries to consider alternative locations.

(a) Suggest which representatives from the UK should be invited to a meeting with the management and give reasons for your choice.

(b) Roles should then be allocated to students according to the suggestions agreed upon in (a). A meeting is then held with the Japanese company to discuss the factors that will play an important part in the decision to locate in the UK and to recommend a site for their operations.

(c) At the end of the meeting each student should produce a report which covers the following points:
   (i) the main issues discussed at the meeting;
   (ii) the possible effects upon the UK's balance of payments.

**Table 10.1: World prices of selected commodities**

| | Crude[1] oil | Copper[2] | Tin[2] | Rubber[3] | Cotton[3] | Coffee[3] | Sugar[3] | Wheat[4] |
|---|---|---|---|---|---|---|---|---|
| 1976 | 11.90 | 782 | 4260 | 35.5 | 79.8 | 142.2 | 11.56 | 329.0 |
| 1977 | 12.80 | 750 | 6196 | 37.2 | 72.2 | 228.5 | 8.11 | 255.6 |
| 1978 | 13.09 | 709 | 6692 | 45.0 | 72.3 | 155.8 | 7.82 | 317.9 |
| 1979 | 19.01 | 937 | 7292 | 58.2 | 76.5 | 169.3 | 9.63 | 403.2 |
| 1980 | 31.89 | 938 | 7242 | 64.5 | 99.0 | 152.2 | 28.69 | 450.8 |
| 1981 | 35.88 | 864 | 7076 | 49.2 | 89.2 | 115.8 | 16.94 | 423.6 |
| 1982 | 34.39 | 847 | 7315 | 38.3 | 75.6 | 125.0 | 8.42 | 346.6 |
| 1983 | 29.85 | 1048 | 8590 | 47.8 | 84.1 | 128.0 | 8.44 | 353.6 |
| 1984 | 28.61 | 1033 | 9228 | 42.5 | 81.2 | 141.2 | 5.21 | 351.2 |
| 1985 | 27.99 | 1104 | — | 34.2 | 71.3 | 132.6 | 4.05 | 327.2 |
| 1986 | 15.59 | 937 | — | 36.2 | 57.2 | 170.6 | 6.04 | 287.3 |

[1] OPEC average $ per barrel.
[2] $ per metric tonne.
[3] US cents per lb.
[4] US cents per bushel.

Source: *National Institute Economic Review*, May 1987, National Institute of Economic and Social Research.

## INTERNATIONAL TRADE AND COMMODITY PRICES

Changes in the world prices of **commodities** (used here as the collective term for a wide range of raw materials and basic foodstuffs – see Tables 10.1 and 10.2) have a significant impact upon the UK's total import bill. As is shown in Table 9.1 (pages 137–8), these commodities, along with oil imports, account for a very large percentage of UK imports. Higher commodity prices will also affect the production costs of user industries; higher oil prices, in particular, will mean higher prices for a wide range of goods and services.

The impact of higher raw-material or energy prices upon an organisation's **long-run unit costs** depend upon the following:

- the part which they play in total costs;
- the introduction of new technology which makes a more efficient use of raw materials and energy and reduces wastage;
- the development of synthetic materials and alternative sources of energy;
- a rise in the productivity of labour whereby a reduction in unit labour costs helps to absorb the effect of other increases in costs.

**Table 10.2: Percentage changes in the prices of principal commodity exports of developing countries**

| | Food | Tropical beverages | Vegetable oil seeds and oil | Agricultural raw materials | Minerals, ores and metals |
|---|---|---|---|---|---|
| 1976 | −22.3 | +80.1 | −4.4 | +22.3 | +5.1 |
| 1977 | −7.3 | +76.5 | +27.5 | +5.6 | +6.1 |
| 1978 | +9.5 | −28.7 | +10.2 | +11.3 | +6.6 |
| 1979 | +13.1 | +3.7 | +15.5 | +22.8 | +16.1 |
| 1980 | +57.7 | −6.3 | −14.3 | +12.4 | +12.4 |
| 1981 | −19.5 | −18.3 | −4.2 | −12.8 | −13.8 |
| 1982 | −28.3 | −4.7 | −21.8 | −13.7 | −9.6 |
| 1983 | +4.2 | +4.9 | +22.2 | +7.3 | −1.2 |
| 1984 | −13.5 | +14.1 | +26.1 | −2.3 | −4.8 |
| 1985 | −14.1 | −8.2 | −31.1 | −10.5 | −1.2 |
| 1986 | +12.7 | +23.6 | +37.8 | — | −10.1 |

Source: UNCTAD.

**Minerals**
Both developed and developing countries are suppliers of **metal ores**, but for the latter they are usually a vital source of foreign-exchange earnings. The demand for such metals as iron, copper, lead, tin and zinc is determined by the level of economic activity in the manufacturing economies. A sudden upturn in the demand for metal ores is likely to produce very substantial price increases once any existing stocks have

been used up. This is because, in these extractive industries, output cannot readily be increased in the short term. This shortage of
capacity is a reflection of a lack of investment in
previous periods. Suppliers have learnt from
experience that a sudden increase in the demand for their ores can often be followed by an
equally sudden fall in demand because of lower
growth rates in the manufacturing economies.

Investment in new extractive capacity generally involves relatively long-term projects.
There is always the risk that producers may
then be left with excess capacity and much
higher fixed costs. The volatile nature of the
demand makes it very difficult to decide upon
the optimum level of their extractive capacity,
and the very short-lived periods of higher demand have caused them to err on the side of
caution. Between 1976 and 1980 prices rose
again as the manufacturing economies recovered from the first oil crisis. The second oil crisis
then produced another slump in the prices of
metal ores.

The gradual increase in the level of economic
activity in the manufacturing economies will not
necessarily lead to a comparable increase in
mineral prices. This is because, firstly, suppliers
have accumulated stocks and, secondly, the
new technology associated with robotics, information technology and home electronic products, along with new materials, is reducing the
world's demand for many of the traditional raw
materials. Suppliers are therefore seeking to
strengthen their position by cutting their production to levels which are more in keeping
with the generally lower levels of demand. The
lower prices for many of the UK's imports of
raw materials have contributed to the lower
rates of inflation in recent years.

*International agreements*
In some cases the fluctuations in the prices of
metal ores would have been much wider were it
not for the **international agreements** which seek
to establish more stable prices. A sudden fall in
the price of copper, for example, will not only
affect the income of the suppliers, but future
output may be threatened because suppliers are
obliged to run down their capacity because of
exceptionally high losses. These suppliers will
not then be in a position to take advantage of
any future upturn in the level of demand. In the
case of a developed economy such as the USA,

the government will seek to ensure that sufficient stocks of important raw materials are
held to meet the future needs of its own industries, including protecting future supplies to its
defence industries. From the point of view of a
developing country such as Zambia, however, it
will seek to maintain a minimum price by controlling supply to the market, because it is very
reliant upon copper exports for its foreign-
exchange earnings. If the price is kept too high,
this will hasten the introduction of a more
efficient use of copper and the development of
other materials, thus reducing demand and
export prospects.

For such reasons international agreements
may be supported by the major importing countries. These countries have a vested interest in
building up **buffer stocks** to avoid any future
shortages and substantial price increases
brought about by a sudden increase in the
demand for important raw materials.

The success of international agreements in
maintaining a minimum price for a particular
commodity will depend upon each member
being willing to accept a quota of the total
supply put on to the world market. Governments of producing countries have to purchase
excess output and hold it as buffer stocks which
can be released to meet any sudden increases in
world demand. During a long period of depressed demand, however, some developing
countries may break such agreements, finding it
increasingly difficult to finance constant addi-
tions to their stocks and also being in urgent
need of foreign exchange. A country may therefore undercut the agreed price to boost its sales.
Once this happens, other countries may be
tempted to do the same. Soon the agreement
may collapse, allowing the price to fall to its
free-market level. In 1985, for example, the
international tin agreement collapsed because
the drop in world demand was so severe and
prolonged that Malaysia found it increasingly
difficult to finance increases in stocks. Tin trading ceased on the London Metal Exchange,
since stocks amounted to about 60 per cent of
annual output, with no sign of a recovery in
demand.

International minerals agreements are also
difficult to maintain if the members are countries with governments of very different political complexions. Not only will it prove difficult to
negotiate such an agreement, but it is also likely

to break down if they find themselves holding conflicting views on an aspect of international relations or supporting different sides in an armed conflict. Consequently such international agreements have generally been difficult to sustain for long periods. Market forces eventually bring about a fall in the world price that more closely reflects market conditions.

## Oil
The **Organisation of Petroleum Exporting Countries** (OPEC) is perhaps the best known example of an **international cartel**. Between 1972 and 1981 it achieved a fourteen-fold increase in the world price of crude oil. The governments which belong to OPEC agree to impose taxes upon crude oil so that they achieve a uniform export price. This tax is passed on by the oil companies in the form of higher prices to the oil-consuming countries. The members of OPEC agree to quotas for their respective levels of production.

Since 1981 the worldwide recession in the oil-consuming countries has made it increasingly difficult for OPEC to hold the price of oil. A series of OPEC meetings failed to enforce the further cuts in oil production which were necessary to compensate for the fall in world demand and to sustain the price of oil. Some of the OPEC members were desperate to increase their exports. Iran, for example, needed the foreign exchange to finance its war with Iraq; and Nigeria had serious overseas debt problems. These countries were exceeding their quotas. By 1986 OPEC was obliged to relax its controls over oil production; and, for a period, oil prices fell below $8 a barrel as countries competed fiercely to increase their sales. Then, towards the end of 1986, OPEC re-established some control over its members, and the price has tended to fluctuate between $12 and $18 a barrel.

### The UK and OPEC
The UK is not a member of OPEC, but the government's **petroleum revenue tax** has tended to move in line with OPEC prices. The output of oil from the North Sea is not subject to a quota, and OPEC has often been concerned that the UK's output will frustrate its attempts to achieve a higher price for oil.

The problem facing the UK is that, if OPEC embarked upon a price war, this could seriously affect the profitability of the oil companies oper-

ating in the North Sea, since the costs of exploration and development there are much higher than in a major producing country such as Saudi Arabia. It is estimated that the oil companies must be confident of a price of around $18 to $22 if they are to explore and develop other major fields in the North Sea. A further weakening of oil prices will seriously damage the UK's balance of payments and the government's tax revenues.

### Agricultural raw materials
**Agricultural commodities** include rubber, cotton, wool, jute and sisal. Their market demands are closely related to the levels of real income in the manufacturing economies, because they are used in a wide range of products which have a high income elasticity of demand. Apart from the industrial uses of rubber for seals and drive-belts, it is also used in a wide range of consumer durables. A rise in the demand for motor vehicles, for example, will increase the demand for rubber in the manufacture of tyres. An increase in the demand for footwear, soft furnishings, textiles and clothing will also raise the demand for rubber and natural fibres.

A sudden increase in demand for any of these commodities, impacting upon an **inelastic supply**, will therefore lead to substantial price increases. Between 1972 and 1974, for example, the prices of both cotton and rubber rose by about 100 per cent and wool prices increased by the same amount in just one year. Since then, the prices of agricultural raw materials have generally shown the same kind of movement associated with metal ores – falling and rising according to the level of economic activity in the manufacturing economies.

### Depressed prices
The development of **synthetic materials** is progressively reducing the demand for these commodities, while potential supply is continually being increased by improvements in growing methods that raise **productivity** in producing countries. These developments have been reflected in a prolonged period of **depressed prices.**

The US government, for example, is reacting to cotton surpluses by reducing its support prices to avoid any further increase in its stocks and to curb over-production. The Australian and New Zealand state boards have increased

**Fig. 10.4**

# Tin producers agree export quotas

### BY WONG SULONG IN KUALA LUMPUR

THE SEVEN nation Associa-
tion of Tin Producing Countries (ATPC) has worked out
individual quotas limiting
members' total exports to
96,000 tonnes for a 12-month
period.

A statement issued after a
three-day meeting of the
ATPC executive committee
said the matter would be
submitted to member governments "for final endorse-
ment."

It did not specify the individual quotas, but conference
delegates say Malaysia has
been allotted 28,000 tonnes,
Indonesia 24,000, Thailand
19,000, Bolivia 15,000, Australia 7,000 and Nigeria and

Zaire about 1,500 tonnes
each.

The two African countries
did not attend the meeting
but signalled support for the
scheme which will run from
March 1987 to February 1988.

The limitation of exports
is expected to cut the current
world's tin surplus of 71,000
tonnes by another 20,000
tonnes. This should improve
prices, which have remained
depressed since the International Tin Council ran out
of money to support prices
in November 1985.

Without the export quota,
the ATPC members would be
expected to export 110,000

tonnes during the stated
period.

The statement said Brazil
and China, two major non-
ATPC producers, attended
the meeting as observers, and
had agreed to "co-operate to
ensure the depletion of the
overhanging stocks."

Delegates said the ATPC
has requested Brazil and
China to limit their exports
to 21,000 tonnes and 7,000
tonnes respectively.

Southeast Asian mining
companies say Brazilian and
Chinese co-operation is essential for the success of the
scheme. They point out that
effectiveness of ITC-imposed
export controls during 1982-

85 was undermined by
increased production from
non-members.

The ATPC statement also
called on the US to restrict
releases from its strategic
stockpile so as not to undermine the effort of the tin
producers.

The ATPC would also urge
banks and brokers, who are
holding substantial metal
stocks, not to sell their metal
until prices are above 20
ringgit (£5.13) a kg.

On the Kuala Lumpur Tin
Market yesterday, tin was
traded at 17.22 ringgit a kilo,
down 8 cents, on turnover
which was 2 tonnes higher at
92 tonnes.

Source: *Financial Times*, 23 January 1987.

their stockpiles of wool in an effort to protect prices. But in the absence of any significant future increase in the demand, they will eventually be obliged to ensure that production is lowered to more appropriate levels. Rubber producers are also holding very large stocks and have experienced increasing difficulties under the **International Rubber Agreement** to secure finance from the importing countries to buy up additional surpluses. This is because the current price is still far in excess of the more realistic level that would reflect the long-term reduction in the market demand.

### Foodstuffs
Government support schemes and international agreements also find it increasingly more difficult to support the prices of **basic foodstuffs** such as wheat, maize, sugar and vegetable oilseeds and oils. Both the USA and the European Community must eventually face up to the political problem of dealing with an excessive number of producers in their agricultural sectors. In the meantime, there is a possibility that the USA and the Community will engage in a **price war** in an effort to offload their surpluses on to the world market. This will be particularly damaging to producers in the developing countries.

In the case of other products, such as coffee, cocoa and tea from the developing countries, there are international agreements in operation, but they are difficult to sustain in the face of only a slowly increasing demand. In some years the future output of coffee is affected by frosts in Brazil which damage new plantings; this was the case in 1977, when the world price of coffee rose more than 200 per cent above its 1975 level. Over-production generally makes it difficult to enforce export quotas, and the **International Coffee Agreement** is continually under pressure.

**Activity 10.3**
Read the article in Fig. 10.4, then attempt the following:

(a) Describe the developments which have contributed to a decline in the world demand for tin.

(b) Explain why the ATPC may experience problems in achieving an increase in the price of tin.

# 11. Markets, Customers and Clients

## Success and failure in the market-place

It is often said that **marketing** is simply a question of getting the right products to the right customer at the right price. In theory this may appear to be a fairly easy thing to do. However, in practice it is difficult to achieve, because it involves clearly identifying **consumer needs**; ensuring that the best **product** or **service** is available to meet those needs; **informing** potential customers about the product or service and **persuading** them to buy it; determining the best **price** at which to sell the product or service; and identifying the most effective means of **distributing** the product or service.

Some business organisations have managed to get all this right, as in the case of Horn Abbot with its internationally successful game Trivial Pursuit, McDonalds with its ability to identify and cater for people's fast-food needs, Heinz with its long-running domination of the baked-beans market and Cadbury's with its highly successful Wispa chocolate bar. But in other cases matters have gone terribly wrong, as Sir Clive Sinclair found to his cost with his C5 electrical vehicle. A company in Australia experienced a similar problem when it tried to launch a revolutionary aluminium cricket bat, and a United States company ran into difficulties over a cigarette made from synthetic tobacco. In each case of failure the business organisation involved tended to be more concerned with the features of the product than with the needs or desires of potential consumers and so paid the price in the market-place – see Fig. 11.1.

The importance of marketing was stressed in *Business Organisations and Environments* Book 1, where consideration was given to types of market, the mechanics of demand and supply factors interacting to determine prices and the importance of the marketing mix. The first ten chapters of this book have covered the political and economic environment in which business organisations operate. It is now appropriate to give a more detailed treatment of the **marketing strategy** adopted by organisations in providing goods and services within such an environment.

In particular we consider how organisations carry out the **marketing function**, the importance of **marketing information**, methods of **price determination** and the methods of **distributing** goods and services. We look at how these aspects of marketing affect business organisations in both the private and public sectors, and at the special problems experienced by **government organisations** in trying to identify and satisfy social needs.

## THE MARKETING FUNCTION

The allocation of marketing responsibilities and the organisation of the marketing operation vary enormously between organisations both of different sizes and also concerned with different products or services. In a small business the marketing role may be carried out by a single individual who decides upon the market mix regarding product, price, place and promotion. Many **sole traders** have to make these decisions, together with all other business decisions relating to such areas as purchasing, production and finance.

For example, consider the one-man mobile hot-dog stall.

Not only has the owner to purchase his own supplies and equipment, cook the product and control the financing of the operation; he also has to make all the marketing decisions. This will include deciding on the most important features of the product for his target consumers in terms of type and size of roll, sausage and sauces; how much he should charge; where he should locate his mobile unit and how he should promote his business through, say, signs by the roadside or advertising.

In a much larger organisation there may be **specialists** responsible for each part of the marketing operation. Fig. 11.2 shows how marketing could be organised in such a business which has markets both at home and abroad.

**Fig. 11.1: The ups and downs of marketing**

SUCCESSES                                    FAILURES

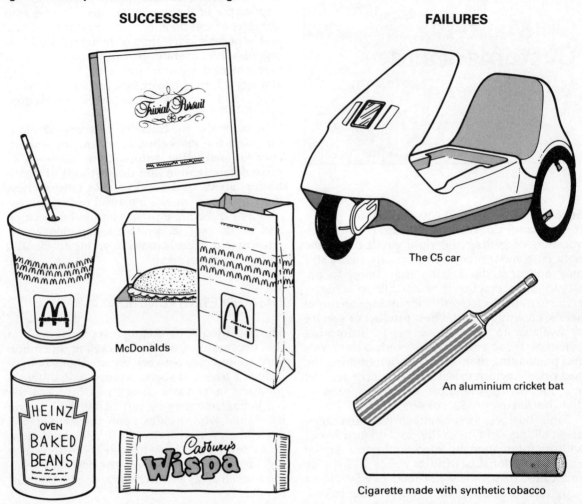

McDonalds

The C5 car

An aluminium cricket bat

Cigarette made with synthetic tobacco

The most important customers at home would be handled by a special key account manager. Some of the work connected with market research, public relations and advertising could be handled by outside agencies.

Whatever the form of organisation of the marketing operation, it must be well co-ordinated and have well-defined lines of communications with other departments. If this is not the case there is always a danger that problems will arise in terms of production, purchasing and finance; costly errors may be made about levels of production and the purchasing of raw materials and components, thus upsetting financial planning.

**Customer- or product-orientated organisations**
The role of marketing within an organisation varies according to whether it is **product-** or **customer-orientated**. In the case of the former there may be an assumption made by those working in the organisation that the existing range of products or services is the best on the market, that sales will follow automatically and that there is no need for product change or modification. Such a complacent view can lead to the downfall of an organisation when it is operating in a rapidly changing business environment. For example, some companies producing towelling nappies were badly caught out by the introduction of the paper-based disposable nappy.

**Fig. 11.2: The marketing operation in a large business organisation**

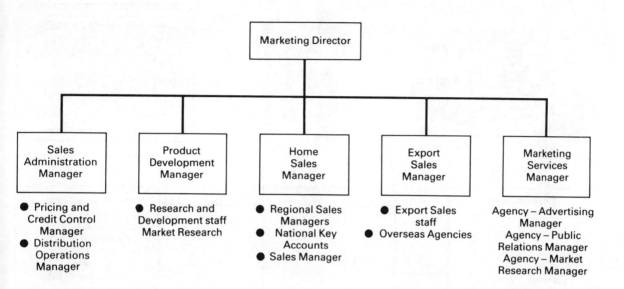

A customer-orientated organisation, on the other hand, is in a constant state of change – assessing, monitoring and responding to alterations in the market-place. It will have a highly developed marketing strategy, which acknowledges and is sensitive to its customers' changing needs and wants. It will strive to find out what the customers want, what causes them to buy and what the product or service really means to them as consumers.

Within the customer-orientated organisation, marketing will feature prominently in the organisation's overall planning. The three major activities of any organisation – **planning, running the organisation** and **controlling its activities** – may be represented as in Fig. 11.3.

In a customer-orientated organisation, any market plan will have its origins in the original overall strategic plan of the organisation and will then be run and controlled by the systems operating within the organisation. For example, if one of the overall objectives of the organisation is to increase profits, this could be done either by reducing costs or by increasing sales. If

the latter is adopted this could be achieved with the help of the marketing function by increasing the organisation's market share in the domestic market and/or entering new foreign markets. These two objectives would then feature as the organisation's marketing plans, and appropriate strategies would be adopted to achieve them – such as increasing the availability of the product or the amount spent on promotion to encourage home sales, or cutting prices to secure a foothold in foreign markets. Such strategies may then be expressed in terms of particular goals, which might include increasing the share of the domestic market by 5 per cent by the end of the year, say. They could then be executed, monitored and possibly revised by the organisation during the course of the year.

### Public and private sector organisations

The role of marketing also varies between public and private sector organisations. This is because in the private sector the organisation can monitor consumer wants and reactions in the market-place, whereas in the case of a state-

**Fig. 11.3: Market planning as part of overall planning**

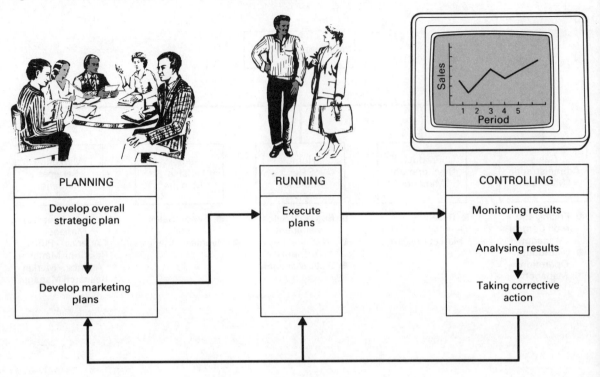

controlled monopoly, such as a nationalised industry, it is far more difficult to identify consumer wants and so to be sensitive to their needs.

*Nationalised industries*
It is felt that **public sector industry** has been removed from the discipline of market forces; so, although it makes use of many traditional market information-gathering techniques, it finds it difficult to assess the requirements and reactions of the market accurately. The problem has probably been worsened by the nationalised industries' centralised form of administration, which is thought to inhibit organisations from responding quickly to the needs of their customers.

The state-owned industries are helped to a certain extent by their **consumer consultative councils**, which act as a watchdog for the consumer and also as a sounding-board for new ideas or proposed changes put forward by the government minister or the board. But since

these organisations by their very nature deal with a minority of consumer problems and issues, it is difficult for them to give an accurate reflection of consumers' wishes.

Even if the nationalised industries manage to identify what the market requires, and then attempt to provide it, they may still find their efforts partly thwarted by **governmental interference** in their activities. Traditionally governments have used the nationalised industries as a means of achieving their macroeconomic objectives and so they have not always been allowed to operate in the way that they wish. For example, in 1984 the Conservative government intervened in the nationalised electricity and gas industries and raised their prices, despite the already relatively healthy state of the two industries concerned. This action was taken by the government because it wished to increase its revenue out of the surpluses of the nationalised industries rather than from other alternative sources.

## Government departments

**Government departments** experience similar problems to the nationalised industries when trying to be customer-orientated and to identify people's wishes and provide services to satisfy 'social' and 'merit' wants. Because there is no market mechanism for these needs and wants, the only way many people can express their feelings about the extent or form of the provision of a particular service is through the political voting mechanism. Then it is a question of voting for a political party which along with a number of other policy considerations is pledged to provide more or less of a particular service. The casting of such a vote can only be a compromise, because the individual is forced to vote for a package of policy measures. For example, an individual may feel strongly about increasing expenditure on health, education, housing and the nationalised industries and reducing that on defence. However, at a general election he or she may be faced by the kind of situation shown in Table 11.1, which shows the expenditure priorities of three fictional parties at the time of an election.

**Table 11.1: Expenditure plans at a general election**

| Areas of government spending | Party A | Party B | Party C |
|---|---|---|---|
| Education | Increase | No change | Increase |
| Health | Increase | No change | Increase |
| Housing | Increase | No change | Reduction |
| Nationalised industries | Reduction | Reduction | Reduction |
| Defence | Increase | Increase | Increase |

In such a situation, whatever party the individual decides to vote for will involve some degree of compromise. This means that although a party is elected to govern the country it cannot assume that even those people who voted it into power necessarily support all of its expenditure plans and the level and type of service it is planning to provide.

Some attempts are made to overcome the imperfections of this system by trying to gauge **public opinion** on particular issues. This may be through Royal Commissions; public inquiries; taking account of the reaction of pressure groups to White and Green Papers; by holding a referendum (as was done with membership fo the European Community); or, as has been the case in education, with the creation of parent governors of schools, by involving more lay-people in decision-making.

Activity 11.1
Select one of the nationalised industries and make out a case for privatising it on the grounds that it fails to meet customers' needs. You should include at least four points of criticism. Illustrate your case with suitable examples.

## MARKET INFORMATION

The key to successful marketing is to develop a proper marketing plan in order to achieve the optimum marketing mix in terms of product, place, promotion and price. This involves developing the right product(s) to meet known consumer needs, and to present it/them in the right place, at the right time, with the right level of promotion and at the right price. Any such plan must be based on up-to-date **market research information**.

### The role of market research

Market research has been defined by the British Institute of Management as 'the objective gathering, recording and analysing of all facts about the problems relating to the transfer and sales of goods and services from producer to consumer'. Market research is concerned not only with the investigation into the consumer market for products, but also with the original concept of a new or improved product, the analysis of existing or new methods of distribution, the sales organisation, advertising and other promotional activities.

Market research is a two-way process. It can originate with changes on the product side, continue through to the analysis of consumer demand or stem from consumer demand itself. A change in any of the aspects of marketing is likely to have repercussions on related activities, and they may need investigation.

Market research is usually associated with the eventual purchase by consumers of goods and services, but producers themselves constitute a market in that they are customers for plant, equipment, components, raw materials and a range of services. Thus producers of these inputs, which assist in the production of consumer goods and services, are also concerned with investigating the market, which in their case comprises the firms to which they sell their output. When this wider concept of market research is taken into account, it is possible to identify several areas which may prove valuable subjects to consider.

### Product research

New or improved products will be put forward on the basis of information derived from other research activities and will then be subjected to a series of **tests**. These tests may be aimed at such features as design, materials or ingredients, colour, durability, ease of handling, fitness for purpose, reliability, operating capacity or any other factor likely to be considered by the final user.

Products will also be analysed from the point of view of the extent to which they will meet other demands of a **psychological** nature. This is because consumers can be motivated in their selection or purchases by the status or prestige which they believe the good or service confers upon them. Even the brand name given to an item can be important in this respect.

Similarly tests will be directed at how the product is presented to the consumer in its **container** or **package**. Several such factors can be important, e.g. material, design, labelling, robustness, weight and ease of storage. Comparable tests may be run on **competitors' products** to highlight any advantage or deficiencies in the new or improved product.

Testing of both the product and packaging may produce features which prove to be superfluous and provide scope for greater standardisation in production. The company may also be concerned with ensuring that it has a sufficient **range of output** to allow it to compete in all areas of the market that may prove profitable. **After-sales service records** may indicate areas for improvement or means of raising the quality of the service provided.

### Sales and distribution research

Opportunities may exist to reorganise the **sales force** both to make it more effective and to eradicate wasted effort. Greater efficiency may be achieved by altering the sequence of calls by sales representatives and by comparing the number of calls with the corresponding number and size of orders. **Sales figures** from various areas when compared with the sales force employed may provide useful information, particularly when some area supposedly had the same market potential. New markets may also require a review of the most efficient way of organising the sales force.

Existing methods of **distribution**, such as selling direct to the customer or using a wholesaler or independent retail unit, may leave scope for improvement or alteration in the light of changes in customer habits or other marketing activities. Different methods of distribution and the performance of individual units may be investigated in order that strong areas are built upon, while unprofitable products and services, customers, orders and territories may be eliminated.

Contact with those purchasing on behalf of distributive outlets or trades will provide useful opinions on the company's marketing techniques when compared with those adopted by competitors.

Sales staff will generally be operating under some form of **incentive scheme**. New schemes may lead to greater effort on the part of those seeking orders from customers or distributors, and the most effective incentive scheme will be a subject of research.

### Communication research

This can help to establish the effectiveness of **advertising material** and the **media** used, such as television, national press, periodicals, trade journals and posters. The sales force also use advertising material; after consideration of its effectiveness, **descriptive brochures** may need to be reviewed. Companies may also organise **exhibitions** and **demonstrations**. Their contribution to sales will be indicated by the number of inquiries and orders placed as a result of these special events.

Companies want not only to introduce their products to the market but also to create a favourable image in the eyes of the public that could help foster future sales. Thus **public relations** and **image-building** exercises will be related to any change in the general opinion of the company held by both consumers and the public in general.

## Economic and business research

This type of research is very important for any organisation involved in planning its existing and future activities. It will help the organisation to identify the existing and predict the future behaviour of the economic, political and social variables which may influence the demand for its product and its position in the market.

### General economic forecasts

The activities of the company will be influenced by the general economic climate and by forecasts concerning the general level of economic activity. This will require analysis of **key economic indicators**. Such information is normally readily available from government, academic and business sources. Table 11.2 shows a comparison of the predictions of some of the major economic forecasting organisations.

Such forecasts as those in Table 11.2 provide information for organisations concerning what is likely to happen during the year to economic growth, levels of business activity, investment, consumption, overseas trade and the rate of price inflation in relation to earnings. This information helps to provide an overall view of the economy, with obvious implications for the position of an organisation's customers, suppliers and competitors and hence for its own future plans.

There are a number of reasons why the forecasts in Table 11.2 differ:

- The forecasts are based on different econometric models and theoretical judgements. For example, the London Business School takes an essentially monetarist line, whereas the National Institute of Economic and Social Research has a more Keynesian approach.
- The forecasts do not appear on the same date, and events can change between the publication of each forecast.
- The forecasts are based in some cases on different sources of statistics.
- The forecasts involve the use of different methods for measuring particular economic indicators.

The fact that the forecasts differ does not detract from the value of using such information when drawing up future plans. Adopting a reasonably scientific approach to planning is far better than just instinctively reacting to present events, taking note of past events or guessing at what is likely to happen in the future.

### Sector forecasts

Data relating to **sectors of the economy** which are closely connected with the prospects of the company concerned will be a subject of investigation. In particular, a company will be interested in any information which it can gather concerning the activities of its competitors, suppliers and trade customers.

**Table 11.2: Forecasts for 1986 – a comparison (annual change %)**

|  | Treasury | National Institute of Economic and Social Research | London Business School | Henley Centre for Forecasting | Liverpool Research Group | CBI | Oxford Economic Forecasting | City average |
|---|---|---|---|---|---|---|---|---|
| (Date of forecast) | (March '86) | (August '86) | (June '86) | (Sept '86) | (Sept '86) | (Sept '86) | (July '86) | |
| GDP | 3 | 1.8 | 2.0 | 2.1 | 2.7 | 2.2 | 2.2 | 2.2 |
| Consumers' expenditure | 4 | 3.8 | 3.1 | 3.4 | 3.1 | 4.8 | 3.7 | 3.6 |
| General govt consumption | 1 | 1.1 | 1.1 | 2.2 | 0.0 | 1.8 | 1.5 | 1.5 |
| Gross fixed investment | 5 | 1.1 | 2.0 | 3.0 | 4.7 | 1.0 | 2.1 | 2.5 |
| Public | — | 0.2 | −9.5 | 1.5 | — | −5.5 | 1.0 | 2.0 |
| Private | — | 2.2 | 5.2 | 3.4 | — | 2.8 | 2.4 | 2.9 |
| Stockbuilding (£ b.) | 0.8 | 1.4 | 1.0 | 0.7 | — | 0.9 | 1.5 | 1.1 |
| Exports (goods and services) | 5 | 0.9 | 2.2 | 1.8 | — | 1.7 | 1.6 | 1.3 |
| Imports (goods and services) | 6 | 3.9 | 4.1 | 4.1 | (3.7) | 5.3 | 3.8 | 3.7 |
| RPI (CPI), 4th quarter | 3.5 | 3.3 | 2.8 | 3.0 | 7.0 | 3.0 | 2.5 | 2.8 |
| Average earnings | — | 7.3 | 8.0 | 7.6 | | 8.6 | 7.7 | 7.7 |

Source: *Economic Progress Report*, HMSO, 1986.

## Fig. 11.4: Major socio-economic trends in the late 1980s

DEMOGRAPHIC: An expansion of the consumer market among the 25 – 44 age group, which has been caused by the boom in the birth rate between 1946–51 and 1961–66; this has encouraged businesses to try to tap this market.

SOCIAL: An increase in the number of single-parent families which has been caused by the increase in the divorce rate and the number of births outside marriage; this has changed the pattern of demand for housing and created a larger demand for government services.

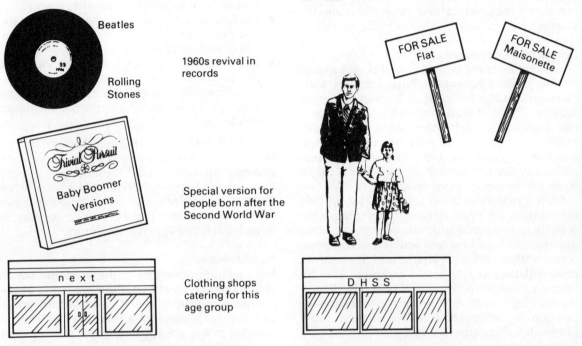

1960s revival in records

Special version for people born after the Second World War

Clothing shops catering for this age group

LEISURE: An increase in the amount of time people spend at home, which has been caused by people viewing their homes as entertainment centres; this has caused an increase in the demand for consumer durable goods.

DISTRIBUTION OF WEALTH: An increase in the number of middle-aged people inheriting fairly substantial amounts of wealth, which has been caused by people inheriting their parents' homes; this has caused an increase in the demand for luxury goods, second homes and personal investment plans.

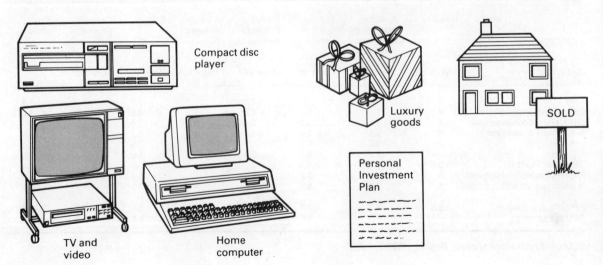

Compact disc player

TV and video

Home computer

Luxury goods

Personal Investment Plan

*Government policy*

The economic and business climate in which the company operates may be influenced by the government's **economic policy** in terms of its approach to managing the level of demand in the economy, policies dealing with company taxation and investment and the extent and nature of government intervention in the form of legislation dealing with consumer protection and other business activities.

Changes in government economic policy which have a direct impact on the organisation's potential customer will also have to be monitored. For example, changes in personal taxation and benefits may have a direct impact on the distribution of income and wealth. As we saw in Book 1, Chapter 2, since the late 1970s there has been a slowing down of the move towards greater equality. In fact, there has been a more distinct polarisation of rich and poor groups. This has been acknowledged in food retailing, where Sainsbury, Asda and Tesco have gone for the upper end of the market and Shoppers' Paradise and Kwiksave the lower end.

A change of government may produce a different emphasis in areas such as these. But even during the lifetime of the same government, attitudes may change and so have to be regularly monitored.

*Social and demographic change*

Research will also take account of **social and demographic trends**. For example, growing consumer awareness and consumer organisations are developments that will influence company policy. Similarly, changes in people's living, working and leisure habits all contribute to a changing life-style that will be reflected in patterns of demand. Such research means that social cults and fashions can be identified and perhaps related to profitable business activities. For example, researchers in the late 1980s will have to take account of some of the trends illustrated in Fig. 11.4. (Some of these changes have already been explored in Book 1, Chapter 2.)

**Consumer or user research**

A company must accurately identify and assess the needs of a consumer in the context of **changing tastes and preferences**. This aspect of market research applies not only to consumer goods and services, but also to capital goods and other inputs which assist in production. This is because the demands placed upon such items by user industries may make it necessary to accommodate changes in specifications, technical requirements and other features associated with such inputs. As with other objectives of market research aimed at consumers or users, this must be an ongoing activity, so that the company is aware of market trends and their implications as soon as they develop.

Research into final markets will allow the producer to assess the potential for new, improved or existing products. Such research should provide information relating to such features as design, quality, price, convenience, size and other physical characteristics of products and packaging which the consumer may consider before selecting a final purchase. The company will also wish to know the **background** of consumers in terms of sex, marital status, family size, socio-economic class and other elements that are important in product development and promotional activities.

There are also less easily identifiable factors which influence the behaviour of individuals as consumers, and hence their pattern of expenditure. These relate to the individual's **psychological make-up**, which leads to a certain expression of attitudes, opinions, reactions and personality when a purchase is made. Surveys aimed at these psychological factors will have to take account of images, social standing, standards of value and other aspects as they affect consumer behaviour.

The company will wish to discover from what type of **retail outlet** certain purchases are made and also **when** they are generally made. Sales will also be analysed from the point of view of the **total market share** and the share of sales among certain groups of consumers.

**Capital producers**

We later consider in detail the methods employed by producers of *consumer* goods and services, rather than user research in the field of **capital goods and other inputs.** The latter is not less important, but the problems which need to be investigated in capital production are largely different from those which arise in the field of consumer goods and services. Producers of capital goods, for example, are often involved in a highly technical and specialised market where there are relatively few customers but with whom in many cases close contact exists. Buyers of such products tend to be motivated by factors which are readily identifiable in terms of technical capability, working capacity, reliability and price, rather than the more subjective factors that influence the tastes and preferences of consumers.

Consumer goods manufacturers allocate a much larger proportion of their total expenditure to various forms of market research than producers of industrial inputs do. In particular, the proportion spent on consumer research is much larger than that spent on user research by industrial producers. The latter, however, do spend vast sums on the **research and development** ('R and D') of products and processes of a technical or scientific nature.

### Independent market research units

The highly specialised nature of industrial production is reflected in the relatively small part of market research work allocated to outside organisations, whereas the demands of consumer goods producers can more readily be catered for by **independent agencies**. Independent market research organisations can provide facilities for large-scale consumer research, and this is often required by those companies dealing with mass-produced consumer goods. The research staff will be highly specialised and experienced in dealing with consumer research projects, and they will employ specialists on psychological influences upon consumer choice and the methods of assessing and analysing these. The agency will have developed research techniques using highly trained analysts and statisticians, assisted by specially developed data-processing systems using computers.

An independent organisation allows the client company the advantage of not making its research objectives known to its competitors. The agency can also take an unbiased approach when reporting direct to the client company at management level. This will be important if some of the company's marketing activities are shown in an unfavourable light. If such research was conducted by an internal unit, it could produce an emphasis in the results which hides deficiencies in the company's marketing department.

### Why consumer research is possible

Specialist research organisations have developed their techniques and accumulated their data over a long period. Information which both contributes to and results from consumer surveys can be a valuable guide to assessing the buying habits and life-style of those who make up the market. This is possible because both economic and social developments have led to a greater uniformity in certain aspects of human behaviour. The ability to place larger numbers of people into fewer income and social groupings, as well as the general improvement in real incomes, have contributed to this greater **uniformity in consumer behaviour**.

These developments, along with mass production, have led to the mass consumption of many products, with the result that a very large part of the population has experienced a wide range of consumer goods and services. It is thus possible to accept the results derived from a survey of a **cross-section of the market** as being a fairly reliable guide to the characteristics of the market as a whole. Even so, the research, analysis and drawing of conclusions must be done carefully and accurately.

### Constraints upon marketing activities

Before attempting to discover where the market lies, and the relative strengths of various influences upon the consumer, there are some **constraints** imposed upon producers which will already be known to them. These constraints may be imposed by **legislation** relating to consumer or environmental protection that prevent the company from embodying certain features in its product or packaging. Such legislation may also control other aspects of marketing, such as **advertising** or **promotional tactics**, and may oblige the company to incorporate certain characteristics into its products and advertisements.

However, some constraints may be imposed by the **physical and business environment** – by the physical properties of homes, say, and by the existing stock of consumer durables to which the product may be complementary. The design of a refrigerator, for example, will have to take account of the kitchen space available in those households which are likely to form a large part of the market. Producers of perishable foodstuffs will have to pay attention to shelf space and the dimensions of refrigerators.

# Desk research

The first stage of any research will be the gathering of factual information from **existing publications.** A useful range of publications stems from the **Government Statistical Office**. This provides data on broad aggregates in the economy such as national income and expenditure, industrial production, investment, international trade, prices, demographic and social trends; these are then broken down into a more detailed presentation to provide more specific information. An official guide to statistical sources is also provided to assist the researcher in discovering certain facts and figures. This is called *The Guide to Official Statistics* and is published by HMSO. The General Statistical Office also publishes *Government Statistics: A Brief Guide to Sources*, which gives details of the government organisations which produce particular data.

**Trade publications** are produced on behalf of firms that constitute an industry or particular trade. These journals contain data, information and articles on subjects and developments of relevance to the industry as a whole. They contain informed opinion of how political, economic and social trends can be expected to affect the product or service around which the industry's activities are concentrated.

There are journals of a more general nature produced by various institutes and professional organisations. *British Business*, published by the Department of Trade and Industry, contains key economic indicators and articles of interest to various sections of industry and commerce. A researcher can also make contact with a specific organisation to seek certain types of information, and directories exist which can be used for this purpose. For example, publications such as Kelly's *Manufacturers and Merchants Directory* can provide the initial contact for researchers seeking information and possible outlets for advertising material.

The individual company's own **records** of past sales may provide valuable data for research purposes as, for example, establishing a connection between the company's own performance and outside influences identified as possible reasons for fluctuations in sales. The results of economic and business research previously described will also be available for further analysis.

# Field research

When all existing sources of information have been tapped, it will then be necessary to supplement general trends and influences on sales with a more detailed analysis of the factors that eventually lead the consumer to select purchases from the choice available. At this stage **field research** must be undertaken, which is the way the company tries to be customer-oriented in its marketing activities. Some form of contact will then be made with consumers, and generally a **questionnaire** of some form will be employed. The vast majority of people do not intentionally distort their answers to a questionnaire, but the final conclusions drawn from research will not prove reliable if the consumer sample selected is not a representative cross-section of the market under investigation.

*Samples*

The market – or 'universe', as the researcher calls it – is first determined; then a number is decided upon to constitute a **sample**. If this sample is too small it will not be a useful guide, whereas if it is too large it will mean an unwarranted use of money and effort. Ideally, the sample should be a microcosm of the 'universe' in that it is selected to reproduce exactly the characteristics of the 'universe' itself. In the sample there should be the same proportion of people with certain characteristics that form particular sub-groups in terms of sex, age, marital status, income groups and so on. The group to be interviewed should be a scale model of the 'universe' whose opinions are sought.

The larger the number of sub-groups that a researcher wishes to identify, the larger the sample required. If, for example, the 'universe' is estimated at 1 million and the consumer sample is to be 3000, while a sub-group of the 'universe' is 2 per cent, then this will make up only 60 of the sample. It may be that from the statistician's point of view such a number is too small to give a reliable indication of opinions held by those in the 'universe' where they number 20,000. In this event, the number in the sub-group could be increased and this disproportionate number taken into account when analysing the results. If the number of such sub-groups is relatively high, the sample will need to be correspondingly larger, and this will raise the cost of the research.

This demonstrates one of the problems facing the researcher. The less uniform the 'universe' and the greater the number of sub-groups he or she wishes to identify, the larger the sample must be. Having decided upon the size of the sample, the researcher will select a method of making up the sample and its constituent parts that lends itself to contacting the categories of consumers involved. The various methods are illustrated in Fig. 11.5 and described below.

*The probability system*
This involves obtaining a list of the 'universe' to be researched. Sources of names and addresses may be available from trade and telephone directories, electoral registers and subscribers to

**Fig. 11.5: Methods of sample selection**

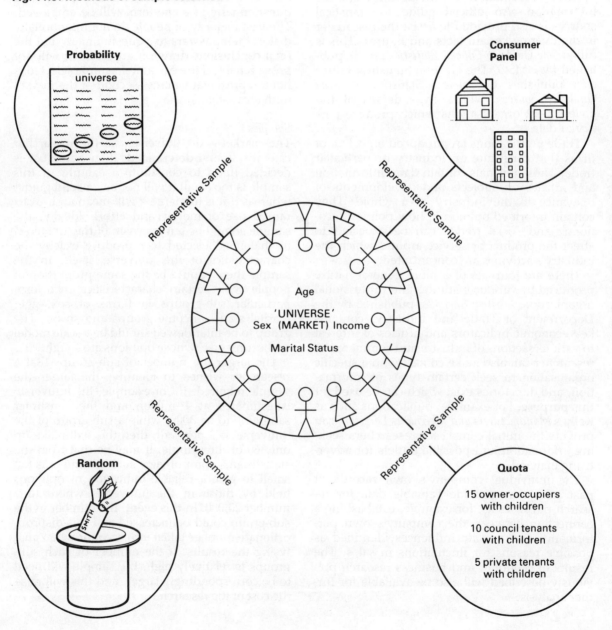

journals and professional organisations. Although names and addresses may be available from many such sources, it is not always possible to identify them as falling within the 'universe' or a particular sub-group. This will depend very much on having access to relevant lists, which even then will often not indicate enough of an individual's personal background to allocate them to a specific sub-group.

The researcher will select the sample by taking perhaps one name in thirty from lists and allocating them to interviewers, who must then adhere to their quotas, otherwise their own bias in terms of the people they would like to interview will make the results unrepresentative. This selection and interviewing will have to continue until the various subsections are complete, and this will not necessarily be at the same time that the number of contacts reaches the number prescribed by the sample. This is because lists themselves may not be a cross-section unless they were selected on the basis that they were essentially the whole 'universe' or a uniform part of it.

### The random selection system

This involves contacting households selected largely on a random basis, rather than allowing the interviewer to make a conscious choice. The interviewer may select contacts by requesting co-operation from passers-by, perhaps asking every tenth person until a contact is established. Any such random selection would be more acceptable than the interviewer being allowed to decide, because of personal preference entering into the exercise. This may be predetermined to a certain extent by basing the random selection upon homes which are capable of being placed into sub-groups. For example, areas may be placed into categories in terms of region, rural or urban location, and types of dwelling, from which random selection is then made. This will be particularly useful when the sample is to contain sub-groups based upon such characteristics.

### The quota system

This can be more clearly defined and is a very popular means of consumer research. Once the size of the sample is decided upon, the sub-groups are defined, and interviewers are allocated a quota of individuals which they must contact according to certain characteristics of the sub-groups. For example, an interviewer may be required to trace and interview a certain number of households in an urban area which are owner-occupied, with two children of school age and both parents working.

With the probability and random methods, the interviewer was obliged to contact those listed or adhere to a uniform random selection basis, such as every tenth house, if the representative nature of the sample was to be achieved. With the quota system, however, the interviewer is not obliged to adhere to such a process of selection as long as the respondent meets the requirements of a sub-group. Thus the interviewer is not obliged to call again on those who were not at home when first called upon and can have greater flexibility in selecting alternative contacts.

### Consumer panels

A continuous flow of information can be derived from households which agree to report on certain items which form a part of their pattern of expenditure or living habits. This will allow the researcher to identify trends in their early stages and possibly relate them to fluctuations in demand or suggest new markets. A cross-section of households is requested to make up a panel designed to be a representative sample of the market. They are asked to submit details of their spending or other information on a regular basis, dealing with such matters as products, their prices and sizes, place and time of purchase or allocation of leisure time between various alternatives.

Such panels are expensive to establish and may require continuous attention if they are to be maintained for a sufficiently long period to make the results from participants worthwhile. Results from a panel with a large turnover will not give an accurate impression of longer-term trends and hence changes in the pattern of expenditure and living habits. The longer a household remains on the panel, the more accustomed they become to making returns. They may then become less self-conscious when making purchases and not continuously consider the implications which their spending will have on their report. They may then act more naturally in accordance with their personal tastes and preferences, and for these reasons the information submitted to the researcher will be more valuable.

### Interviewing techniques

The information which the researcher seeks is usually derived from the answers which consumers are willing to give to some form of **questionnaire**. It is important that the contact with the **respondent** makes full use of the questionnaire and permits as much accuracy as possible. The various methods are illustrated in Fig. 11.6 and described below.

#### Personal interview

A **personal interview** is generally the most successful method in that it achieves the greatest response. A personable and experienced interviewer will acquire a technique which not only encourages participation in the questionnaire but generally leads to more complete and accurate answers. The interviewer's approach can be adapted to put the respondent at ease; the value of their participation can be explained in the light of the researcher's objectives, and any difficulty in interpreting a question or areas of response can be dealt with by verbal alternatives. Where the quota system is employed, the interviewer will gain experience of certain types of household and more readily identify areas where they can be located. The interviewer may become accomplished in identifying other general characteristics concerning the individual or household and therefore submit information that could not be obtained from questions since they would have to be of a more personal nature.

Personal interviews are expensive, however, in terms of salaries and travelling costs, particularly when the probability and random systems mean that they must recall on people who were originally not at home, because substitutes would destroy the nature of these techniques. Even in the quota system, a subsection may contain a group with characteristics which it proves very time-consuming and difficult to

**Fig. 11.6: Interviewing techniques**

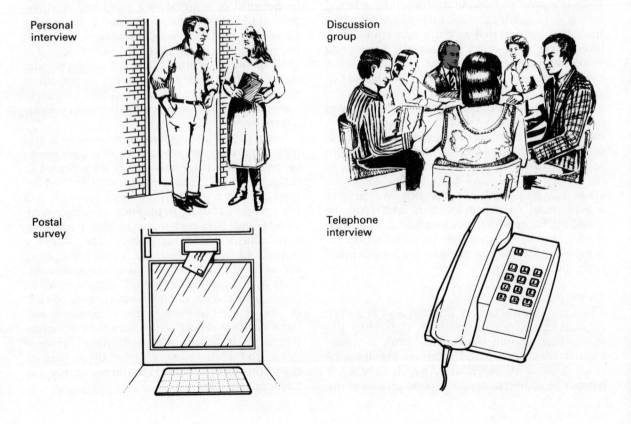

Personal interview

Discussion group

Postal survey

Telephone interview

trace within a particular area, and this will add to travelling expenses. Interviewers themselves may subconsciously allow bias to enter into their choice of respondents and/or may distort the results by 'helping' respondents complete the questionnaire. If questionnaires are completed face to face, the respondents may try to give the answers expected of them, or those they believe will create the best impression on the interviewer.

## The discussion group technique

In this case a group of people representing a cross-section of the 'universe' is invited to participate in a **discussion** to express their tastes and preferences in relation to certain goods and services or give their views on household activities. The chairman of the meeting will be an experienced researcher who will be able to create an atmosphere in which the participants feel free to express their opinions. The chairman will introduce topics and guide the conversation. The whole exercise can be recorded and analysed at a later stage, and the tone of conversation will also help indicate the strength of certain opinions and attitudes. This may prove a limited exercise, because the more vociferous person will play a disproportionately large part, and the shy and more retiring person will not be well represented.

## Postal surveys

**Mailing** questionnaries to households will be less expensive than the personal interview. But this may be partly offset by the number which must be sent out to achieve a sufficient number of replies and the extra literature which must be enclosed to describe the purpose of the research. The questionnaire must be expressed in simple terms and readily understood, since the questionnaire must be completed without assistance. The answer technique should be of a nature that reduces the amount of effort involved on the part of the respondent. Answers must therefore be of the 'yes/no' type, or boxes which require ticking, one of them covering the respondents' activities and opinions. Such postal communications need to be made as attractive as possible so that they are not thrown away.

## Telephone interviews

Less than 80 per cent of homes have a telephone. This would not present a problem if it were not for the fact that such households are not likely to provide a representative sample in terms of important subsections, since telephones may be heavily concentrated in a narrow range of households. The telephone may prove a relatively cheap method of contacting respondents, but the subscriber may be unwilling to provide personal information to an unknown, unseen caller.

## Questionnaires

Having decided upon the area to be researched, the questions must be designed so that the answers allow respondents to be classified into the desired subsections of the 'universe'. The initial questions will seek **personal facts** about the respondent such as sex, age, marital status, family and occupation. Some of the early questions can be designed to arouse the **participants' interest** in the survey and to create an impression that his or her **contribution** will play an important part in the research. Other questions of a more personal nature, necessary to identify subsections in terms of income and important items of personal expenditure, may follow at a later stage when the respondent has become more relaxed. The researcher may also need to. design questions which seek to gain information concerning not only patterns of expenditure but also **related household** activities, and to gain **opinions** on certain features of goods and services.

Although the majority of people will have no reason for giving **false information**, the possibility of this happening does arise with questions where the participant might hesitate to give an answer that would affect his or her personal standing or show him or her in an unfavourable social light. Where such questions are necessary, they can be checked against **control questions** included in the questionnaire with the intention of obtaining the same information using a different style of question. If control questions indicate contradictory answers, then it can be supposed that for personal reasons the answers provided are not a true reflection of the individual's activities or opinions.

Such an individual's questionnaire can then be omitted from the sample used in the eventual analysis. The need for control questions in sensitive areas can be avoided if the question is constructed so that issues of guilt or social standing do not arise.

Questions should not be too exacting and should follow **logically** upon one another, not changing direction. The sentence construction and choice of words should **avoid ambiguity** and strike an acceptable balance between the **vocabulary** and **powers of expression** of various groups of the community. Similarly, answers should not make a great demand upon the respondent's ability to communicate orally.

The easiest question for both parties, and for the analyst, is the one which simply demands a **'yes/no' response**. In areas which do not lend themselves to such answers it is possible to give a **range of responses**, which can also help to remind the participant of the choices available. For example, the question may be: 'If you were to buy a newly built home, what type of central heating would you prefer?' The following responses could then be contained in boxes, one of which could be crossed through: 'oil, gas, solid fuel, storage heaters, under floor, warm-air'. This **multiple response** is also useful where the respondent cannot be expected to give a precise answer, but an approximate indication would prove acceptable. In this case the individual selects an answer which most closely reflects his or her activities or views.

Some questions may be **open-ended** in that they allow the respondent greater scope in the answer, but they are more time-consuming for both respondent and interviewer. They are also more difficult to process using computer techniques, because they require analysing before being given a code. Personal judgement may have to be used in allocating some open-ended answers to certain codes. The interviewer may assist by writing a summary of the answer, but this again leaves scope for personal interpretation of the respondent's remarks. The interviewer must also take care that the question is posed in such a way that the **tone of voice** does not create undue emphasis on certain words or parts of the question.

A problem may arise if the potential respondent wishes to know both the name of the company sponsoring the research and further details of the purpose of the investigation. If the identity of the company is disclosed, this may prejudice answers; they may be deliberately flattering or very critical, rather than a rational assessment of opinion. If the activities of the company became known to competitors, it may lose some initial advantage and provoke early competitive reactions. If too much detail of the purpose of the research is revealed, this can create a bias by influencing answers in a particular direction which the respondent believes will assist the researcher.

### Consumer motivation research

Questionnaires can easily be designed and used to obtain factual data on the characteristics of consumers and what they regard as important influences in their selection of products. The important aspect of *why* they hold these opinions, or are influenced by certain features of a product, is a much more complex area of investigation that enters more deeply into the field of psychology. It is a difficult matter to research into **consumer motivation** in selecting between alternatives for expenditure and between various retail outlets, and into what influences the timing of expenditure. Consumer motivation research seeks to identify the features that should be incorporated into the product, packaging and other marketing activities so that a consumer will select in favour of the company concerned. The choice of a brand name and advertising are areas where there is often an attempt to appeal to the inner feelings and emotional make-up of consumers. Some such attempts may be obvious to the consumer, but others may be of a more subtle nature.

These aspects of research are more difficult to deal with in the form of a questionnaire, because consumers are often unwilling to discuss their inner motives and desires, even if they are conscious of them. Specialist research units may concentrate upon this aspect of human behaviour and then relate it to consumer behaviour and marketing activities.

## TEST MARKETING

When a large capital investment is involved in the development of a new or improved product, some form of **test marketing** will generally be an important pre-condition for a national sales effort. Test marketing applies not only to the product itself, but also to all the marketing activities supporting the product – the sales organisation, the distribution system, advertising and promotional aids. It allows the company to experience the realities of competitive pressures in a market, to make accommodating changes in the product and to discover any deficiencies. Test marketing has a very impressive record; products launched on a national scale after having been corrected in the light of test-market findings have a success record of about 90 per cent.

### The test area

The **test area** selected must be representative of the marketing 'universe' so that results can be a reliable guide for the basis of a national campaign. The residents of the area must be a cross-section in terms of their personal characteristics, and all other factors must be typical of those elsewhere. The quality of the marketing force and the strength of competition must be typical of those existing in other areas. Even the level and type of employment should approach those existing in the economy as a whole.

The **size of the test market** is an important factor. If the product by its very nature is not expected to sell in vast quantities, the area selected must be sufficiently large to produce sales that can be used for statistical purposes. It must also take account of the market share which the firm believes will make the product a viable proposition. If, for example, the company anticipates that 10 per cent of a market of 1 million will be viable, then an area yielding sales in the region of 10,000, but not less, will prove a workable basis for a test.

The area must also be typical as regards the organisation of **sales and distribution networks**. The selection of an area that is too large for the prospective sales organisation may produce disappointing results that are not due to deficiencies in the product itself.

If **advertising** is to be tested, the area for the product test should as far as possible coincide with the coverage of the media being used. The area for test should also be considered from the point of view of retail outlets using **point-of-sale** promotions and demonstrations, as they will have certain catchment areas. If national advertising is likely to play an important part in the total market, the area selected to test such media must be one where, for example, regional television or editions of national newspapers are available. This will allow a test of the anticipated advertising media.

Producing output for test purposes and set-

ting up a marketing network for new product can be a costly exercise, because the company will not yet be geared to high levels of output in terms of the type and size of productive capacity. The **unit costs** of the product may thus be very high, and the company will be particularly keen to deal with a test market that is small yet practical. A large area runs the risk of a substantial financial loss if the test is unsuccessful, but such a loss may be justified if the company reduces the risk of launching a national sales effort on the basis of statistical evidence taken from such a small area. The larger the area selected for the test, the more difficult it becomes for a competitor to obscure the results by engaging in concentrated competition in that area.

### The test factors and results

Test marketing should not attempt to test too many **factors** at the same time in the same area. If, for example, an advertising technique is being tested, then altering other factors – such as special offers and packaging – will not allow the researcher to assess the relative importance of any single factor on sales. The response of competitors must be monitored, since this may not necessarily be a type of competition which a rival could be expected to maintain on a national scale.

If test marketing is used for what is considered to be an improved product or a more effective marketing technique, the **results** should be compared with those in a similar area in order to identify changes in sales peculiar to the test area itself. A similar yardstick can be obtained by initial consumer research in the test area which is then repeated at a later date to assess changes in tastes and preferences.

If test plans are changed, it may be a wise precaution to change the test area. Results of new factors introduced into the original test area will be distorted by those that may still be working their way through. The company must take care that the **total effort** which it exerts in the area is one which can be maintained on a national scale; otherwise conclusions drawn from the test area results may be unduly optimistic.

### The test period

The length of the **test-market period** should be long enough to cater for all the possible seasonal fluctuations in demand and perhaps confirm the trends which have been identified in consumer research. The test area should be kept under continuous scrutiny even after the national launch has commenced and has been running for some time. This monitoring process will give an early indication of trends as they develop and lead the company to check them on a national scale.

The initial response of consumers to new or improved products will in any case not be a true indication of future spending habits on a more permanent basis. The initial purchase may have been on a promotional offer to encourage a consumer to make the first purchase, or simply curiosity on the part of the consumer. The test period must therefore be sufficiently long to allow changes of a more permanent nature to show themselves as the consumers eventually place the product within their scale of tastes and preferences.

## MEASURING AND FORECASTING DEMAND

### The value of measuring and forecasting demand

Deciding on markets to enter and what parts or segments of those markets to concentrate on requires organisations to try to **measure and forecast demand.** Such measurements and forecasts can be short-, medium- or long-term, covering local to world sales, from individual items to an organisation's total product range.

In all cases the objective is to provide information to aid the organisation's planning. Short-term forecasts of demand are of value to an organisation trying to make the optimum decisions concerning the purchasing of raw materials and components, scheduling production and financing. Profits may be sacrificed if the market is either over- or underestimated. The extent to which organisations engage in these activities is almost directly proportionate to the size and sophistication of their operations.

### The market

Any measurement or forecast requires a fairly sound understanding of the **market** involved. The 'market' refers to the actual and potential consumers who satisfy the following conditions:

- they have expressed an **interest** in owning the product;
- they have the **income** to afford to buy the product;
- they have the **opportunity** to buy the product.

All the consumers satisfying the first condition are said to make up the **potential markets.** The second and third conditions mean that only some of the potential market are able to make themselves available as consumers; they are said to make up the **available market.** The organisation may then decide to serve only part of the available market; the part(s) or segment(s) it concentrates on are known as the **target market**. Those consumers who are already buying the organisation's or its competitors' products are said to make up the **penetrated market**.

Fig. 11.7 illustrates these definitions in terms of the sale of Superior Lager. This sort of information is very useful for market planning. In the case of Superior Lager, if it wanted to increase its sales it might do this by trying to attract more consumers in the target market. It might expand to other available markets, such as outside London. It could lower the price of lager to increase the size of the available market. Or it could increase the size of the potential market by running a large promotional campaign.

### Methods of measuring demand

Market planning requires the measurement of the following:

(a) the total sales of the industry as a whole;
(b) the share of sales going to the particular organisation in question ('market share');
(c) the total demand in the market;
(d) the level of demand in particular areas within the market.

In the case of (a), **total industry sales,** this information is often available through the industry's trade association or from private market research firms. By expressing its own sales as a percentage of the figure obtained from these sources, it is possible for the individual organisation to calculate its own **market share** (b).

The **total demand in the market** (c) must be viewed as the total volume that would be purch-

**Fig. 11.7: The market for Superior Lager (an upmarket drink)**

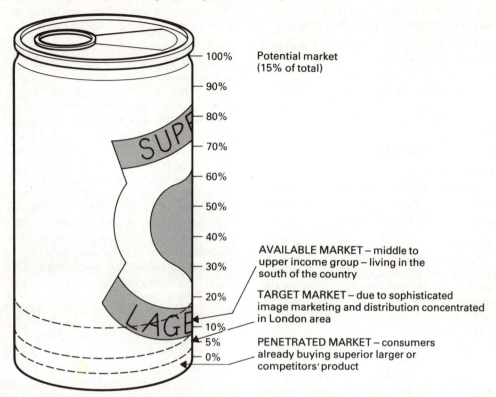

Potential market
(15% of total)

AVAILABLE MARKET – middle to
upper income group – living in the
south of the country

TARGET MARKET – due to sophisticated
image marketing and distribution concentrated
in London area

PENETRATED MARKET – consumers
already buying superior larger or
competitors' product

ased at a particular point in time, by a specified consumer group, in a defined geographical area, under particular economic conditions and a defined level of marketing in the industry. One of the most common ways of estimating this level of demand is by the formula:

*total market demand = number of buyers in the specific market × quantity purchased by an average buyer per year × the average price per unit of the product.*

For example, if the manufacturers of Superior Lager estimate that within the specific market they are interested in there are 800,000 buyers, that they purchase on average 75 cans of lager each year and that the average price is 45p per can, then the total market demand may be estimated as:

800,000 × 75 × 45p = £27,000,000.

In our example, Superior Lager initially concentrated its marketing efforts on the London area. To make this sort of decision, a company must be able to estimate the **level of market demand** in a particular area (d). This is often carried out by identifying the most important factors influencing the buying power in the market, such as the percentages of disposable income, total retail sales and population in the area. The relative importance of these different factors is then indicated by allocating weights to them, depending upon the type and state of the marketing environment in which the organisation operates. The weighted factors are then combined into a mathematical model which can be used to establish a weighted index of buying power for the whole area.

For example, if a food chain selling health foods was expanding its operation on a national basis it would need to look at the relative buying power of different areas before deciding where it should locate any new outlets. One of the areas it might be considering could be Westshire, with 0.05 per cent of the nation's disposable income, 0.08 per cent of retail sales and 0.055 per cent of population. If income was weighted as the most important factor at 0.5, retail sales next at 0.3 and then population at 0.2, the following model might be developed:

% national buying power = 0.5 (% of national disposable personal income in the area) + 0.3 (% of national retail sales in the area) + 0.2 (% of national population in the area)

% national buying power = (0.5 × .05) + (0.3 × .08) + (0.2 × .055)

∴ % national buying power = 0.06.

If the chain has estimated that total national sales could reach £1000 million, then Westshire could yield

1,000,000,000 × .0006 = £600,000.

This could then be compared with figures from other areas in order to make a decision.

The accuracy and value of this kind of calculation depend upon the weights selected and the quality of statistics used.

### Forecasting demand

It is more difficult to forecast **future demand** accurately than it is to measure current demand. This is because it involves predicting what buyers are likely to do under a given set of circumstances in the future. A general approach that can be taken to sales forecasting involves three stages. The company starts by making an economic forecast as to the future levels of gross national product. This is then used along with a number of other indicators to make a forecast as to the future levels of industry sales. The company then bases its own sales forecast on the assumption that it will achieve a certain proportion of industry sales.

There are a number of more specific approaches that can be taken to sales forecasting. First, it is possible to carry out a survey of **potential buyers' future intentions** and determine the probability of a particular group of people buying a product in the future. Second, it is possible to carry out a survey of **expert opinion** within the industry. This could involve contacting sales representatives, suppliers, distributors and trade associations in order to build up a picture of what they think might happen in the future. Such an approach is often taken by car producers who survey their dealers in order to forecast short-term future demand. Third, a more scientific and mathematical approach to forecasting makes use of **time series analysis.** This involves analysing past data on sales in order to predict probable future trends.

Activity 11.2

For over ten years Rachel Daniels has been employed in the catering industry as a chef. Two months ago the restaurant she had been working for was forced to trim its staff, and she was made redundant, receiving redundancy pay of £13,500. Rachel has a house which has a market value of £65,000, with an outstanding mortgage of £25,000. She had decided to use her assets, knowledge and skills to set up in business on her own. Suggest three areas that she might consider moving into and in each case identify the market information that would be of value to her and describe how she might collect it.

Activity 11.3

Working in groups of four, examine a particular product in as much detail as possible. The product selected should be one which would normally be expected to fall within the current expenditure pattern of the average student's financial resources.

Each group should adopt the role of manufacturer of the product. The rest of the class, acting as potential customers, should ask questions about various features of the product. Tape-record the proceedings. An analysis of the discussion can then be conducted, with the following objectives in mind:

(a) information that could be of use to the manufacturer's market research department;
(b) the extent to which customers' opinions may have been unduly influenced by irrational factors arising out of the discussion itself rather than their experience with the product.

## METHODS OF PRICE DETERMINATION

It is extremely important for organisations to develop the optimum **pricing policy**, because pricing is the only element within the marketing mix that produces **revenue**; all the others represent costs. As we saw in *Business Organisations and Environments* Book 1, the organisation can be selling its product in a number of different types of market, covering competitive, imperfectly competitive, oligopolistic and monopolistic situations. In a highly competitive market, prices are basically determined by market forces. In the case of the other market types, there is an opportunity to influence prices to some degree. So organisations need to develop some sort of pricing policy.

### Developing a pricing policy

There are a number of stages that any organisation needs to go through in developing its pricing policy.

1. It has to decide upon its own **pricing objectives**, which will reflect the organisation's overall objectives, as discussed in Book 1, Chapter 1. If its overall objective is to maximise current profits, then it will estimate the potential demand and costs and select a price which maximises current profits. But if it is more interested in achieving security, then it may do this by trying to achieve a larger market share, thus setting a lower price. Again, if it is concerned ultimately with status and prestige, it may attempt to produce a product of the highest possible quality and so will need to set the price at a higher level in order to cover the necessary research and development costs.

2. Through market research the organisation needs to establish the **level of demand** for the product at different prices. From this it may be possible to derive a demand schedule and determine the degree of **price elasticity**. The more inelastic the demand for the product, the higher the company can set its price.

3. The organisation needs to identify and state clearly the **costs** associated with the project. Ultimately the price that is set must in the long term recover the costs of producing, distributing and selling the product, plus some sort of return. As we saw in Book 1, Chapter 6, total costs are made up of both fixed and variable elements. **Fixed costs** are those that do not vary no matter what changes occur in output; they might include plant, machinery, rent and rates. **Variable costs** vary directly with the level of output and are incurred only when output takes place. For example, if output increases so will the variable costs associated with such inputs as

labour, raw materials and energy. In formulating a pricing policy it is necessary to study the behaviour of such costs in the short, long and very long run.

4. Pricing has to be **competitive**. So it is important to analyse possible competitors' prices and offers. Information may be gathered directly by sending out researchers to compare prices and offers in the shops or by studying the price lists of competitors.

5. The organisation is now in a position to select a **pricing method**. It must produce a price which reflects the organisation's objectives, the price elasticity of demand for the product, the organisation's costs and competitors' prices. There are four main approaches to this problem, as follows.

*Cost-plus pricing*
**Cost-plus pricing** is a rather elementary and crude method of pricing. It involves establishing the total costs of producing a particular product, adding a standard margin or mark-up and pricing the product accordingly. For example, it may cost a manufacturer of electrical goods £6 to produce an electric kettle. If the firm then added a $33\frac{1}{3}$ per cent mark-up, it would then set the price at £8 to the electrical retailer. This is a method widely used by many construction companies; in some areas a **standard mark-up** exists, as in the case of books sold by retailers, which normally have a 33⅓ per cent mark-up.

The major weakness of this system is that it fails to reflect market forces. If the price has been set too high, the level of sales will suffer; whereas if it has been set at too low a level, some profits may be sacrificed. The system works reasonably well if all the firms within a particular industry broadly use the same methods, so that prices move together.

*Break-even charts and the target level of profit*
This method uses the concept of a **break-even chart** as shown in Fig. 11.8. You will have studied these in your Finance Module in year 1. It shows total costs and total revenues at different volumes of sales. **Fixed costs** occur irrespective of whether production takes place, and total **variable costs** rise with the level of output. The price must be set at a level at which the firm at least covers its variable costs, otherwise there is no point in continuing production.

**Fig. 11.8: Break-even chart and target profit level**

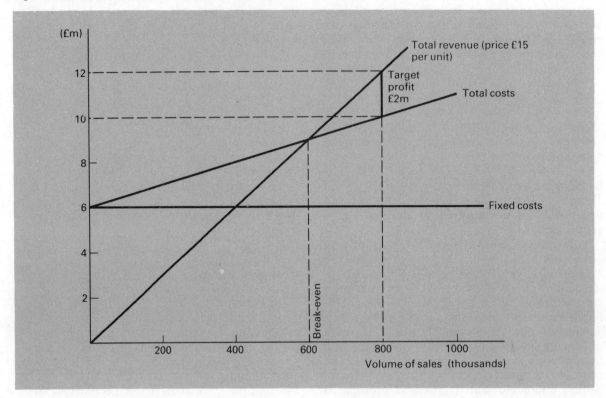

Profits will arise only at a volume of sales above the break-even level, because only at this point have fixed and variable costs been covered.

In the case of the example in Fig. 11.8, at a price of £15 per unit and with the given cost structure, the firm will break even at a volume of sales of 600,000. If the firm's objective is to achieve a target profit of £2 million then it would have to achieve a level of sales of 800,000 at a price of £15 per unit. It is possible that by charging a higher price the firm may achieve its objective of £2 million profit with a lower volume of sales. This is because the slope of the total revenue curve would be steeper, and so the firm would break even at a lower volume of sales. Ultimately the price and volume of sales at which the firm will achieve this target level of profit will depend upon the firm's demand schedule and the price elasticity of demand. So this break-even analysis is of value only if it is viewed in the context of the demand situation facing the firm.

*Perceived value pricing*
By working on the non-price variables in the marketing mix it may be possible for the organisation to raise the consumer's perception of the product. The price may then be set at a level to capture this **perceived value.** For example, take a simple product like fish and chips. If they were served up in newspaper in a fish bar then a consumer might be prepared to pay £1.25 for them. If, on the other hand, the consumer ate them off a plate in a café he or she might accept a price of £2.50. In the atmosphere of a restaurant the same fish and chips might appear on the menu for £5.50, and in a hotel restaurant a resident might happily pay £7 for them as part of the evening meal. The higher price can be charged due to the different surroundings and atmosphere in which the fish and chips are being consumed.

This method of pricing relies upon very accurate research into how people view a particular product and put a value on the non-price variables in the marketing mix.

The consumer's perception of the value of a product may in fact be lowered if the organisation *reduces* its price. This is because the consumer may view a lower price as being synonymous with a product of a lower quality. Such an attitude is often taken towards electrical goods, where the consumer may feel that if the product is priced below the expected range, then there must be something wrong with it technically, or it must be accompanied by a poor standard of after-sales service. This view is further supported by the fact that some products, such as Heinz baked beans, are more expensive than other brands; but consumers are prepared to pay the higher price because they feel the product is of a higher quality.

*Market-rate pricing*
In the case of many smaller organisations which lack the sophisticated research techniques to determine their own prices, a simple solution is merely to charge what is considered to be the going **market rate** amongst their competitors. Then at least their price reflects the collective wisdom of the industry overall.

**Fig. 11.9**

# Teenage rampage

Teenagers have become an increasingly exciting market for the media. Despite their declining numbers and the effects of unemployment and recession, teenagers clearly have money to spend, the result of which is a steady flow of new magazines.

Towards the end of the Seventies, the 'Big Four' weeklies (*Melody Maker, Sounds, New Musical Express* and *Record Mirror*) dominated the market. Today the picture looks completely different. While more people than ever are buying pop magazines, [Fig. 11.10] shows that the circulation of the tabloids has declined.

What people are buying now is a different type of publication. At the younger end of the music market the growth started seven years ago with the launch of *Smash Hits*.

Every time circulation figures are published, *Smash Hits* breaks its record for selling more pop magazines than any other publication. In 1983 *No.1* was launched and in 18 months improved on its first audited circulation figure by 40 per cent. Between them, *Smash Hits* and *No.1* reach one in four of the country's young people. These pop glossies now dominate the market.

Catering for somewhat older readers are *Blitz*, the *Face* and *i-D*: stylish, innovative and very glossy titles, all launched by small and independent publishers.

# The tabloid response

One result of the changing market has been to make the tabloids fight to regain their lost sales. Given the increase in the number of competitive titles and their very wordy format, they had to try harder than ever to appeal to the young. *Sounds, NME* and *Melody Maker*, however, still don't seem to have made sufficiently dramatic differences to their editorial styles.

Source: Wight Collins Rutherford Scott, 'Mediabank: the Music Press', *Marketing Week*, 2 August 1985.

Activity 11.4
Carefully study the extract and charts in Fig. 11.9 and 11.10, then write brief notes on the following:

(a) The general trends in the UK music press.
(b) The factors which influence the demand for the music press.
(c) The type of editorial and commercial strategy that might be adopted by the *NME, Sounds* and *Melody Maker*.

**Fig. 11.10**

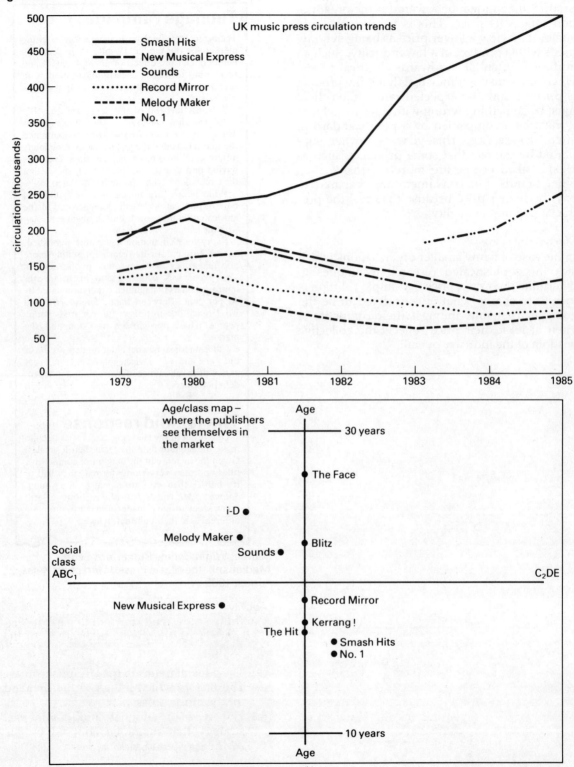

Source: Wight Collins Rutherford Scott, 'Mediabank: the Music Press', *Marketing Week*, 2 August 1985.

## Pricing policy of the nationalised industries

The pricing policy of the **nationalised industries** has traditionally been rather confused. This is largely because of the conflict they face between their commercial and social objectives. Commercially they have been supposed to finance their own activities by charging for the services that they provide. However, their **social obligations** have often been in conflict with this, because of the responsibility to provide services throughout the whole country at a price that people can reasonably afford. For example, electricity may have been provided to rural areas at less than full cost and subsidised out of the proceeds from a more profitable part of the service.

This is really a question of deciding whether the pricing policy of the nationalised industries should reflect marginal or average costs. This is something that governments have found extremely difficult to clarify. Following the post-war nationalisation period, the industries were required to break even, which meant that they were able to set their prices equal to average costs at any level. However, it was felt that such a system was not particularly efficient and led to cross-subsidisation.

So in 1967 the White Paper *Nationalised Industries: A Review of Economic and Financial Objectives* emphasised the need for marginal cost pricing. This focuses on the pricing of individual goods and services and avoids cross-subsidisation. The White Paper also tried to distinguish social from commercial objectives, by the government giving subsidies or grants for non-commercial operations. This approach led to some improvements in the late 1960s which were then wiped out, firstly, by the price restraint of the early 1970s, and then by rapid price increases following the change of government in 1974.

Another attempt was made to clarify the situation in 1978, when the White Paper *Nationalised Industries* was published. This tried to reintroduce the approach advocated by its predecessor in 1967. The election of a Conservative government in 1979 added a further element to the pricing position of the nationalised industries. The new government attempted to put pressure on the nationalised industries' prices, first by increasing market competition and subsequently by privatisation.

## METHODS OF PRODUCT DISTRIBUTION

The selection of the most effective means of **distribution** is an essential part of the responsibilities of the marketing department of a company. Not only should the distribution costs be kept at a competitive level, they should also encourage the consumer to re-purchase, not solely on the basis of price, but also because the selection of distributive outlet can increase the extent to which the product is consumer-orientated. This is one of the reasons for the increased tendency for manufacturers to bypass the wholesaler and deal direct with retail units or consumers themselves, because of the savings in costs which such a move may produce, and the closer connection with market trends.

Four such channels of distribution will be examined.

### The wholesaler

Although often accused of simply taking a cut and contributing to higher prices, the **wholesaler** plays a vital role in many areas of distribution. Since independent wholesalers still exist, it can be concluded that both manufacturers and retailers still see advantages in using their services. If either the manufacturer or retailer believe that they can perform these services, a wholesaler will be avoided in the interests of both profit and competitive sales. It is difficult to imagine manufacturers and retailers allowing wholesalers a mark-up if no benefits accrue to either of them.

*Advantages*
The advantage of wholesalers are as follows.

1. The wholesaler is prepared to **buy in bulk**, which allows the manufacturer to benefit from fewer but larger orders, with resulting economies of scale for production, and the avoidance of what may be a high minimum outlay for sales and transport facilities. Producing a multitude of small and perhaps differentiated orders will not allow long production runs unless the producer is prepared to tie up capital in large stocks of finished goods and warehousing or storage facilities.

2. **Less costly administrative work** in that fewer but larger accounts will have to be dealt with.

3. An experienced and effective **sales force** takes time to build up, and the advantages of a

market trend will not be fully exhibited if the firm is a newcomer to the market.

4. The **delivery costs** of small consignments to a large number of retail outlets or consumers widely dispersed may weaken the product's competitive position.

5. The wholesaler can assist the manufacturer in avoiding **seasonal fluctuations in output** which would otherwise involve the accumulation of stocks if capacity was to be utilised so that unit costs of production were kept to an acceptable level. If the manufacturer was obliged to install capacity to meet a peak demand, spare capacity would raise unit costs in the slack periods.

6. From its retailers' point of view, by using a wholesaler they avoid the necessity of dealing with **a large number of widely dispersed manufacturers**; they can also obtain supplies in more acceptable quantities which can readily be replenished. This is particularly important for the small retailer unable to hold large stocks and without premises for storage. If they dealt direct with the manufacturer, they would have to pay higher prices for small quantities.

7. Retailers may also receive **credit** from the wholesaler as well as benefiting from advice on window displays and sales in other areas where a new product is involved. As will be seen, it is in the interest of the wholesaler that the small independent retailer does survive, because the expansion of large-scale production and retailing is bypassing the independent wholesaler.

8. The wholesaler may undertake **specialist activities** involving blending, processing or packaging, which when conducted on behalf of many producers can be carried out on a more economic scale. As with many aspects of wholesaling, the facilities and staff are spread over a larger and wider range of products, and these are opportunities not available to some small manufacturers.

9. Large wholesalers may be willing to purchase the product and market it under their **own brand name**. This will reduce the need for promotional activities by the original producer, since the wholesaler will undertake this aspect of marketing.

10. **Speed of distribution** may be vital with perishable products, such as fruit and vegetables. The specialist activities of wholesale traders may be advantageous for reaching a scattered market.

11. A new company with very limited trading experience and financial resources may initially use a wholesaler who will have a greater **knowledge of local customers** in terms of creditworthiness and size and frequency of orders.

The independent wholesaler still survives, along with the small independent retail unit, particularly in the field of groceries and hardware and where the blending and processing of commodities such as tea, coffee and wool has produced specialist skills. The development of the **cash-and-carry** trade has led to the provision of facilities that allow both wholesalers and retailers to remain competitive in the face of rapidly changing market conditions.

## The retailer

*Direct contact with manufacturers*
The growth of both the size and scale of operations of retail units and the growth of consumer spending has brought about increased opportunities for both retail units and manufacturers to **deal direct** with each other. Large supermarkets and chain stores mean fewer retail units but they are prepared to buy in bulk as well as conducting their own blending, processing, packaging and in particular branding of foodstuffs. Direct contact with these retail units proves very attractive to manufacturers. The wholesaling function does not disappear but is absorbed by either the retailer or the manufacturer, to whom such activities now become more economic.

Manufacturers have also **diversified**, so that the costs of dealing direct with a retailer are now spread over a wider range of products. Many of these products have achieved a hard-won **brand image**. This will have created a degree of brand loyalty and thus a consistent demand, which is of primary concern to retailers because such a product will have a relatively short **shelf life**.

The reputation for **freshness** associated with a brand of food will be better protected by avoiding the wholesaler. Dealing direct with retail units allows great influence over the product. The appeal of particular brands is maintained by **advertising** on a national scale, and the resulting demand must be met by an adequate shop distribution; whereas wholesalers promoting their own brands will be in direct competition with such manufacturers.

*Limitations of wholesaling*
The sales staff of a wholesaler may be primarily concerned with maximising total sales, whereas the **manufacturers' representatives** will be pushing their own brand. These representatives, via the retailers, will have a more direct contact with the market; and trends that develop can be more effectively communicated to the manufacturer, which allows a better co-ordination of marketing activities. Where **new or restyled products** are involved, the wholesaler may prove to be rather conservative and prefer to deal in well-known lines until the product becomes established, by which time the producer will have developed an alternative means of distribution.

Some products by their very nature are distributed direct to retailers. This includes relatively expensive products where distribution costs can be borne by the producer without a severe impact upon the competitive position or profit margins. It is not necessary for retailers to deal in large and varied stocks of consumer durables; they are not expected to buy television sets or washing-machines in bulk. Manufacturers may perhaps conduct their own wholesaling function in such products where **after-sales service** is required, and where close contact with retail units giving such services will be necessary.

*Mobility*
The increasing popularity of manufacturers dealing direct with retailers has been given added momentum by the increased **mobility of consumers**, allowing them to shop in cities and towns for the bulk of their purchases. This has increased the turnover of fewer but larger retail units. Where congestion in city centres has created problems, retail units have responded by taking sites in out-of-town shopping centres and establishing **hypermarkets.** This also assists in deliveries and increases warehousing facilities. Manufacturers have themselves benefited from the building of **motorways** and from the development of larger commercial vehicles. Some of these vehicles are of a specialist nature, according to the product in question, such as frozen food.

**Mail order**
With the use of **mail order** both the wholesaler and the retailer are bypassed. The manufacturer deals direct with the consumer. Methods of distribution change in accordance with social habits and pressures, and recent years have seen rapid growth in the mail-order business. This would seem an obvious means of selling to a market where the consumers are widely dispersed and where access to urban shopping areas for a wide selection of products is not readily available. Such a description does not apply to many areas of the UK, yet mail order has still increased significantly. This growth can be attributed to several factors.

*Reasons for growth*
An important element may be the **time and effort involved in travelling** to what may be crowded shopping centres, and even then with no guarantee that a particular requirement can be satisfied. The growth of **branded products** with an established reputation provides the consumer with increased security concerning the quality of the product purchased via a mail-order system.

There may be the possibility that a **lower price** can be paid, because the manufacturer or dealer may be able to make significant savings in the marketing of the product. The warehouse and administrative centre can be sited outside an urban area, and the lower property prices may permit a more extensive service to be provided. A large sales force is not required, but this must be balanced against postal, advertising and delivery charges.

The products selected for mail order must not incur large **transport costs**, particularly if a national market is being served. The costs of **packing** fragile goods would be an additional consideration.

Some consumers are attracted by the sense of being regarded as a **personal customer**, especially where the product has an exclusive appeal; this is a common feature of mail-order advertisements in the more expensive magazines. In fact, one of the main advantages of mail order is that a postal approach or an advertisement in a particular publication can concentrate upon the **sector of the market** where the bulk of the demand is expected to arise. If the product is not expected to have a wide popular appeal, then neither a sales organisation nor widespread advertising will be justified; nor will either the wholesaler or retailer express a strong interest in the product. The **advertising cost** will be high if the product is to be adequately described; a colour picture may be important, and space must be available for instructions for purchasing and the order form itself.

There is a tendency to associate mail order with the well-established companies such as Great Universal Stores and Littlewoods, but in fact there are more than 2000 UK firms dealing with consumers via mail order. Their products range from clothing, motor-vehicle accessories, limited editions of prints and silverware, to double glazing, DIY products and chest expanders. Virtually anything that is reasonably economic to transport lends itself to mail order.

Activity 11.5
Make a survey of the magazine supplements of the quality newspapers and identify those advertisements which display goods that are being offered for distribution via mail order. Describe the main features of these advertisements and any common characteristics you can identify in both the style of the advertisement and the goods themselves.

### Marketing boards

**Marketing boards** are designed to strengthen the bargaining position of many widely dispersed producers by co-ordinating their marketing, by administering price-support schemes and by standardising output. They play an important part in the marketing of milk, hops, potatoes and wool and have been used for pigs, bacon, tomatoes and eggs. Members sell their output to the relevant marketing board at a price fixed by the board, which in turn sells to the market. If the price is set too high, this can lead to over-production and the creation of a surplus which may be both difficult and expensive to store.

With some products supported by schemes in the **European Community** this has led to the continued accumulation of **surpluses**, which cannot be released within the Community since this would defeat the object of guaranteed prices. High prices have been necessary in the Community because its farms are on the whole much smaller and less efficient than those in the UK, and the agricultural workforce is larger in number and hence in political strength. As yet the Common Agricultural Policy has not managed to avoid the continual build-up of surpluses.

Marketing boards have an unenviable task. They must adopt a system of marketing which, by reducing price competition, meets the needs of producers, consumers and is in the interests of the economy as a whole.

# 12. Contract Law

This chapter offers a brief examination of the **contracted relationship** between a business organisation and its clients. Studying the law can be daunting if it is regarded as a dry and tedious subject. What is presented here is factual, but the text is supported by some lively activities which you are encouraged to resolve. In this way you can appreciate the application of contract law to everyday situations.

## WHAT IS A CONTRACT?

### The contract as a voluntary bargain

A contract is a **legally binding agreement** made between two (or more) parties. Agreement means a 'meeting of minds', i.e. parties to a contract must agree to all the terms and must intend that their agreement shall be upheld and legally enforceable. While every contract is an agreement, not every agreement is a contract.

The contract is the basis of all commercial transactions, whether for sale of goods, credit, the provision of services, insurance policies, the establishment of a business, owning shares or starting work with an employer. Contracts are very much part of our daily lives, and people often undertake them without realising it. The popular conception of a contract is that it has to be a complex legal document containing difficult clauses, with seals attached and bound up by the lawyers' red tape. In some cases this is true, but none of it is necessary just to buy a cup of tea in the college refectory – and that act is just as much one of contract as, say, asking Taylor Woodrow to build an airport terminal, or importing raw materials which you then sell to ICI. Certainly there is no comparison between buying a railway tricket for £1.20 and selling machine tools to Saudi Arabia for £120,000 except that contract forms the inescapable **foundation of agreement.**

*The essentials of a valid contract*
The following elements must be present if a contract is to be made – see Fig. 12.1.

- There must be a clear and certain **offer** made by one party and a clear **acceptance** of it made by the other.
- The parties must **intend** their agreement to have legal effect.
- Each party must enjoy the legal **capacity** to make a contract.
- There must be some **consideration**, i.e. the exchange of mutual advantage.
- There must be genuine **consent**; the agreement must not be obtained by fraud or duress.
- The object of the contract must be **legal**.
- The contract must comply with any laid-down **formalities**.
- The contract must be **possible** to perform.

These elements are explained below.

## THE CONTRACTUAL AGREEMENT

Having stated the basics, it is necessary to explore in more detail the major constituents of any contract, regardless of its simplicity or complexity. The majority of the fundamental contractual rules have been developed largely by the courts as the need for regulation has become evident. *A contract arises when the parties involved make an agreement which is to be enforceable at law.* In simple terms, this occurs when one party (the **offeror**) makes a firm offer to another party (the **offeree**), who **unconditionally** accepts.

### Offer

In the majority of cases, an **offer** is made to a clearly defined offeree, but offers can also be made to the 'world at large'. Where an offer is made to a person or a group of persons, only that person or group is entitled to accept (or reject) that offer. In the case of an offer being made to the 'world at large', then *anyone* may accept so long as the terms of the offer are complied with. This situation can arise when a company is attempting to promote a product or

**Fig. 12.1: Making a contract**

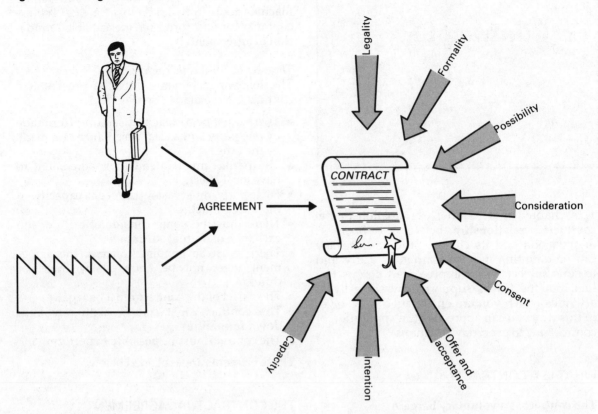

service and those buying it are entitled to claim, for example, a prize, or a 'money off next purchase' voucher (subject to the performance of some task, like sending off so many wrappers) or money back if the product fails to satisfy (subject to being used according to instructions).

A court of law will want to be certain that an offer has in fact been made and is capable of being accepted to form a binding contract. An offer needs to be distinguished from what is known as an **invitation to treat**. In other words, is the seller really offering goods for sale or is he or she just inviting offers? Goods on display in a shop window or on the shelves of a supermarket are an invitation to treat and not an offer to sell. When a customer selects an item and takes it to the cashier with the intention of paying, the customer's action is an **offer to buy**. The cashier accepts the offer and takes the money in payment.

If a mink coat is displayed in the window and priced at £25, the seller is under no obligation to sell that coat at the stated price. If the coat has been wrongly priced, the seller is entitled to say so and refuse to sell it. Equally, he or she is under no obligation to sell at all. The same principles can be applied to prices set out in price lists, catalogues and circulars, and to a prospectus issued by a company inviting the public to subscribe for its shares.

An invitation to treat is often merely a **statement of a price** which need not be construed as an offer to sell, but this is not always a straightforward matter. Sellers cannot always hide behind invitation to treat in all cases. The Trades Descriptions Act 1968 provides that 'persons exposing goods for supply or having goods in their possession for supply shall be deemed to offer to supply them'.

A seller is legally protected if he or she genuinely and inadvertently misprices an item. But he or she is subject to prosecution under Section 11 of the Trades Description Act should he or she seek deliberately to mislead customers over prices.

*Options*

An **option** is an offer to keep a contract *open* for a specified period of time. It is not binding unless supported by some form of consideration. It is not enough to secure a bare promise from a seller that you have first refusal and that he or she won't sell until you have had the opportunity of making up your mind or making your arrangements. Suppose Watts wants to buy Glew's business. Glew may give Watts an option to buy the business subject to a consideration of, say, £1000 to keep the offer open for one month, during which time no other contract for sale of the business shall be entered into. The £1000 binds Glew not to sell his business but to keep it available for one month in case Watts decides to buy it. Thus if Glew revokes the option, having received £1000, by selling to Wells within the agreed time, then Watts can seek remedy through the courts.

*Termination of offer*

An offer is terminated:

- on the **death** or either offeror or offeree before acceptance (if death should occur after acceptance, the contract may still be held to be valid, and the deceased's personal representative may insist on performance);
- by **non-acceptance** within the time stipulated for acceptance, or within reasonable time (if a time has been stipulated, the offer lapses when the time has expired; the term 'reasonable time' will be determined by a court from the circumstances of the case);
- when **revoked** before acceptance (the withdrawal or revocation of an offer must be communicated to the offeree before acceptance; revocation has no effect until it is brought to the attention and notice of the offeree);
- when **rejected** by the offeree (this may take two forms: (a) where the offeree communicates his or her rejection to the offeror, or (b) where the offeree makes a counter-offer).

## Tenders

The **tender** is commonplace in business and very much part of competition. The party inviting the tenders is clearly looking for the supply of the best materials, equipment, services, etc. at the keenest prices.

The essential features of tender are:

- Where tenders are invited for the supply of specified goods or services, and *each* tender is an **offer**, then the party inviting the tenders may accept any tender of his or her choice and thus bring about a binding contract. It is usual for the tenderer meeting the specifications at the lowest price to be accepted.
- Where tenders are invited to supply a party **as and when demanded**, the party submitting a tender is making a **standing offer**. The acceptance of a standing offer does not have the same effect as the acceptance of a definite order, since there is a **separate acceptance** each and every time an order is raised. Thus a new and distinct contract is made on each occasion.

## Acceptance

An offer must be communicated to an offeree before it can be **accepted**. No one can be said to have accepted an offer of which he or she is ignorant. Once the existence of an offer has been established, the court must be satisfied that the offeree *actually accepted the offer*; otherwise there is no contract.

It may be difficult to state exactly when a contract is formed. Offer and acceptance can be made **orally**. If a party does not wish to be legally bound until a **written** agreement has been prepared, he or she must clearly state his or her position and intention. The term **'subject to contract'** is in wide use (particularly by estate agents) and means that the parties to a proposed contract do not *yet* wish to be bound. Perhaps, for example, one of the parties has still to raise the finance.

A contract cannot arise until and unless there is a **firm offer** and a **positive unconditional acceptance**. Difficulties can occur if the terms used in a contract are imprecise or vague, resulting in ambiguity or uncertainty. A court will not enforce a contract if it is without meaning or definition, but if a court can see beyond reasonable doubt that the parties *intended* legal relations, then maybe the agreement will be enforced. Statements and/or conduct will be carefully scrutinised in the context of the express and implied meanings; particular attention will be paid to any previous dealings between the parties, customs of the trade, codes of conduct or any other relevant factor.

*Terms of acceptance*

Sometimes an offeree responds to an offer by attempting to introduce a **new term or condition**; e.g. the offeror wants to sell a car 'as seen' for £2000, and the offeree agrees to the price subject to the car being fitted with a new set of tyres. This additional term is really no part of the proposed contract, and its legal effect is to reject the offer. This is known as **counter-offer**, and the offeror has the right then to withdraw the car from sale. If the offeree then backs down and agrees to the terms, the offeror has the right not to deal, simply because he or she has already been rejected. In day-to-day transactions of this nature, bargaining inevitably takes place, and many contracts would not arise if every attempt by a buyer to gain some advantage was rejected out of hand. Requests for further information about an offer must not be construed as counter-offers.

Acceptance may be subject to **specific terms** prescribed by the offeror. It follows that for acceptance to be recognised those terms must be followed. If the offeror makes it clear that only one particular method will suffice, there is no contract unless the offeree accepts by the prescribed method. Thus, if acceptance is demanded by letter sent first-class post, acceptance by telephone would be insufficient, as it would not comply with the terms.

*Rules of acceptance*

The basic **rules of acceptance** can be summarised thus:

- Acceptance must be communicated by the person(s) authorised to make it.
- Acceptance must be clearly communicated, e.g. it may be made orally but it is not enough that it be spoken; it must be *heard* by the offeror.
- Mental acceptance (consenting in one's mind) is not legally acceptable; e.g. 'If I don't hear from you by Saturday I shall assume that the house is mine.'
- Where the offeror makes no stipulation of terms of acceptance, the offeree is free to choose his or her own method.

If the offeror demands that the proper means of communication between the parties should be **by post**, the following additional rules apply:

- An offer has no effect until it **reaches** the offeree.
- The contract is made the moment the letter accepting the offer is **properly posted** (even though it might not reach its destination).
- **Revocation** of an offer is communicated when the letter of revocation is received and read by the offeree.

These days 'properly posted' would mean recorded or even registered post; otherwise there is no proof of posting. The second point above may seem curious, but any organisation not wanting to run any risks of postal delays and doubtful claims can state that no contract will be formed until the offeror has received communication of the offeree's acceptance.

For some organisations the post is far too slow a method of doing business. Those dealing in, say, commodities or currency expect to be able to contact other dealers or market-makers wherever they are in the world at a moment's notice. The telephone, the telex and computer system are all examples of **instantaneous communication**. In such cases a contract is complete only when the acceptance is received by the offeror at his or her end of the line.

## Intention to create legal relations

The intention that the agreement shall have **legal effect** is an essential element in any contract. Where no intention to be bound can be attributed to the parties, there is no contract. The test of intention is *objective*; that is, a court will seek to give effect to the **presumed intentions** of the parties.

In commercial agreeements there is a presumption that the parties intended to create legal relations. To rebut this presumption it must be shown that the parties did not intend to be legally bound. Parties are not contractually bound where an agreement is expressed to be binding in *honour* only, or where it is expressed to be 'subject to contract'.

Because a contract is an agreement that is intended to have legal consequences, agreements of a purely social or domestic nature cannot be termed contracts, although some may have legal implications. There is the presumption that the parties did not intend legal relations to arise, but this is rebuttable by an evidence to the contrary.

Although it is possible for parties to make an

agreement which does not impose contractual rights and obligations, it is not possible to make any agreement which ousts or challenges the jurisdiction of the courts. The question as to whether the parties intended to create legal relations is always for a court to determine.

## Capacity

**Capacity** refers to a party's legal status to make a contract. Essentially the law recognises that any party may enter into a binding contract, with the following exceptions:

### *Infants or minors*

This category includes all parties under the age of 18. **Young people** can make contracts but only for **necessaries** – food, clothing, medical attention and educational books. They cannot make contracts for loans of money; if they do, the law will not help adults to recover the loans.

Valid contracts are of two kinds:

- contracts for necessaries – these will be for goods suitable to the condition in life of the young person and to his or her actual requirements at the time of sale and delivery;
- contracts for the minor's benefit – contracts of apprenticeship, training or education fall within this category.

### *Aliens (foreigners)*

An **alien** has the same contractual capacity as a British subject in peacetime (except that he or she may not acquire property in a British ship). In wartime an enemy alien cannot enter into a contract with a British subject. The test of whether a person is an enemy alien is not his or her nationality but the place where he or she resides or carries on business. A British subject resident in a hostile country may be classed as an enemy alien.

### *Insane and drunken persons*

A contract entered into by an **insane person** is voidable, but a liability exists to pay a reasonable price for necessaries. The contract may be repudiated at the will of the insane person. **Drunken persons** are treated in the same way, regarding contract, as those suffering from insanity.

### *Corporations*

**Corporations** are unable to make contracts of a personal nature.

- **Registered companies**: their powers are determined by the memorandum of association. These days a company will define its powers and activities so widely that it cannot be accused of acting *ultra vires*.
- **Statutory corporations**: they derive their powers from the statutes which create them. Any contract or act made *ultra vires* is void.
- **Chartered corporation**: their powers are to be found in the Royal Charters granting their corporate status. There are no limits to the contractual capacity of these organisations.

## Consideration

The rules governing **consideration** are rather complex, but every contract must be supported by consideration. Consideration can be defined as *the mutual exchange of advantage or the price for which the promise of another is bought*. A bare promise is not legally binding, as a promise without consideration is a gift; but one made for consideration is a bargain. A court will therefore be concerned with what the parties bargained to do and not with empty promises. Any contract for the sale of goods offers a good example of consideration in a contract – the goods are exchanged for money, and thus each party benefits.

### *Rules of consideration*

The rules of consideration can be summarised as follows.

1. It must be **genuine**. Consideration must have some value. A court will not enforce any vague or even sham promise or those promises in which there is no advantage or benefit at all.

2. It must not be **vague**. The promise made by a contracting party must be clear and definite. A vague promise cannot be binding unless the vagueness can be cured by the implication of terms.

3. It must be **legal**. Unlawful agreements are void. Where the consideration is either contrary to the rule of law or immoral, a court will not as a rule allow an action on the contract. If a party were to sue, the likelihood is that he or she would be charged for criminal conspiracy. The point applied under this head is that no action can arise from a base cause.

4. It must be **possible of performance**. The court cannot enforce any agreement which is outside human capability. An impossible or outrageous proposal would make a court ques-

tion whether the parties were genuine in their desire to be bound. However, a promise to undertake an impossible condition must be distinguished from a promise which, although possible of performance at the time when the contract was raised, subsequently becomes impossible, e.g. through outbreak of war.

5. It need not be **adequate**. Parties are generally regarded as being free to make their own bargains. So aggrieved parties cannot seek the assistance of a court just because they realise they have made a bad bargain. If a consumer buys goods at a price which he or she then discovers is markedly higher than he or she might have paid elsewhere, a court will entertain no case. Generally the adequacy of consideration is of no interest to a court except where there is any suggestion of fraud, duress or undue influence. So it is possible for a person to acquire a mink coat for £1 without incurring the displeasure of a court. But if a worthless vase should be sold as a genuine Ming, then the price or consideration becomes a material point, because the seller has the intention of deceiving a buyer.

There are perhaps two notable exceptions to this general rule, which are provided by consumer protection. The Consumer Credit Act 1974 introduced the concept of the *extortionate agreement*. Any credit agreement may be examined, amended and altered by a county court if the agreement appears to be grossly exorbitant or is contrary to the principles of fair dealing. The rate of interest will be scrutinised. The Act also includes sections to combat the more offensive aspects of door-to-door selling by allowing a customer who has signed a document **away from trade premises** after **oral persuasion** to cancel the agreement within five days, commencing usually after signing or after receiving the second statutory copy. This is the important exception to the rule that a party cannot back out of a contract once it is made.

6. It must not be **past**. This means that any benefit conferred in the past is not consideration for a present promise. Moral obligations of indebtedness have nothing at all to do with this matter.

7. It must **move from the promisee**. The relationship which exists between the parties of a contract is known as **privity of contract**. No stranger to a contract can sue one of the parties, since he or she would have provided no consid-

eration in return for the promise. Any action for a breach of contract must be brought by a party who gave consideration. To illustrate the point, if a person buys a gift for another and it turns out to be defective in some way, the recipient of that gift is a stranger to the contract and would not be able to take legal action. This situation is not to be confused with the code of conduct which any particular seller might support; e.g. on the evidence of a receipt a defective item will be exchanged, or the purchase price refunded.

## FORMS AND TERMS OF CONTRACT

### Forms

*Written*
The following contracts must be made **in writing** as demanded by Statute:

- Bills of exchange, cheques and promissory notes.
- Contracts of marine insurance.
- Contracts of hire purchase.
- An assignment of copyright.
- The transfer of shares in a registered company

These contracts must be **evidenced in writing**:

- Contracts of guarantee.
- Contracts of employment.
- Contracts for the sale of land.

*By deed*
These contracts are required to be made **by deed**:

- Transfers to title of land.
- Transfers of British ships.
- Leases of land for more than three years.
- Those contracts not supported by valuable consideration (e.g. promise of gifts).

*Defective contracts*
Unless contracts are **valid** they may be considered **defective**, i.e. lacking legal effect. There are three categories of defective contract:

- **Void**: a void contract is destitute of all legal effect and thus cannot confer any legal rights on the parties. In fact, a void contract is not a contract at all.

**Fig. 12.2: Example of standard terms and conditions**

## STANDARD CONDITIONS & REGULATIONS AS TO LETTING THE THEATRE

**1. APPLICATIONS AND FEES**

All applications for the hire of the Theatre shall be made to the Theatre Manager in writing. The hirer will be personally responsible for the payment of all fees and for compliance with all conditions of hiring and must therefore be a person of responsibility over the age of 18 years of age.

Hirers shall be liable to pay a deposit of 50% of the total hire charge when making a reservation for the Theatre. This deposit will be offset against the total hiring fees the balance of which will be payable immediately after the use of the Theatre has occurred, unless the hirer wishes to pay before that time or the Theatre Manager deems it necessary to obtain full payment in advance of the function taking place.

The Theatre Manager, on behalf of the Bancroft Players, reserves the right, after giving not less than two months notice, to alter the scale of charges for the hire of the Theatre.

The Theatre Manager, on behalf of the Bancroft Players, reserves the right to refuse any application for the use of the Theatre without specific reasons having to be given.

**2. CANCELLATION OR BOOKINGS**

**(a) By the Theatre Manager on Behalf of Bancroft Players**

In the case of long term periodic bookings the Theatre Manager reserves the right to review such bookings from time to time and to terminate such bookings by three months' notice to the hirer.

In the case of any booking, the Theatre Manager reserves the right to close the Theatre while any function is in progress in the event of any accident or emergency rendering this necessary.

Upon any cancellation of a booking or termination of periodic bookings by the Theatre Manager any hiring fees paid for bookings cancelled will be refunded but the Bancroft Players shall not be liable to pay any compensation.

**(b) By the Hirer**

If the hirer cancels the reservation of the Theatre less than four weeks before the date of the function for which it has been booked, a cancellation charge of 50% of the total hiring fee will be payable by the hirer at the discretion of the Theatre Manager unless the Theatre is re-let on that date.

**3. NUMBER OF PERSONS TO BE ADMITTED**

The Theatre Manager reserves the right to place a limit on the number of persons who may be admitted to any function.

**4. CONDUCT OF PATRONS**

The hirer shall be responsible for the proper conduct of persons using the Theatre and, in the event of any persons acting in such a manner as to cause annoyance or inconvenience to other persons, the hirer shall take all necessary steps to deal with the offender.

**5. SEATING**

All arrangements as to the placing of seats and means of ingress and egress, including gangways, shall be under the control of the Theatre Manager.

**6. APPARATUS**

All furniture, fittings, apparatus, or appliances brought or sent to the premises by the hirer must be unloaded, placed in position and removed by persons employed by the hirer, at such time as shall be agreed with the Theatre Manager's representative at the Theatre, having regard to any other function for which the Theatre is being used or has been let and except insofar as the Theatre Manager may otherwise agree, every hirer shall remove all property belonging to him or brought into the Theatre for use at the hirer's function immediately upon the termination of a letting. The hirer will be liable to a further charge for each hour that such property is left upon the premises and the Theatre Manager also reserves the right if he deems it necessary to remove such property whereupon the hirer shall be liable for the cost incurred by the Theatre Manager in such removal.

Use and/or management of the Theatre's own specialist lighting and sound facilities should only be by specific arrangement with the Theatre Manager and/or his appointed technical advisor.

The hirer shall not bring in to the Theatre any obnoxious chemicals, explosive devices, or such material and equipment which may cause damage to the Theatre or persons present.

**7. DAMAGE**

The hirer will be responsible for the cost of making good any damage caused in the course of the function for which the Theatre has been booked or of replacing any furniture or fittings afterwards found to be lost or missing from any part of the building.

The hirer shall ensure that no nail, screw or other fastening is driven into the walls, floors, platforms or furniture of the Theatre.

No electrical fittings or appliances in the Theatre may be altered, removed or interfered with in any way, or additional fittings or appliances installed without the prior approval of the Theatre Manager at the time of hiring.

**8. FILMS**

No cinematograph or film projection apparatus shall be used without the prior permission of the Theatre Manager. If such permission is granted all apparatus in connection therewith must at all times, when in use in the Theatre, be enclosed in a metal housing which must be approved by the Theatre Manager and the hirer shall comply, where applicable, with the requirements of the Cinematograph Acts 1909 and 1952 or any statut... modification thereof, and all Regulations thereunder.

**9. EXITS**

All doors giving egress from the Theatre shall be kept unfastened and unobstructed and immediately available for e... as the hall is in use...

...risk of fire o...

Source: The Queen Mother Theatre, Hitchin.

- **Voidable**: such a contract may be repudiated at the will of one of the parties. If the contract is affected by fraud, undue influence or duress, the party adversely affected has the right to set aside the contract. However, the contract remains valid and binding until it is repudiated.
- **Unenforceable**: this type of contract is valid and binding, but it cannot be enforced in the courts because of (a) evidence of the contract, or (b) the form prescribed by the law.

**Standard form contracts**

In recent years organisations within certain industries or trades have collaborated to produce **standard form contracts.** These tend to contain all the relevant **terms and conditions** of the contract to be made – see Fig. 12.2. Generally, all that the parties are required to do is to complete the minimum of detail, e.g. names, price, description of goods or services.

These standard form contracts highlight the unequal bargaining powers of the contracting parties. The seller is in the stronger position, for it is he or she who dictates the terms, and the buyer has little alternative but to comply. The terms are not open to any negotiation, and the buyer can be in a 'take it or leave it' situation. As a rule, buyers do not have the necessary knowledge to analyse contractual terms, nor do they have the confidence to try. The terms and conditions of a car-hire contract are formidable; how many hirers want to read all that small print, especially in front of an impatient assistant? Buyers mostly sign the contracts, hoping that all will be well. Standard form contracts are fairly common in insurance and mortgages.

The aims of the standard form contract are:

- to reduce an organisation's risks;
- to offer the maximum protection from liability.

**The terms of a contract**

If a dispute arises, a court will want to scrutinise the terms upon which the contract was formed. Initially the attention will focus on the **express terms**, and since most business contracts will be in writing the court will consider questions of interpretation. Oral evidence is admissible if the contract was made orally; but if the contract is written, oral evidence is rarely admissible unless it can be established that the oral terms are clearly part of the written agreement.

To determine liability, the court in examining an alleged breach of contractual term will classify it as either:

- a **condition**, i.e. a term which goes directly to the 'root' of a contract, the 'essence' of the contract; or
- a **warranty**, i.e. a subsidiary term of the contract, one which does not reflect the main purpose of the contract.

This classification and distinction is imperative, because the remedies available to the injured party depend upon it. A **breach of condition** allows an injured party to repudiate the contract or to continue with the contract and yet claim compensation for any losses incurred. A **breach of warranty** entitles the injured party to an action in damages.

Distinguishing between a condition and a warranty is not always an easy matter for the court. It must rely upon the obvious intentions of the parties, but there is a tendency to consider just how serious the alleged breach is *in fact* before deciding whether the breach is one of condition or warranty.

## BREACH AND DISCHARGE

**Breach of contract**

Perhaps the most common form of dispute in a contract is a **breach** – see Fig. 12.3. If this occurs, the injured party can treat the contract as discharged and sue for damages. If there is a breach of condition, the whole contract can be treated as discharged, and a claim for damages may be made.

In all contractual breaches the parties are expected to take reasonable steps to minimise the loss, mitigating any claim that may eventually be made. A court will look favourably upon an injured party who, although suffering loss, has made every attempt to help him- or herself; e.g. a hotel ought to make an attempt to relet room cancellations.

*Remedies*

The remedies for breach of contract are:

- **Specific performance**: the court instructs the parties to carry out the terms of their agreement.
- **Injunction**: this is an order of the court restraining a party from the doing of an act.
- *Quantum meruit*: the injured party may claim in addition to damages a payment for what he or she has done under the contract.
- **Refusal of further performance**: on the breach of a condition, the injured party may of his or her own volition treat the contract as at an end and refuse to perform or fulfil his or her part of the contract.
- **An action for damages**: the object is to compensate the injured for loss caused by the breach of contract, i.e. to restore the injured party to his or her previous position.

**Discharge of contract**

When a contract is at end it is said to be **discharged**. There are five methods by which a contract may be discharged:

- **Agreement**: since the parties enter into a contract by agreement, it follows that they may also release each other from their contractual obligations.

**Fig. 12.3: Breach of terms**

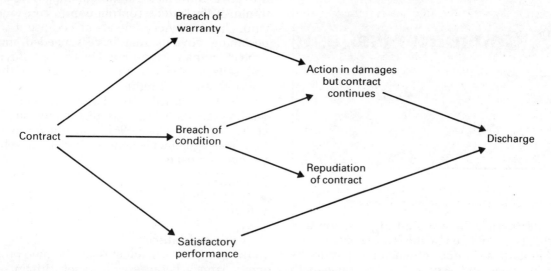

- **Performance**: each party completely fulfils his or her obligations under the contract.
- **Breach**: a breach of condition will entitle the injured party to treat the contract as discharged.
- **Operation of law**: examples of factors which may bring about a discharge are bankruptcy, death, lapse of time and material alteration.
- **Frustration**: when a contract subsequently becomes impossible to perform, it is said to be frustrated. Impossibility may arise, for example, if there is a change in the law, because there is a vital change in the circumstances or where the contract depends on a certain event taking place.

Activity 12.1
(a) Each member of the course should find an example of a standard form contract.
(b) Study the terms and conditions of your contract.
(c) Comment upon whether or not it is easy to understand.
(d) Do the terms and conditions seem to be fair and reasonable?
(e) How do you think they could be improved upon?

Activity 12.2
Read the following case and then suggest what action Guinevere should take.

*The blouse*
Guinevere saw a china tea set in the window of Camelot Chinawares, and it was priced at an unbelievable £15. Guinevere entered the shop and was met by a polite and helpful assistant, who showed her a selection of china tea sets priced from £40 to £150.

Guinevere could not afford those prices but as she had noticed the tea set in the window, she said she would buy it. She was surprised to be told that it was not for sale.

Guinevere argued that since the tea set was on display it must be for sale and at the price stated. The assistant disagreed and said that the price ticket was a mistake and it should have read £75.

Guinevere insisted on her right to buy the tea set at £15. The assistant was equally firm in her view that Guinevere had no such right.

# 13. Consumer Issues

The relationship between an organisation and its clients is regulated by the law of contract, but that in itself is insufficient when it comes to the sale of goods and services. In the nineteenth century **freedom of contract** was upheld and in sales situations reinforced by the doctrine of *caveat emptor* ('let the buyer beware'). It was widely thought (particularly by the courts and Parliament) that it was unnecessary and unreasonable to regulate sale-of-goods contracts, because people buying defective goods had only themselves to blame. Buyer and seller were expected to know their own minds, to act in their own best interests and to come freely to agreement without any legal guidance or intervention.

## CONSUMER PROTECTION AND THE LAW

The idea of **consumer protection** is not a new one, however, although the growth of interest in and legislation governing the sale of goods and services has been a feature since the early 1960s. It could be argued that the foundation of consumer protection was laid in **1844**, when the Rochdale Pioneers opened the first successful Co-operative Society, operating it according to a **code of practice** (the Rochdale Principles); or in **1893**, when the first piece of consumer legislation was entered in the statute book, namely, the **Sale of Goods Act.**

### Sale of Goods Act 1893
In terms of impact on the law and the buyer–seller relationship, the 1893 Act has made more impression than the beginnings of the Co-operative Movement (although that is not to diminish the latter's contribution to consumerism). The 1893 Act came about because it was becoming obvious that buyers needed more protection than was afforded by the law. Buyers and sellers needed a clear statement of their positions and their rights.

The Act defined three basic conditions regarding goods which, despite many specific consumer laws since 1961, still remain at the root of all agreements between buyer and seller; i.e. goods must be:

- of merchantable quality;
- as described;
- fit for purpose.

### Post-war legislation
In the late 1950s consumer issues became prominent, largely because as a nation Britain was better off and people were buying more goods and services. The growing prosperity produced a change to the general pattern of life (e.g. the increased ownership of cars, television, refrigerators, etc. and the growth of the package holiday business); this naturally threw up new legal problems.

The Molony Committee was set up in 1959 to investigate the whole question of consumer protection. Its interim report resulted in the **Consumer Protection Act 1961**, which gave the minister responsible delegated powers to take action on certain consumer matters without having to produce specific legislation. Since then Parliament has addressed itself with some interest to legislating to improve consumer rights.

It is impossible to discuss each Consumer Act that has been passed since 1961, but two Acts are of immediate concern:

- **Supply of Goods (Implied Terms) Act 1973.**
- **Sale of Goods Act 1979** (which replaces the 1893 Act).

These two Acts share a common objective in that they emphasise and define these points:

- **Merchantable quality**: goods must be as fit for the purpose or purposes for which goods of that kind are commonly bought as it is reasonable to expect having regard to the description applied to them.
- **Correspondence with description**: nearly every sale will involve some kind of description;

if the buyer makes a purchase relying upon description, then the goods must be as described. If, however, the goods do not correspond with description then there is a breach of implied condition, and the goods can be rejected by the buyer.

- **Fitness for purpose**: this right covers any sales where the buyer clearly informs the seller of the particular purpose for which he or she requires the goods. If the seller is not confident that the goods will meet the buyer's requirements, he or she must make it clear that the buyer cannot rely upon his or her skill or judgement.

*Implications of the Acts*
Several issues emerge from the above.

1. Fitness for purpose cannot apply when defects are specifically drawn to the buyer's attention *before* the contract is made, or if the buyer examines the goods before purchase and there are defects which his or her examination should have revealed.

2. It is reasonable to expect a seller to select his or her stock with skill, and to assume that goods are in good condition. It is also reasonable to hold a seller answerable for the merchantability of the goods sold in the course of his or her business.

3. The contract of sale is made between the seller and the buyer. The seller is made liable to the buyer.

4. Increasingly buyers are relying on manufacturers' claims in advertising, but in any sale the buyer is said to be dependent upon the seller's skill.

5. In the case of hire purchase or conditional sale agreements involving a finance company, the buyer's rights will be against the finance company and not against the seller.

6. The law recognises a buyer's implied right as being either a condition or a warranty. If there is a breach of condition the buyer may reject the goods, but if he or she accepts goods which are later found to be defective then the breach of an implied condition will be treated as a breach of warranty.

7. A claim that goods are defective can be dealt with in these ways: (a) a refund of the price paid; (b) an offer to repair the goods free of charge. Under (b) the buyer may be able claim compensation for loss of use, for the cost of hiring a replacement or for any other loss which he or she may have suffered because of the breach of warranty.

## The Office of Fair Trading (OFT)

This is an agency set up under the **Fair Trading Act 1973** to monitor the effectiveness of competition and to help protect the consumer against unfair trading practices. The office is run by the Director-General of Fair Trading, whose task it is to collect detailed information about consumer matters. The OFT is advised from time to time by the many consumer bodies and is active in publishing its advice to consumers.

The OFT's role can be summarised thus:

- to encourage trading organisations to draw up voluntary codes of practice;
- to publish information on consumers' rights;
- to recommend new regulations and procedures to close any loopholes in current legislation;
- to recommend new regulations to stop unfair trading practices;
- to take legal action against those traders or sellers who commit offences against, and/or who break their legal obligations to, the consumer.

*Complaints to the OFT*
The complaints procedure follows this pattern:

1. A complaint is made by an individual, an organisation or a consumer group to the OFT.
2. The OFT will consider the complaint and may refer it to the Consumer Protection Advisory Committee.
3. If there is a case of unfair trading practice, then the Advisory Committee may refer the matter to the Secretary of State for Trade and Industry.
4. The Secretary of State may make an Order before Parliament which will have the force of law.
5. The resultant regulation or law will be enforced by the Trading Standards Departments of the local authorities.

## The Department of Trade and Industry (DTI)

The **Department of Trade and Industry** is the government department which, among many activities, is responsible for consumer protection. The Secretary of State appoints the Director-General of the Office of Fair Trading. The

DTI has responsibility for government policies on such issues as

- fair trading;
- home and consumer safety;
- monopolies and mergers;
- consumer credit;
- competition.

It also administers such legislation as:

- Prices Act 1974.
- Unsolicited Goods and Services Acts 1971 and 1975.
- Weights and Measures Acts.
- Consumer Credit Act 1974.

## CODES OF PRACTICE

A **code of practice** is a set of rules drawn up by a trade association (or even an individual company) for their members to follow. Such codes are often written with the advice and help of the Office of Fair Trading.

### Aims and objectives
The aims of a code of practice are:

- to improve standards of service;
- to provide the consumer with a better deal;
- to offer protection additional to that provided by the law;
- to offer an acceptable method of dealing with complaints;
- to offer low-cost independent arbitration schemes.

Reputable firms are always conscious of their duty towards the consumer, knowing very well that a dissatisfied customer means lost business. Some firms will offer, through their codes, rights additional to those offered by the law. A good example is that of Marks & Spencer, which has earned a fine reputation for customer service. There is no provision under consumer legislation for a buyer to demand a refund or an exchange if he or she has changed his/her mind about the goods, yet M & S will accommodate its customers in this way. Consumers know that they will get a fair deal from the company.

The basic object of a code of practice is to reassure the public that **consumer rights** are being observed and upheld – see Fig. 13.1. By far the majority of the retail business transacted in the UK is completed to the evident satisfac-

tion of both buyer and seller. The reason why there is so much consumer law now and so many codes of practice is because there is always that element within the retail industry which fails to meet consumer expectations. Some traders will sell defective goods, cheat people and conduct their business unethically. The law and the codes are to protect not only the consumers but also the honest sellers.

Codes of practice cover goods and services such as: cars, catalogue mail order, funerals, furniture, glass and glazing, holidays, household electrical appliance servicing, motor cycles, photography, postal services and telecommunications – see Fig. 13.2. Some of the codes are now explained.

### Shoes
One area of considerable concern for the consumer is the purchase of **footwear**. This ought to be as straightforward as buying any other product, but many people seem to have some horrific story concerning faulty shoes and the refusal of the retailer to make any refund or exchange on the grounds that 'the shoes have been worn'. Shoes and other footwear must be

**Fig. 13.1: Foreword from the British Telecommunications Code of Practice for Consumers, November 1984. The Code is regularly revised.**

British Telecommunications plc wants to give you, its customer, the best possible service at all times. We are a very large company with millions of customers throughout the United Kingdom but we aim to deal fairly with every individual customer.

This Code of Practice explains many of the services offered by British Telecommunications plc, sets out our commitment to our customers and tells you where and how to get advice and help.

The contents of this Code of Practice do not form part of a contract and do not create a collateral contract between British Telecommunications plc and any of its customers. The Code does, however, include an explanation of the arbitration arrangements for the resolution of simple disputes offered by British Telecommunications plc within many of its contracts.

Source: British Telecom PLC.

**Fig. 13.2: Examples of signs displayed by retailers showing their support for codes of practice**

Sources: National Association of Retail Furnishers, The Society of Master Shoe Repairers, Footwear Distribution Federation.

**as described** and **fit for any particular purpose made known to the seller**. If a buyer requests a pair of wellington boots they would not be of **merchantable quality** if they let in water. Consumer protection is available on footwear as it is on any product, but a consumer has no entitlement in law for:

- those faults pointed out by the seller at the time of purchase;
- those faults which could have been seen by the buyer at the time of purchase;
- a change of mind, e.g. the buyer decides that the shoes do not suit him or her.

The footwear industry is covered by two codes of practice: one for repairs and the other for retailing. The general objectives of the codes are to:

- improve the quality of footwear;
- improve the standards of service;
- improve the quality of workmanship;
- improve the quality of materials;
- encourage the employment of trained staff who can advise and help customers.

*Complaints procedure*
If a consumer has a genuine complaint, he or

she must go back to the repairer or retailer and attempt to resolve the problem. Sellers concerned for their customers (and for their reputation) will settle with the minimum of fuss and will offer either a cash refund or an exchange. However, if a seller proves to be unhelpful and difficult, the consumer has several ways of complaining and getting something done about the problem:

- complain to bodies like the Trading Standards Department, Consumer Protection Department or local consumer adviser;
- seek advice from the Citizens Advice Bureau;
- agree to the shoes being sent to the Footwear Testing Centre for an independent report (the seller must abide by the centre's findings);
- go to court.

### Cars

*Legal protection*
Car buyers are protected in law in this way:

- **Sale of Goods Act 1979**: new or used cars must be of merchantable quality, as described and fit for any particular purpose made clear to the seller; the seller cannot avoid these legal obligations.

- **Trades Descriptions Act 1968**: new and used cars must be described accurately whether in writing, speech or by illustration; this Act is enforced by the Trading Standards Department.
- **Road Traffic Act 1972**: it is an offence to sell an unroadworthy car.
- **Unfair Contract Terms Act 1977**: a buyer is protected from 'exclusion clauses', e.g. when the seller refuses to accept responsibility for loss or damage to the car through his or her negligence; such an exclusion would be effective only if the seller could convince a court that the clause was reasonable; a seller cannot limit or exclude his or her responsibility if personal injury or death is caused through his or her negligence.

*Codes of practice*

In addition to the law, the buyer is further protected by two codes of practice. One is a common code for the motor industry and is supported by the Motor Agents' Association, the Society of Motor Manufacturers and Traders and the Scottish Motor Trade Association – see Fig. 13.3. The other code covers vehicle body repairs for cars and caravans and is issued by the Vehicle Builders' and Repairers' Association – Fig. 13.4. The codes cover such provisions as pre-delivery inspection, written estimates and quotations, and price structures.

**Fig. 13.3: Motor-industry association logos**

Sources: Motor Agents' Association, Society of Motor Manufacturers and Traders, Scottish Motor Trade Association.

**Fig. 13.4: Vehicle Builders' and Repairers' Association logo**

Source: VBRA.

*Complaints procedure*

If a buyer is not satisfied owing to condition or warranty problems, he or she is advised to:

- make a formal complaint to the seller;
- contact the customer relations department of the manufacturer if the remedy is beyond the seller;
- seek advice from, for example, the Trading Standards Department, if the matter remains unsettled;
- contact the trade association, particularly if the seller is what is known as a **code trader**;
- take the case either to court or to arbitration.

If the seller is not a code trader, the buyer should obtain advice from one of the many sources now available, including the AA or RAC.

**Package holidays**

The trade association for the holiday industry is the **Association of British Travel Agents** (better known as ABTA), which represents most of the well-known tour operators and travel agents – Fig. 13.5.

The package holiday business has grown

**Fig. 13.5: ABTA logo**

Source: ABTA.

markedly in the last ten years or so. It is estimated that each year more than 16 million Britons take their holidays abroad (with about 36 per cent of them going to Spain). The appeal of the package holiday is easy to appreciate. People want to buy a holiday inclusive of travel, accommodation, food, organised trips, entertainment, service charges and company representation in the hotel or resort. The vast majority of such holidays are successful, and the customers return home well satisfied with the arrangements. However, every now and again a problem arises, and the case comes to court.

In consultation with the Office of Fair Trading, ABTA has drawn up a **code of conduct** which is supported by its members. The code is there to offer protection to holiday-makers and also to give them an avenue of complaint should the need arise. The code provides, among other things, regulations covering:

- cancellations by either agent or customer;
- alterations to the holiday arrangements by the agent;
- surcharges;
- overbooking;
- booking conditions;
- complaints procedure.

*Complaints procedure*
If consumers have a complaint about their holiday, they are advised to attempt to remedy the problem at the hotel or resort. They should raise the matter with the tour operator's representative and/or the hotel management. If the consumer's complaint is not resolved, then they can take up their problem with the travel agent or tour operator on their return from holiday. It helps complainants if they keep a detailed record of the complaint, money spent, receipts, dates, what was said and so on. If a reasonable course of action does not work, ABTA will help, providing **conciliation facilities** free of charge. If that should fail, the consumer may use ABTA's **arbitration scheme** (all ABTA members are obliged to go to arbitration and to accept the final decision) or take legal action through the county court.

## Buying by post
The newspapers and magazines are full of advertisements offering the opportunity to buy goods and services through the post. The term generally applied to this business is **mail order**.

*Catalogue shopping*
Firms selling through catalogues are referred to as **mail-order catalogue houses**. The largest of these belong to the **Mail Order Traders' Association**, which has a code of practice and the symbol in Fig. 13.6.

**Fig. 13.6: Mail Order Traders' Association logo**

Source: MOTA.

The companies send out well-produced, illustrated catalogues. Recognising the difficulties of 'distance buying' (the inability to feel the goods, check the colour in daylight, etc.), they offer the customer the chance to examine the goods **on approval**. Unwanted or faulty goods can be returned, and the money is refunded. Substitute goods may be sent if the goods ordered are not available but these can be returned at no cost to the customer.

The code of practice promises that accurate information should be given in regard to the goods' size, colour, materials, installation, any restrictions on use, delivery dates, surcharges and restricted availability.

*Books and records*
The companies engaged in publishing and selling books and records by post generally belong to the **Association of Mail Order Publishers** (Fig. 13.7), and adhere to a code of practice supervised and administered by the **Mail Order Publishers' Authority** with an independent chairman. The code sets out standards and procedures governing every aspect of the members' relations with the public, including for instance:

- advertising – the main terms of any offer must be clear;
- prices – postage, packing, delivery or any other extra charges must be indicated;
- information – quantity, quality, price and terms must be clearly stated;

**Fig. 13.7: Assocation of Mail Order Publishers logo**

Source: AMOP.

- contracts – (1) the commitment undertaken by a book or record club member must be clearly shown in material retained by the club member. (2) A member of the public subscribing to a series can withdraw if prices are increased, or after one year.

*'Postal bargain' advertisements*

In general, consumers buying from newspaper and magazine advertisements are protected by the **Mail Order Protection Scheme** (MOPS). This means that if an advertiser, i.e. seller, becomes bankrupt or stops trading the newspaper or magazine will refund the money. Fig. 13.8 explains the purpose of the scheme; this advertisement, or similar, is published frequently in the press.

The protection scheme applies only when a customer is asked to send money in advance. The exclusions are:

- advertisements under a classified heading;
- sellers who advertise a catalogue from which goods may be bought.

*Complaints procedure*

The steps to follow in the event of a complaint are:

- contact the seller in the first instance; if there is no satisfaction, then:
- seek advice from, for example, the Trading Standards Department or the Citizens Advice Bureau; if as a result of that there is still no satisfaction, then:
- contact one of these bodies: Advertising Standards Authority, Mail Order Traders' Association, Mail Order Publishers' Authority, the newspaper or magazine; if that fails, then:
- decide whether to go to court or to arbitration.

*Arbitration*

**Arbitration** involves both parties to a dispute putting their case to an independent person, i.e. the arbitrator, whose task is to consider the evidence and to determine who is in the right. A buyer having a problem settling a dispute with a code trader (a seller who is a member of a trade association which operates a code of practice arbitration scheme) may well be advised to go to arbitration. However, a court of law will not be appropriate in certain circumstances.

*The best advice to give a consumer is to take reliable advice!*

## CREDIT

**Credit** is a means of acquiring goods and services by deferred payment. When credit was increasing in popularity in the 1950s it was described as 'buy now, pay later'. At one time debt would have been despised, but nowadays credit is respectable and very difficult to resist. Inflation has encouraged people to get goods

**Fig. 13.8: The Mail Order Protection Scheme**

**Shopping by post?**

# Play it safe

Readers who reply to cash with order advertisements in national newspapers or colour supplements are safeguarded by the National Newspapers Mail Order Protection Scheme. This covers all categories of goods and services with the exception of: those advertised under classified headings, perishable foodstuffs, horoscopes, lucky charms, non durable gardening and medical products.

The MOPS protection guarantees that your money will be refunded if a member advertiser stops trading and does not deliver your order, or refund your payment.

Advertisements covered by the Scheme may include the MOPS symbol or the initial letters MOPS in their layout.

For full details send a 9" × 6" stamped addressed envelope to:
The National Newspapers' Mail Order,
Protection Scheme,
16 Tooks Court, London, EC4A 1LB

*Play it safe—look for the symbol*

**THE NATIONAL NEWSPAPER**

MAIL ORDER PROTECTION SCHEME

Source: National Newspapers' Mail Order Protection Scheme.

when they can budget for them on a credit system rather than wait until they can pay cash, when the price may have risen. There is a considerable opportunity element with credit; so much can be acquired and enjoyed now with the question of paying for it being a future problem.

*Sources and forms of credit*

Credit is available from many **sources**: mail-order catalogue houses, banks, building societies, insurance companies, finance companies, moneylenders, retailers, cheque trading companies and credit unions. And it takes many **forms**: hire purchase, personal loans, free-flow or budget accounts, credit cards, mortgages, overdrafts, charge cards, conditional sale agreements, credit sale agreements, trading cheques and vouchers, insurance policy loans.

## Consumer Credit Act 1974

All the aforementioned activity is regulated by the **Consumer Credit Act 1974**, a very extensive piece of legislation which has rationalised and updated the law relating to credit. The oversight of this Act rests with the Director-General of Fair Trading. With so much credit activity, there is a need for regulation, and the credit consumer (or debtor) must be protected.

The Act is highly technical, but some of its more obvious points are:

- Every credit agency must obtain a licence from the Director-General of Fair Trading.
- There is control over advertisements for credit which may be misinterpreted, i.e. be misleading.
- The credit agreement must be properly drawn up and contain terms laid down in regulations by the Secretary of State, e.g. the debtor's principal rights and duties.
- The debtor is entitled to a copy of the agreement at the time of the contract, and a second copy within seven days if the agreement is accepted at a later date.

The Office of Fair Trading produces excellent explanatory leaflets on credit, so consumers can be well informed.

## APR

APR has been in use since 1980. It stands for **annual percentage rate** (of the total charges for credit). The points to note about APR are:

- It is the *true cost* of credit.
- It includes *all* the costs.
- It is not to be confused with interest rates.
- The consumer has the right to ask for a written quotation regarding a prospective credit agreement, and this must contain the APR.
- Where APR is shown in advertisements, it must be given greater prominence than any other rate, e.g. the annual flat rate.
- If a trader is not giving the correct APR, the matter should be reported to either the OFT or the Trading Standards Department.

*An important point for all credit-consumers to bear in mind is that they are buying not only the goods or services but also the credit itself.*

## Credit reference agencies

A **credit reference agency** keeps files about credit agreements, and they are available for consultation by traders. If a person applies for credit, his or her name may be referred to an agency to determine whether or not he or she is credit-trustworthy; e.g. has there been a county court judgement against him or her for a previous agreement? A trader is not obliged to tell a consumer why he or she cannot have credit, but the consumer has these rights:

- to be given the name and address of the agency consulted;
- to ask the agency for a copy of his or her file (this must be done in writing and accompanied by a £1 fee);
- to write a note of correction, if there is an error in the file.

## MANUFACTURERS, GUARANTEES, MONOPOLIES AND RESTRICTIVE PRACTICES

### Duties of a manufacturer

Essentially there is no contract, no legally enforceable agreement, between a consumer and the manufacturer where there is no direct sale. However, this does not mean that no contract can exist between them. Two areas may give rise to obligation:

- **advertising** by (a) itinerant sales representatives, (b) direct mail or (c) mass media;
- a promise to repair or replace contained in a manufacturer's **guarantee** or **warranty**.

As far as advertising is concerned, there is no general acceptance by the law that it creates an agreement. But there may be a specific instance when an advertisement can be construed as having a contractual objective. The *Donaghue* v. *Stevenson* (1952) case established the principle that in certain circumstances a manufacturer owes a duty to be careful to the ultimate consumer.

If a consumer buys goods as a result of a sales representative's statements, then a contractual relationship may exist between buyer and manufacturer. There is a reasonable assumption that a manufacturer knows more about his or her product than any consumer; so a sales representative's statements may be regarded as contractual promises unless they are vague and imprecise.

Catalogues and leaflets are examples of invitation to treat. Should a consumer complete an order, the descriptive passages within the catalogue or leaflet may form part of the contract. A court may not necessarily recognise descriptive claims in catalogues as intentions towards contractual promises. In certain circumstances, mass-media advertising may create contracts between buyers and producers.

### Guarantees

It is often the practice to include a **guarantee** in the sale of a product, particularly a durable good (e.g. a video, iron or toaster). *A guarantee cannot take away or diminish a consumer's rights*:

- A manufacturer cannot use a guarantee to limit his or her liability for damage or loss where this results from a defect in the product caused by neglect.
- The Supply of Goods (Implied Terms) Act confers rights on a buyer against a seller – not against the manufacturer. In a consumer sale, nothing in a manufacturer's guarantee or warranty can take away any of the rights a buyer has against a seller.

It is not necessary to complete a manufacturer's **guarantee registration card**, but a buyer is well advised to do so because:

- It registers the buyer's purchase of the product.
- It may offer additional rights.
- It will therefore complete a direct contractual link between the consumer and the manufacturer.

### Monopolies and anti-competitive practices

Two Acts are of immediate interest as far as **monopolies and restrictive practices** are concerned:

#### Competition Act 1980

This Act provides for the scrutiny of practices of single firms which are neither monopolies nor in collusion with other firms for the purpose of **restrictive practices.** The Director-General of Fair Trading may set up a preliminary inquiry, and is required then to report publicly the findings as to whether any practice constitutes an anti-competitive practice and, if so, whether it should be reported to the **Monopolies and Mergers Commission.**

The task of the commission is to assess and report whether there is an anti-competitive practice and whether it is against the public interest. If the conclusion is adverse, i.e. against the practice, the Secretary of State may then make an order requiring the firm to desist from or amend the practice concerned. It may ask the OFT to monitor the firm's activities.

The Act seeks to deal with restrictive practices such as where a manufacturer refuses to supply goods to certain outlets.

#### Fair Trading Act 1973

This Act extends previous legislation on monopolies and mergers and gives certain functions to the Director-General of Fair Trading. The Act defines a monopoly as the control of one-quarter of the sales in a market, not one-third as formerly.

## OTHER EXAMPLES OF CONSUMER PROTECTION

As the chapter has demonstrated, there are many organisations and laws looking after the interests of consumers. The following are worthy of note.

### British Standards Institution

This is an independent and non-profit-making body which publishes British Standards for many areas of industry. The standards specify how a product should be made to be fit and acceptable for its purpose. Goods made to British Standards bear a symbol, e.g. the Kitemark, BSI or BEAB.

### Advertising Standards Authority

All advertisements should be 'legal, decent, honest and truthful', and if any fall short of that then consumers are entitled to lodge complaints. There is no specific law relating to advertising, although all advertisers are subject to the law in general. The advertising profession has adopted a code of practice which sets out what may be advertised and what may not; it also defines what may not be said and claimed. The Advertising Standards Authority is there to ensure that advertisements are not misleading and, if any should be, it offers a channel of complaint for consumers.

### The nationalised industries

Because of the monopolistic position of the public utilities there has been a determined effort to strike a relationship between each utility and its customers. Legislation setting up, say, the electricity industry provides that the rights of the consumer are not denied and should be protected. In a situation where there is no choice of supplier, it is imperative for the consumers to know that their position is fully protected and that they have an avenue of complaint should the need arise. The consumer has access to **Consumers' Consultative Councils**, which will investigate genuine problems and complaints. The councils are not part of the industry they serve but are independent.

### Consumer Safety Act 1978

This legislation provides legally enforceable **safety standards** for certain goods. It covers such areas as labelling, packaging and design and applies to such products as toys, nightdresses and domestic heating.

### Trades Descriptions Acts 1968 and 1972

It is an offence for sellers to describe inaccurately or falsely the goods they are selling or the services they are offering. This is an attempt to control misleading descriptions. The 1972 Act makes it an offence not to give an indication of origin where goods bearing a UK name or make have been produced or made outside the UK.

### Misrepresentation Act 1967

The main object of this law is to protect people from **false inducement**, i.e. untrue statements presented as facts in order to bring about a contract. There are three main types of actionable misrepresentation:

- **Innocent misrepresentation**: this is where the maker of a false statement had reasonable grounds for believing it to be true; the injured party may cancel the contract, and both parties may be restored to their respective pre-contractual positions.
- **Negligent misrepresentation**: this is a false statement made by a party who had no reasonable grounds for believing the statement to be true; a court can allow the injured party to rescind the contract and may also make an award of damages.
- **Fraudulent misrepresentation**: this is often very difficult to prove; fraud is committed where the statement is made knowing that it is false or where it is made recklessly; the injured party may be awarded damages and can rescind the contract.

### Unsolicited Goods and Services Acts 1971 and 1975

The 1971 Act was designed to control what is known as **'inertia selling'**, i.e. sending unsuspecting people goods through the post which they hadn't ordered and relying on their ignorance and/or apathy to extract payment. Fines can be imposed on those persons making demands for payments for goods and services which are unsolicited.

The Acts provide that any unsolicited goods may be kept by the recipient without payment **after a period of 30 days** provided that the recipient gives notice to the sender asking that the goods be collected. Alternatively, the recipient can do nothing – that is, give no notice to the seller – and the goods become his or hers, as an unconditional gift **after six months**.

### Labelling

**Labelling** is an important area of consumer protection. Since January 1983 we have been subject to new regulations on food labelling, part of the European Community's consumer protection programme. The object of the labelling regulations is to update and improve the law and to give consumers more information.

Generally speaking, pre-packed foods must have labels which show: the name of the food; ingredients; net quantity; date-mark; place of origin, when necessary; name and address of manufacturer, or packer, or of a seller in the European Community; instructions for use, when necessary; any claims for the product, e.g. 'made especially for diabetics', must be backed up with supporting information on the label; labels must be easy to understand.

There are some interesting points on the question of the **food names**. Any food which does not have a name prescribed by the law, or a customary name, must have a descriptive name which will tell the consumer the true nature of the food. It is not permissible for brand names, trade marks or other invented names to be used on their own – only in addition to the proper name of the product. Names must also indicate the condition of the food, e.g. powdered, smoked or dried.

*Product liability*
This means that a manufacturer (or anyone else in the marketing process) is liable where a product is defective and that defect causes injury, loss or damage. **Product liability** law exists in the USA, France and West Germany. In July 1985 the UK Parliament approved a European Community directive on product liability which will require legislation to be enacted within three years. All Community member states must have law on the subject not later than July 1988. The effect of such legislation on British manufacturers has yet to be assessed, but it is generally felt that insurance premiums will rise as a result of the additional cover required by industry.

Those opposed to the doctrine of product liability cite US examples were manufacturers are held liable for the general stupidity of consumers. For example:

- Car batteries are required to carry a notice warning people that drinking battery acid may be harmful.
- Aluminium ladders carry a notice warning people not to lean a ladder against a high-tension power cable.

**Activity 13.1**
Read the following case and then suggest what action Robin should take.

*The power drill*
Robin bought a power drill from Do-it-yourself Stores. The price was £24.99, marked down from £34.99. When he got home, Robin unpacked the drill, fixed a plug to the cable and began to drill a hole in the bathroom wall. The drill had been in operation for no more than ten seconds when it began issuing blue smoke and the electric motor burnt out with a frightening flash. Robin was so startled that he dropped the drill into the washbasin, which sustained some damage as a result.

The manager at Do-it-yourself Stores listened to Robin with sympathy but declared that he could do nothing to remedy the situation for these reasons:

- The price had been reduced.
- There was a sign clearly saying that sale or reduced goods could not be exchanged.
- The firm had no legal responsibility towards Robin.
- Robin has a contract with the manufacturer who had issued the guarantee.
- Robin did not ask a qualified electrician to fix the plug on the cable.

**Activity 13.2**
Read the following case and then suggest what action Ruth should take.

*Unwanted books*
The postman brought Ruth an unexpected parcel which she eagerly opened, discovering inside a set of novels by Edwin Snood. The set was accompanied by a statement showing that Ruth owed £5.99 plus £1.35 postage and packing, payable within 14 days.

Ruth hadn't sent for the books so she rang up Smears Book Distributors, who told her that she was under an obligation to buy them. The company said that it didn't matter whether or not Ruth had actually ordered them, but since she had accepted the parcel from the postman she had therefore assumed full responsibility for them.

Ruth doesn't want the books. She is most unhappy at the thought of having to buy something she didn't order and probably won't read.

# Suggestions for Integrated Assignments

**Situation**: Students should investigate the main issues surrounding the question of nuclear energy; produce a campaign leaflet to enlist the support of the general public for one side or the other; and determine a strategy to achieve the desired objective.

## Indicative content

Pressure groups

Social benefits and social costs

Formulating rational and persuasive arguments

## Student activity

1. Research media for relevant material.

2. Adopt either a pro- or anti-stance.

3. Design a suitable leaflet which incorporates the following:

   (a) the arguments to support the case;

   (b) an appropriate use of colour, charts, diagrams and pictures;

   (c) action that the recipient of the leaflet might take to give further weight to the campaign.

4. Recommendations concerning the distribution of the leaflet and supporting action.

## Skills

Numeracy

Identifying and tackling problems

Learning and studying

Design and visual discrimination

Information gathering

Communicating

## People in Organisations

G Recognise factors which contribute to efficient workings within an organisation and ways in which this can be assessed and influenced.

## General Objectives

R Identify how the resource decisions of organisations are affected by external factors.

V Investigate and analyse interrelationships between organisations, community and the state, in the process of policy making and policy implementation.

Assignment 2
The expansion of a local business

**Situation**: Students should look at a local business, research its activities and assess the relative merits of expansion on either its existing or an alternative site.

## Student activity

1. Identify a suitable local business and research its structure, activities and markets.

2. Investigate possible government financial asistance relating to investment projects and regional investment support schemes.

3. Adopt the role of an assistant in the planning department of the chosen organisation.

4. Write a report which outlines options available to the organisation and implications for the activities of the various departments.

## Indicative content

Government departments

Regional policy

Locational factors

The effect of change upon the organisation

## Skills

Numeracy

Identifying and tackling problems

Learning and studying

Information gathering

Communicating

## People in Organisations

J  Analyse changes that affect the work of individuals and groups within organisations.

## General Objectives

P  Analyse the major factors creating change and the response of business organisations to change.

Q  Assess the impact of change upon the operation of business organisations and their environments.

R  Identify how the resource decisions of organisations are affected by external factors.

S  Analyse how major institutions at local and national level have an impact upon organisations.

U  Explain and evaluate government policies.

## Assignment 3    The Budget

**Situation**: Students should analyse the effects of the latest Budget upon either their own company or a well-known company of their choice.

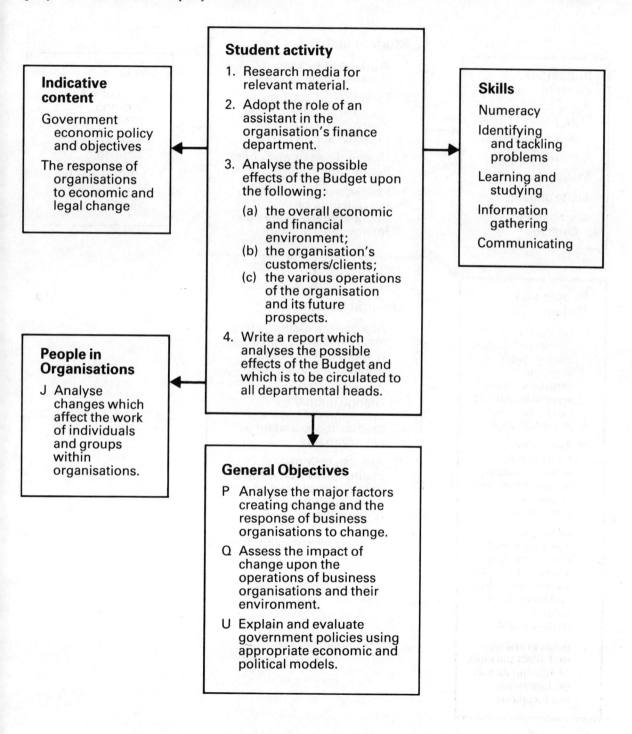

**Indicative content**

Government economic policy and objectives

The response of organisations to economic and legal change

**Student activity**

1. Research media for relevant material.

2. Adopt the role of an assistant in the organisation's finance department.

3. Analyse the possible effects of the Budget upon the following:

   (a) the overall economic and financial environment;
   (b) the organisation's customers/clients;
   (c) the various operations of the organisation and its future prospects.

4. Write a report which analyses the possible effects of the Budget and which is to be circulated to all departmental heads.

**Skills**

Numeracy

Identifying and tackling problems

Learning and studying

Information gathering

Communicating

**People in Organisations**

J Analyse changes which affect the work of individuals and groups within organisations.

**General Objectives**

P Analyse the major factors creating change and the response of business organisations to change.

Q Assess the impact of change upon the operations of business organisations and their environment.

U Explain and evaluate government policies using appropriate economic and political models.

Assignment 4    Annual pay negotiations

**Situation**: Students should divide into representatives and employees to negotiate the annual pay rise for production-line workers in a motor-vehicle manufacturing plant. The management offer is 5 per cent to match productivity while the trade union has asked for an average rise of 10 per cent plus a shorter working week.

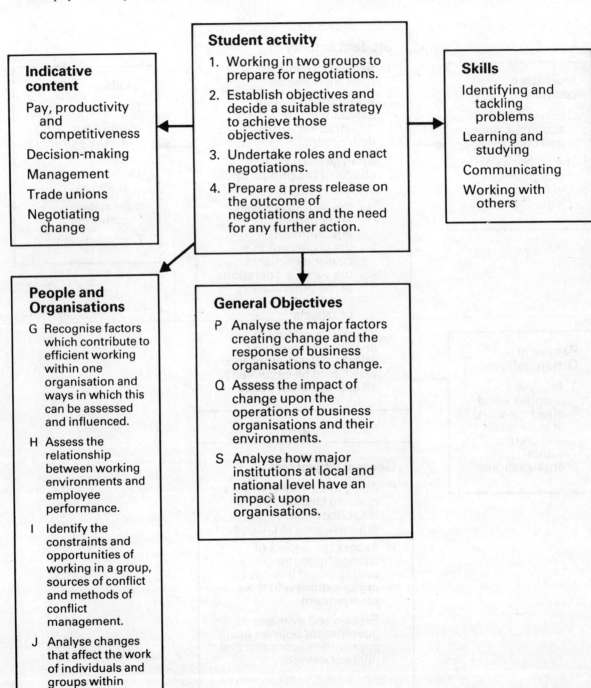

**Student activity**

1. Working in two groups to prepare for negotiations.
2. Establish objectives and decide a suitable strategy to achieve those objectives.
3. Undertake roles and enact negotiations.
4. Prepare a press release on the outcome of negotiations and the need for any further action.

**Indicative content**

Pay, productivity and competitiveness

Decision-making

Management

Trade unions

Negotiating change

**Skills**

Identifying and tackling problems

Learning and studying

Communicating

Working with others

**People and Organisations**

G  Recognise factors which contribute to efficient working within one organisation and ways in which this can be assessed and influenced.

H  Assess the relationship between working environments and employee performance.

I   Identify the constraints and opportunities of working in a group, sources of conflict and methods of conflict management.

J   Analyse changes that affect the work of individuals and groups within organisations.

**General Objectives**

P  Analyse the major factors creating change and the response of business organisations to change.

Q  Assess the impact of change upon the operations of business organisations and their environments.

S  Analyse how major institutions at local and national level have an impact upon organisations.

Assignment 5
International competitiveness

**Situation**: Students should investigate the market for stereo-radio cassette players and identify the market potential for a new producer.

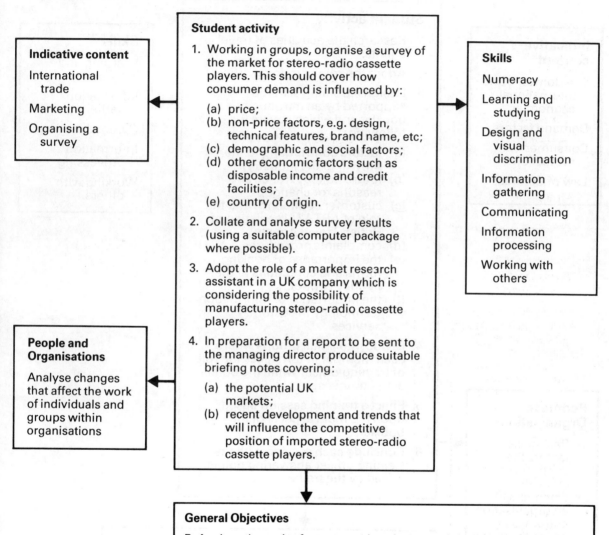

**Indicative content**

International trade

Marketing

Organising a survey

**Student activity**

1. Working in groups, organise a survey of the market for stereo-radio cassette players. This should cover how consumer demand is influenced by:

   (a) price;
   (b) non-price factors, e.g. design, technical features, brand name, etc;
   (c) demographic and social factors;
   (d) other economic factors such as disposable income and credit facilities;
   (e) country of origin.

2. Collate and analyse survey results (using a suitable computer package where possible).

3. Adopt the role of a market research assistant in a UK company which is considering the possibility of manufacturing stereo-radio cassette players.

4. In preparation for a report to be sent to the managing director produce suitable briefing notes covering:

   (a) the potential UK markets;
   (b) recent development and trends that will influence the competitive position of imported stereo-radio cassette players.

**Skills**

Numeracy

Learning and studying

Design and visual discrimination

Information gathering

Communicating

Information processing

Working with others

**People and Organisations**

Analyse changes that affect the work of individuals and groups within organisations

**General Objectives**

P  Analyse the major factors creating change and the response of business organisations to change.

T  Investigate and analyse how interdependence between the UK and international agencies affects organisations in the UK.

Y  Analyse the methods organisations used to affect the demand for their goods and services.

Z  Recognise the importance and cost to the organisation of information about the market, and examine how public sector and non-commercial organisations seek to meet customer/client wants.

Assignment 6    Training for travel

**Situation**: Students should adopt the role of training officer in a travel company and design and run a short introductory training session.

## Indicative content

The domestic and international economies

Demand factors

Consumer protection

Law of Contract

## Student activity

1. Research the activities of travel agents.

2. Adopt the role of training officer.

3. Design a training scheme supported by an introductory booklet and which covers the following:

   (a) factors contributing to the growth of the industry;
   (b) future holiday trends and reasons for change;
   (c) customer confidence and the role of ABTA (Association of British Travel Agents);
   (d) complaints procedures;
   (e) the importance of booking forms and conditions of the holiday contract;
   (f) the importance of information technology in customer services.

4. Divide into small groups where each member in turn takes the role of training officer while the others act as trainees.

5. Enact a training session based upon the main aspects of the booklet.

6. Conclude each session with the training officer answering points raised by the trainees.

## Skills

Learning and studying

Information gathering

Communicating

Information processing

Working with others

## People in Organisations

G  Recognise factors that contribute to efficient working within an organisation, and ways in which these can be assessed and influenced.

J  Analyse changes that affect the work of individuals and groups within organisations.

## General Objectives

P  Analyse the major factors creating change and the response of business organisations to change.

Q  Assess the impact of change upon the operation of business organisations and their environments.

X  Assess the effect that the legal system can and does have on the nature and working of markets and customer-client relationships.

# Index